THE CASE FOR AN INTERNATIONAL COURT OF CIVIL JUSTICE

When multinational corporations cause mass harms to lives, livelihoods, and the environment in developing countries, it is nearly impossible for victims to find a court that can and will issue an enforceable judgment. In this work, Professor Maya Steinitz presents a detailed rationale for the creation of an International Court of Civil Justice (ICCJ) to hear such transnational mass tort cases. The world's legal systems were not designed to solve these kinds of complex transnational disputes, and the absence of mechanisms to ensure coordination means that victims try, but fail, to find justice in country after country, court after court. *The Case for an International Court of Civil Justice* explains how the ICCJ would provide victims with access to justice and corporate defendants with a non-corrupt forum and an end to the cost and uncertainty of unending litigation – more efficiently resolving the most complicated types of civil litigation.

Maya Steinitz is a Professor and Bouma Family Fellow in Law at the University of Iowa College of Law and has taught courses at Harvard Law School, Columbia Law School, Tel Aviv University, and the Hebrew University of Jerusalem. She served as a litigator in one of the nation's top law firms, Latham & Watkins LLP, and clerked for the Hon. E. Hayut, currently Chief Justice of the Israeli Supreme Court. Steinitz led the representation of the government of Southern Sudan in drafting its national and subnational constitutions and regularly serves as an arbitrator, expert, and counsel in international and domestic arbitrations.

The Case for an International Court of Civil Justice

MAYA STEINITZ
University of Iowa College of Law

CAMBRIDGE
UNIVERSITY PRESS

University Printing House, Cambridge CB2 8BS, United Kingdom

One Liberty Plaza, 20th Floor, New York, NY 10006, USA

477 Williamstown Road, Port Melbourne, VIC 3207, Australia

314–321, 3rd Floor, Plot 3, Splendor Forum, Jasola District Centre, New Delhi – 110025, India

79 Anson Road, #06-04/06, Singapore 079906

Cambridge University Press is part of the University of Cambridge.

It furthers the University's mission by disseminating knowledge in the pursuit of education, learning, and research at the highest international levels of excellence.

www.cambridge.org
Information on this title: www.cambridge.org/9781107162853
DOI: 10.1017/9781316678428

© Maya Steinitz 2019

This publication is in copyright. Subject to statutory exception and to the provisions of relevant collective licensing agreements, no reproduction of any part may take place without the written permission of Cambridge University Press.

First published 2019

Printed and bound in Great Britain by Clays Ltd, Elcograf S.p.A.

A catalogue record for this publication is available from the British Library.

Library of Congress Cataloging-in-Publication Data
Names: Steinitz, Maya.
Title: The case for an international court of civil justice / Maya Steinitz, University of Iowa College of Law
Description: Cambridge, United Kingdom; New York, NY, USA: Cambridge University Press, 2019. | Includes bibliographical references and index.
Identifiers: LCCN 2018027874 | ISBN 9781107162853 (hardback)
Subjects: LCSH: Tort liability of corporations. | Liability for human rights violations | Liability for environmental damages. | Complex litigation. | Class actions (Civil procedure) | International courts.
Classification: LCC K1329.5 .S74 2019 | DDC 346–dc23
LC record available at https://lccn.loc.gov/2018027874

ISBN 978-1-107-16285-3 Hardback

Cambridge University Press has no responsibility for the persistence or accuracy of URLs for external or third-party internet websites referred to in this publication and does not guarantee that any content on such websites is, or will remain, accurate or appropriate.

To Nate, Romy and Jonathan

Contents

Acknowledgments		*page* xi
List of Abbreviations		xiii

Introduction   1
    I   Adjudicating Cross-border Mass Torts: A Problem of Forum, Not Just of Law   3
   II   Incentives and Feasibility of a New Court   5
   III   The Proposal   10

1   How New International Courts Come into Being   14
    I   Theoretical Models   17
   II   The Case Histories   21
      A   The International Criminal Court   21
        1   Legal and Institutional Precedents – Experimentation and Idea Contagion   22
        2   Change Agents   25
        3   Geopolitical Change and Constitutional Moments   26
      B   The World Trade Organization Dispute Settlement Understanding   27
      C   The Iran–United States Claims Tribunal   29
      D   The Jerusalem Arbitration Center   35
   III   Holdouts?   37
      A   The United States   37
      B   China   39
   IV   Gathering Winds   42

2		**The Human Toll: The Bhopal Disaster, the Devastation of the Ecuadorian Amazon, and the Abuse and Murder of Dr. Kiobel**		45
	I	A Tragedy in Bhopal, India		47
		A	The Disaster and Its Decades-Long Aftermath	47
		B	The Inconvenient Forum	50
		C	Enterprise Liability	59
		D	Aftershocks	60
	II	The Devastation of the Ecuadorian Rain Forest		62
		A	Background	64
		B	Round One: In the Courts of the United States	65
		C	Round Two: In the Courts of Ecuador	67
		D	No Clear Winner: Seeking and Defending Against Enforcement the World Over	67
	III	Human Rights Abuses in Nigeria		70
		A	Oil, Unrest, and Violence	70
		B	A Clear Path to US Courts?	72
		C	The Closing of the Courthouse Doors	73
	IV	Systemic Flaws in Transnational Litigation		76
		A	Boomerang, Parallel, and Sequential Litigation	77
		B	The Effects of Corporate Structures on Transnational Litigation	78
		C	Moral Hazards	79
3		**The Problem of the Missing Forum**		83
	I	Multinational Corporations' Home Courts		84
		A	US Courts and Foreign Plaintiffs	85
			1 Declining to Act as Global Courts	87
			2 The Overall Decline of Access to Justice in US Courts	89
		B	The Courts of Europe	93
	II	Litigating in Courts of the Jurisdiction Where the Mass Injury Occurred		99
	III	International Arbitration		100
	IV	Single-Issue International Courts, Alternative Dispute Resolution, and Corporate Social Responsibility		102
	V	A Better Solution: The International Court of Civil Justice		104

4		**The Business Case for the ICCJ**	108
	I	Rising Direct Litigation Costs	111
		A Forum Shopping, Parallel and Sequential Litigation	112
	II	The Indirect Costs of Litigation	113
		A Uncertainty and the Restraint on Business Activities	114
		B Distracted Management and Criminal Prosecution	117
		C Harms to Reputation and Goodwill	118
		D Change in Investment Climate	119
	III	The Cost of Corruption and the Value of the Rule of Law	120
	IV	The Global Peace Premium	123
	V	Backlash and the New Transnational Litigtionscape	127
		A The Rise of Litigation Finance	127
		B The Rise of the Global Entrepreneurial Lawyer	128
		C Blocking Statutes and Other Pro-Plaintiff Legislation	130
		1 Blocking Statutes and Litigation-Enabling Legislation	131
		2 Class Action Goes Global	133
	VI	Business Ethics	134
	VII	Global Growth as the Tide That Lifts All Boats	137
5		**Institutional and Procedural Features of an ICCJ**	141
	I	Institutional Relationships	145
		A With States Parties	145
		1 The Two-Tiered Structure of an ICCJ and Its Effect on Institutional Arrangements	145
		2 Dependent or Independent?	147
		3 Composition of the Court	147
		B With Other International Organizations	149
	II	Jurisdiction and Admissibility	150
		A Temporal Jurisdiction	151
		B Subject Matter Jurisdiction	152
		1 Mass Claims and Mass Torts	152
		2 "Cross-Border" Claims and Enterprise Liability	153
		3 Applicable Law	154
		C Personal Jurisdiction	157
		D Admissibility – Relationship of the ICCJ to National Courts	158

III	Procedural Features		161
	A	Civil Law–Common Law Hybrids	163
	B	Claim Screening and Routing	164
	C	Alternative Dispute Resolution	166
	D	Nonrepresentative Collective Litigation	166
	E.	Representative Actions	167
	F	Supervision and Administration of Aggregate Settlement	174
	G	Remedies	175
	H	Appellate Review	176
IV	Financing the Operation of the Court		177

Conclusion 179

Notes 183
Index 231

Acknowledgments

Many colleagues, students, and family members contributed to the effort of making this book a reality and I wish to thank them wholeheartedly. I owe a special debt of gratitude to Nathan Miller, my better half, for supporting me every step of the way; for commenting on the entire manuscript and especially on Chapter 5, which touches on his area of vast expertise in the field of international courts and tribunals; and for editing the manuscript with vigor. I am also very grateful to Mark Osiel, who read and commented on each chapter as it was completed. I also owe a debt of gratitude to many colleagues who commented on various chapters of the book: Catherine Kessedjian, Pam Bookman, Amelia Kessler, Karen Alter, Stacie Strong, Paul Gowder, Theodor Rave, Marc Galanter, Nora Engstrom, Christoph Herpfer, Ronen Avraham, Christopher Whytock, Michael Goldhaber, Emilia Justina Powell, and Joelle Adda. I am also thankful to Dan Miller, Nathan's dad, who commented on the Introduction before he passed away.

A very special and heartfelt word of acknowledgment and gratitude goes to my children, Romy and Jonathan Steinitz-Miller, who had to give up mommy time while I was writing the book. I hope that when they are older and able to understand the thrust of the book, it will make them proud. I also thank my parents, Benjamin and Rivka Steinitz, for babysitting Romy and Jonathan while I was off writing the book and for cheering me along over the course of three summers in Rehovot, Israel.

I also thank the organizers and participants of the Harvard International Law Journal Symposium on An International Jurisdiction for Corporate Atrocity Crimes, Northwestern's Global Capitalism and Law Colloquium, and the Iowa Legal Workshop and Iowa Law's Food for Thought for giving me an opportunity to present my work while it was still in progress.

A small army of students have lent their research assistance in the years this book was written and they, too, deserve special thanks: Nick Schnell, Paul Covaleski, Sara Gardner, Rosa Newman, Susanne Wejp-Olsen, Bria Davis, Ziyad Al-Mutairi, Erick Orantes, Amanda Rolon, and Carly Thelen.

The core idea of the book was first developed and presented in a short essay, "The Case for an International Court of Civil Justice," 67 *Stanford Law Review Online* 75 (2014). Meanwhile, the argument that judicial corruption or perceptions thereof causes a prisoner's dilemma, discussed in Chapter 3, was first fleshed out in Maya Steinitz & Paul Gowder, "Transnational Litigation as a Prisoner's Dilemma" (2016) 94 *North Carolina Law Review* 751. In that article we also described in detail the Chevron-Ecuador litigation and that description formed the basis of the discussion of the same litigation in Chapter 2. The argument that arbitration is not an appropriate mechanism for resolving transnational mass torts, which appears in revised form in Chapter 2, first appeared in Maya Steinitz, "Back to Basics: Public Adjudication of Corporate Mass Atrocities," *Harvard International Law Journal* (2016).

Abbreviations

ADR	Alternative Dispute Resolution
ATS	Alien Tort Statute
BIT	Bilateral Investment Treaties
CAT	Rules of the Competition Appeals Tribunal
CJEU	Court of Justice of the European Union
ECHR	European Convention on Human Rights
ECtHR	European Court on Human Rights
EDNY	United States District Court for the Eastern District of New York
EEC	European Economic Community
EU	European Union
FDI	Foreign Direct Investment
GATT	General Agreement on Tariffs and Trade
GCCF	Gulf Coast Claims Facility
IACHR	Inter-American Commission on Human Rights
ICC	International Criminal Court
ICCJ	International Court of Civil Justice
ICJ	International Court of Justice
ICSID	International Centre for Settlement of Investment Disputes
ICTR	International Criminal Tribunal for Rwanda
ICTY	International Criminal Tribunal for the Former Yugoslavia
IEEPA	International Emergency Economic Powers Act
ILC	International Law Commission
ISDS	Investor-State Dispute Settlement
IUSCT	Iran–United States Claims Tribunal
JAC	Jerusalem Arbitration Center

MSOP	Movement for the Survival of the Ogoni People
MNC	Multinational Corporation
New York Convention	Convention on the Recognition and Enforcement of Foreign Arbitral Awards
NGO	Non-Governmental Organization
OPA	Oil Pollution Act of 1990
OPT	Occupied Palestinian Territories
Rome Statute	Rome Statute of the International Criminal Court
SDNY	United States District Court for the Southern District of New York
Section 1983	Section 1983 of Title 42 of the United States Code
UN	United Nations
UNCC	United Nations Compensation Commission
UNWCC	United Nations War Crimes Commission
WTO	World Trade Organization
WTO DSU	World Trade Organization Dispute Settlement Understanding

Introduction

More than thirty years have passed since courts in the United States and India denied adequate compensation to the victims of the most tragic industrial disaster in history for the catastrophic harms they suffered – the Bhopal industrial accident, which took the lives of many thousands. And we still do not have a system of global civil justice that gives victims a meaningful day in court against the multinational corporations (MNCs) responsible for those kinds of injuries. That does not (and should not) stop victims from trying to obtain relief, however. When they do, as is happening with increased frequency, the corporations defending against those claims can incur massive direct and indirect costs – not just once, but in one country after another, as plaintiffs pursue their case in multiple national courts, in what can amount to a never-ending game of global whack-a-mole. Courts in developed countries where MNCs are based do not want the cases, and frequently pass the buck to the countries where the injuries happened. But the courts in those countries often lack the resources to handle complex mass tort litigation and the rule of law culture to generate judgments that courts in the MNC's home jurisdiction, where its assets are often found, would enforce. The small numbers of victims fortunate enough to get a judgment in their favor, therefore, find it all but impossible to enforce. The stakes are high enough for them to try, however, increasingly with backing by deep-pocketed financiers, in as many places as the global corporate defendants have assets. This process can stretch for years or even decades, the irresolution hanging over the heads of plaintiffs and defendants alike. There is no easy fix at the domestic level; the inability to handle cross-border mass torts is a feature of a patchwork system of national courts applying doctrines never designed to handle the kinds of transnational claims produced by our global economy.

Starting with the dual premise that access to justice is a human right that must become a reality and that foreign direct investment (FDI) undertaken by MNCs is a powerful economic force that can reduce poverty and increase global welfare,

I argue that the best solution for both victims and corporations is an International Court of Civil Justice (ICCJ).

On December 3, 1984, a gas cloud from a chemical plant in Bhopal, India, killed thousands of the city's residents and injured approximately half a million more. A New York judge dismissed the case brought by survivors of the disaster, ruling that the Indian judicial system, despite being notorious for its inefficiency, was better placed to handle what would be a hugely complex litigation: The plaintiffs eventually accepted a settlement of less than half a billion dollars, translating to approximately five hundred dollars for the "lucky ones" who managed to get at least some compensation.

Little has changed since. Claiming decades of sickness and death from environmental contamination, residents of the Ecuadorian rain forest sued Texaco for causing the pollution. In 2002 a New York court sent the case to Ecuador, specifically rejecting the allegation that its judicial system was corrupt. Yet when the plaintiffs went back to New York a decade later to collect on an $8.6 billion judgment they obtained in Ecuador, the very same court ruled that the award was unenforceable because of judicial corruption. The plaintiffs in that case have yet to see a dollar of their judgment. Maria Aguinda, the original plaintiff in the class action against Chevron (which acquired Texaco), was in her late teens when Texaco began its operations in the Orienté. She is now in her late sixties. Compensation in her lifetime is unlikely.

Conversely, on April 20, 2010, the Deepwater Horizon oil rig, operated by British Petroleum (BP), a foreign corporation, caught fire and poured millions of barrels of oil into the Gulf of Mexico. Mere days later, BP announced a $20 billion trust that backed an uncapped commitment and an administrative program to compensate fully all victims of the spill. By its second month of operation the program had paid more than $27 million a day, for a total of $840 million, in emergency advance payments. By the end of its eighteen-month tenure it had processed more than a million claims and paid more than $6 billion to individuals and businesses. The discrepancy between the prompt settlement of claims arising from the Deepwater Horizon spill and the persistent inability of the Ecuadorean plaintiffs to secure compensation is prima facie unjust.

The lack of accountability for MNCs is a matter of great public concern. As the importance of MNCs increases so does the urgency of solving what I call "the problem of the missing forum." Today, MNCs are global governance players whose influence can at times equal or exceed that of some sovereigns.

> Transnational businesses have seen incredible growth over the last forty years. In 1970, there were approximately 7,000 transnational corporations [] in the world; that number grew to 30,000 by 1990, 63,000 by 2000, and to 82,000 by 2009. Today,

there are more than 100,000 multinational corporations with 900,000 foreign affiliates... [FDI has increased] more than ten-fold between 1990 and 2000.[1]

Currently, of the world's 100 largest economies, 51 are companies while only 49 are countries. For example, G.M. is larger than Denmark.[2] As MNCs' activity rises, so do the mass harms attendant on their activity.[3] MNCs simply can no longer be above the law.

In addition to the need to advance the goals underlying tort law – namely, deterring behavior that presents risks that exceed its social value and compensating innocent victims – access to justice is a human right. It is "guaranteed as a legal right in virtually all universal and regional human rights instruments, since the 1948 Universal Declaration, as well as in many national constitutions."[4] The right to bring a suit has also been described by some as derived from freedom of expression, and participation in mass tort trials, in particular, has been regarded by some as an aspect of democratic participation.[5]

I ADJUDICATING CROSS-BORDER MASS TORTS: A PROBLEM OF FORUM, NOT JUST OF LAW

Three cases help to illustrate the problems an ICCJ could help resolve. The cases are Bhopal, an industrial disaster case; the Chevron–Ecuador litigation, an environmental dispute; and the Kiobel litigation, a human rights case.[6] I selected Bhopal because it is the largest industrial disaster of all time. I chose Chevron–Ecuador because it is the largest and longest-running transnational environmental dispute, and has yielded the largest-ever judgment in an environmental suit. And I decided on *Kiobel*, a human rights case, because the United States Supreme Court's recent decision in that case represents the end of an era in which it seemed that the United States would progressively provide a forum for transnational mass tort litigation for harms created by MNCs. Kiobel is generally considered to be the death knell of transnational human rights, environmental, and similar cross-border mass tort litigation in US courts.

In brief summary, the plaintiffs in Bhopal, as mentioned, suffered from one of the largest industrial disasters of all time. US courts refused to hear the case (against a US company) and transferred it instead to India. There, problems with the Indian court system and vigorous resistance from the defendant led the plaintiffs to accept a settlement that was paltry in comparison to the harms they suffered. In Chevron–Ecuador, US courts again refused to hear a case against a US corporation and instead sent it to Ecuador. Against all odds, the plaintiffs secured a multibillion-dollar judgment in Ecuadorian court. But Chevron's assets are located in the United States, and US courts refused to enforce the Ecuadorian judgment, finding it was tainted by fraud and judicial corruption. That was not the end of the story, however.

The Ecuadorian plaintiffs continue to try to enforce the judgment anywhere and everywhere Chevron has assets. In *Kiobel*, survivors sued Royal Dutch Petroleum (Shell) for its alleged complicity in the extrajudicial execution of environmental activists in the oilfields of Nigeria. In deciding the case on appeal, the US Supreme Court ruled that the Alien Tort Statute (ATS)[7] – the vehicle through which foreign plaintiffs had for decades brought lawsuits in US courts for human rights violations in their own countries – did not apply outside the territory of the United States.

I make no claim that these illustrations are representative of the universe of transnational mass harms or of transitional mass litigation. Legal scholars have long known that, because of the unavailability of data as well as other methodological challenges "the behavior of the tort litigation system is ... unknown[] or unknowable."[8] Rather, I offer these because they bring to life known problems that are the natural consequences of the procedural characteristics of contemporary legal systems in both the developing and the developed world, as well as known coordination problems between national legal systems. In other words, the case studies are vivid, real-world examples of the procedural difficulties that an analytic approach to the characteristics of cross-border mass litigation reveals to be systemic. While, like all litigation, each of these cases is unique, involving specific facts and idiosyncratic procedural twists and turns, they are all largely representative of the main, relevant features of the contemporary transnational litigationscape.

Bhopal, Chevron–Ecuador, and Kiobel all highlight what I call "the problem of the missing forum": The courts of MNCs' home state will often not hear cases based on activities in developing countries, and the courts of the host state where the injuries happened are often ill equipped to handle complex litigation.[9] Even when they attempt to do so the resulting judgments are often unenforceable in the home jurisdictions of the defendant MNCs, where assets which can satisfy the judgment are often found. The lack of capacity of the courts in host states is caused by, among other things, corruption (real and perceived), bias, lack of judicial capacity, antiquated tort law, and the absence of procedures to handle mass claims. The unavailability of US and European courts results from the operation of doctrines such as *forum non conveniens*, which gives judges the discretion to decline to hear a case when it would more easily and naturally be tried elsewhere. Those doctrines, in turn, are underpinned by concerns about judicial resources, the inefficiency of trying a case far from the location of evidence and witnesses, and the foreign relations implications of such litigation. There are also good, legitimacy-based reasons why the courts of the United States, or any other nation, should not serve as a world court.

But if not US or European courts, perhaps some other existing mechanism would work? I explain why arbitration is inappropriate for mass tort cases. And I similarly explore other alternative solutions to the access to justice deficit in the area of transnational tort – such as single-issue courts, Corporate Social Responsibility, and self-regulation initiatives – and explain why an ICCJ represents a superior solution. An ICCJ would successfully address the normative and practical problems posed by attempts to adjudicate such cases in national courts, or through arbitration or single-issue courts.

This is a good opportunity to note that while the problem of the missing forum that this book seeks to solve applies with equal force with respect to all MNCs, there are a number of reasons I choose to focus (albeit not exclusively) on United States–based MNCs and on US law. First and foremost, American businesses, responsible for a quarter of the world's FDI,[10] have a leading stake and potentially a leading role in opposing or supporting the ICCJ. In addition, the United States has long been considered the most open forum for mass claims by non-American plaintiffs. The reason for this perception was twofold. First, the United States is a relatively plaintiff-friendly jurisdiction because of a combination of juridical features (including, but not limited to, the existence of juries, punitive damages, and an "each party pays its own" approach to legal costs) and economic features such as the existence of an entrepreneurial plaintiff bar willing to take cases based on contingent fees. Second, during the years when the ATS was interpreted to permit claims for human rights abuses occurring overseas, prior to *Kiobel*, US courts did in fact provide one of the only places in the world where such claims could be adjudicated. The *Kiobel* decision sent access-to-justice advocates back to the drawing board to consider new possible ways to provide victims of human rights and other violations their day in court.[11] This book is part of that effort.

II INCENTIVES AND FEASIBILITY OF A NEW COURT

Even with all the problems of the current system, would businesses and governments ever agree to the establishment of an ICCJ? I answer "yes." MNCs may be persuaded to support its establishment because an ICCJ would solve many problems they face doing business internationally. First, it is important to understand the magnitude of the costs, direct and indirect, of transnational litigation for MNCs. Direct costs include, for example, attorneys' fees, travel costs, investigation and evidence gathering, witness preparation, experts, and translation. They also include the cost of any preliminary injunctions, for instance, when a court orders a defendant to post a substantial cash bond, or freezes corporate assets, as well as any permanent injunction that may preclude certain forms of doing business. When litigating in the courts of developing countries, those costs are compounded by real and perceived corruption.

As high as they are, direct costs can be dwarfed by indirect costs. Corporations facing large lawsuits may find that their share price falls for the duration of the litigation, that raising capital becomes more expensive in the face of lenders' uncertainty about the outcome of the litigation, or that they are forced to refrain from undertaking business activities such as expansion or mergers, to name but a few of the cascading effects. These and other indirect costs can threaten a company's very existence. Furthermore, direct costs can be replicated many times over, and indirect costs persist for years and decades because the decisions of the courts in one country are not binding on the courts of another country. As I mentioned previously, a final decision in the courts of one country does not mean that the litigation is definitively ended. So even though the Chevron–Ecuador plaintiffs lost their enforcement case in the United States, the story is not over; they continue to seek enforcement in other countries such as Canada and Brazil. And even though Mrs. Kiobel lost her case in the United States she is now relitigating it in the Netherlands. It is important to note that direct and indirect costs, compounded by corruption and multiplied by successive rounds of litigation, are independent of any judgments for the plaintiffs; MNCs are forced to pay the costs even if they never pay a judgment.

In the past, MNCs could perhaps have counted on avoiding the pernicious effects of litigation, confident that the combination of resource-poor plaintiffs and friendly host governments would insulate them. But those days are ending.

The lack of corporate accountability for harms gives rise to a host of backlash effects that compound both the direct and indirect costs of litigation, while systemic changes in the global legal system make it less likely that MNCs will be able to avoid costly litigation and relitigation. Backlash effects include, for example, the increasing adoption by foreign jurisdictions of pro-plaintiff procedural features, at times tailored to apply only to cases brought against MNCs; statutes designed to block the application of *forum non conveniens* in US courts; the use of domestic criminal procedures against corporate executives and employees in host states; and even contribution to regime change (from pro-FDI to populist). These backlash effects, and the contemporary "transnational litigationscape" they create, intersect with three important developments that increase the potential transnational litigation risk that MNCs face: the rise of litigation finance, the development of global lawyering, and the increasing adoption of claim aggregation devices worldwide.

An ICCJ would alleviate such problems for MNCs by providing a final, once-and-for-all decision in cross-border mass tort cases. Direct costs would be incurred only once, and indirect costs, driven for the most part by uncertainty, would end when the trial and appeal, if any, were over. This "global legal peace" would in and of itself be an immense benefit to MNCs. In addition to that, the ICCJ would offer them a neutral forum, based on the rule of law and applying clear, previously disclosed law. I will summarize the ways the ICCJ would do all that later. But first, a brief look at the incentives of states to join and an examination of what the theory of international courts and tribunals tells us about whether the time is ripe for an ICCJ.

II Incentives and Feasibility

Beyond plaintiffs and defendants, nations would benefit from the ICCJ as well. Governments of capital importing nations – such as India and Ecuador – would be incentivized to join the ICCJ because it would offer their citizenry a forum capable of holding MNCs accountable. That, in turn, should deter practices that are likely to result in mass torts. In addition, such nations would be more competitive as investment hosts than nations that declined to join the ICCJ and therefore could not offer foreign investors the prospect of global legal peace should they find themselves defending against mass claims. Governments of capital exporting nations – such as the United States, European countries, and China – on the other hand, would have a different set of incentives. They might wish to provide their businesses with the advantages described without ceding the power of their own courts. The two-tier structure for the ICCJ that I propose (which I discuss in more detail later in this Introduction) would give capital exporting countries the ability to join the enforcement regime, thus helping the ICCJ fulfill its promise of enforceable judgments (for plaintiffs) and global legal peace (for defendants), but to remain separate from the ICCJ's jurisdiction so that, for example, US federal courts would retain the power to adjudicate cross-border mass torts that occur in the United States.

Despite concerns that they may decide to hold out, there are reasons to believe that both the United States and China would support an ICCJ. Certainly, there is a kind of "schizophrenia" evident in American attitudes toward international courts. Successive administrations' views oscillate between cosmopolitanism and institutionalism, on the one hand, and "exceptionalism" and unilateralism, on the other. This may suggest that an ICCJ, sure to be many years in the making, may only be joined by the United States when the pendulum has shifted from the stark isolationism of the contemporary Trump administration to an equally authentic American desire to participate and even lead international governance and rule of law through support of its institutions. This view is bolstered by empirical work that documents the consistent support by American citizens of international courts, a consistency that may help explain why the United States has, in fact, been instrumental to the establishment of most international courts over the course of the past two centuries.

As to China, I acknowledge that the ICCJ may join the large group of international courts designed and launched without China's participation. That said, there is evidence that China is increasingly willing to submit to international regimes that might limit its sovereignty in order to foster economic growth. These include the dispute resolution regimes of the WTO, the International Centre for Settlement of Investment Disputes (ICSID, which resolves investment disputes arising under bilateral investment treaties BITs), and the New York Convention mentioned later. To that evidence I would add that participation in either one of the two tiers of the ICCJ – the jurisdiction regime or the enforcement regime – would serve the economic interests of China, which is both a significant capital importer and a capital exporter. The competitive disadvantages of holding out will increase as more capital importing nations join the court, making it more likely that China will be a late joiner, even if it is not a founding member.

The feasibility of the ICCJ becomes clearer when placed in the context of the development of international dispute resolution, the international judiciary, and the resolution of transnational mass torts in the past century. The international judiciary in the twentieth century has grown from a handful of courts to more than a hundred.[12] In parallel, international arbitration – where private parties contractually agree to settle their disputes through a private process rather than through litigation in court – has also gained acceptance and has grown exponentially.[13]

The body of theory on the question of how new international courts come into being suggests that creation of new courts is preceded by the confluence of a dizzying array of factors. These include states' self-interests; democracies' desire to spread ideals of democracy and the rule of law; the desire of states transitioning out of illiberal regimes to bind their own hands lest they lapse back; a desire to enhance the credibility of international commitments, as well as many others. The explosive growth of the international judiciary has given scholars many opportunities to study real-world examples. Those analyses show that factors that affect whether a new court will be created include the use of legalist arguments by Western leaders that limit the range of nonjudicial responses acceptable to their constituencies; a "constitutional moment," such as the end of a world war or the collapse of Communism; and the desire to cement a new world order in the wake of such historical moments. Governments' lack of credibility in terms of their willingness or ability to solve legal problems ignites social movements that push for international courts. Social entrepreneurs, visionaries, and leaders can also be instrumental. The desire to avoid incurring the diplomatic costs of setting up an ad hoc tribunal, in particular, has been identified as a reason to set up a new permanent court. All these factors, and others, help explain the emergence, often over the course of decades, of new courts.

Examining the emergence of several previously unimaginable courts shows how the theory plays out in practice. The creation of the International Criminal Court (ICC), for instance, is a remarkable development in human history because it has the power to impose criminal liability on heads of states as well as the soldiers and military leaders they send to battle. The combination of individual criminal liability and the subject matter, namely, the conduct of war, which goes to the very heart of state sovereignty, can hardly lead to greater resistance to delegation of judicial sovereignty to the international level. Yet, after a century of striving, and despite a lack of participation by the United States, the ICC became a reality in 2002. The WTO, with its Dispute Settlement Understanding (WTO DSU), developed over nearly half a century to become a lynchpin of today's global trade regime. Among other things, it attracted China – generally hostile to international courts – as a member beginning in 2001. The Iran–United States Claims Tribunal (IUSCT) was set up by two nations in an active state of hostility; indeed, it was the consequence of and was set up during the height of the 1979 hostage crisis to adjudicate thousands of private claims arising from the Iranian Revolution. Qualitative explorations of the coming into being of those institutions highlight the broad array of historical, economic, political, and other forces that converge to make international courts a reality, often over the course of many decades and despite reluctance by or within some of the world's superpowers.

Similarly, cross-border mass claim aggregation by ad hoc international tribunals is not new. Its origins can be traced at least to the Jay Treaty of 1794,[14] which established commissions that dealt with claims of US and British nationals against the other state. More contemporary examples of such claims facilities include the United Nations (UN) Compensation Commission, which was created to adjudicate claims arising from the 1990–1991 Gulf War, and the Claims Resolution Tribunals for Dormant Accounts in Switzerland, which were set up in the 1990s to resolve claims regarding assets deposited in Swiss bank accounts.[15] "Governments ... have intervened to facilitate ... [transnational mass tort claims in] situations where the numbers of parties affected is too large to ignore or resolve through informal or diplomatic means. During the nineteenth century, approximately eighty claims commissions adjudicated private litigant cases arising out of war and civil unrest... Between World War I and World War II nearly thirty commissions and arbitral bodies adjudicated private litigant disputes."[16] The proposal to establish a permanent ICCJ builds on that institutional history, providing a permanent institution to deal with such claims. That will help to ensure that like cases are treated alike, and will save states the high costs and inefficiencies of negotiating and setting up new ad hoc institutions every time there is enough political will to adjudicate transnational mass claims.

Many of the preconditions for the creation of a new international court identified in theory and practice already exist in the context of cross-border mass torts. These include, among other things, the growing discontent with the existing, asymmetrical international investment dispute resolution system, which by design offers protections to foreign investors (MNCs) but not to those harmed by them, and which takes the form of private arbitration; discontent with the lack of access to justice for plaintiffs and due process deficit for defendants in existing fora; the growing calls to regulate business and human rights, which include calls for permanent international single-issue courts (for human rights, environmental disputes, or corruption); and systemic changes engendered by the growth of litigation finance and the global rise of national collective redress and class action regimes.

III THE PROPOSAL

I propose a new international court, the ICCJ. A single global court would reduce direct and indirect costs by streamlining procedures, ensure global legal peace, and eliminate corruption by providing a neutral forum operating according to the rule of law. It would make FDI more predictable and hospitable in participating host states, and alleviate backlash by giving plaintiffs a viable way to hold MNCs accountable.

At the heart of the proposal is a two-tiered structure, implemented through two separate treaties, reflecting the differing incentives of capital exporting and capital importing countries. The former would be primarily concerned with providing their businesses global legal peace (because their own courts provide a viable forum for their own plaintiffs) whereas the latter would be primarily concerned with providing their citizens with a forum to adjudicate their claims. The first treaty (the ICCJ statute) would create the court and establish its jurisdiction in the territory of states parties. The second would set out the enforcement regime (the ICCJ enforcement treaty), but would not grant the ICCJ jurisdiction in the territory of states parties. All members of the ICCJ statute would also be part of the enforcement regime, but not the reverse. The two treaties would be designed to come into force together, but only after garnering enough support – especially for the enforcement regime – to ensure a reasonable expectation of success.

I argue that the ICCJ should have exclusive jurisdiction over the cross-border mass tort claims arising within the territory of states parties to the ICCJ statute. The grant of exclusive jurisdiction would mean that if, say, Peru were a party, then plaintiffs injured in Peru would only be able to bring their cross-border mass tort claims in the ICCJ. Exclusivity has several advantages. It would remove cross-border mass torts from the morass of transnational litigation and therefore guarantee an end to parallel and sequential litigation. It would also protect both parties from the pernicious effects of real and perceived corruption and bias in national courts. But complementarity, where the ICCJ would defer to the jurisdiction of a national court that was willing and able to take on the case, would be a plausible, albeit inferior, fallback position. The territorial nexus meanwhile would mean that the ICCJ would have jurisdiction over any defendant operating in Peru – no matter that defendant's nationality, and no matter whether its home country were or were not a member of the ICCJ statute.

The ICCJ would grant defendants global legal peace (in legal jargon, "global preclusion") through the operation of the enforcement treaty. States joining the enforcement regime would commit to enforcing the decisions of the ICCJ. The mechanism I propose for this regime is similar to the one that already exists in international arbitration. There, the Convention on the Recognition and Enforcement of Foreign Arbitral Awards (the New York Convention),[17] generally regarded as one

III The Proposal

of the most successful commercial law treaties of all time, requires every state that joins the treaty to give full effect to arbitration decisions (with some rarely invoked exceptions).

Since the ICCJ would adjudicate cross-border mass torts, it is worth defining those terms, as I use them throughout the book. By "cross-border" (or "transnational") I am referring to cases in which plaintiffs from one jurisdiction sue defendants (usually, MNCs) in the courts of another jurisdiction. A "tort" is "an act or omission that gives rise to injury or harm to another and amounts to a civil wrong for which courts impose liability. In the context of torts, 'injury' describes the invasion of any legal right, whereas 'harm' describes a loss or detriment in fact that an individual suffers."[18] In order to provide both plaintiffs and defendants with maximum predictability, to integrate modern advances in tort law, and to ensure fairness the ICCJ should define and apply its own law, defined in the ICCJ statute. The alternative, applying existing national laws, would maintain the unpredictability of the current system and furthermore might deprive injured plaintiffs of their day in court if the country in question lacked, for instance, modern environmental standards. "Mass" means litigation involving a number of claimants that exceeds a numerical (such as twenty) or discretionary (such as when the judges decide efficiency will best be served) threshold.

These are complex cases that can arise from a variety of circumstances such as a single mass disaster, myriad individual contacts with a hazardous product, or environmental contamination over decades. Therefore, the claims may all arise at once or be latent for years, maturing in waves. However, the hallmark of mass tort claims is that they involve identical or near-identical issues, and are brought against the same defendant or group of defendants. Mass torts can be dealt with through a range of options, with individual adjudication on one end of the spectrum, collective redress (also known as claim aggregation) somewhere in the middle, and class actions (in which one or few plaintiffs represent a larger group of unnamed, sometimes unknown, plaintiffs and to which I will also refer as "representative actions") on the other end of the spectrum. The ICCJ should offer procedures all along that spectrum, so that each group of claims can be dealt with in the most efficient way possible. In that way, it will resemble a "multidoor court," offering alternative dispute resolution (ADR), aggregate litigation (coordinating and consolidating part but not all of the trial), representative actions, and supervised settlements. Judges will manage routing the parties through these multiple options.

As a general approach, I propose that the ICCJ adopt streamlined procedures derived from the increasing convergence of common law and civil law approaches in the areas of adjudicating mass claims. That would mean, among other things, that the ICCJ's version of the representative action would be structured differently than the American class action (which is generally regarded with skepticism outside the

United States). Also, I argue that the ICCJ should opt for the more managerial and inquisitorial approach to adjudication favored in countries with a civil law system, as opposed to the system in common law countries, where the judge is more passive and the parties' attorneys drive the process. Among other benefits, this will permit judges to dismiss cases early on, something they are not easily able to do in jury-based systems.

The hybridization means that some of the most controversial features of the American legal system would be restricted or dispensed with altogether. Among those features are expansive discovery, punitive damages, and juries. Discovery would be limited, along the lines of what is permitted in international commercial arbitration. Punitive damages, too, would be restricted; they would only be available where provable beyond a reasonable doubt (as opposed to the more lenient standard of preponderance of the evidence used in most parts of civil trials). The ICCJ would have no juries; all trials would be bench trials. Further efficiencies for MNCs would accrue through the predictability of a single body of law, known *ex ante*; a neutral forum free from actual or perceived corruption; and state-of-the-art aggregation procedures tailored to the specific needs of each case. By adopting a hybrid of common law and civil law procedures, drawing on cutting-edge thinking coupled with freedom from path-dependent domestic legal arrangements, and creating specific solutions custom-designed for mass torts that do not operate as precedent domestically, the proposal should assuage MNCs concerns that justice and efficiency for defendants, as well as plaintiffs, would be served by the new institution.

An ICCJ would not, of course, be a panacea. All international courts are the products of political compromises, sometimes painful ones. They are imperfect institutions and the ICCJ will be no different. I invite the reader to ask not whether all problems of mass claims and transnational litigation would be resolved by this proposal. They will not. Aggregate litigation, in particular, is an area characterized by unhappy trade-offs between justice and efficiency; both it and tort law are ideological battlegrounds where competing worldviews cannot all be satisfied. Rather, I ask readers to consider whether the ICCJ will significantly improve on the existing reality – leaving transnational mass tort resolution to flawed, reluctant national courts that were never designed to serve as world courts. The proposal for an ICCJ is an exercise in nonideal theory and as such it inherently seeks to not let the very best be the enemy of the good enough.

Finally, as implied by the institutional histories of other international courts, this is self-consciously a project with a long view. Arriving at a treaty to create the court may take years or decades. And decades more would be needed for the court to build institutional expertise and maturity, to become efficient, and to develop nuanced and predictable jurisprudence. Such is the nature of building an international (or domestic) legal order. Nonetheless, I suggest that we should not let the

III The Proposal

formidable challenges that would be involved both in setting up and running an ICCJ, or the fact that it will inevitably be an imperfect compromise, be a barrier to getting started today.

In that vein, I will conclude the book with the outline of an action plan, consisting of steps that academics, activists, policy makers, and others can take to lay the groundwork for the establishment of an ICCJ.

The book proceeds as follows: In Chapter 1, I set out the theory of how international courts come into being, identifying the range of circumstances that have historically merged to spur their creation. This is the first part of the argument that an ICCJ would be feasible, not just desirable. I will then spend much of the rest of the book attempting to show that many, if not most, of those circumstances exist today in the context of transnational civil justice. (Readers less interested in this theoretical exposition may wish to skip to Chapter 2.) In Chapter 2, I offer three case studies – Bhopal, Chevron–Ecuador, and *Kiobel*, to highlight the limits of the ability of the current system to deal with cross-border mass torts committed by MNCs. That discussion continues in Chapter 3, where I elaborate on the legal underpinnings of the problem of the missing forum and show how no existing forum can adequately solve it. In Chapter 4, I offer the second part of the argument for feasibility: the business case for an ICCJ. MNCs, their home states, and the states that host FDI all have economic incentives to prefer an ICCJ to the existing transnational litigationscape. In Chapter 5, I offer a blueprint for the ICCJ, addressing issues such as jurisdiction and procedure. The Conclusion provides ideas for action that can be taken to make the ICCJ a reality.

1

How New International Courts Come into Being

> *Thirty-four years ago, when the organization of which I am secretary formulated a plan for the establishment of a "High Court of Nations," we were laughed to scorn as mere theorists and utopians, the scoffers emphatically declaring that no two countries in the world would ever agree to take part in the establishment of such a court. Today we proudly point to the fact that the Hague Tribunal has been established; and notwithstanding the unfortunate blow it received in the early stages of its existence by the Boer War and the attempt on the part of some nations to boycott it, there is now a general consensus of opinion that it has come to stay.*
>
> Randal Cremer, Laureate of the 1903 Nobel Peace Prize and the lead architect of what is today known as the Permanent Court of Arbitration, 1905

Author's Note: This chapter covers the theoretical approaches to the question of when and under what conditions states agree to create new international courts and tribunals. Some readers may wish to skip the theory and instead begin with Chapter 2, which presents the current broken system for adjudicating cross-border mass torts.

New international courts and tribunals are the products of complex historical, political, moral, and intellectual factors that defy easy categorization. Existing theories of the behavior of states vis-à-vis international law and international legal institutions – whether rationalist, constructivist, or Kantian (to name a few) – all address important aspects of the process of creation. But none of them fully accounts for the broad range of social forces that empirical studies suggest must come together to create the conditions for new international courts and tribunals to emerge. Readers not already familiar with the contemporary international legal landscape might suppose that such a confluence happens only rarely and that international courts and tribunals are few and far between. And prior to the twentieth century that would have been true. But since the end of World War II and with greater force since the conclusion of the Cold War, the pace of the development of international legal institutions has accelerated. Today, there are approximately a hundred international courts and tribunals, a number that challenges common notions of the scarcity of political will of states to submit to international adjudication and that provides scholars with a wealth of data to draw on in understanding what generates that political will.

In this chapter, I will provide the first part of the answer to the question of whether or not the establishment of an ICCJ is a politically and otherwise viable proposal. In so doing, I will also establish the theoretical foundations upon which the rest of the book rests. First, I will summarize existing theories of international law and states' engagement with international institutions in order to develop a schematic of the types of factors that each theory tends to point to as especially influential in the creation of new international courts and tribunals. Loosely, these are some version of self-interest/rational choice for the rationalists, liberal democratic norms for contemporary Kantians and socialization through interaction for constructivists. Then, I will turn to recent empirical literature on international courts and tribunals to show that, generally speaking, versions of the especially influential factors identified by the different theories, taken together, tend to precede the successful establishment of new international courts and tribunals. In this section of the chapter I will examine the creation of the ICC, the WTO Dispute Settlement System, the Iran–United States Claims Tribunal (IUSCT), and the Jerusalem Arbitration Center (JAC). These qualitative analyses will highlight the wide range of forces that converge to make international courts a reality. They are offered as qualitative illustrations of the complex (and often unforeseeable) confluences of sociohistorical global forces that converge to make international courts a reality, often over the course of many decades, and despite reluctance by or within some of the world's superpowers.

There is no magic recipe, repeatable on demand, for the establishment of a new international court or tribunal. But the histories teach us that several factors commonly appear as part of a new institution's backstory. States' self-interest and economic incentives feature heavily in explaining the decision to join. As complexity and specialization increase in areas such as trade, human rights, and the environment, joining an international court serves a functional purpose. A desire to enhance the credibility of international commitments, especially those of new or returning players and of nations transitioning into democracy, is another explanation. And the strength of states' desire to avoid diplomatic and political interventions to resolve disputes is particularly important to keep in mind. Such a desire has been observed in particular in the establishment of tribunals designed to deal with transnational mass claims. Overlapping jurisdiction over given matters on the national, regional, and international levels, coupled with dissatisfaction with advancement on the national or regional levels with respect to the matters subject to the overlapping jurisdiction, is often observed as a catalyst for establishment, as is blockage of political change at the national or regional level. Distrust of governments and disappointment in their ability or willingness to solve the problems that end up adjudicated internationally are also contributing factors. The existence of similar, earlier institutions that serve as prototypes is another. Discontent with such institutions can propel a movement to replace them with a new court. Conversely, the existence of successful courts at a different governance level, a different region, or a different area of law can create idea contagion. The existence of "blueprints" can assist, whether or not a prototypical institution already exists. Such blueprints have been known to develop over decades, sometimes collecting dust until the time is ripe.[1] Global initiatives, charismatic visionaries, and social entrepreneurs have all been observed to play key roles in the creation of new courts. "Constitutional moments,"[2] such as the conclusion of a major war or the decline of Communism, that bring a new world order led in the twentieth century to the establishment of courts that consolidate and reinforce the new order. Finally, social movements of scholars, jurists inside and outside academia, practitioners, politicians, and others, and converging interests of various constituencies of support, some stronger than others, all play an important role.[3]

Next, I analyze what the theory and case studies might teach us about the possible positions of two states that are, prima facie, likely to hold out on becoming members of an ICCJ – the United States and China – and about what might be the effects if either or both hold out. The chapter then concludes the lessons learned from all the aforesaid with respect to the question whether or not the establishment of an ICCJ is plausible and whether conditions are ripe to initiate an advocacy program calling for its establishment.[4]

Before delving into the arguments this chapter seeks to make, and at the risk of stating the obvious, it should be acknowledged that new international courts and tribunals are the result of political compromises and are therefore imperfect institutions (to say the least) – imperfect, but nonetheless tasked with some of the most formidable challenges facing humanity. I do not intend to idealize and suggest that any of the existing international courts and tribunals, or the one suggested in this book, is a perfect solution to the complex global problems that they endeavor to address. Rather, a goal of this chapter is to suggest that we should not let the formidable challenges that would be involved both in setting up and in running an ICCJ, and the fact that an ICCJ will also be an imperfect compromise in its structure and performance, be a barrier to embarking on such a project. The proposal for an ICCJ is an exercise in nonideal theory, and the standard against which to judge the viability and desirability of an ICCJ is whether it would present significant progress over the existing reality – leaving transnational mass tort resolution to flawed (sometimes deeply) and reluctant national courts – as described in Chapters 2 and 3. The approach offered here follows the adage "not to let the very best be the enemy of the good enough."

I THEORETICAL MODELS

Since Randall Cremer gave the Nobel lecture excerpted at the beginning of this chapter, the international judiciary has seen explosive growth. It has gone from a handful of courts a century ago to more than a hundred today.[5] The puzzle of when and why states support the creation of new international courts is one that occupies the interest of jurists, political scientists, international relations scholars, and historians. Because complex phenomena have complex, multifactor explanations, their answers vary. A reasonable conclusion from the rich literature on the topic is that a web of interests and values informs the decision to create or join an international court. Doing justice to all of the nuanced explanations is beyond the scope of this book, but a humble survey of some of the leading theories follows.

There are, very roughly speaking, three categories of theories. Theories in the first category posit that states' decisions on whether or not to join (or support the creation of) a new international court or tribunal come down, in the end, to self-interest. The second category posits that democracy, once established, prompts states that have adopted liberal norms to uphold and propagate those norms via international law (among other routes). And a third category emphasizes the importance of the fact that states' decisions are embedded in a larger network of interactions with other states, with citizens, and with international civil society – among other groups. Theories in this category argue that those interactions can influence states' views, change their incentives to act, and even overcome the imperative of short-term self-interest.[6]

In the first category, realist and critical legal theories maintain that participation in international courts and tribunals is an expression of power and self-interest. Hegemons join for their own reasons, then coerce or entice weaker countries to accept new courts in furtherance of the hegemons' goals.[7] Various rationalist reasons have been advanced for why states might choose to cede authority to international courts. For example, powers victorious in major wars may create international courts, as well as other international organizations, to cement a new world order. "Powerful states can use international courts to stabilize relationships with weaker powers, pacify weaker states by giving them a voice in the international order, and stabilize the order by locking in the hegemon's preferences."[8] One explanation, advanced predominantly in the context of interstate disputes, focuses on information sharing and uncertainty reduction. According to this view, international courts are useful for sharing information about the law and facts of a dispute in situations where states are interested in cooperating to resolve the dispute and, in turn, to reduce uncertainty in treaty interpretation.[9] Closely related is an explanation that exacts that bargaining in the shadow of the law, namely, in the shadow of courts that can issue binding rulings, benefits overall bargaining.[10] Desires to address important concerns of domestic actors, to deflect blame, and to acquire economic benefits have all been advanced as self-interest based explanations.[11] Power-based explanations have broad appeal because they have at least partial explanatory power. But they have their limits. For example, power cannot account for "why two major powers with similar capabilities would adopt distinct levels of support for new international courts."[12]

Functionalist accounts are an important strand of rationalism, according to which new international courts and tribunals are created to satisfy specific needs that emerge as global interactions change in frequency and form and that the founding states believe need to be addressed. Functional needs often include increasing complexity and specialization in trade, the environment, and human rights, to name a few examples. The European Court of Justice (ECJ) was created as the judicial organ of the European Community to ensure that the interpretation and application of European Union (EU) treaties and EU law are observed and the WTO's DSU was created "to fill a dispute settlement purpose that was lacking in the prior General Agreement on Tariffs and Trade (GATT)" regime, for example.[13] Politicians desire to avoid the need for diplomatic interventions to resolve disputes.[14] A primary example of this last function is in the realm of mass claims resolution, where, currently, states incur high costs negotiating new ad hoc mass claim resolution tribunals.

In the second category, on the other hand, ideational theories "maintain that transnational processes of diffusion and persuasion socialize less-democratic governments to accept norms."[15] Here, one finds the view that the expansion of a system of international organizations, including courts, represents a movement toward Kantian peace. As the number of democracies increases, according to this view, democracy's preference for legalized dispute resolution, as part of the rule of law, makes its mark in the form of international courts.[16] Consistent with, but separate from the ideational view is the view that the proliferation of international courts is a function of social contagion. "One sees a process of court contagion as new courts partially emulate existing courts and as the increasing number of cases and 'sound' judgments leads to further utilization of existing courts and demands for new ones."[17] Relatedly, and more broadly, the development of new ideas at the international level has been described as a "norm cascade" that culminates in a moment when an idea becomes irresistible. "A cascade is an area of turbulence and transition in a longer riparian metaphor. Such a stage seems to have been reached in the area of international justice in the 1990s. The river has had normative tributaries, eddies, currents, and dams, as well as a cascade or two already, and it is reasonable to imagine that more of these will be reached."[18]

A middle ground between rationalist and ideational views is occupied by the view that international law is simultaneously instrumental and resistant to the pursuit of power by dominant states because international law is "important for powerful states as a source of legitimacy, but in order to provide legitimacy, it needs to distance itself from power and has to resist its mere translation into law. [It] then occupies... [a] secure position between the demands of the powerful and the ideals of justice held in international society."[19] In this context, one finds explanations that focus on reputation building versus reputational costs: creating and joining courts allow states to enhance the credibility of their international commitments.[20] In that vein, it has been demonstrated empirically that governments delegate authority to international bodies, and bind their own hands, to protect and consolidate democratic gains. Newer and weaker democracies will therefore favor the enforcement of human rights obligations more strongly than strong and established democracies.[21] More broadly, theories in the third category focus more on the interactions among states and their officials inside and outside international organizations. For constructivists, state interests are not given and therefore are determinative of their approach to international law and international legal institutions. Rather, state interests are *determined by* international legal norms, which, among other things, specify which actors get to play the game and how they should play it. "Nations thus obey international rules not just because of sophisticated calculations about how compliance or noncompliance will affect their interests, but because a repeated habit of obedience remakes their interests so that they come to value rule compliance."[22]

Of course, there are overlaps between the categories. One could define building and maintaining a reputation as "good" actors to be in a given state's self-interest, and therefore to be more in line with realism. And the process described by constructivists whereby liberal norms are propagated and enforced through interaction and sociocultural dissemination is compatible with contemporary Kantian notions of democracy's normative pull. Irrespective of categorization, most of those theories were developed to explain states' broader international legal commitments at a time when international judicial institutions were scarce and when the few international courts and tribunals that did exist were scarcely used. In the thirty-plus years since the end of the Cold War, however, states have created ever-greater numbers of international courts and tribunals and have used them with ever-greater frequency.

Historically, the international judiciary develops in waves and those waves can be traced to moments in human history when the world order has been transformed. To borrow a concept from constitutional theory, a constitutional moment in world affairs might be necessary for nations with widely divergent interests to join and form a new multilateral organization to which some sovereignty is delegated. "Growth spurts" in the international judiciary in the twentieth century, for example, can be traced to the end of World War I, when the PCIJ was created, the end of World War II, when the ICJ was created, and the end of the Cold War, when the ad hoc and permanent international criminal courts as well as the WTO with its dispute resolution body were created.[23] At such moments, new international organizations are set up to help cement a new international order. Legal change, more generally, "can occur at varying paces," observed one legal scholar, with "long periods of gradual evolution [] sometimes punctuated by brief moments of rapid, irregular change."[24]

The proliferation of international courts and tribunals – particularly "new style" international courts with compulsory jurisdiction that allow nonstate actors to initiate litigation[25] – has provided scholars with a previously unimaginable wealth of examples against which explanatory theories can be tested. In an exhaustive study of the rise of new-style international courts, the political scientist Karen Alter has identified five general political factors that render governments willing to concede authority to international courts. These factors cut across the three types of theories described previously, suggesting that the real-world behavior of states in deciding whether to support and join new international courts and tribunals defies easy categorization. The first factor is distrust of governments. "Governments only sign on [] once their legitimating suggestions of other options ring too hollow to be convincing. Europeans' experience of World War II and Communist rule, Latin Americans' experience with brutal military dictatorship, and Africans' experience with corrupt nationalist governments that become increasingly violent"[26] are all examples of disappointments that propel the establishment of new-style courts. "When alternatives are exhausted, and [] politicians are willing to agree that something needs to change, advocates [who stand ready to promote international judicial models that address the problems of the existing regime] will put forward their proposals."[27]

The second factor is the existence of global initiatives that help facilitate the spread of an "embedded approach" to where international law is explicitly imported into domestic legal systems that then serve as the primary enforcers of international norms. The EU and the European human rights system are paradigmatic examples of the embedded approach; for the most part national courts are called on to enforce EU law, and the European Convention on Human Rights, the CJEU, and the ECtHR exist to oversee domestic implementation. Since the end of the Cold War, "global initiatives have aided the implantation of international law in domestic legal systems, and thus facilitated the spread of the embedded approach to international law enforcement."[28] These initiatives include The Washington Consensus (economic reform prescriptions developed by the International Monetary Fund, World Bank, and US Treasury Department), the Rome Statute, and the international development goals developed by the UN and endorsed by all of its member states known as the "Millennium Development Goals."[29] The third factor is the overlapping nature of jurisdiction at the national, regional, and international levels, coupled with dissatisfaction: dissatisfaction with advancement in one level propels developments in another overlapping jurisdiction. The fourth factor is "legal and political dynamics [that] interact to produce institutional change between conjunctural moments."[30]

More simply stated, legal changes are sometimes propelled by a blockage in political change. And fifth, the United States and Europe "facilitate the spread of international law and [] adjudication when [their] leaders articulate, accept, and respond to legalist arguments."[31]

To identify these factors is not to say that all previous theoretical models should be discarded – quite the contrary. It is, rather, to suggest that no one lens is sufficient to understand the complex phenomenon of the creation of new international courts and tribunals. The kinds of things that realists point to as important – economic incentives, advancing domestic prerogatives, acquiring information – do play a significant role. But, so do the kinds of interactions that ideational theories point to, such as the propagation of democratic norms and idea contagion. And so do constructivist notions of participation in similar institutions and robust dialogue among governments and nongovernmental actors in academia, civil society, and professional practice.

The upshot is that reasoning backward from a single theory of states' participation in international legal institutions to those states' likely view of a new international civil court will not produce a good answer to the question of whether the time is ripe for the ICCJ. Rather, a good answer requires a careful and nuanced analysis of the extent to which some or all of the factors identified by the whole range of theories as contributing to the creation of other international courts and tribunals are present in the context of international civil justice. Throughout the rest of this book I will try to show that they are, and that an ICCJ is therefore a viable idea. But first, I will turn to some case studies to illustrate how new international courts and tribunals are born when several disparate elements merge, often over a significant amount of time.

II THE CASE HISTORIES

A *The International Criminal Court*

This section will explore the long journey of an idea that first emerged at the Hague Peace Conferences of 1899 and 1907 and became a reality a full century later with the creation of the International Criminal Court (ICC) in 2002.[32] The emergence of international criminal law enforced by ad hoc and permanent international criminal tribunals is arguably the most important legal development of our time. It represents humanity's emerging willingness to end the state of affairs in which the murder of a single individual is punishable, but genocide is not.

In the following paragraphs, I will highlight several aspects of the history of the creation of the ICC in order to illustrate how the preceding theoretical discussion explains what played out in practice. In brief summary, like other, apparently novel international courts, the ICC is actually the successor of earlier institutions, which can be viewed as experiments or prototypes. In addition to offering lessons to be learned from their successes (and failures), earlier international criminal tribunals can be understood as contributing to idea contagion. In addition to their knowledge of the history of earlier international criminal tribunals, the drafters of the Rome Statute were informed by nearly a century of academic, professional, and diplomatic discourse. The massive geopolitical shifts occasioned by, among other things, the end of the Cold War helped generate the political will to create accountability for the worst crimes.

The Rome Statute of the International Criminal Court (the Rome Statute) entered into force on July 1, 2002.[33] Thus, the ICC was established (the first judges took their oaths in March of 2003) with a mandate to counter impunity by prosecuting the perpetrators of "the crime of crimes," genocide, as well as crimes against humanity and war crimes. Those who remember the shock of the first concentration camps to emerge in Europe since World War II during the Balkan war(s) of 1991–1995, or the horrors of the 1994 genocide in Rwanda, which developments in media enabled to be broadcast daily worldwide for the first time, might recognize these wars as constitutional moments. A liberal institutionalist would reason that the ICC is a reflection of the rise of a global epistemic community that espouses the norm that impunity for war crimes, crimes against humanity, and genocide are unjust and that sees a need for a permanent international organization to enforce the prohibition against such crimes. A constructivist might emphasize that "new justice norms were incorporated into the Statute because state decision makers, informed by civil society, came to believe that a modern justice system had to take greater cognizance of victims' interests and social reconstruction following massive crimes than did traditional justice."[34] And a realist would reason that joining the ICC promoted the self-interest of the states who chose to join and, in particular, provided them with some comparative advantage. Such an account might reason that "it is conceivable a state concerned about its citizens being subject to international crimes, or convinced that genocide, crimes against humanity, and war crimes contribute to potentially costly regional threats, would join efforts to prosecute international criminals to deter future criminal behavior. A state might join the ICC succumbing to pressures exerted by other state supporters of the Court. Or a state might believe that it could manipulate the ICC's resources to contribute to its individual advantage."[35]

1 Legal and Institutional Precedents – Experimentation and Idea Contagion

The ICC did not appear out of thin air. Its roots can be traced back to the development of humanitarian law in the mid-nineteenth century and the establishment of military war crimes courts after World War II. One of the earliest proposals for an international criminal court came from Swiss jurist Gustave Moynier, who

II *The Case Histories* 23

cofounded the predecessor of the International Committee of the Red Cross. Moynier argued in 1872 that international criminal courts be created in order to deter and adjudicate violations of the 1864 Geneva Convention. Although Moynier's proposal was never implemented, during the interwar years the international community again took up the idea. The League of Nations began to consider the notion of an international criminal court in 1920, and in 1937 opened for signature a treaty establishing just such an institution.[36] The League of Nations international criminal court never entered into force, but the idea continued to gain traction. As World War II drew to a close, the Allied powers set up several intergovernmental and quasi-intergovernmental bodies to study the question. These included the London International Assembly (1941) and the International Commission for Penal Reconstruction and Development (1942).

All of the earlier attempts, stretching back to the League of Nations, created the ideational backdrop that turned into the reality of the Nuremberg and Tokyo military tribunals. In the 1943 Moscow Declarations, the Allies declared that "Germans who had committed war crimes would be sent for trial to the countries where they had committed their atrocities" and that the "'major criminals whose offenses have no particular geographical location' would be punished by the Allies."[37] Shortly after the Moscow declaration, the Allies established the United Nations War Crimes Commission (UNWCC) (1943).[38] The Charter of the International Military Tribunal (Nuremberg) was promulgated in 1945; it incorporated many of the ideas of the UNWCC. General MacArthur created the International Military Tribunal for the Far East unilaterally in 1948, using his power as Allied supreme commander in the area. The Nuremberg and Tokyo tribunals adjudicated and penalized, respectively, Nazi leaders who planned and carried out the Holocaust and other war crimes and the leaders of the Empire of Japan who participated in a joint conspiracy to start and wage war,[39] and who planned, committed, or failed to prevent atrocities or crimes against humanity.

The institutional momentum of the post–World War II years continued for only a short time. In 1950, the UN General Assembly tasked the International Law Commission (ILC) – a body created by the UN Charter to promote the codification and progressive development of customary international law – to codify the Nuremberg principles and to develop a draft code of offenses against the peace and security of mankind. The following year, the ILC presented to the UN General Assembly the draft code and a proposal for an international criminal court. "The ILC's projects to develop a criminal jurisdiction – to design a court and its procedures – and to develop a code of offenses ... flowed intermittently and in parallel, but with little interconnection, thereafter. The ILC submitted a draft international criminal court statute and a revised draft code of offenses in 1954, but the General Assembly then shifted its attention away from the statute and code ...

"ostensibly pending the sensitive task of defining the crime of aggression. In fact, political tensions associated with the Cold War had largely dammed progress on the war crimes agenda."[40]

That lack of progress largely persisted until the end of the Cold War. The 1960s and 1970s produced little visible progress for the cause of establishing an international criminal court. However, during that time, international civil society came of age with organizations such as Amnesty International being founded and environmental and human rights activism, such as the global antiapartheid movement, gaining momentum and influence. The concept of a "crime against humanity," which first emerged to describe the massacre of Armenians during World War I, had been used by the UN General Assembly in a 1973 resolution that declared apartheid as such a crime. In 1981, the ILC under the direction of the General Assembly resumed its work on a draft code of international war crimes.

The dam broke at the end of the Cold War. The most significant development at that time was the creation by the UN Security Council of two new, ad hoc international criminal tribunals. Under the UN Charter, the Security Council has broad power to act when it determines that a situation presents a threat to international peace and security. Using that power, it decided that the conflict in the former Yugoslavia, and the genocide in Rwanda, presented such threats. At the time, a typical response of the Security Council in such a situation would have been, taking two common examples, to deploy peacekeeping troops or to impose sanctions. Instead, however, it chose to create two brand-new international judicial institutions: the International Criminal Tribunal for the Former Yugoslavia (ICTY) in 1993 and, a year later, the International Criminal Tribunal for Rwanda (ICTR). These were closely followed by "hybrid" or "internationalized" criminal courts and tribunals, institutions that combined national and international law and that included both local and international judges. They included the Special Court for Sierra Leone, the Extraordinary Chambers in the Courts of Cambodia, and the Special Panels of the Dili District Court in East Timor.[41] At the same time, in 1993, the ILC began work on a new draft statute for an international criminal court, under the direction of the influential thinker Professor James Crawford.

The early, never-realized permanent international criminal courts, the Nuremberg and Tokyo tribunals, as well as the ICTY, ICTR, and their immediate successors in Sierra Leone, Cambodia, and East Timor can be seen as instances of "idea contagion" as well as forms of institutional experimentation through which the international community was testing the viability of different ways of implementing international criminal justice. The military tribunals that followed World War II and the critiques of these tribunals inspired the ad hoc tribunals for Rwanda and the former Yugoslavia, which, in turn, inspired both the hybrid tribunal and the permanent ICC. And each of these "waves" served as a prototype, and a basis for improvement for the one that followed. By the late 1990s, the public debate had been reframed, to a large degree, from a debate about whether to internationalize criminal law, to what form of internationalization is most effective, just, and efficient: domestic, international, or hybrid? Ad hoc or permanent? If international, in what kind of relation to national systems? In that vein, another way to look at this institutional history is as a form of experimentation. The ICTY and ICTR incorporated many of the principles of the Nuremberg and Tokyo tribunals while consciously trying to avoid some of their pitfalls (such as their military nature). The hybrid tribunals of the late 1990s and early 2000s were an explicit reaction to the size, slow pace, expense, and vulnerability to charges of neoimperalism of the ICTY and ICTR. And the nature of the ICCs, as will be discussed in detail in Chapter 5, was designed in reaction to dissatisfaction with the relationship between the international jurisdiction of the ICTY and ICTR and the national jurisdictions of the Balkan states and Rwanda.

2 Change Agents

The rise of an international civil society organized around human rights and accountability for atrocities played an important role in setting the stage for the creation of the ICC. This change began in the late 1970s, and accelerated through the 1980s and 1990s. Helsinki Watch was established in 1978. Shortly thereafter, a growing cadre of human rights activists launched sister organizations such as Americas Watch, Africa Watch, and Asia Watch. In 1988 the network merged into the global Human Rights Watch. At around the same time, a group of activists in London founded Amnesty International, a membership-based organization that would go on to create chapters in nearly every country in the world. Amnesty International and Human Rights Watch came to define a global agenda that both drew inspiration from and inspired local activists and nongovernmental organizations (NGOs) worldwide.

Like other developments in the 1990s, the global human rights movement gathered steam and force with globalization and, particularly, the communication and information revolution that underlies it. The end of the Cold War led to transitions, some bloody, to many nations. Bloody transitions, wars, and genocide in a world in which international human rights ideology, and a global network of human rights NGOs, have greatly expanded led to the new "atrocities law" and the academic and discursive field of transitional justice,[42] as well as to a toolbox of responses that included national criminal prosecutions, truth commissions, and international or internationalized (national–international hybrid) criminal tribunals. The limitations of national prosecutions and of truth commissions highlighted the need for international prosecution as a viable and permanent option. (And vice versa: the limitations of international criminal prosecution highlighted the continuing need for domestic responses including national trials and truth and reconciliation programs.)

International NGOs were not the only important players (outside governments) in the normative, legal, and institutional development of international criminal law; other social change agents carried the international criminal court idea from one international sphere to another. For example, Professor Schiff describes the work of Professor M. Cherif Bassiouni, an expert in international criminal law, who proposed in 1989 that the idea of an ICC be reexamined by the ILC, including a mandate to consider a mechanism for international adjudication of crimes such as drug trafficking. When the Balkan wars broke in 1991 and news of the mass atrocities they involved shocked the conscience of many worldwide, Professor Bassiouni proposed and then headed the UN Commission of Experts on the Situation in Yugoslavia. The commission's work led to the 1993 establishment of the ICTY. Professor Antonio Cassesse, a specialist in international criminal law, advanced the notion in numerous writings over several decades that the international community could, and should, provide accountability for atrocities. He served as the first president of the ICTY and, later, as the president of the Special Tribunal for Lebanon, a hybrid tribunal set up in 2009 to adjudicate responsibility for the attack that killed Rafik Hariri, Lebanon's prime minister. Professors Bassiouni and Cassesse and countless others created and advanced scholarly, diplomatic, and professional discourses in international criminal law – discourses that informed the designers of the ICC.

All the political, diplomatic, legal, scholarly, and advocacy efforts came to fruition when the UN Diplomatic Conference of Plenipotentiaries on the Establishment of an International Criminal Court was held in 1998 in Rome. Early drafts of the statute had circulated widely, drawing commentary from scholars, lawyers, activists, and others.

> In the initially becalmed post–Cold War diplomatic environment, new atrocities and growing international attention added momentum to what had been the project of a small group of international lawyers to convert conceptual agreement into generally accepted positive international criminal law. The many streams of [international humanitarian law, international criminal law], retributive, restorative, and transitional justice poured into draft texts to be discussed and considered at formal and informal meetings leading up to the Rome Conference. To the surprise of many participants and observers, on July 17, 1998, the negotiators at Rome broke through the final blockages to agreement, and their efforts enabled the Rome Statute of the ICC to be open for signature and ratification.[43]

3 Geopolitical Change and Constitutional Moments

The end of the Cold War, the advent of globalization, and the increase in the number of both emerging and stable democracies also helped to set the stage for the creation of the ICC. The effect of the Cold War on international relations, and in particular on the UN and international adjudication, is well documented and need not be repeated here. In the late 1970s, in parallel with the rise of an international civil society focused on human rights, President Jimmy Carter adopted human rights as a core tenet of his foreign policy. "As the 1980s wore on, the Cold War system began to crack, and by 1991, it had disintegrated. The international lawyers who had been working to consolidate international human rights, humanitarianism, and criminal law under the shadow of the Cold War were about to enjoy a confluence of opportunities and crises that vastly accelerated the current."[44] Ideas about accountability for international crimes encountered a constitutional moment at the conclusion of World War II, when the horrors of that war galvanized who sought to outlaw and punish war crimes, and another at the end of the Cold War, when Western nations sought to consolidate the new, postcommunist world order. In the latter case, several changes in international relations increased the possibility of international criminal adjudication. These included more cooperation among previously distrustful Western and Eastern bloc states, more acceptance by former Soviet countries of international law, and "unprecedented agreement in the Security Council and increasing convergence in the views of its five permanent members."[45]

B The World Trade Organization Dispute Settlement Understanding

The story of the WTO DSU is a story of institutional experimentation and development from prototype to court. The predecessor of the WTO, the General Agreement on Trade and Tariffs (GATT), came into being in 1947. At the outset, GATT established a dispute settlement procedure although it could not be called an international court or tribunal in any modern sense of the word. Rather, its proscribed process would begin with consultations between the complaining state(s) and the state(s) alleged to have violated GATT. If the parties could not settle the disputes through consultations, they could refer the dispute to the GATT Council, the plenary body of the contracting parties. The GATT Council had wide leeway in how to handle disputes referred to it; commonly, it would establish a panel of outside experts or convene a working group of representatives of contracting parties. If the experts or working group failed to resolve the dispute, they would send their findings to the GATT Council, which could use those findings either to urge further mediation and settlement or to make a ruling. Although it rarely happened, the members of GATT could authorize retaliation if they believed the circumstances warranted it. One of the features of the GATT process most widely criticized was the consensus-based model: any action taken to settle a dispute had to attract a consensus of contracting states; thus, any state, including the state against which the complaint was brought, could veto action.

Although states regularly called on the GATT Council to convene panels in the 1950s, by the 1960s the dispute settlement system fell into disuse. This reflected what one scholar termed a shift from a legalistic approach to an antilegalistic – or diplomatic – approach.[46] During this period, states shied away from filing formal disputes in favor of negotiation, consensus building, and political solutions. "Accordingly, consultation-style diplomacy became glorified as the ideal of regulatory policy."[47] This turn away from law toward politics was an instance of institutional experimentation. The experiment lasted, however, only as long as the political commitments of GATT members were broadly in line with the goal of fostering free trade.

Increasingly protectionist politics in the 1970s thus prompted a round of negotiations focused, among other things, on reforming the dispute settlement system (the Tokyo Round). Negotiators at the Tokyo Round advanced some significant reforms, most notably a series of "surveillance bodies" tasked with continually monitoring government compliance with their respective GATT agreements. Ultimately, the Tokyo Round kept most of the central elements of the previous system intact, but made changes to facilitate access by complaining states – primarily by discouraging respondent states from engaging in the kinds of excessive delaying tactics that had been common – and modifying the panels' operating procedures to place a stronger emphasis on mediation, early settlement, and other ways to avoid issuing final decisions.

Although they increased confidence in the dispute settlement system in the short term (at least as measured by the frequency of states' use of the system), the reforms of the Tokyo Round proved inadequate. For one thing, the GATT retained the consensus-based model, which created a chilling effect, where states might not bring a complaint at all for fear that their opponent could veto action. It also undermined confidence in panel findings, which at times were perceived as tainted by the panelists' consciousness that their decision needed to garner political consensus. For another thing, each additional agreement beyond the original GATT included its own dispute settlement provisions, leading to dispute settlement a la carte and providing the opportunity, where the subject-specific code and the GATT covered the same material, for forum shopping. The Uruguay Round marked the transition from GATT to the WTO, from a la carte to a single agreement, and from politicized panels to a quasi-judicial model. The two most important innovations of the Uruguay Round for the dispute settlement system were the reversal of the consensus rule and the creation of an appeals process. Panels would now be established and their findings adopted automatically, unless there was a consensus against formation or adoption. And while panels would continue to be ad hoc, the Appellate Body would be composed of permanent judges.

The institutional experimentation of the Tokyo and Uruguay Rounds occurred against the backdrop of major geopolitical trends that both highlighted and exacerbated the inadequacies of the existing system. Beginning shortly after the establishment of GATT, the wave of decolonization and the consequent rise in the number and influence of developing countries strained the established rules by drawing in a large number of new members that demanded to be excused from many of their trade obligations owing to their lack of economic development. At the same time, the creation of the European Economic Community (EEC) created a bloc with enough power to challenge the United States and to permit deviation from strict trade rules with a low potential for adverse legal consequences. Furthermore, as one commentator pointed out, the global economic instability of the late 1960s and early 1970s prompted a desire for a more stable and predictable international trade regime. Those three forces led to the reforms adopted in the Tokyo Round. Almost immediately, however, it became apparent that the reforms were inadequate. In the context of dispute settlement, the Tokyo round reforms did not fully address the drawbacks of the GATT system. The fall of the Soviet Union was a pivotal moment in that it both created additional strain on the system with the addition of the former Soviet republics and removed a main obstacle to the long-standing policy goal of the United States to radically revise the whole international trade regime. This, then, was the main agenda of the Uruguay Round. But dissatisfaction with the dispute settlement system, even after the Tokyo reforms, remained.

In addition to a changing geopolitical context and evolving state attitudes, the creation of the modern WTO DSU was spurred by "change agents" – in particular, by academics credited with creating the field of international trade law (much as Bassiouni and Casesse were credited with inventing modern international criminal law). Two prominent examples in that regard were John H. Jackson and Robert E. Hudec. About Professor Jackson, one former colleague and collaborator wrote that he "bestrode the world of international trade law like a Colossus ... [He] created a new law school course and introduced thousands of students around the globe to international trade law.... His analysis of GATT infirmities convinced certain influential governments to push for a new international trade organization, which eventually saw life as the World Trade Organization."[48] Similarly, Professor Hudec's influence on the field is difficult to overstate. He was a scholarly authority on GATT and the WTO, and "government officials from all over the world sought his counsel on issues regarding the law and governance of international trade."[49] He worked directly with both the United States government and the GATT Secretariat, and served on numerous panels under several different international trade regimes.[50]

C *The Iran–United States Claims Tribunal*

The establishment of the Iran–United States Claims Tribunal (IUSCT) also bears the hallmark confluence of economic incentives, geopolitical change, inadequate existing fora, and a history of institutional experimentation. To be sure, the background of the agreement creating the IUSCT distinguishes it from many other examples. Given the scale of the claims it was set up to settle, it may be more accurate to describe the economic incentives as imperatives, and the backdrop of US citizens held hostage in Tehran lent a certain urgency to the negotiations missing in other contexts. Nonetheless, the example of the IUSCT shows how a new international court can come into being notwithstanding gargantuan diplomatic and political obstacles. In that sense, it lends support to the contention that the ICCJ can overcome its own obstacles.

The genesis of the IUSCT can be traced to the Islamic Revolution in Iran in 1978 and 1979 – a major geopolitical shift if ever there was one. Typically, one might imagine that the kinds of geopolitical shifts – constitutional moments – that presage the creation of new international courts and tribunals would be in the direction of liberalism. Certainly, that was true at the end of World War II and, later, at the end of the Cold War. But the IUSCT shows that even the ascendance of illiberalism can create fertile conditions for new international judicial institutions. The reign of the shah in the mid-twentieth century, and his vision for the economic development of Iran, led to decades of close economic ties between the two nations and to large-scale investments by American firms in Iran. This era in the two nations' relations ended, however, with the 1978–79 Islamic Revolution, which culminated with the proclamation of the Islamic Republic of Iran on February 11, 1979. In its stead began a deeply hostile relationship symbolized, among other things, by the designation of Iran by the United States as a state sponsoring terrorism as well as by the economic sanctions regime the United States initiated and still imposes upon Iran.

During the revolution, American investments in Iran were disrupted, contracts with American businesses were terminated, American assets in Iran were confiscated or abandoned, and most Americans hastily fled the country – often leaving valuables behind.[51] On November 4, 1979, what became known as the hostage crisis began when a group of revolutionary Iranians enraged that the deposed shah had been allowed to enter the United States, seized the America Embassy in Tehran taking fifty-two Americans hostage.[52] During the depths of the crisis, Iran officially announced that it intended to "withdraw all of its funds from United States banks and to repudiate its financial obligations to U.S. nationals."[53]

In reaction, on November 14, 1979, President Carter issued the first in a number of freezing orders attaching all Iranian assets that were then subject to US jurisdiction.[54] Simultaneously, American businesses, banks, and individuals who had suffered losses due to the revolution rushed to federal courts to initiate claims and to obtain attachments of Iranian property located within the United States. While many attachment orders had been issued by federal courts, in general, lawsuits did not progress past the interim relief stage because the presidential freezing orders forbade the "entry of any judgment or of any decree or order of similar or analogous effect" against Iranian assets and because the Department of Justice requested that the courts effect a standstill pending the resolution of the hostage crisis.[55]

So here were two states that were hostile to one another, but whose affairs were inextricably intertwined as a result of Iran's frozen assets and the United States' hostages – much the same way that states exist today in an inexorable web of globalized relations that persist without regard to any two states' posture toward one another. In this case, both the United States and Iran had incentives to cooperate despite their mutual hostility: Iran for the return of its assets and the United States for the return of its hostages and compensation of its nationals. And so, among other avenues, they engaged in indirect negotiations to settle the crisis through the mediation of the Government of Algeria.[56] But because attachment orders had been issued by courts (in addition to the executive freezing orders),[57] the US government's ability to unfreeze the assets as part of a negotiated solution was limited. In any event, neither the United States nor Iran was likely to trust the other's courts or to allow them to adjudicate the disposition of billions of dollars. In other words, Iran and the United States faced the problem of a missing forum – a phenomenon I explore in detail in Chapter 2, where I show that victims of cross-border mass torts have nowhere to take their claims with any expectation that they would get enforceable judgments.

The hostage crisis lasted 444 days and came to an end on January 19, 1981, when, on President Carter's final day in office, the United States and Iran had reached an agreement, later known as the "Algiers Accords,"[58] to release the hostages, to dismiss all lawsuits against Iran then pending in US courts, and to order the release of all of the attached Iranian assets.[59] Consequently, some $8 billion USD (more than 20 billion in today's dollars) held by American banks and the New York Federal Reserve Bank were transferred into escrow accounts with the Government of Algeria acting as escrow agent. The hostages were released minutes after President Reagan took office and the Reagan administration ratified the Algiers Accords.[60]

As a substitute to litigation in US federal courts, the United States and Iran had agreed in the Claims Settlement Declaration, a component of the Algiers Accords, to establish an arbitral tribunal, later known as the IUSCT, at the Hague to adjudicate claims by US nationals against Iran, claims by Iranian nationals against the United States, and claims between the two governments.[61] Of the approximately $2 billion USD in frozen Iranian funds $1 billion USD were deposited in a special "Security Account" serving as security of awards to be issued by the new tribunal in favor of American claimants.[62] The security account was to be replenished promptly if it fell below $500 million USD. If ever there was an executive intervention in the judicial sovereignty of American courts in favor of an international tribunal, this was that time.

As unusual as it may seem at first glance, the idea of an international claims tribunal to settle disputes between states and their nationals has a rich history:

> Mixed claims commissions are bodies founded ad hoc on the basis of international agreements usually consisting of a majority of nationals of the States Parties to the agreements and established with the purpose of settling claims which have arisen between citizens of different States, between citizens of one State and the other State, or between the States themselves in formal and final proceedings. Such commissions played a very prominent role in the peaceful settlement of international disputes in the 19th century. Typically, the task assigned to these commissions in the past was to decide a multitude of claims which arose after internal disturbances or international conflicts during which aliens suffered damages.[63]

Mixed claims commissions are generally traced back to the Jay Treaty of 1794, which established commissions that dealt with claims of US and British nationals against the other state. In the nineteenth century, states agreed to approximately eighty mixed commissions and another thirty at the beginning of the twentieth century (through the end of World War I).[64]

The United States has had a particularly robust experience with mixed commissions; it agreed to several over the course of nearly a century of tension and open hostilities with Mexico. In 1839, for instance, the two states agreed to submit to a claims commission "all claims of the Government and Citizens of the United States against the Republic of Mexico" that were timely submitted by the injured individuals to the US authorities.[65] After the Mexican-American War (1846–48), the Treaty of Guadalupe Hidalgo (1848) created a "board of commissioners" to consider claims by US nationals against Mexico (with the United States appointing the commissioners and agreeing to pay any awards made by them).[66] The McLane–Ocampo Treaty, never ratified by the US Senate, envisioned "payment of the claims of citizens of the United States against the Government of the Republic of Mexico, for injuries already inflicted" through a law later to be drafted by Congress.[67] In 1868, the two countries again agreed to establish a claims commission in light of the fact that "claims and complaints have been made by citizens of the United States on account of injuries to their persons and their property by authorities of [Mexico], and similar claims and complaints have been made on account of injuries to the persons and property of Mexican citizens by authorities of the United States."[68] After the tumult of the Mexican Revolution, the United States and Mexico agreed to create two commissions – one to settle outstanding claims going back to 1868[69] and one specifically to settle claims by US nationals against Mexico for damages suffered as a result of "the revolutions and disturbed conditions which existed in Mexico" from 1910 to 1920.[70] It is important to note that these commissions were not altogether successful, although the Special Commission, after requiring several extensions, did manage to adjudicate nearly three thousand claims in a very short amount of time.[71] In 1941 the remaining general claims, with some exceptions, were settled by a lump sum payment.[72]

But the success of these tribunals is not the most important aspect of this context (although it is certainly not unimportant); rather, the point is to emphasize that, while groundbreaking in many respects, the IUSCT was part of a lineage of claims commissions stretching back nearly two centuries. In addition to the United States–Mexico examples already mentioned, countries that established mixed commissions included France after the Napoleonic Wars; Chile after war with Peru and Bolivia; Venezuela after a civil war (to compensate nationals of its neighbors) and the Mixed Claims Commission set up by the United States and Germany after World War I, which adjudicated more than twenty thousand claims.[73] After World War II, claims commissions fell somewhat out of favor, with states seeming to prefer lump sum settlements.[74] According to some, the IUSCT "placed claims commissions back into the diplomatic tool bag."[75]

To say that obtaining the agreement of Iran, and the US Senate, to the IUSCT was an uphill battle would be to understate the case. Challenges to the constitutionality of the Algiers Accords, and specifically to the release of assets attached by US courts and the suspension of litigation in these courts in favor of the newly formed tribunal, which some regarded as a violation of Article III of the Constitution, were mounted by various claimants. The US Supreme Court promptly granted certiorari, in *Dames & Moore v. Reagan*,[76] to consider the constitutional challenges. It resolved those challenges in favor of the executive action and against the petitioning corporation. In an opinion authored by Justice Rehnquist[77] the Supreme Court held that the presidential order nullifying the attachments was authorized by the International Emergency Economic Powers Act (IEEPA). The Supreme Court noted that it "has previously recognized that the congressional purpose in authorizing blocking orders is to put control of foreign assets in the hands of the President [and that] such orders permit the President to maintain the foreign assets at his disposal for use in negotiating the resolution of a declared national emergency. The frozen assets serve as a bargaining chip to be used by the President when dealing with a hostile country."[78] It also found that the president's actions with respect to the attachments were "supported by the strongest of presumptions and the widest latitude of judicial interpretation"[79] given that they were taken pursuant to specific congressional authorization (namely, the IEEPA).

This important conclusion was bolstered by the fact that the president had provided another way to settle the claims of American nationals in an alternative forum capable of providing meaningful relief, namely, the IUSCT. Moreover, the Supreme Court accepted as support for its conclusion the solicitor general's argument that the establishment of the IUSCT would enhance, rather than diminish, the opportunity for claimants to recover their losses because it would remove some of the jurisdictional and procedural impediments claimants faced in US courts.[80]

Even once it was established, many doubted the IUSCT would be able to achieve its aims. Commentators often start their review of the IUSCT with statements to the effect of the following:

> Never before was an international arbitration launched with so much antecedent acrimony between the High Contracting Parties, attracting such genuine skepticism among professional participants and observers. Even the few incorrigible optimists who believed in the resilience and relevance of international arbitration gasped for breath when on some subjects the [IUSCT] delivered awards that were obviously insensitive to the well-publicized position of one Party and were clearly questionable in terms of doctrine and logic.[81]

And yet, although born, according to some, in sin,[82] through an unusual process that entailed indirect negotiation only and which resulted with an international instrument issued in the name of a third party, Algeria,[83] and while not without its flaws and not without its critics, the IUSCT managed to resolve nearly 4,000 claims, representing more than 95% of the claims before it, awarding some $2 billion USD in compensation.[84] It did so despite numerous, severe political challenges including the Iran-Iraq war, the US bombing raid in Libya, and the physical attack on and death threats issued to the Swedish Judge Mangrad by the two Iranian arbitrators, Judges Kashani and Shafeiei.[85] In addition:

> The litany of reasons why the tribunal might have failed is long. The enduring absence of diplomatic relations between Iran and the United States throughout its proceedings has provided the base note. A succession of actual hostilities, however, periodically have sounded the theme: military confrontation between the two countries in the Gulf in the late 1980s, in particular, resulted in the sinking of the Iran Ajar, an attack on offshore Iranian oil platforms, and the downing of an Iranian Airbus. Add to this the persistent American belief that Iranian authorities were responsible at least in part for the prolonged detention of American hostages in Lebanon, and the Iran-Contra debacle, and you have a prescription for potential disaster.[86]

During all of these events, the tribunal continued hearing cases and issuing awards, which were paid out, and Iran continued to replenish the security account as needed. And thus, the first mass claim institution to be set up between a Western country and a non-Western one, which also has the distinction of being the largest bilateral international claims adjudication mechanism at the time, managed to fulfill its mandate.

The success of the IUSCT, despite significant obstacles, gives reason to be hopeful about the prospects of the ICCJ. They are, after all, mirror images of one another. The IUSCT was established, like ICSID, to vindicate the rights and protect the property of (American) investors investing abroad. It is part of the FDI regime that provides foreign investors causes of action, a forum, and remedies. The ICCJ's core mission would be to deal with the "negative space" created by the existing international investment dispute resolution regime, which leaves unattended the claims of local stakeholders in the host states, providing them neither causes of action, nor forum, nor remedy. The IUSCT provides an illustration of what the United States could, and did, do in the reverse scenario to the Chevron–Ecuador dispute – namely, when United States–based businesses sought redress for harms (contract breaches, violations of property rights, and expropriation) inflicted upon them overseas. The establishment of the IUSCT required incredible flexibility and creativity, intense diplomatic effort, and an unusual (and, according to some, unconstitutional) presidential intervention – all to ensure that Americans were compensated by a foreign government. And the IUSCT is not the only institution created by strong action from the US executive branch.[87] Nor is the IUSCT the only modern dispute settlement body to be established amid hostilities among the parties.

D *The Jerusalem Arbitration Center*

Perhaps the most recent example of a dispute settlement body that "could never be" is the Jerusalem Arbitration Center (JAC). The JAC differs in important respects from the other examples in this chapter. It is a private initiative to settle commercial disputes via arbitration created under the auspices of the International Chamber of Commerce and does not involve states in its establishment or as parties. Notwithstanding these differences, the JAC is a useful example because it suggests that some of the same factors Alter has identified as influencing states may also influence private actors. That is important for the overall project of the ICCJ since the buy-in of MNCs is as important as that of states. The example of the JAC also shows both how much committed "change agents" can accomplish, as well as the limits of what is possible if geopolitical conditions fail to align.

The JAC, as with our other examples, is a product of a combination of factors, including economic incentives, a perceived need for dispute settlement according to the rule of law coupled with deficient existing fora, and the social entrepreneurship of a small set of committed individuals. Trade between Israel and the Occupied Palestinian Territories (OPT) amounts to around $5 billion USD per year,[88] yet there is *de facto* no place for business owners to settle commercial disputes. Most residents of the OPT are physically barred from accessing Israeli courts, which they would hardly trust in any case. The judicial system of the Palestinian Authority is chronically understaffed, has an immense backlog, and has a very low rate of enforcement of its judgments. But even if it were in better shape, Israelis would be hard pressed to trust Palestinian courts to adjudicate disputes neutrally. Here, again, we encounter the problem of the missing forum. That absence, according to the founders, depressed the level and types of commerce and trade possible between the neighboring communities. Tenacious social entrepreneurs on both sides – senior, high-profile members of their respective communities – traded on their social capital, gained in other arenas (military and business), to persuade, cajole, garner support, or, at least, remove opposition. The JAC, then, opened its doors in 2013 to address the problem by offering international commercial arbitration to resolve commercial disputes between Israelis and Palestinians.

Neutrality is ensured through the principles of equality and international dominance. At every level – of individual tribunals, the overseeing court, and the board of directors – there are a majority of third-party nationals and an equal representation of Israelis and Palestinians. In addition to identifying a need recognized by the business communities on both sides, the JAC was structured to ensure enforcement, the lynchpin of any international dispute resolution regime. Its goals are self-consciously modest and well defined; limited to contract disputes, it was designed to sidestep issues that could politicize its awards or create a perception of politicization. The Rules of the JAC reflect pragmatism over ideology.[89] For example, the founders drafted the procedural rules so as to try to insulate the arbitrators and court members from having to touch on lightning-rod political questions such as who has sovereignty over East Jerusalem or who counts as an "Israeli" or a "Palestinian" for the purposes of personal jurisdiction. In so doing, the founders employed what is known in diplomacy as "constructive ambiguity." Constructive ambiguity allows international deal makers to "kick the can down the road" in order to strike a deal, in this case on the very establishment of the JAC, leaving it to the wisdom of the arbitral tribunals in any given case to exercise prudence in the hope of allowing the JAC to gain a track record of success without, or at least before, decisions in contentious issues proving to be necessary.

As noted, the JAC was set up under the auspices of the International Chamber of Commerce International Court of Arbitration, the leading international arbitration institute, and draws on the institutional know-how and reputation of its parent organization. Shortly after its launch, the 2014 Israel–Gaza conflict erupted, setting back its operation and leaving it an open question, as of this writing, whether, in the long run, it will be successful despite the active state of hostilities between Israelis and Palestinians. Nonetheless, the decade-long process from the emergence of the idea of the JAC to the creation of an institution ready, willing, and able to resolve contract disputes is a story worthy, at a minimum, of study by theorists of international courts and tribunals.

III HOLDOUTS?

The value proposition of the ICCJ to developing nations (the majority of the world's nations) is quite straightforward, and is set out at length in Chapters 2 and 3. Ideally, Chapters 4 and 5 provide a similarly compelling explanation of the value proposition for developed nations as well. Nonetheless, readers may have hesitations, in particular, as to whether the United States and China – two superpowers who, unlike the EU and its strongest member states (Germany, France, and the United Kingdom), are not known for unwavering support of the international judiciary – are likely to support the creation of such a court. This section explores what these two nations' potential informed positions might be in light of their historical and contemporary approaches to the international judiciary.

A *The United States*

Readers may suspect that the United States would be opposed to an ICCJ, but the complexity of the attitudes of the United States toward international adjudication belies that easy intuition. Certainly the United States' rejection of the jurisdiction of the International Court of Justice (the ICJ), the principal judicial organ of the United Nations and the only permanent international court of general jurisdiction, and its famous refusal to accede to the ICC are reasons for skepticism. But the American position toward international courts is not fixed; it oscillates among realism, exceptionalism, and unilateralism, on the one hand, and cosmopolitanism and institutionalism, on the other.[90] A review of shifting American attitudes toward various international courts or any individual international court paints a much more complex picture. A nuanced understanding of US attitudes, and of the oscillation between the two aforesaid poles, must begin with an understanding that both approaches are authentic and have deep roots. Therefore, I start this analysis with the premise that "long-lasting factors such as American culture and history, the U.S. constitutional structure, and the unique post-Cold War position of the United States in the international community, rather than the view of this or that administration, probably have greater explanatory power over trends and fundamental attitudes of the United States toward international courts and tribunals."[91] The first part of this section explores the historical-cultural roots of both.

It is worth starting out by pointing first to a correlation between the rise of the United States as a superpower and the growth of international organizations generally and courts specifically.[92] Some see not only correlation but also causation:

The United States has been instrumental in or, at a minimum, has encouraged the creation of most of these international judicial bodies. The United States has a tradition of commitment to adjudication of international disputes that dates back more than two hundred years, the intellectual roots of which draw deep into the philosophical and religious movements that shaped the early days of the American republic... During the twentieth century, the United States showed dedication to the resolution of economic disputes through specialized tribunals.[93]

This is true not only of international courts and tribunals, but of international organizations generally. The role of the united States in establishing the United Nations is well known. Its support was also indispensable in fostering European integration, promoting human rights in Latin America, transforming GATT into the WTO, and even in the early stages establishing the ICC. After initial ambivalence about the ICTY the United States was instrumental in the passage of the Security Council Resolution 955 creating the ICTR. As one commentator noted, "The United States is a divided nation that includes deep wells of support and highly mobilized opposition to international law and international courts.... [Ultimately, t]he U.S. (and European) commitment to legalism ends up contributing to the spread of international adjudication."[94]

Empirical evidence from the second half of the twentieth century and the first decade of the twenty-first century paints a picture of consistent, widespread support among Democrats and Republicans alike.[95] This may be surprising for those expecting confirmation of the apparent ambivalence (at best) displayed by successive US administrations. The empirical research shows that a large majority of Americans, irrespective of political orientation, support participation in and compliance with international courts.[96] Kull and Ramsay conducted a study of public opinion data from 1942 through 2005. They concluded that data show a clear pattern:

> The American public has long had an open and positive attitude toward the United States participating in [international courts] and accepting their decisions, although awareness of them has been low. The public seriously considers counterarguments to U.S. participation in international courts when they arise in poll questions, but it has a settled predisposition favoring international institutions for the settlement of disputes under the rule of law...
>
> Overall, the existing public opinion record shows large majorities supporting the principle of international adjudication and modest majorities agreeing to accept adverse decisions. There has been strikingly little fluctuation in these basic attitudes across the decades and little evidence of trends – with the possible exception of a warming to international adjudication as the Cold War ended.[97]

Importantly, Kull and Ramsay reported on a 1993 Americans Talk Issues Foundation (ATIF) poll in which respondents were asked to opine on the idea of amending the

UN Charter to create an international criminal court. One of the subhypotheticals posed to respondents posited that "it is conceivable that a President of the United States or leaders of U.S. corporations might someday be arrested by the UN under this charter revision."[98] A majority favored such a court, which, of course, would entail a much more severe (criminal) sanction than the proposed ICCJ could impose.

Kull and Ramsay's own polling, conducted during the second term of the George W. Bush administration, showed strong popular support for international adjudication. Their polls were designed to test American attitudes towards international adjudication when faced with American exceptionalism arguments.[99] They presented respondents with hypotheticals regarding a wide range of disputes and found that

> in every case, a majority expressed support, and in all but one case, a large majority did so. The highest support was for adjudication of disputes over whether states are abiding by treaties governing human rights (79 percent)... There were also strong majorities supporting the use of international bodies to adjudicate disputes over whether countries are enforcing environmental laws (69 percent) ... [and] whether countries are enforcing labor laws (64 percent).[100]

This strong public support is not, of course, always reflected in US policy. As already mentioned, the United States signed the Rome Statute but declined to ratify it; later, the George W. Bush administration purported to "de-sign" it – a move of dubious legality that was eventually reversed. The question then becomes: Which United States will show up for ICCJ negotiations? The cosmopolitan liberal institutionalist or the unilateralist hegemon? The answer to that may depend, in part, on the extent to which US policy is identical to the preferences of its MNCs; and, by implication, the extent to which MNCs themselves are open to an ICCJ. In Chapter 4 I provide an argument for why MNC might indeed prefer a world with an ICCJ rather than the current one without it. While this book is written at a time when a highly isolationist administration is in place, American history gives us reason to believe that the pendulum will at some point once against shift toward multilateralism and, perhaps, even a renewed desire to lead rather than trail developments in international governance. Given the long development arc of international courts' coming into being, the views of a given administration are less dispositive than the United States' overall approach to international institution and dispute resolution.

B *China*

China, and indeed, the rest of Asia, is generally characterized as being skeptical of international law, wary of joining multilateral regimes, and reluctant to cede sovereignty to supranational institutions. That overall characterization is borne out by the data, which show consistently lower participation of Asian countries in international treaties as compared to their counterparts in the African, Latin American, European, and North American blocs.[101] China's disinclination to submit to international adjudication – most recently displayed in its refusal to participate in arbitration to settle the dispute over the South China Sea – is well documented and entrenched. And the argument that may serve with respect to other states – that regulation of the private sector implicates sovereign interests much more weakly than regulation of sovereign activity – applies with less force to China since many of its enterprises remain state-owned or state-controlled. This is especially true of China's largest enterprises.[102] It is therefore important to acknowledge at the outset that the ICCJ may well be another in a long line of international courts designed and launched without China's participation.

But like most generalizations, the one about China's reticence is not axiomatically true in each case; it is susceptible to nuance. Furthermore, it is not obvious that China's current level of (dis)engagement will persist into the future. Although the obstacles remain significant, there are some factors that could influence China to consider joining the ICCJ statute and might suggest that a cautious optimism with regard to China's potential participation in the ICCJ enforcement treaty is justifiable. China's incentives to join the ICCJ statute may well depend on the extent to which it wants to continue to maintain or grow foreign direct investment in its economy, or to shift resources to the continued growth of its outbound direct investment. Historically, China has been capital importing, but as its engagement with the global economy has increased that has started to change. In 2015, for the first time, China's outward direct investment surpassed its inbound FDI – $145.7 billion USD and $135.6 billion USD, respectively.[103] That trend continued in 2016, with $170 billion USD in outflows and $126 billion USD in inflows.[104] At the same time, however, fears over capital flight caused Chinese authorities to increase restrictions on capital outflows at the end of 2017, a move that many analysts believed would hamper outbound direct investment in 2017.[105]

To the extent that China wants to continue to attract FDI, then it would have the same incentives to join the ICCJ statute (i.e., accept its jurisdiction) as other capital importing countries. Put simply, those incentives – discussed at length in Chapter 4 – include offering its citizens a means to pursue accountability for harms caused by foreign enterprises (thereby reducing the likelihood of political unrest directed at the FDI-enabling regime), the ability to offer foreign investors the certainty and predictability of a settled regime, and the assurance that their cases would be litigated in a neutral international forum and not in China's government-controlled courts. As other capital importing nations join the ICCJ, a failure by China to do so would put it in a comparative disadvantage in the competition for inbound FDI. Further, under the regime proposed in the previous chapter, Chinese companies would be subject to the jurisdiction of the ICCJ if they committed alleged torts in member states. Therefore, China may perceive it to be in its interest to be able to influence the court's statute and rules and to have representation among the judges.

China may also opt into the enforcement treaty only. In doing so it would be offering investing companies the prospect of global legal peace under the ICCJ without the delegation of sovereignty involved in joining the ICCJ statute and conferring jurisdiction. The enforcement regime would, as discussed in the Introduction, be very similar to the New York Convention, which China has already joined.

There is evidence that China is increasingly willing to submit to international regimes that might limit its exercise of sovereign prerogative in order to foster economic growth. The most notable example in this regard is, of course, China's membership in the WTO, which includes the dispute settlement system. China's decision to seek membership in 2001 was driven by a number of factors, about which entire volumes have been written. The space available in the present context is hardly sufficient to do such an analysis justice, but one or two aspects of China's decision making are worth highlighting. The first is that one of the major drivers was the desire of some leaders – especially President Jiang Zemin and Premier Zhu Rongi – to reform China's economic sector. Facing inertia and internal resistance, they elected to induce reform and to promote efficiency by joining the global economic order and fostering competition. A second reason was that joining the WTO, with its established rules, would protect the Chinese economy from ad hoc retaliatory and protectionist measures (especially from the United States) to which it might otherwise be subject. Doing so, however, meant, among other things, accepting the jurisdiction of the WTO's dispute settlement system. Ultimately, China decided that participating in international competition in a free market under the shadow of international law was in its best economic interests.

The WTO is not the only context in which China made that decision. In 1987 (a year after applying for membership in the GATT, which preceded the WTO), China became a contracting state to the Convention on the Recognition and Enforcement of Foreign Arbitral Awards, which it has enforced domestically.[106] It also became a member of the ICSID Convention – which requires enforcement of ICSID awards[107] – in 1993 and has more than one hundred bilateral investment treaties, which, since 1998, routinely include international arbitration clauses for investor-state disputes.[108] Recently, China was the respondent in an ICSID arbitration over the construction of a golf course by a Korean investor; the panel issued an award in which it found the claim to be time-barred and awarded costs to China.[109] This was the first ICSID arbitration with China as the respondent to proceed to an award, but it was the respondent in at least one other proceeding that ended prior to an award.[110]

China's willingness to participate in the WTO, ICSID, and the New York Convention is in line with other signs that point to its emerging preference to leave behind its role as "rule taker" in favor of actively participating in shaping international law and international institutions. Thus it played a strong role in the drafting of the draft Optional Protocol to the Convention against Torture, "rather than simply failing to accede to it once it was formally adopted," and, although it objected to the content, helped to create and ultimately voted in favor of the ILO's 1998 Declaration on Fundamental Principles and Rights at Work.[111] Whether the preceding considerations and China's recent desire both to participate in and to be a leader of the global economy would be sufficient to overcome China's antipathy for international adjudication is impossible to answer; the purpose here is merely to point out that its antipathy is not the beginning and end of the story. Countervailing considerations do exist.

IV GATHERING WINDS

As this book goes to print at the dawn of the Trump era, which is characterized by stark isolationism and unilateralism of the leading superpower, pessimism regarding the plausibility of a new international court is high. Nonetheless, as this section explains, it is reasonable to argue that the time is ripe to embark on the process of developing a blueprint and advocating for an ICCJ. A "returning China" and a reengaging United States may wish in the future to join and, indeed, shape, such an institution; to enhance the credibility of their international commitments and blunt the appearance of brute force; to afford their MNCs the "global peace" only an ICCJ can offer; and, in the case of China, to enhance its competitiveness as an FDI host while offering its citizens a forum to bring their claims against non-Chinese defendants. Let us examine some of existing tail winds that might propel such an initiative.

First are growing calls for reforming the existing system for resolving disputes arising from FDI. That system was explicitly set up to protect foreign investors only, without affording rights of action for host states and local constituencies. For more than two decades, capital importing nations as well as human rights, labor, consumer, and environmentalist groups have criticized a skewed system of asymmetric accountability in which "privately contracted adjudicators ... award public funds to businesses that sustain loss as a result of government regulation."[112] While investors enjoy a high degree of protection in the form of a system purposefully created to protect them, other constituencies such as host countries and their populations must make do with the vagaries of legal systems and doctrines that evolved in the preglobalized world and that, at best, struggle to deal with transnational disputes. Latin American nations have started defecting from the system, leading some to predict that a critical mass of discontent might lead to a breakdown of the system giving way to a new institution.[113] Indeed, as this book goes to print, calls to revise the Investor-State Dispute Settlement (ISDS) system, including calls to create a new global court for international investment disputes, have been sounding not only from the global South but also from the centers of power: from the EU, France, Germany, and prominent American politicians.[114]

Next is the growing global embrace of collective redress and class actions, as well as third-party funding and contingency fees that finance them, once considered uniquely American (described at length in Chapters 4 and 5). This is an express recognition of the rise in mass harms and the growing need to find ways to adjudicate them. For example, the EU, via the European Commission, is also currently looking to identify common legal principles on collective redress and analyze how such common principles could fit into the EU legal system and into the domestic legal systems of its twenty-seven member states.[115] In the common law world, in Asia, in Latin America, in the Middle East, and in Continental Europe mechanisms for collective redress are emerging for the first time.[116] This emergence is a global recognition of the current gaps in the infrastructure to address mass harms. But those emerging solutions are ad hoc and national in character and as such are unlikely to be able to solve the unique transnational problems posed by the kinds of cross-border harms that currently go without redress and may even exacerbate some of them. The increasing complexity involved in resolving mass claims in a world with a growing number of overlapping jurisdictions outside the United States willing to provide claim aggregation, on the one hand, and a growing discontent and disillusionment with unwillingness of domestic courts (especially in the United States) to do so (discussed, respectively, in Chapters 4 and 3) may also portend a growing social mobilization toward an institutional, global solution.

In addition, NGOs, IGOs, academics, and even corporate responsibility initiatives supported by businesses are all focusing on the need to improve adherence to human rights, environmental, and other norms. This is evident in the debate in the UN Human Rights Council on whether or not to adopt a binding treaty creating human rights obligations for MNEs.[117] Other examples include ongoing calls to establish single-issue courts for human rights and environmental disputes[118] and advocacy for an international anticorruption court from organizations as disparate as the Brookings Institution,[119] Human Rights Watch,[120] and lawmakers involved in Ukraine's very active domestic anticorruption courts.[121] All of those initiatives, taken together, can be viewed as tributaries on their way to join a single river that leads to an ICCJ.

In addition to all these, as the remaining chapters of this book explain, the self-interest and economic incentives of both capital importing and capital exporting nations for joining the ICCJ – especially with the two-tiered membership (discussed in Chapter 5) that tailors the extent of the obligations imposed to the degree of rule of law offered by prospective member states' domestic legal systems – are served by an ICCJ. Similarly, the changing transnational litigationscape (described in Chapter 4), the converging interests of business, and potential plaintiffs (and the law firms that represent them) all point in the same direction. Finally, the efficiency and justice that can be gained from an ICCJ are enhanced by the fact that for about a century nations have been spending diplomatic currency reinventing the wheel with ad hoc mass claims commissions. It is time to replace these prototypes with a permanent solution applied equally to like cases irrespective of the political strength of the victims of any given mass tort.

In sum, far from being a futile utopian enterprise, it appears that many of the preconditions for serious consideration of a new international court are already in play and that, with the right academic and policy discourse, blueprints developed now may meet their constitutional moment in the first half of the twenty-first century.

2

The Human Toll

The Bhopal Disaster, the Devastation of the Ecuadorian Amazon, and the Abuse and Murder of Dr. Kiobel

This chapter tells the stories of three cases that illustrate the problems an ICCJ could help resolve. It focuses on two dimensions: first, the human tragedies that lie at the heart of transnational private harms; and second, the court cases themselves, with an emphasis on the procedural twists and turns that create the problem of the missing forum: a reality in which, *de facto*, there often is no forum that can and will issue enforceable judgments against those who commit the most extensive, and at times most heinous, torts – even if, de jure, they should be able to do so. The three cases are the Bhopal litigation, which stemmed from an industrial disaster in Bhopal, India, that killed an estimated ten thousand people and injured approximately half a million more; the Chevron–Ecuador litigation, which stemmed from the devastation of the Ecuadorian Amazon; and the *Kiobel* litigation, which resulted from human rights abuses in furtherance of oil production operations in Nigeria. I make no claim that these three cases are representative. There are simply no systemic data on the phenomenon of cross-border mass tort cases that would reveal their numbers and characteristics.[1] Furthermore, it is impossible to know how many cases currently do not get filed.[2] Similarly unknowable is how many cases are initiated and settled before a complaint is filed.[3] In all likelihood, the three illustrative cases are not representative in terms of the scope of devastation involved. They do, however, reveal the *systemic* problems that make pursuing cross-border mass tort cases difficult and often futile.

And while comprehensive data of the number of cross-border mass torts are not available, evidence of the need for a forum in which to raise them is available. For example, approximately 40 cases against corporations for human rights abuses were pending in US federal courts in 2014 (most were subsequently dismissed after the Supreme Court's decision in *Kiobel*, discussed in detail later).[4] And during the *Filartiga* era, more than 150 ATS cases had been filed in US courts.[5] Or, one could look at the several hundred complaints filed with "national contact points" (NCPs) alleging violations of the Guidelines for Multinational Enterprises since the mechanism for receiving and mediating complaints was established in 2011.[6] Some of the allegations include harm to the environment and to livelihoods from destroyed fisheries as a result of pollution from a coal plant in Indonesia; the deaths of more than eleven hundred people and injury of twenty-five hundred more in the collapse of the Rana Plaza factory building in Bangladesh; and forced eviction and land grabbing at sugar plantations in Cambodia.[7]

The point of presenting the illustrations, in sum, is not to claim they are typical. Rather, I have chosen Bhopal, Chevron–Ecuador, and *Kiobel* because they highlight specific, systemic problems with our current way of dealing with cross-border mass torts. Taken together, those cases provide a foundation for the claim that MNCs operate with overall impunity for the injuries their activities cause. The final part of this chapter will draw the outlines of that claim from the examples, setting the stage for a more systematic examination of the legal barriers that compose what I call "the problem of the missing forum," described in the Chapter 3.

The stories in this chapter illustrate the kinds of harms that this book is ultimately concerned with – what I call "cross-border mass torts." "Cross-border" in this context refers to cases in which plaintiffs in one country are injured by defendants (often, MNCs) from another country. For reasons discussed in this chapter and Chapter 3 the problem of the missing forum is most pervasive and acute when plaintiffs in the developing world seek redress from corporations based in the developed world. So, while the BP oil spill arose from cross-border mass injuries, since BP is a British company and the spill occurred in the United States, the following examples involving United States–based corporations and mass injuries in the developing world are more representative of the problem addressed here.

By "mass" I mean a large number of injuries (read: potential claims) arising from the same set of underlying facts and characterized by a commonality of issues and actors.[8] In the United States, there are two main ways to aggregate large numbers of claims: the class action and the mass action. A class action is brought on behalf of unnamed members of the class who are not parties and do not themselves participate in the litigation (though they are bound by it and, at least nominally, benefit from any settlement or judgment it yields). In a mass action, by contrast, named plaintiffs' claims are aggregated in one of the following ways: filing a joint suit against a common defendant, filing separate claims that are fully or partially consolidated by the court, or, if the litigation is dispersed in multiple districts, consolidated or coordinated by a multidistrict judicial panel. Other jurisdictions worldwide, to the extent they allow for claim aggregation, pursue somewhat different aggregation procedures.[9]

"Torts" is a legal category that, in its broadest sense, covers injuries to person or property that occur outside the context of a contract. Indeed, the word "torts" is most frequently used in the United States, the United Kingdom, and countries that inherited their legal systems from the latter. In civil law systems, similar harms are usually referred to as "noncontractual harms." (In Chapter 5 I will make specific proposals about which kinds of harms the ICCJ should address, mindful of the fact that some limits will be necessary to avoid overwhelming the court with a flood of claims.)

I A TRAGEDY IN BHOPAL, INDIA

The story of the Bhopal disaster and its legal aftermath illustrates the gaps in our existing system for redressing cross-border mass torts. Despite catastrophic injuries, the Bhopal litigation ultimately ended when the Government of India settled the claims for a pittance, without the victims' consent. How did this come to pass? The Bhopal litigation demonstrates characteristic legal barriers that explain the global legal system's current failure to address and remedy cross-border mass harms. These obstacles include the operation of the doctrine of *forum non conveniens*; the ease with which multientity corporate structures can be abused in the transnational context to evade liability; the sprawling parallel and sequential litigation of mass claims that result from the inability to harmonize and coordinate national legal systems; the role of host state governments as coventurers of MNCs and thus as conflicted actors when mass harms occur; and the roles of the same governments in their citizens' cross-border litigation, including, critically, in settling such cases and purporting to grant MNCs preclusion (all of which are described later). All these are common causes for the repeated, systemic failures to properly remediate mass harms caused by MNCs across national boundaries. This section, therefore, begins with a description of the Bhopal catastrophe. It then describes the parallel and sequential litigation that ensued as a result of the inability of the Indian courts to handle the litigation and American courts' unwillingness to do so.

A *The Disaster and Its Decades-Long Aftermath*

Just before midnight on December 2, 1984, forty tons of methyl isocyanate (MIC), a deadly gas, escaped from a manufacturing plant run by Union Carbide India Ltd. (UC-India), the Indian subsidiary of the United States–based Union Carbide Corporation (UC-US).[10] According to one journalistic account, the accident originated from myriad hazards at the plant, including a tank of MIC that was almost 90 percent full despite a rule that it should never be more than half full.[11] In addition, a "faulty valve had allowed the methyl isocyanate to become contaminated with water. The cooling system had been turned off in an attempt to cut costs of roughly $40 a day. Safety checks were desultory. Staff on the night shift at the methyl isocyanate unit had been cut from six to two."[12]

As the cloud of white gas subsumed the city of Bhopal, India, thousands died instantly.[13] According to a *New York Times* report of that week, "the plant [was] almost surrounded by thickly populated and largely poor communities of huts built of clay, thatch, tin and wood that sprang up during and after the plant's construction. These are the communities that suffered the worst casualties as the gas was swept through the area by a night breeze."[14]

The effects of the gas leak were extensive and gruesome. According to *Time* magazine, some victims thought they were afflicted by the plague; others thought a nuclear explosion or an earthquake had taken place. Others simply believed the end of the world had come.[15] "As in some eerie science-fiction nightmare, hundreds of people blinded by the gas groped vainly toward uncontaminated air or stumbled into one another in the darkness."[16] Many died in their sleep; others asphyxiated as they attempted to flee.[17] "When methyl isocyanate breaks down," explained another journalistic report, "it produces hydrocyanic acid, which ravages internal organs, especially the lungs, heart and brain, halting transmission of oxygen in the blood. Victims literally drown in their own body fluids."[18] The *Time* Magazine report further described the horrors:

> The disaster struck hardest at children and old people, whose lungs were either too small or too weak to withstand the poison... Six days after the accident, patients were still arriving at Hamidia Hospital at the rate of one a minute, many of them doubled over with racking coughs, gasping for breath or convulsed with violent spasms that brought a red froth to the lips.... Thousands of animals were also killed by the gas. As the days passed, a sickly stench of decay arose from the bloated carcasses of water buffalo, cattle and dogs that clogged the city's streets. Finally, the army removed them with cranes. But as long as animal and human corpses decomposed in the open air, the threat of contamination increased, and with it the specter of cholera. Meanwhile, rats scurried around the dead bodies, awakening fears of bubonic plague. For days, vultures and wildeyed pariah dogs roamed through the piles of rotting flesh, feasting.[19]

Estimates of the death and injury tolls resulting from the disaster vary. When the Southern District of New York dismissed a class action suit by the victims, in 1986, it acknowledged more than 200,000 injured and as high as 2,100 deaths.[20] In 2010, the *New York Times* reported 3,000 instant deaths, thousands more from the aftereffects, and 578,000 people affected by illnesses.[21] Amnesty International estimated that between 7,000 and 10,000 people died in the days immediately following the disaster and a total of 15,000 to 20,000 more died as a result of illnesses from 1985 until 2003.[22] As of October 2014, the Bhopal Gas Tragedy Relief and Rehabilitation Department, India's official commission for distributing relief funds, had given awards to 574,366 individuals and families affected by the disaster.[23]

As is often the case with mass accidents, it is difficult to generalize the total damage caused by the gas leak. Injuries from exposure ranged from nausea and vomiting blood to blindness and lung, kidney, and liver illnesses. Other common illnesses victims reportedly suffered include posttraumatic stress disorder, severe pulmonary edema, heart ailments, cancer of the esophagus, persistent diarrhea and abdominal pain, increased pregnancy loss, and newborn abnormalities such as cleft palate, pediatric cancer, and polydactyly (extra fingers or toes).[24] The total amount claimed by victims and the Government of India in their complaints filed in American courts totaled many billions of dollars.[25] According to one estimate, had the Bhopal victims been paid at the same rate as asbestosis claimants in US courts, UC-US's liability would have exceeded $10 billion USD.[26]

Further, in the complaint filed by the Government of India in the ensuing US litigation, it claimed damages for harms beyond death and personal injuries, such as the harms suffered by the families of the victims; environmental damage; damage to personal and business property; impairment to the future earning capacity of thousands; disruption to industrial, commercial, and government activities throughout Bhopal and the surrounding region; and the costs of emergency and ongoing aid provided by the government (that is, by the Indian taxpayers).[27]

These devastating accounts are even more heartbreaking because the disaster was predictable. Just five months before the leak, a local journalist published an article titled "Bhopal on the Brink of a Disaster," which detailed the risks the plant posed to the impoverished communities surrounding it.[28] A number of accidents had been reported in the Bhopal plant since it first began operations. Specifically, reports detailed six accidents in the six years prior to the disaster. When slums started developing around the plant, a municipal administrator recommended that the plant be removed. Instead, government authorities removed the administrator and left the plant intact.[29]

According to the plaintiffs, UC-US contributed to the design of the plant, provided for storage of excessive amounts of the gas at the plant,[30] and, as the majority owner of UC-India, generally exerted control over managerial decisions and operations. But, as we shall see, no court adjudicated the merits of their case and, accordingly, no court has ever made findings of liability.

The Government of India advanced both claims of negligence, a tort doctrine where defendants are held liable for injuries caused by acts and omissions that fall short of the usual standards (fault-based liability), and strict liability, where defendants must pay for harms resulting from certain types of activity even if their behavior met all applicable standards (no-fault liability).[31] India pleaded that at all relevant times, UC-US "designed, constructed, owned, operated, managed and controlled" the plant in Bhopal through its UC-India subsidiary, and it manufactured, processed, handled and stored" the ultrahazardous MIC "at its Bhopal plant."[32] In more detail, it alleged that UC-US:

> recommended, encouraged and permitted storing MIC in dangerously large quantities ... [that] the MIC storage tanks were not equipped with dual temperature indicators to sound alarms and flash warning lights in the event of an abnormal rise in temperature ... [that it] failed to provide even basic information with regard to protection against or appropriate medical treatment in the event of MIC exposure ... [that it] failed to disclose the internal safety survey of its plant in Institute, West Virginia, dated September 10, 1984, which acknowledged that a runaway reaction in MIC storage tanks could occur [and that it] failed to provide specifications for determining what constituted either stable or unstable MIC.[33]

A generation later, the damage persists. In 2002, the *Jerusalem Post* described a "chemical in search of immortality; having ravaged one generation, it is now deforming the next. Men and women who were children in 1984 are now marrying and conceiving. Conception to birth is a period of mortal dread in the slums of Bhopal because babies with terrible abnormalities are being born."[34]

B *The Inconvenient Forum*

In short order, several different entities initiated several different processes for different but overlapping groups of victims. Within ten days of the disaster, American lawyers traveled to Bhopal to begin the process of filing lawsuits on behalf of the victims in various American courts. As of May 1986, 145 personal injury class actions involving approximately 200,000 plaintiffs were filed, consolidated, and transferred to the United States District Court for the Southern District of New York (the "District Court" or the "SDNY"). The plaintiffs claimed that the accident was caused, in part, by the negligence (fault) of the American parent corporation, UC-US. In 1985, the Indian government enacted the Bhopal Gas Leak Disaster (Processing of Claims) Act (the "Bhopal Act").[35] The Bhopal Act purported to provide the Government of India with the exclusive right to represent Indian plaintiffs in India and elsewhere in connection with the disaster. Shortly after its enactment, the Government of India (through its organ, the Union of India), acting *in parens patriae*, filed a complaint in the SDNY on behalf of all victims of the Bhopal disaster, asserting similar claims to those in the consolidated complaint of the individual plaintiffs' class actions. Despite India's claim to speak for all victims, the consolidated class actions remained active.

In parallel, and also pursuant to the Bhopal Act, the Government of India set up a system in India for processing claims arising out of the disaster. At the time the SDNY was considering the *forum non conveniens* motion described later, more than 487,000 claims had been filed in India through this scheme.[36] Finally, as of 1987, some sixty-five hundred lawsuits had been instituted by victims against UC-India in Indian courts.[37]

Union Carbide moved to dismiss the litigation initiated by individual victims and by the Government of India at the SDNY on the basis of the *forum non conveniens* doctrine, which grants judges discretion to decline to hear a case when a better alternative forum (India, in this case) can be found. India argued that the SDNY should deny the motion and retain the cases for four reasons. First, there is a presumption of deference to the plaintiffs' choice of forum that generally pervades in American law. Second, Indian courts were insufficiently equipped for the task of adjudicating such a complex tort case. American federal courts, in contrast, had vastly superior experience and more developed procedures designed to handle just such complex actions. Third, UC-US's principal place of business was in New York. Finally, the evidence that plaintiffs deemed most probative of their negligence and causation claim was all located in the United States.

Three years earlier, the United States District Court for the Western District of Washington had rejected a similar *forum non conveniens* motion in *In re Air Crash Disaster near Bombay*. In that case, a district court found that India was not an adequate forum for *forum non conveniens* purposes. That case involved a plane crash in which all passengers, the vast majority of whom were Indian nationals, were killed.[38] The defendants were American corporations, and the accident occurred on the high seas. The District Court for the Western District of Washington recognized the validity of many of the defendants' arguments: that the presence of evidence overseas and the challenges involved in compelling the testimony of witnesses presented substantial difficulty; that a US court was powerless to compel discovery or testimony of witnesses in India; and that discovery in India is so limited as to restrict defendants' ability to significantly develop their defense. Nonetheless, the court decided India did not provide an adequate forum, relying heavily on the fact that a prompt resolution in India's courts was unlikely. In so doing, it accepted the plaintiffs' expert witness's opinion that the case might take a decade to resolve in Indian courts.[39] That recent precedent was cited by the Bhopal plaintiffs.

Nonetheless, in May of 1986, the District Court rejected all of India's arguments, granted UC-US's *forum non conveniens* motion, and dismissed the lawsuit. It found that the plaintiffs did not present sufficient evidence to support their claim that the Indian legal system had insufficiently developed since the British-colonial days. The judge came to that conclusion even though one of the plaintiffs making the argument was the Government of India, discussing its own court system. The District Court relied heavily on the Bhopal Act, which (perhaps aspirationally) provided that cases were to be treated "speedily, effectively, equitably and to the best advantage of the claimants."[40] The SDNY also perceived the enactment of the Bhopal Act as evidence of the innovation and agility of the Indian legislature and legal system. The court was, therefore, by extension, unpersuaded by the plaintiffs' contention that the Indian legal system lacked the wherewithal to deal effectively and expeditiously with the Bhopal litigation.

The District Court placed a number of conditions on the dismissal. First, UC-US had to agree to be bound by the judgment of its preferred Indian court and to satisfy any judgment rendered by that court (and affirmed on appeal). The only exception would be the denial of "minimal" due process.[41] Second, UC-US had to waive defenses based on the statute of limitations and agree to be subject to discovery in accordance with the American Federal Rules of Civil Procedure.[42] In June of 1986, UC-US accepted the District Court's conditions, subject to its right to appeal them, and the District Court entered its dismissal order.

Meanwhile the individual plaintiffs and UC-US cross-appealed the District Court's decision. The Government of India changed its position on appeal and endorsed the District Court's dismissal order.[43] The individual plaintiffs opposed the dismissal. The Court of Appeals for the Second Circuit upheld the *forum non conveniens* decision, finding it "just and fair" to both parties.[44] The Second Circuit affirmed that the District Court did not abuse its discretion given that all but a few of the 200,000 individual plaintiffs were Indian citizens located in India and the defendant had consented to the jurisdiction of Indian courts. It also dismissed the requirement that UC-US consent to the enforcement of a final Indian judgment because it was duplicative of New York's Foreign Country Money Judgments Law. Further, the appeals court overturned the requirement that UC-US consent to an American scope of discovery since UC-US would not have similar access to evidence from the plaintiffs and codefendants under Indian law.[45]

Forum non conveniens is very important for understanding transnational litigation arising out of cross-border mass torts, both because of the role it plays in the resolution (or irresolution) of specific cases, and because of what the structure of the *forum non conveniens* analysis says about how transnational litigation is conceptualized in the current system. Hence, the following paragraphs will first discuss the factors courts must consider when deciding on a *forum non conveniens* motion, then examine how those factors played out in the Bhopal case. At the end of the chapter, the implications of *forum non conveniens* – along with characteristics of transnational litigation of cross-border mass torts drawn from the other case studies – will be tied into a larger story of corporate impunity.

The *forum non conveniens* doctrine allows a court to decline jurisdiction, even when it is properly seized of a case. Generally speaking, the *forum non conveniens* analysis focuses on factors such as adequacy: whether the alternative forum has a functioning court system that offers plaintiffs a reasonable remedy; public policy; and convenience. As the District Court in the Bhopal case explained,[46] when deciding such a motion a court must first determine whether an alternative forum exists and whether the proposed alternative forum is "adequate." As part of this inquiry, a court looks at the substantive and procedural differences in the law that would be applied in the alternative forum if the case is dismissed and refiled there. The existence of more favorable law in the United States – including on such matters as the availability of strict liability for tort, juries, contingency fees, and extensive discovery – is not a consideration to maintain jurisdiction and hear the case. If such considerations were to be taken into account, the District Court worried, "American courts, which are already extremely attractive to foreign plaintiffs, would become even more attractive. The flow of litigation into the United States would increase and further congest already crowded courts."[47]

However, "if the remedy provided by the alternative forum is so clearly inadequate or unsatisfactory that it is no remedy at all," the *de facto* absence of a remedy may be given substantial weight, and a court may conclude that dismissal would not be in the interest of justice.[48] There is a fine distinction to be drawn, then, about what, conceptually, is an "adequate" forum and whether, as a matter of fact, a specific alternative forum is, indeed, adequate. Much hangs on the outcome of those determinations.

The next step in a *forum non conveniens* analysis is to identify and analyze relevant public interest factors. Public interest factors typically include the administrative burdens posed on the court seized of jurisdiction; a public's interest in having local controversies adjudicated locally; and the efficiency created by holding the trial in a court that is familiar with the governing law, and by avoiding the complexities confronting judges who would have to engage in international conflict of laws analysis or who would be called upon to apply foreign law. Finally, burdening local citizens with jury duty in such cases is often perceived as unfair.

Finally, convenience or private interest factors typically include the relative ease of access to sources of proof (documents and witnesses), the availability of a compulsory process for attendance of witnesses, the cost of attendance of witnesses, the possibility of viewing the scene of the harm, and similar practical considerations that may affect the ease, length, and expense of trial.[49]

The inadequacy of the Indian legal system – its laws, its courts, its bar – was at the heart of the individual plaintiffs' and, importantly, the Government of India's plea that the American court should exercise the jurisdiction granted to it. According to the plaintiffs, Indian procedural law had not evolved to deal with complex tort litigation. Discovery was very limited. Lawyers were not trained to handle such cases. The plaintiffs explained that local lawyers lacked specialization and practical investigative techniques, shortcomings that limited their ability to handle this kind of litigation. Further, Indian law prohibited them from organizing in large firms of the size that could handle the task of litigating such a complex case. The Indian legal system lacked broad-based legislative activity and innovativeness in legal practice and education. Legal information was inaccessible and legal services were similarly inaccessible because of, among other factors, burdensome court filing fees.[50]

In January of 1985, a *Wall Street Journal* reporter visited India and reported on the pending question of whether an American court would find India's legal system "adequate." The assessment of the Indian lawyers he interviewed was that such a finding was very unlikely. At the top of the Indian judicial system he found "a prestigious supreme court, viewed as a bulwark of constitutional freedom."[51] However, just beneath the supreme court level, he learned, India's court system was on the verge of collapse. "Even without Bhopal litigation, the country's chaotic district and high courts labor with a backlog of a million cases, many of which will drag unresolved into the 1990s," he wrote.[52] The journalist interviewed the chief justice of the Supreme Court of India, who told him, that "it is my opinion that these cases must be pursued in the United States… It is the only hope these unfortunate people have."[53]

In a prescient paragraph that seems to anticipate the reasoning of the District Court for the Southern District of New York, the journalist reported that "despite some anti-imperialist mutterings over the arrival of American damage lawyers in Bhopal … many Indians believe that only the American courts could grant the kind of damage awards that would help deter such accidents in the future."[54] At least some Indian jurists believed that the litigation strategy behind the *forum non conveniens* motion brought by UC-US was to place the plaintiffs in a position where they had no choice but to bring suit against its majority-owned subsidiary, UC-India. UC-US knew that UC-India was financially unable to satisfy the expected damages (UC-India was reported to have assets totaling less than 100 million USD).[55]

The *Journal* article went on to explain the inadequacy of the Indian forum, pointing to the fact that tort actions are alien to Indian legal culture. "Indian newspapers routinely report deaths from scaffolding collapses, train wrecks, fires and explosions, yet rare is the calamity that provokes a suit. Why? Many rural Indians accept death as a God-willed event without remedy. More-sophisticated Indians don't necessarily agree, but they are reluctant to pursue the suits because they find the legal system hopeless."[56] The characteristic hurdles faced by tort victims illustrate India's underdeveloped tort system:

> Klaus Mittelbachert… dived into the swimming pool at New Delhi's Oberroi Intercontinental Hotel and hit his head on the bottom. He is now a quadriplegic… Asserting negligence on the part of the hotel, he sued… The courts require a non-refundable filing fee of up to 5% of total damages sought. Mr. Mittelbachert's filing fee of more than $8,400 would have kept all but the richest Indians from filing a similar suit. Lawyers' fees, too, must be paid in advance – about $84 for the simplest case, more than a judge earns in a week far more than what poorer Indians earn.

1 A Tragedy in Bhopal, India 55

Contingency fees linked to eventual awards are unethical in India. And ... there is a plethora of other fees... In the 10 years since his complaint, no essential progress has ensued despite the filing of hundreds of pages of documents... Trial is years away and appeals could take decades... [If he prevails,] he probably would get only one-tenth [of the damages claimed], or $42,000... Still, that would be the largest tort award ever made in India.[57]

The cultural, procedural, and institutional barriers to asserting tort claims result in a dearth of legal precedent that can guide tort litigation. Over the course of five decades, only 613 tort cases were reported in India's national case gazette – this, in the world's largest democracy.[58] India also had no law governing complex product or design liability – the issue at the heart of the Bhopal litigation.[59] Further, "what little precedent exist[ed]," at the time of the Bhopal litigation, "derive[d] from English cases dating to the 1920s and earlier and ignore[d] the radical changes ... that have taken place since then in English and American law,"[60] according to the *Wall Street Journal* report. "Although Indian courts could attempt to set precedent in Bhopal cases, if they are tried in India, that would create even more delay in the system. And delay, says Chief Justice Chandrachud, "is the overwhelming problem facing the judiciary."[61] Judicial errors – which are common and result in interlocutory appeals (appeals taken during a trial of any of a judge's decisions) from nearly every decision – further extend litigation in Indian courts. During such common interlocutory appeals, the case would stop for however long (often years) it took for the appeals court to rule. Then the case would resume – until the next interlocutory appeal. These lead to reversals and remands that can extend the life of a case by decades. Last but not least, like much of the developing world, the lower echelons of the Indian judicial system were, at least at the time, rife with bribery.[62]

The District Court for the Southern District of New York rejected the plaintiffs' and their expert's opinion that the substantive tort law of India was insufficiently developed to address the Bhopal claims. The absence of a class action procedure in India, similarly, did not equate, in the eyes of the District Court, to an absence of remedy either in isolation or in combination with the deficiencies of India's tort law.[63] Far from being deemed inadequate, the District Court concluded, the Indian legal system appeared "to be well up to the task" of handling the litigation stemming from the worst industrial disaster of all time.[64]

Remarkably, upon succeeding in persuading the District Court that Indian courts provided an "adequate" forum, UC-US then immediately proceeded to argue before the Second Circuit that Indian courts do not observe adequate due process standards. On appeal, it requested that the District Court retain jurisdiction to ensure that any denial of due process by the Indian courts could be remedied promptly rather than at the enforcement stage, upon the conclusion of the Indian court proceedings and appeal. As evidence, it pointed to how the Indian court hastily issued a temporary freezing order against it and the possibility of prejudice that stemmed from the government's dual, conflicting status as both plaintiff and codefendant. Specifically, UC-US worried that the Indian government might, as a plaintiff, voluntarily dismiss its claims against itself as a defendant or, as UC-US's codefendant, place the blame on UC-US.[65] As to the freezing order, the Bhopal court had issued a temporary order freezing all of UC-US's assets worldwide, an interim remedy that UC-US claimed would irreparably injure it. It was on these grounds that UC-US requested that the District Court retain jurisdiction to "monitor the Indian court proceedings and be available on call to rectify" any due process violations that might occur in India.[66]

However, the Second Circuit rejected UC-US's wish that a trial court in New York, which declined to hear the case, monitor its Indian counterpart. In so doing, the Court of Appeals admonished that

> [UC-US]'s proposed remedy is not only impractical but evidences an abysmal ignorance of basic jurisdictional principles, so much so that it borders on the frivolous. The district court's jurisdiction is limited to proceedings before it in this country... The concept of shared jurisdictions is both illusory and unrealistic. The parties cannot simultaneously submit to both jurisdictions the resolution of the pre-trial and trial issues when there is only one consolidated case pending in one court.[67]

Despite the holdings of the courts in the United States, the inadequacy of India's forum became quickly apparent. As is nearly always the case, the *forum non conveniens* dismissal in the United States was not followed by a trial in India. In 1989, five years after the disaster, UC-US entered into a global settlement agreement with the Government of India.[68] Under the terms of the agreement, UC-US paid a total of $470 million USD and in return received full waiver of all past, present, and future civil and criminal claims arising from the disaster.[69] Without consultation with – let alone the consent of – the victims, the Government of India granted global preclusion to UC-US in exchange for what turned out to be an average of $510 USD per known victim. (As already noted, the Government of India stopped tracking Bhopal-related deaths in 1992.) The individual compensation amount was less than a tenth of that paid by Exxon following the 1989 *Valdez* oil spill in Alaska, in which no one was killed.[70]

Unsurprisingly, many criticized the settlement agreement. It was widely viewed as constituting an ineffective remedy and as devaluing human life in the developing world. "'This amount is a joke,' says Abdul Jabbar ... a gas victim himself ... 'The World Trade Center victims were given $500,000. Look at the difference. Yes, the standard of living is higher in the US, but are Indian lives worth so little?'"[71] Victims immediately attacked the validity of both the Bhopal

Act and the settlement agreement.[72] Both deprived the victims of authorizing, or even having a say in, the settlement. Both, instead, vested full authority to settle the claims in the Government of India, which, as a major shareholder of UC-India, a codefendant, and a government interested in attracting FDI, had multiple conflicts of interest with the victims it purported to represent. In contrast, in the United States, the principle that only a plaintiff can settle his or her own claim is sacrosanct in all fifty states. Retainer agreements, for example, in which attorneys purport in any way to encroach upon such exclusivity are considered unethical and unenforceable.

Another critique centered on the fact that the full effects of the accident and many of its repercussions were unknown at the time the settlement was entered into, preventing even an approximation of the true damage sustained. More than thirty years after the disaster, experts still cannot agree on approximations for the number of deaths and victims.[73] The fact that uncertainty still exists decades after the disaster illustrates how estimations made just five years afterward could not have been accurate. When the Indian Supreme Court entered the settlement order, there were only 205,000 claimants that were considered eligible for compensation under the Bhopal Act.[74] In contrast, as of November 2008, the Bhopal Gas Tragedy Relief and Rehabilitation Department had awarded settlement funds to 574,366.[75]

The Government of India's advocacy against *forum non conveniens* dismissal (before it later changed its position) also focused on a prong of the doctrine that was ultimately not addressed by the District Court. It pointed out that a *forum non conveniens* analysis must ask what outcome – dismissal or case retention – serves "the ends of justice."[76] Perhaps astonishingly, the Government of India took the position that there was a real likelihood that American courts would refuse to enforce, on due process grounds, a judgment issued by the courts of India.[77] It then explained that because it predicted that American courts would find Indian court processes to be violative of basic due process requirements, and therefore refuse to enforce a judgment in favor of the plaintiffs, the outcome would be that the victims of the worst industrial catastrophe of all time would receive no redress.

The District Court did, however, address the significant public policy issue of the extent to which the courts of developed nations should exercise jurisdiction over claims arising from conduct in developing countries (itself a problematic framing of the problem; see later discussion). Empathizing with the human suffering caused by the catastrophic accident, Judge Keenan opened his opinion acknowledging that the Bhopal disaster was the largest industrial disaster in history. He concluded the opinion with a recognition that "it is difficult to imagine how a greater tragedy could occur to a peacetime population than the deadly gas leak in Bhopal."[78] The judge also concluded by acknowledging a paradox presented by the case and the plaintiffs' legal position in the *forum non conveniens* proceeding:

> The Court thus finds itself faced with a paradox ... To retain the litigation in this forum, as plaintiffs request, would be yet another example of imperialism, another situation in which an established sovereign inflicted its rules, its standards and values on a developing nation. This Court declines to play such a role. [] India is a world power in 1986, and its courts have the proven capacity to mete out fair and equal justice. To deprive the Indian judiciary of this opportunity to stand tall before the world and to pass judgment on behalf of its own people would be to revive a history of subservience and subjugation from which India has emerged.[79]

The extent to which the SDNY and the Second Circuit got the public policy questions at stake in the Bhopal case right is a matter of considerable controversy.

The District Court's attempt to resolve the paradox of imperialism, according to many, reflected the very imperialist sentiment it sought to avoid. As one commentator stated:

> The irony of this is, of course, that Justice Keenan's stated desire to allow India's courts the opportunity to "stand tall" had a fundamentally imperialist result – United States–based multinational corporations do not have to operate according to their home state standards, are able to attach less value to the peoples and environments of hosts states than that of the United States, and are not accountable in the United States for the damage they cause in their transnational operations... The modern foreign investor is again protected by the development and manipulation of legal doctrine, reproducing the links between law and the interests of capital-exporting states and their nationals that were established in the seventeenth to early twentieth centuries.[80]

The *Wall Street Journal*'s report echoed this sentiment in reporting that Indian lawyers were supportive of American lawyers' efforts to try the case in the United States. Aware that the American lawyers were motivated, at least in part, by profit motive, they told the journalist, "What does it matter so long as they provide substantial relief to the victims?... But for the American lawyers, there wouldn't be any litigation against Union Carbide. I say God bless them. They deserve to be thanked by the Indian nation."[81]

Of primary concern to the court, in terms of private interest factors, was the source of proof. The District Court found that most of the documentary evidence relating to the key factual questions of design, training, and safety were located in India. Similarly, it found that most witnesses who would attest to causation and liability were in India. A minor, yet noteworthy, consideration was the possibility of viewing the site of the accident. An Indian court, the District Court stated, was in a much better position than an American court to direct and supervise a site viewing should one be required.[82]

C Enterprise Liability

One of the reasons the Indian government advocated keeping the case in the united States was that Indian courts did not have jurisdiction over UC-India's American corporate parent, UC-US.[83] This is a common problem in transnational litigation, where MNCs, often for valid and legitimate business reasons, organize and do business through local subsidiaries.[84] When harms occur, courts in the host state may have jurisdiction over the local subsidiary but not the faraway parent that never actually conducted activities in the host state. This was the case in India. UC-US owned 50.9 percent of the stock of UC-India. Another 22 percent was owned or controlled by the Government of India.[85] But that ownership stake alone did not give Indian courts jurisdiction over the American MNC.[86]

The Government of India, in its complaint, explained the generalizable problem posed by the structure of the modern MNC: "Key management personnel of multinationals exercise a closely held power which is neither restricted by national boundaries nor effectively controlled by international law. The complex corporate structure of the multinational, with networks of subsidiaries and divisions, makes it exceedingly difficult or even impossible to pinpoint responsibility for the damage caused by the enterprise to discrete corporate units or individuals."[87]

As a result of the distributed power of corporate networks, India argued, courts should consider the entire enterprise – parents and subsidiaries alike – as a single enterprise for the purposes of determining jurisdiction. In support of the position that treating UC-US and UC-India as completely separate entities was a legal fiction at best, the individual plaintiffs provided evidence and extensive analysis of the alleged effective control UC-US exerted over its subsidiaries worldwide and over UC-India in particular. For example, they quoted UC-US's Corporate Charter, which articulated its global purpose. They produced corporate policy manuals that detailed worldwide policies governing subsidiaries, which could not be altered without UC-US's approval. They quoted UC-US's "comprehensive control system" with respect to the "critical management issues" of health, safety, and environmental affairs. Under that system, the company's US divisions had the duty to issue policies and procedures for product lines in the international affiliates. UC-US's personnel safety policy required that the parent entity take steps to ensure that all operations are conducted according to superior standards of safety; to maintain management control systems; and to share safety-related information and practices between units with similar operations worldwide.[88] They described the movement of engineers and others, described by UC-US as "international employees," between the different Union Carbide entities generally and, in particular, their role in the design of the Bhopal plant and in implementing UC-US's global objectives.[89]

The plaintiffs offered evidence that previous safety incidents in Bhopal were reported back to, and ultimately handled by, UC-US One accident in December of 1981 resulted in a plan to train Bhopal personnel at the American facilities of UC-US. When the catastrophic 1984 accident occurred, it was UC-US who attempted to respond, by sending personnel to dispose of remaining MIC and to investigate the cause of the accident.[90]

UC-US took a more conventional approach to the issue of enterprise liability, arguing that UC-India was entirely independent. UC-US claimed that the plant was entirely managed and operated by Indians in India; that it was financed entirely by Indian financial institutions controlled by the Indian government; and that the Indian government approved the plans for the establishment and construction of the plant as well as its operations and products. It further claimed that it was the Indian government that required that MIC be produced locally, in India. UC-US pointed out that the Government of India regulates all business in India. And it contended that the local governments of Madhya Pradesh and the Municipality of Bhopal permitted and, indeed, encouraged the development of the hutments in the areas surrounding the plant.[91]

The District Court explicitly avoided making any findings on the key issue of enterprise liability. Discovery at that point had been limited to the question of convenience of venue, and the court was not presented with evidence on liability. Nonetheless, for the limited purpose of *forum non conveniens*, it sided with UC-US and found that UC-US's participation in the design and construction of the plant was limited and that its involvement in plant operations terminated long before the accident. Specifically, the SDNY held that under agreements negotiated at arm's length with UC-India in the 1970s, UC-US provided process design for the construction of the plant and the services of its technicians to monitor the progress of the construction of the plant. Nonetheless, UC-India independently and exclusively had authority over detail design and engineering data, as well as over the erection and commission of the plant. These designs were executed by UC-India engineers, using Indian engineers and subcontractors.[92]

D *Aftershocks*

Although UC-US procured global preclusion from the Government of India, litigation "aftershocks" persisted well into the twenty-first century. Civil suits were filed, and failed, in both the United States and India. For example, after the Indian Supreme Court upheld both the Bhopal Act and the settlement, two dissatisfied victims then filed separate class actions in Texas state courts in 1990.[93] They attempted to attack the settlement collaterally, claiming it constituted grossly inadequate remedy and violated their due process right to opt out of a settlement.[94] After being removed from state court to Texas federal court, the judicial panel on multidistrict litigation transferred the suits to the Southern District of New York.[95] Judge Keenan, once again, dismissed the actions on *forum non conveniens* grounds.[96] The Second Circuit Court of Appeals affirmed the decision in 1993, holding that the plaintiffs lacked standing.[97] Specially, it addressed the question of whether American courts (both state and federal) should defer to the judgment of the Government of India, as a democratic foreign government, that disputes arising from the mass accident that occurred within its borders are best resolved through a statute according it exclusive standing to represent the victims in the courts of the world. In concluding it should do so, the Second Circuit reasoned, "Were we to pass judgment on the validity of India's response to a disaster that occurred within its borders, it would disrupt our relations with that country and frustrate the efforts of the international community to develop methods to deal with problems of this magnitude in the future."[98]

In November 1999, a different group of victims filed another action in the Southern District of New York.[99] This civil suit sought damages for violation of international norms and the Alien Torts Claims Act, for Union Carbide's failure to honor the conditions of the 1989 settlement, and for environmental harms.[100] This case, too, was dismissed. The District Court held once more that the plaintiffs lacked standing. It also held, in the alternative, that the claims were barred by the 1989 settlement.[101] In 2006, the Second Circuit affirmed the District Court's dismissal of all claims.[102] Additional property and environmental lawsuits concerning the disaster all met a similar fate and failed to make it to trial.[103]

In 2010, India's attorney general filed an action against Dow Chemical, which had bought Union Carbide in 1999, seeking to increase the $470 million settlement reached in 1989. According to the Indian government, more than 15,000 additional victims died in the years following the accident and nearly 600,000 were otherwise affected.[104] Some advocates placed the death toll at 25,000 lives and "say the effects of the gas continue to this day."[105] As of this writing, in 2017, this litigation was still pending.[106]

Attempts to impose criminal liability were similarly largely unsuccessful. Although Union Carbide's chairman, Warren Anderson, was arrested days after the spill, he paid bail within twenty-four hours of his arrest and never returned to India.[107] In 1992, an Indian magistrate judge declared Anderson a fugitive; however, the executive still successfully eluded subsequent extradition attempts from the United States and many subpoenas for civil liabilities.[108] In 2010, the Supreme Court of India found eight former employees of UC-India, all Indian citizens, guilty of negligence.[109] For those who waited more than twenty-five years for criminal justice, the two-year prison sentences and $2,100 fines handed down to the seven surviving defendants were a bittersweet victory, as many felt the penalties were inconsequential.[110] Anderson passed away at the age of ninety-two in 2014.[111]

In sum, the unwillingness of American courts to hear the claims of Bhopal's victims and the Indian courts' inability to do so led to an outcome familiar to observers of the legal aftermath of cross-border mass torts that occur in developing countries. The litigation never reached trial on the merits, no findings of liability were ever made by a judge or jury, nor were damages ever assessed by a court of law. Many victims received no compensation, and those "lucky" few who did received woefully small amounts.

Similar is the fate of the indigenous population of the Ecuadorian Amazon whose land was rich with oil coveted by the American-based Texaco. Their story is next.

II THE DEVASTATION OF THE ECUADORIAN RAIN FOREST

In 1964, Texaco (later acquired by Chevron) discovered oil in a part of the Ecuadorian Amazon called the Oriente.[112] Part of the Amazon, the Oriente is a rain forest roughly equivalent in size to the state of Rhode Island. It has been described as the richest biotic zone on Earth.[113] It is home to eight groups of indigenous people, who have inhabited it for thousands of years, living harmoniously in its rain forest environment.[114] The indigenous communities have always relied on the rain forest for subsistence. In particular, they relied on the "waters, groundwater, flora, and fauna for fishing, bathing, cooking, drinking, washing clothes, and transportation.... [and on its resources for] the preparation of traditional medicine."[115]

The environmental catastrophe that unfolded over the next twenty-eight years, until Texaco left Ecuador in 1992, has earned the moniker the "Rain Forest Chernobyl." According to AmazonWatch, a not-for-profit started in 1996 to advance the rights of indigenous peoples in the Amazon basin:

> In a rainforest area roughly three times the size of Manhattan, [Texaco] carved out 350 oil wells, and upon leaving the country in 1992, left behind some 1,000 open-air, unlined waste pits filled with crude and toxic sludge. Many of these pits leak into the water table or overflow in heavy rains, polluting rivers and streams that tens of thousands of people depend on for drinking, cooking, bathing and fishing. [Texaco] also dumped more than 18 billion gallons of toxic wastewater called "produced water" – a byproduct of the drilling process – into the rivers of the Oriente. At the height of Texaco's operations, the company was dumping an estimated 4 million gallons of [produced water] per day, a practice outlawed in major US oil producing states like Louisiana, Texas, and California decades before the company began operations in Ecuador in 1967.[116]

According to the Government of Ecuador, in order to save on production costs, Texaco Petroleum (TexPet), a subsidiary of Texaco, used inferior equipment and methods to those used by its parent and affiliates in the United States and elsewhere around the world.[117] According to the government, TexPet bears the responsibility for an excess of 300,000 barrels of oil that "it admits spilled or leaked from the pipeline during that period of time. TexPet was responsible for numerous crude oil spills."[118] The Government of Ecuador's position is that TexPet's oil operations led to the release of "numerous toxic contaminants into the air, surface water, groundwater, and land through crude oil and its residues, drilling mud, diesel emissions, and flares. The subsistence living of adults and children in the Oriente means they were exposed to this contamination via multiple pathways – including inhalation, ingestion, and dermal exposures."[119] In 1992, TexPet relinquished its interests in the consortium, and PetroEcuador, the state-owned company, became its sole owner.[120] Texaco left Ecuador that year "amidst growing international pressure for it to clean up the damage it had done to the Oriente."[121] Even today, decades after Texaco ceased operations, the land of the Oriente is viscous with oil and effluvient.

Chevron, for its part, contends that much of the damage complained of occurred after Texaco ceased operations (in 1992). From that point onward, the state-run oil company took over. According to Chevron:

> [TexPet] operate[d] in Ecuador, mostly in minority partnership with Ecuador's state oil company, Petroecuador, which owned 62.5 percent. TexPet left Ecuador in 1992, and at that time it fully remediated its share of environmental impacts arising from oil production. The $40 million remediation operation was certified by all agencies of the Ecuadorian government responsible for oversight, and TexPet received a complete release from Ecuador's national, provincial and municipal governments. Chevron acquired TexPet in 2001.
>
> For more than two decades, Petroecuador has been the sole owner of the operations TexPet left behind, and the state oil company has greatly expanded them. Petroecuador has been slow to remediate its majority share of pre-1992 impacts and has amassed a poor environmental record since that time. All remaining environmental conditions in the region are the sole legal responsibility of Petroecuado.[122]

The effects of the contamination on the lives and livelihoods of the indigenous residents of the Oriente are sprawling. Some studies, which Chevron contests, have shown increased rates of cancer, miscarriages, birth defects, and other ailments. Furthermore, the ecosystem on which the traditional life depended no longer exists. Fish no longer swim in, and wildlife no longer drink from, contaminated rivers and streams. Plant life has suffered as well. The impossibility of living off the land has forced many members of indigenous communities into cities to find low-wage work to support a significantly lower standard of living than they enjoyed in the rain forest.

The multidecade, multijurisdiction set of litigations arising from the contamination of the Oriente, known collectively as the "Chevron–Ecuador litigation," is singular in many respects: an $8.6 billion judgment, Chevron's seemingly endless litigation budget, sordid episodes of corruption. Having said that, exploring the Chevron–Ecuador litigation in more detail will help make the problem of the missing forum clearer. It shows how little has changed in the decades since Bhopal, despite widespread recognition of the faults of that process. Also, precisely because the enormous stakes have driven both parties to seek out every possible, plausible, and even impossible legal avenue imaginable, the saga establishes that the worst nightmares of both victims of cross-border mass torts and defendants can come true. Corporations can evade accountability even after a court has found them liable, and claims can live on – in country after country – despite successive defeats. Like a stress test, the Chevron–Ecuador litigation has pushed the current system of transnational litigation to its limits and thereby laid bare its weaknesses.

"The story of the conflict between Chevron and residents of the Lago Agrio region of the Ecuadorian Amazon must be among the most extensively told in the history of the American federal judiciary," according to the Second Circuit.[123] It has, as this book goes to print, been ongoing for a quarter of a century. The extent of the resources devoted by the parties, especially by the defendants, who, it is estimated, had spent much more than a billion dollars on the litigation as of 2012, with no end in sight,[124] means that the dispute is unusual in scope and character. Chevron has vowed to litigate the case "until hell freezes over and then fight it out on the ice."[125] It had also warned that "the Ecuadorian Plaintiffs will endure a 'lifetime of litigation' if they dare pursue their claims."[126] The aggressive litigation went, as we shall see, as far as petitioning a national court for extraterritorial relief that does not exist.

A Background

When Texaco Petroleum Company (TexPet), a subsidiary of the then-California-based Texaco, began oil drilling in the Oriente region of Ecuador, the country was under military rule. Importantly for our purposes, in 1974, the dictatorship, through its state-owned oil company Petroecuador, purchased a 25 percent share in the consortium.[127] Two years later it acquired the shares of another coowner to become the majority stakeholder.[128] TexPet was designated as the consortium's operator, a position it held until 1990. As the operator, TexPet conducted the exploration and production for the consortium and, according to the Government of Ecuador, the republic relied on TexPet's expertise to make use of appropriate technology and production methods as required by the contract between the government and TexPet and by Ecuadorian law.[129] In 2001, Chevron acquired Texaco. As Texaco's successor, it "inherited" its liabilities, including any lawsuits stemming from TexPet's operations in Ecuador.

Despite the damage in the Oriente, relations between Texaco and the government remained friendly. In 1995, TexPet entered into a settlement agreement with the Republic of Ecuador and Petroecuador. In it, TexPet agreed to perform certain remedial environmental work and community development projects in the total amount of $40 million in exchange for a release of all claims by the Republic of Ecuador.[130] The release covered Texaco and all of its related companies, including its successors. The Government of Ecuador represented that all of the claims raised in the Aguinda litigation (discussed in the following section, Round One: In the Courts of the United States) belonged to it "under the Constitution and laws of Ecuador and under international law."[131] According to Chevron, Ecuador and PetroEcuador retained responsibility for all the remaining impact from the consortium operations. Chevron also claims that those parties remained responsible for any future impact caused after TexPet's 1992 withdrawal from any ongoing operations.[132]

Meanwhile, Ecuador's government became more populist and less friendly to foreign corporations. In 1999, Ecuador passed the Environmental Management Act, an environmental law that created a new private right of action for damages for the cost of remediation of environmental harms. It was that law that made the plaintiffs success in Ecuador possible. According to the *New York Times*, "as the case snaked its way through American courts, Ecuador seemed to fall to pieces, going through 10 presidents in a decade by 2006."[133] In 2006, the leftist Rafael Correa was elected president. Correa "has repeatedly sided with the plaintiffs, calling Chevron's Ecuadorian past 'a crime against humanity.'"[134]

B Round One: In the Courts of the United States

In November 1993, Maria Aguinda Salazar and a group of Ecuadorian individuals filed a class action against Texaco under the Alien Torts Claims Act in the United States District Court for the Southern District of New York on behalf of all residents of the Oriente (the "Aguinda litigation").[135] Remedies sought included damages for injury to persons and property and "equitable relief to redress contamination of the water supplies and environment; ... creation of a medical monitoring fund; ... and restitution."[136] Texaco requested the dismissal of the Aguinda complaint on various grounds, including *forum non conveniens*. It argued, among other things, that Ecuador's courts were not corrupt, would offer the plaintiffs due process, and therefore could, legally, be considered an adequate forum. Indeed, as late as 2000, Texaco submitted affidavits from no fewer than fourteen distinguished experts, who all attested that the Ecuadorian court system was fair and that it constituted an adequate alternative forum.[137] Among other things, these sworn testimonies represented that "Ecuador's judicial system is neither corrupt nor unfair; that the courts of Ecuador … treat all persons … with equality and in a just manner; and that the Ecuadorian judiciary was fully independent."[138]

The plaintiffs counterargued that the case should remain in US courts because it was Texaco's senior officials in New York and Florida who had supervised the decisions made by its Ecuadorian subsidiary, TexPet, and because the Ecuadorian legal system was ill equipped to handle a litigation so complex. They also claimed that Ecuadorian courts had unclear jurisdiction over the company – which had withdrawn all operations from the country – that plaintiffs who litigated against oil companies in Ecuador faced harassment and physical harm, and that the Ecuadorian judicial system had "wide-scale procedural deficiencies" and lacked independence.[139] In addition, the plaintiffs argued the United States had a strong interest in regulating the conduct of its national corporations and that imperative evidence was located in the United States, not Ecuador.[140]

The District Court sided with Texaco. It concluded that the case had "everything to do with Ecuador and nothing to do with the United States"[141] and dismissed it. After the Second Circuit's admonishment that the dismissal was inappropriate in the absence of certain conditions, most importantly, a requirement that Texaco consent to the jurisdiction of Ecuadorian courts over the claims,[142] the District Court dismissed a second time.[143] As conditions for the second dismissal, Texaco agreed in writing and represented to the court that it would accept Ecuador's jurisdiction over the dispute and that it would satisfy any final Ecuadorian judgment.[144] The agreement was subject only to a right to appeal the District Court's decision and a reservation of the right to challenge an adverse Ecuadorian judgment on due process grounds.[145] In 2002, the Second Circuit affirmed the dismissal. The appellate court agreed with Texaco that Ecuadorian law was sufficiently developed and that Ecuadorian courts were adequate to hear the types of claims advanced by the plaintiffs.[146]

It is commonly assumed that Texaco, like other similarly situated defendants, presumed that the dismissal of the case in the United States meant that the plaintiffs would not refile the litigation in Ecuador – perhaps because of lack of resources, litigation fatigue, or "because there was no class action mechanism and little if any judicial experience [in Ecuador] with massive environmental litigation."[147] After all, "empirical data available demonstrate that less than four percent of cases dismissed under the doctrine of *forum non conveniens* ever reach trial in a foreign court."[148] "And if Plaintiffs somehow were able to re-file in Ecuador, Texaco still had the comfort that its experience in Ecuador's courts had been singularly favorable, both in private party suits and even in direct litigation with the Government itself."[149]

That comfort proved to be short-lived.

C Round Two: In the Courts of Ecuador

In 2003, the case was refiled in Ecuador. A group of forty-seven plaintiffs brought a "popular suit" – the form of aggregation available under Ecuadorian law – on behalf of some thirty thousand indigenous peoples in the Amazonian rain forest of Ecuador (the "Lago Agrio litigation").[150] The claims and the plaintiffs were substantially the same as those brought by and through the *Aguinda* litigation. Although Texaco agreed as a condition of the dismissal of the *Aguinda* case not to contest the jurisdiction of the Ecuadorian court,[151] on the very first day of the proceedings in Ecuador its successor, Chevron, argued that the Ecuadorian court did not have jurisdiction to hear the action.[152] The Ecuadorian court rejected the argument and heard the case. Chevron contested at the time and still does contest liability. Substantively, it contends that much of the claimed damage was caused by Petroecuador's operations after TexPet withdrew in 1992. Also central to its defense is the argument that the plaintiffs' claims were precluded by the settlement agreement between Ecuador and TexPet, the certified remediation that followed, and the resulting release of liability.

Some eight years after the initiation of the case, on February 14, 2011, the Lago Agrio court issued an $18.2 billion judgment against Chevron. This was the largest-ever judgment in an environmental contamination dispute.[153] Half of the amount was assessed for the damage that the Ecuadorian court found to be a result of Texaco's operations. The other half represented punitive damages. Chevron appealed the judgment, but its appeal was rejected by the court of appeals, the Provincial Court of Justice of Sucumbíos, which reviewed the case de novo. Chevron then requested extraordinary review by the National Court of Justice, Ecuador's highest court. The National Court of Justice overturned the punitive damages, thus reducing the judgment to $9.5 billion, but otherwise upheld the judgment.[154]

The judgment by Ecuador's highest court was hardly the end of the matter; rather, it was the opening of the second act. This one would be even more elaborate and global than the first. The plaintiffs developed an aggressive enforcement strategy, contemplating, for instance, freezing and attaching Chevron's assets in more than seventy jurisdictions.[155] For example, in 2011, plaintiffs commenced recognition and enforcement actions – at the trial and appellate level – in Argentina, Brazil, and Canada.[156]

D No Clear Winner: Seeking and Defending Against Enforcement the World Over

The Chevron–Ecuador case shows the difficulty of enforcing a foreign judgment against a determined corporate defendant. Although the story is far from over, in the years since the judgment was issued and upheld, Chevron has successfully evaded having either to pay or to settle. It did so by seeking a global injunction of the enforcement of the Ecuadorian judgment in both American courts and international arbitration, launching a collateral attack alleging fraud and corruption on the part of Ecuadorian judges and the plaintiffs' counsel, and leveraging Chevron's political connections to pressure the Ecuadorian government.

Anticipating the global enforcement battle, on March 7, 2011, Chevron rushed to the very court it had originally urged to refuse the case – the SDNY. Chevron claimed that the Lago Agrio judgment was procured by fraud, committed by plaintiff's lawyers with collusion by the Government of Ecuador. It also claimed more broadly that the Ecuadorian judiciary was corrupt.[157] Since fraud violates due process, Chevron argued, enforcement should be precluded under New York's foreign judgment enforcement law. It therefore asked the SDNY to declare the courts of Ecuador – the very courts Chevron's passel of experts and amici had praised – to be so corrupt as to render their judgment unenforceable. Specifically, it asked the court to adopt a novel interpretation of New York's Uniform Foreign Country Money-Judgments Recognition Act[158] under which interpretation the court could issue a global injunction against the enforcement of the anticipated Lago Agrio judgment. The District Court in New York obliged, holding that since the election of President Correa in 2006, the Ecuadorian judicial system had become incapable of producing a judgment enforceable in New York courts.[159] The court issued in Chevron's favor a preliminary injunction that purported to preclude plaintiffs from enforcing or preparing to enforce the anticipated Ecuadorian judgment anywhere outside the Republic of Ecuador.[160]

The Second Circuit reversed the District Court's decision. It criticized the factual finding that the Ecuadorian judiciary was categorically incapable of producing an enforceable judgment.[161] It also explained that the lower court's decision was rooted in a misapprehension of the law[162]: "The Recognition Act nowhere authorizes a court to declare a foreign judgment unenforceable on the preemptive suit of a putative judgment-debtor."[163]

In parallel, Chevron commenced an international investment arbitration against the Republic of Ecuador in an arbitral tribunal organized under the auspices of the Permanent Court of Arbitration (PCA) at The Hague (the "PCA arbitration").[164] The arbitration was brought under a 1993 bilateral investment treaty between the United States and Ecuador. Chevron argued that Ecuador colluded with the plaintiffs and their contingency lawyers in violation of the 1995 settlement agreement and associated release, the bilateral investment treaty, and basic international standards of due process and natural justice.[165] As in the New York court so in the international arbitration: Chevron maintained that the Ecuadorian judiciary lacked independence; generally speaking,[166] Chevron therefore requested that the arbitral tribunal declare that Ecuador or Petroecuador was liable for the Lago Agrio judgment; order

Ecuador to "indemnify, protect and defend [Chevron] in connection with the Lago Agrio Litigation"; and order that Ecuador pay all Chevron's legal costs defending against the Lago Agrio litigation and the criminal proceedings and prosecuting the arbitration claim.[167]

While the final outcome of the arbitration is pending, in January of 2012 – a day before the decision of the Second Circuit declining to serve as "a transnational arbiter"[168] – the tribunal granted Chevron interim relief. The order purports to compel the Government of Ecuador, including its judiciary, to take all measures within its power to prevent the judgment from becoming final and enforceable.[169]

As part of its attempts to block the enforcement of the Ecuadorian judgment, in February of 2011, Chevron also launched a civil Racketeer Influenced and Corrupt Organizations Act (RICO) action against Steven Donziger, plaintiffs' lead counsel, and others.[170] In sum and substance, Chevron claimed that Donziger and others conceived, funded, and executed a scheme to extort and defraud Chevron. The scheme consisted of, among other things, fabricating evidence, corrupting and intimidating Ecuadorian judges, and exerting coercive pressure on Chevron to pay money by means of the Lago Agrio litigation as well as by publicly attacking Chevron with false and misleading statements, by inducing US public officials to investigate Chevron, by making false statements to US courts, and by intimidating and tampering with witnesses in US court proceedings.[171]

Following a lengthy bench trial, in an exhaustive decision spanning nearly five hundred pages, the District Court for the Southern District of New York found in Chevron's favor. It ruled that Donziger had, indeed, acted corruptly to obtain the Lago Agrio judgment. The corrupt means included coercion of judges and judicial officials, fraud, deception, extortion, obstruction of justice, and money laundering.[172] Consequently, the court enjoined the plaintiffs from enforcing the judgment in the United States.[173] Donziger appealed the decision but the Second Circuit upheld it.[174]

Chevron has engaged in intense lobbying in Washington. One series of emails that have come to light document that then-CEO of Chevron David O'Reilly personally contacted the State Department. "This is not the first time Chevron has raised this issue with us. Following one approach from Chevron, I spoke with the Ecuadorian Foreign Minister (who was visiting Washington). Also, we will have other high level visitors to Ecuador in the near future... In other words, we will have opportunities to raise this issue and others."[175] Chevron's efforts included urging the State Department to tie trade preferences for Ecuador to a beneficial outcome for Chevron. "Chevron has fought back with trade lawyers and lobbyists, using highly paid talent like the former United States trade representative [] and the former Clinton White House chief of staff [] to push the Obama administration to strip Ecuador of trade preferences, on the grounds that it broke its agreement to absolve the oil company of liability."[176] In addition, years earlier, the Government of Ecuador initially opposed the *Aguinda* plaintiffs' position and, at Texaco's urging, supported Texaco's request that the SDNY dismiss their case. The Government of Ecuador represented to the international tribunal that it allowed Texaco's government relations department to ghost-write a diplomatic note, urging the US government to intervene in the *Aguinda* litigation. The note was then sent from the Ecuadorian Embassy to the US State Department requesting that the State Department advise the District Court that only Ecuadorian authorities have the competence to adjudicate the claims and that the notion that the plaintiffs cannot receive a fair hearing in Ecuadorian court is false. (The Ecuadorian governmental position then changed in 1996 when elections brought a new [leftist] government to power.)[177]

Maria Aguinda was in her late teens when Texaco began its operations in the Oriente. She is, as of this writing, in her late sixties. As the global enforcement wars remain ongoing, with Chevron appearing to have the upper hand, compensation in her lifetime appears unlikely. A combination of corruption in Ecuadorian courts and reluctance to entertain the claims in American ones have conspired to prevent a judicially enforced remediation and compensation. Esther Kiobel of Nigeria seemed likely to suffer similar injustice. Her story is next.

III HUMAN RIGHTS ABUSES IN NIGERIA

Harms suffered as a result of industrial and environmental disasters are not the only kinds of cross-border mass torts. For a brief time, victims of violations of international human rights could sue MNCs that were complicit with host countries in those violations. One such victim was Esther Kiobel, and her case is the one that ended that brief period of potential corporate accountability.

A *Oil, Unrest, and Violence*

The claims of Mrs. Kiobel and her coplaintiffs stemmed from severe human rights abuses in Ogoniland, Nigeria. Ogoniland is a region located in the Niger Delta area of Nigeria. In 1956, oil was discovered in the region. A consortium led by Royal Dutch Petroleum (Shell) was granted extraction rights in Ogoniland. By the early 1990s, residents of Ogoniland and the Niger Delta had organized into groups to protest the mass contamination of their lands and the lack of compensation from the government.[178] The largest and most well known of these was the Movement for the Survival of the Ogoni People (MSOP).[179] In the words of its president:

Ogoni has suffered and continues to suffer the degrading effects of oil exploration and exploitation: lands, streams and creeks are totally and continually polluted; the atmosphere is for ever charged with hydrocarbons, carbon monoxide and carbon dioxide; many villages experience the infernal quaking of the wrath of gas flares which have been burning 24 hours a day for 33 years; acid rain, oil spillages and blowouts are common. The result of such unchecked environmental pollution and degradation are that (i) The Ogoni can no longer farm successfully…; (ii) Fish, once a common source of protein, is now rare… (iii) All wildlife is dead.[180]

The Ogoni people became victims of the "resource curse." The "resource curse" is a paradoxical phenomenon whereby countries rich in natural resources, such as oil, are unable to use those resources to boost their economies. Instead, they experience lower economic growth than countries without an abundance of natural resources. The discovery of the natural resource often leads to conflicts over the control of the resources and extraction of revenues. This, in turn, often leads to armed conflict in regions where the resources are located. Research has demonstrated, in particular, that oil wealth correlates to lower levels of democracy and solidifies autocratic regimes.[181] Corrupt national governments have been known to conspire with extraction companies to circumvent laws and suppress opposition by indigenous populations opposed to the extraction practices.[182] According to the United States Senate Foreign Relations Committee's report titled "Petroleum and Poverty Paradox, "too often, oil money that should go to a nation's poor ends up in the pockets of the rich, or it may be squandered on grand palaces and massive showcase projects instead of being invested productively."[183]

Nigeria did not escape the curse. To this day, the Government of Nigeria relies heavily on oil revenues. Ogoniland's natural wealth has fueled a revolving door of corrupt military dictatorships, with successive regimes embezzling billions of dollars from the public treasury. The most notorious of these rulers was General Abacha, in power during the environmental protests, whose offshore bank accounts are still being uncovered.[184] The reaction of this oil-dependent government to the protests in Ogoni was therefore swift and brutal: "The complaint alleges, Nigerian military and police forces attacked Ogoni villages, beating, raping, killing, and arresting residents and destroying or looting property."[185]

In 1993, MSOP organized a protest of tens of thousands of Ogonis that caused the shutdown of Shell's facilities.[186] According to reporting by Human Rights Watch, Nigerian military forces detained or beat thousands of people and executed hundreds. Among those executed were Ken Saro-Wiwa, the founding father of MSOP, and eight others – known as "the Ogoni Nine." One of the Ogoni Nine was Dr. Barinem Kiobel. His widow, Esther Kiobel, became the named plaintiff in a case filed in US court against Shell for complicity with the Nigerian forces in human rights abuses against the Ogoni people. Specifically, the plaintiffs claimed that the attacks included "extrajudicial killing, torture, arbitrary arrest and detention, cruel, inhuman and degrading treatment, crimes against humanity, rape, forced exile and the deliberate destruction of private property. Shell and [its wholly owned Nigerian subsidiary] financially supported the operations of these military units directly and indirectly, including the purchase of ammunition for the Police," they contended.[187] Shell and its Nigerian subsidiary also, according to the plaintiffs, acted in consort with the Nigerian government to execute a joint strategy to deploy the military to discourage protests, terrorize the civilian population, and depopulate the region.[188] It was with Shell's logistical support and encouragement that the Nigerian military began its campaign of systematic, widespread abuses against MSOP and the Ogoni protesters[189] "by ... providing the Nigerian forces with food, transportation, and compensation, as well as by allowing the Nigerian military to use [Shell's] property as a staging ground for attacks."[190]

Shell and its local subsidiary, the complaint went on to allege, bribed witnesses to procure false testimony and cooperation with a special military tribunal set up to try and punish protesters. Following summary proceedings in the same tribunal, "without adequate counsel, access to witnesses, or the right of appeal," Dr. Barinem Kiobel, Ken Saro-Wiwa, and other Ogoni leaders were executed in 1995.[191] Esther has been detained, beaten, and suffered attempted rape when trying to visit her husband.[192] She was ultimately released but threats to her and her family's lives continued. Esther fled, and ultimately received political asylum in the United States, where she resides today.[193]

In 2002, together with eleven other Nigerian activists from the Ogoniland, Esther filed a putative class action under the Alien Tort Statute (ATS) in the Southern District of New York against Shell, a Dutch corporation; the Shell Transport & Trading Company, a British corporation; and their joint Nigerian subsidiary, Shell Petroleum Development Company of Nigeria Ltd. (Shell Nigeria).

B A Clear Path to US Courts?

The *Kiobel* plaintiffs had every reason to be confident that they would have their day in court, unlike their counterparts in Bhopal and Chevron–Ecuador. That is because their claims fell into the narrow range of harms covered by the ATS, which allowed for lawsuits based on torts committed in violation of international law. Ultimately, the plaintiffs – and the world – were astounded when the United States Supreme Court upended the understanding of the ATS that had persisted since 1980. To understand *Kiobel*, and the American courts' attitude toward the question of which forum should adjudicate cross-border mass torts, a bit of background on the ATS is warranted. The ATS was originally passed by Congress as part of the Judiciary Act of 1789. Its full text reads, "The district courts shall have original jurisdiction of any civil action by an alien for a tort only, committed in violation of the law of nations or a treaty of the United States."[194]

The ATS lay dormant until 1979, when Dr Joel Filártiga and Dolly Filártiga filed a suit in the United State District Court for the Eastern District of New York (the "EDNY") against Americo Peña-Irala, the former inspector general in the Department of Investigation for the Police of Asunsion, Paraguay's capital. The suit charged Peña-Irala with the torture and murder of Joelito Filártiga. Dr Joel Filártiga, Joelito's father, was "a well-known physician, painter, and opponent of Latin America's 'most durable dictator.'"[195] Dolly, his daughter and Joelito's sister, was forced out of her home in the middle of the night to view the mutilated body of her seventeen-year-old brother, Joelito, who had been abducted and tortured to death by Peña-Irala.[196]

The district court initially dismissed the case, but the Second Circuit reversed that decision, holding "that foreign nationals who are victims of international human rights violations may sue their malfeasors in federal court for civil redress, even for acts that occurred abroad, so long as the court has personal jurisdiction over the defendant."[197] The Filártigas' victory launched a new form of human rights advocacy.[198] Soon thereafter, foreign plaintiffs seeking redress from human rights violations overseas were increasingly pressing their grievances in American courts under the ATS. By 2008, federal judges had heard 173 ATS cases.[199] Until the late 1990s, the suits were brought against foreign individuals. The first ATS suit against a corporation was *Doe v. Unocal*, which was filed in 1997.[200] The case settled in 2005, after a trial had been scheduled but before it took place.

The primary significance of the appellate decision was in holding that a corporation could be held liable under the ATS for aiding and abetting a foreign government's human rights abuses. The *Unocal* case's facts were typical of the many ATS complaints against corporations that would follow it; most involved allegations that the corporate defendants encouraged, supported, and benefited from abuses committed by coventures, often host governments.[201] Many such lawsuits were filed in the years after *Unocal*, including, for instance, against Pfizer for drug trials that allegedly killed several Nigerian children, against Coca Cola for complicity in the murder of union organizers in Colombia, and against several companies for their support of the apartheid regime in South Africa.[202]

The rise of corporate liability under the ATS led the Court of Appeals for the Second Circuit, in 2010, and shortly thereafter the United States Supreme Court, to use *Kiobel* to initiate a review of the direction ATS litigation was taking.

C *The Closing of the Courthouse Doors*

Shortly after the plaintiffs filed the complaint in *Kiobel*, the defendants filed a motion to dismiss on the grounds, among others, that the plaintiffs had failed to state claims upon which relief could be granted.[203] At the same time, the Supreme Court issued a decision in *Sosa v. Alvarez-Machain*, limiting the international law claims that could serve as a basis for an ATS claim. The Court held that "federal courts should not recognize private claims under federal common law for violations of any international law norm with less definite content and acceptance among civilized nations than the historical paradigms familiar when [the ATS] was enacted."[204] On the heels of that decision, the *Kiobel* defendants swiftly filed a second motion to dismiss, contending that under the newly pronounced *Sosa* standard the plaintiffs' claims against them were no longer viable.[205] In its ruling on the motion, the district court held that claims for torture, arbitrary arrest and detention, and crimes against humanity were well-established norms of customary international law and as such survived the motion to dismiss.[206] Four other claims – for property destruction, forced exile, extrajudicial killings, and violations of the right to life, liberty, security, and association – were dismissed, however, on the basis of a finding that those were insufficiently definite under the norms of international law and therefore not actionable under the ATS.[207] But instead of proceeding to trial on the approved claims, the district court certified its decision for an immediate, interlocutory appeal over the question of whether these claims were, indeed, actionable under the ATS following *Sosa*, whose legal rule, the Court stated, was too ambiguous to provide guidance.[208]

When the Second Circuit Court of Appeal issued its opinion in September of 2010, it declined to rule on whether the claims in question were indeed actionable under the ATS.[209] Instead, it addressed the question of whether or not ATS jurisdiction extends to actions brought against corporations under the law of nations. In a sweeping decision, it held that corporations could not be sued for civil liability under the ATS at all – an issue that "was never raised, briefed, argued or decided at any point in the … litigation below."[210] The court reasoned that the ATS requires courts to determine which rules are universally accepted by the nations of the world as binding upon them in their dealings with other nations.[211] While it acknowledged that "the singular achievement of international law since the Second World War has come in the area of human rights, where the subjects of customary international law … now include not merely states, but also individuals,"[212] it decided those norms had never been extended to corporations. Under international law, it reasoned, the principle of individual liability for violations of international law is limited to natural, not "juridical," persons.[213]

In a separate lengthy and impassioned concurrence, Judge Leval vehemently disagreed with the majority's conclusion. Judge Leval criticized both the legal rule the decision created and its reasoning. "According to the rule my colleagues have created, one who earns profits by commercial exploitation of abuse of fundamental human rights can successfully shield those profits from victims' claims for compensation simply by taking the precaution of conducting the heinous operation in the corporate form."[214] Without mincing his words, he explained:

III Human Rights Abuses in Nigeria

The new rule offers to unscrupulous businesses advantages of incorporation never before dreamed of. So long as they incorporate ... businesses will now be free to trade in or exploit slaves, employ mercenary armies to do dirty work for despots, perform genocides or operate torture prisons for a despot's political opponents, or engage in piracy – all without civil liability to victims. By adopting the corporate form, such an enterprise could have hired itself out to operate Nazi extermination camps or the torture chambers of Argentina's dirty war, immune from civil liability to its victims. By protecting profits earned through abuse of fundamental human rights protected by international law, the rule my colleagues have created operates in opposition to the objective of international law to protect those rights.[215]

As to the majority's reasoning, he pointed out that the opinion was wholly unsupported by either precedent or scholarship.[216]

The Second Circuit's reasoning in *Kiobel* was rejected by the D.C., Seventh, and Ninth Circuits. All of these found that liability under the ATS extended to corporate defendants.[217] This circuit split made the issue ripe for Supreme Court review. In June of 2011, the plaintiffs filed a petition of certiorari with the United States Supreme Court, asking it to decide "whether corporations are immune from tort liability for violations of the law of nations such as torture, extrajudicial executions or genocide ... or if corporations may be sued in the same manner as any other private party defendant under the ATS for such egregious violations."[218] The Supreme Court certified the case. Numerous governments, civil society groups, and international legal scholars around the world weighed in, filing amicus briefs in support of both the plaintiffs and the defendants.[219] The United States Supreme Court's decision was much anticipated around the world.

In a surprising turn of events, the Court, after oral arguments, ordered that the case be reargued and directed the parties to file additional briefs addressing a totally new question, "whether and under what circumstances the Alien Tort Statute ... allows courts to recognize a cause of action for violations of the law of nations occurring within the territory of a sovereign other than the United States."[220] After hearing reargument, the Court issued its ruling on April 17, 2013. It held that the ATS could not be applied to Shell's actions in Nigeria. More generally, it adopted a new interpretation of the ATS, one that upended decades of precedent. "The presumption against extraterritoriality applies to claims under the ATS, and [] defendants can only be held liable for human rights abuses under the ATS in cases that 'touch and concern' the U.S. with 'sufficient force.'"[221] The presumption against extraterritorial application is a presumption applied by courts, according to which "when a statute gives no clear indication of an extraterritorial application, it has none."[222] Finding no such indication in the ATS, the Court held that the statute did not apply to conduct occurring outside the United

States.[223] This narrow interpretation was, according to the Court, supported by the "text, history, and purposes" of the statute.[224]

The presumption against extraterritoriality "reflects the 'presumption that the United States law governs domestically but does not rule the world.'"[225] The rationale behind the presumption is a desire to protect against unintended clashes between the laws of the United States and those of other nations since such clashes can lead to international discord.[226] In other words, because foreign policy and international relations are implicated, as a matter of separation of powers, courts should not proceed unless explicitly given a green light by Congress. The foreign relations concerns are heightened when the conduct under consideration occurred within the territory of another sovereign. The *Kiobel* litigation, to recap, was brought by Nigerian plaintiffs against Dutch and Nigerian defendants, for conduct that occurred in Nigeria. Thus, *Kiobel* is an example of what has come to be known as "foreign cubed" cases. The policy question whether US courts are an appropriate forum is particularly heightened in foreign cubed cases. Stated otherwise, the United States Supreme Court rejected in *Kiobel* both the notion that it has universal jurisdiction over torts that are committed in violation of the law of nations and any notion that the United States Supreme Court should sit as a world court: "There is no indication that the ATS was passed to make the United States a uniquely hospitable forum for the enforcement of international norms… 'No nation has ever yet pretended to be the *custos morum* of the whole world.' … Indeed, the parties offer no evidence that any nation, meek or mighty, presumed to do such a thing."[227]

The abuses suffered by Esther Kiobel and the eleven members of the MSOP, the Court concluded, were too remote from the United States to give rise to ATS jurisdiction and the case, therefore, had to be dismissed.[228] In so doing, as the Center for Constitutional Rights (which launched modern ATS litigation with Filártiga and assisted the *Kiobel* plaintiffs) explained, the Supreme Court "undercut 30 years of jurisprudence to limit U.S. courts' ability to hear cases on human rights violations committed outside the U.S."[229] It did so at its own initiative, without prompting by Shell.

Mrs. Kiobel's quest continues. On June 28, 2017, she filed a suit, along with three other widows, against Shell in the courts of the Netherlands (Shell's home country),[230] and is seeking to have the documents Shell was prepared to turn over in the US litigation, had it proceeded, made available to her for the Dutch case.[231]

IV SYSTEMIC FLAWS IN TRANSNATIONAL LITIGATION

The Bhopal, Chevron–Ecuador, and *Kiobel* cases illustrate several pernicious flaws in the current transnational system for adjudicating cross-border mass torts. Those

IV Systemic Flaws in Transnational Litigation

flaws include different standards for deciding on *forum non conveniens* motions and motions to enforce foreign judgments; the inability or unwillingness of courts to deal with the implications of multinational corporate structures; and the difficulty of navigating public policy concerns in light of, on the one hand, corruption (real or perceived) in the courts of developing countries and, on the other, the specter of imperialism when the courts of developed countries purport to judge for the rest of the world. Taken together, those flaws fatally compromise the current patchwork system, leading to a status quo that minimizes the welfare of all involved – plaintiffs, defendants, and tribunals alike.

A *Boomerang, Parallel, and Sequential Litigation*

Bhopal and Chevron–Ecuador illustrate a problematic feature of transnational mass tort litigation: so-called boomerang litigation. The term refers to a pattern in which corporate defendants sued in the United States seek and obtain a dismissal based on *forum non conveniens*, but then "still escape liability by thwarting the enforcement proceeding in the United States if they can successfully argue that the case was not fairly litigated in the foreign forum. Alternatively, defendants may attempt to launch a collateral attack via international arbitration. After several rounds of this 'boomerang litigation,' in which the merits of the case are never actually tried, the plaintiff may ultimately be barred from recovery."[232] In addition to bouncing the main case among international jurisdictions, filing satellite RICO litigation against plaintiffs' attorneys (and others working with and for the plaintiffs) appears to be another defense tactic.[233]

Boomerang litigation is an example of a larger problem of parallel and sequential litigation. Parallel litigation – trying the same case simultaneously in different international jurisdictions – as well as sequential litigation – litigating the same case over and over in different jurisdictions – are both consequences of the disaggregated nature of transnational litigation and the lack of cross-border preclusion. Boomerang, parallel, and sequential litigation are among the key drivers of what can be staggering costs of transnational litigation to both plaintiffs and defendants (something I discuss in detail in Chapter 4).

The Southern District of New York discussed the dangers of parallel and sequential litigation in its order purporting to enjoin all global attempts to enforce the Ecuadorian judgment against Chevron. The court showed concern over the potential irreparable harm that Chevron would sustain from the parallel enforcement proceedings:

> The evidence establishes that the [Lago Agrio Plaintiffs] and their allies intend quickly to pursue multiple enforcement actions and asset seizures, including ex

parte remedies where possible, around the globe. Absent a preliminary injunction, Chevron would be forced to defend itself and litigate the enforceability of the Ecuadorian judgment in multiple proceedings... Chevron would be put to the cost, distractions and other burdens of defending itself in multiple fora, probably simultaneously... Injunctions to restrain a multiplicity of suits [in cases of vexatious litigation] ... are not only permitted, but favored, by the courts. This is so largely because a multiplicity of suits has in terrorem value – it forces its target needlessly to defend itself in many fora... There would be no adequate remedy at law for this coercive effect.[234]

B *The Effects of Corporate Structures on Transnational Litigation*

The use of multiple entities serves many legitimate business goals. Operating through subsidiaries allows the parent company to spread risk, e.g. by selling part of the ownership to owners other than the parent company. Thus, separate legal entities can facilitate the creation of joint ventures, mergers and acquisitions, and the sale of separate business lines. The practice of using separate business entities for different parts of the business can provide tax and accounting advantages, as when different jurisdictions impose different tax rates and different accounting standards. Subsidiaries can enable a conglomerate to calibrate its operation to different regulatory environments in different jurisdictions better. The use of subsidiaries can enhance specialization and produce other efficiencies, for example, by having a local management team with better knowledge of the local market, culture, and law manage the local business of the parent. Or, by separate branding for the separate units. But first and foremost, operating through subsidiaries is intended to limit the liability of the parent. The corporate law doctrine of limited liability shields shareholders' assets from liability for the actions and debts of the corporation. When those shareholders are individuals, the doctrine protects their personal assets (house, car, college funds). Since business entities often own other business entities, limited liability can also protect the assets of parent corporations from liability for acts, including torts, of their subsidiaries. The ability to limit liability through the use of legal entities, and the separate legal personhood of each legal entity, is a cornerstone of the modern economy. It enables individuals, and businesses, to engage in economic activity by providing protection to their assets that are not invested in the corporations. Without it, most business activity would be too risky to undertake.

However, limited liability can be abused. Delineating the line between legitimate and illegitimate use of limited liability is a preoccupation of much of business law.[235] For example, it can be seen in the development of the doctrine of "piercing the corporate veil" – where courts disregard the corporate form under certain, very limited, circumstances such as when the corporate form is used to perpetrate fraud.

Important for our purposes, the practice of using multiple entities to conduct foreign investment can, and routinely does, also shield MNCs from tort liability by, among other things, allowing them to "judgment-proof" their local subsidiaries. "Judgment-proofing" is the practice of undercapitalizing a business entity in order to insulate the entity against debts resulting from judgments. In other words, the judgment-proof entities (and individuals) can commit torts with impunity because their bank accounts are virtually empty; there is no money for potential plaintiffs to recover. In economic terms, judgment-proof debtors have suboptimal incentives to exercise care and therefore impose above-optimal levels of risk on third parties.

Meanwhile, the parent company remains insulated because it is, legally speaking, completely separate from the local subsidiary and therefore cannot be held responsible for the latter's independent actions. Under current US law, as well as the laws of other developed nations, even if a subsidiary engages in the most egregious torts and the subsidiary in the host country is judgment-proof, the parent remains shielded by the limitation of liability provided by the business form "even though the parent gains immense benefits from having a subsidiary operate in a foreign nation."[236]

C Moral Hazards

These flaws in the system of transnational adjudication of transnational mass torts are welfare-minimizing. The welfare minimization to the victims is clear from the preceding accounts. Some of the welfare minimization to corporations, and by extension their shareholders, is also evident from these examples and the topic is more fully explored in Chapter 4. There are also other ways in which the problem of the missing forum is welfare-minimizing. The fact of a missing forum, and the consequent *de facto* immunity that MNCs enjoy from liability over mass torts committed in low-income nations with impaired legal systems, create a moral hazard. A "moral hazard" is a situation where the behavior of one party (e.g., an MNC) may harm another (e.g., of local constituencies), but the potentially harming party has no incentive to minimize the potential damage. The party insulated from risk – here, the risk of successful litigation leading to an enforceable judgment – behaves differently than it would if it bore the full risk. The MNC makes a decision about how much risk to take, while the local constituencies bear the costs if things go wrong. The effects of insurance are a classic example of a moral hazard: an individual who has taken out an insurance policy for her home will be less cautious than she would be without insurance because now someone else – the insurance company – bears the risk of damage to the house. Because they enjoy *de facto* immunity for cross-border mass torts, MNCs have little incentive to act with the kind of care they would exercise if they were to internalize the costs of their management decisions, except that in the context of global business activities the risk is not shifted to an insurer – understood in economic terms to be a superior risk bearer – but rather to the world's poorest. The standard economic view is that "*all* of moral hazard represents a welfare loss to society because its costs exceed its value."[237]

We can consider the Bhopal example in that light. In order to save costs such as extra nighttime shift workers and the expenses associated with proper safety measures in the MIC manufacturing process, UC-US took action that led to billions of dollars worth of damage to the victims, their families, their communities, and the Indian taxpayer at large. The effects of environmental disasters such as the Bhopal catastrophe are often incalculable. As noted before, in addition to deaths and personal injuries, the disaster caused damage to personal and business property; impaired the future earning capacity of many; disrupted industrial, commercial, and governmental activities throughout the surrounding region; and caused long-lasting environmental damage. According to experts, the Bhopal disaster dramatically affected all aspects of the nearby cities and the entire state of Madhya Pradesh, especially the economy. Some have suggested that MNCs, which provided many jobs, have become hesitant to invest in Bhopal and Madhya Pradesh because the city now has a negative stigma.[238] In 2009, twenty-five years after the disaster, Madhya Pradesh's economic struggles were reflected by its "extremely alarming" rating in the India Hunger Index. According to this study, approximately 23 percent of Madhya Pradesh's citizens were undernourished, ranking last in the Indian state hunger index.[239] Yet for all that harm, UC-US paid only half a billion dollars. Had it been likely to be forced to pay the full cost of such a catastrophe, and based its operational decisions on the risk of that happening, perhaps it would have managed the Bhopal site differently.

In sum, the absence of workable avenues for litigation of cross-border mass harms, and the resulting inability to compensate the victims of such harms, mean that those who are least able to do so – host states and their citizens – bear the cost of cross-border mass torts. That is nothing less than a massive, albeit incalculable, transfer of wealth from the world's poorest to MNCs.

MNCs externalize the cost of their business activities onto the citizenry of their home countries as well. Cross-border mass torts impose political and diplomatic costs (which are the focus of concern for federal courts in the *forum non conveniens* analyses). MNCs with enough political clout to do so pressure their governments to spend political capital – a public good – to help them avoid liability. For example, as discussed earlier, Chevron mobilized the US government vis-à-vis Ecuador. In another example, in the *Dole* litigation, the defending corporation requested and received intervention by the US embassy to prevent the enforcement of a new statute, Ley 364, which imposed liability upon them for alleged mass torts against banana workers:

[T]he U.S. embassy intervened, pressuring Nicaragua's Attorney General to block enforcement of the law. The Attorney General in turn submitted the law for review to the Nicaraguan Supreme Court, which found it unconstitutional in March of 2002. The Nicaraguan Supreme Court's ruling ignited the NGOs and activists in Nicaragua, who felt their democratic processes were being undermined by foreign corporate interests. Thousands of workers from around the country converged in Chinandega, the site where a majority of the injuries occurred, and from there marched for days to the capital of Managua in protest. The workers gained more support in Managua, and eventually the President and members of Parliament signed [a] Resolution [], which directs Nicaraguan courts to enforce Ley 364. In October 2003, the Nicaraguan Supreme Court issued an advisory opinion, not connected with any litigation, stating that Ley 364 was indeed constitutional.[240]

Spending American political power in this way hamstrings the United States' ability "to seize and maintain the moral high ground in the international arena, a necessity if America wants to lead the world by persuasion and not coercion."[241] According to US Senator Dick Durbin, "American families are harmed when human rights abuses and instability in oil-producing regions result in higher oil prices. Our reputation suffers when U.S. companies are complicit in human rights abuses committed by security forces."[242] The same logic extends to other powerful FDI exporting nations.

Governments also, at times, intervene on behalf of victims. We have seen an example in the discussion of the Chevron–Ecuador dispute, and more examples are provided in Chapter 4, which discusses a new trend of legislation aimed directly at blocking litigation in the host state in order to force the home state to retain jurisdiction; creating favorable procedures for suing in the host state; and changing the substantive law to make it more rewarding to sue foreign corporations in the host nation's courts.

Powerful nations also intervene on behalf of their victims of mass torts. Given their ad hoc and à la carte nature, they represent high costs to the polities whose diplomatic capital is spent on those interventions. Perhaps the most low-cost example of such a political intervention was the intervention by President Obama on behalf of American victims of the BP oil spill, which led to a compensation scheme set up with unprecedented speed. "The deal was announced four hours after four BP executives ... marched up to the west wing, allowing the cameras of cable television networks a clear view of what was immediately dubbed a 'perp walk'– the US slang term for a police parade of suspects."[243] The meeting, which was described as "tense" and which resulted in the said measures, was seen as the beginning of a "truce" between BP and the White House.[244]

On the other end of the spectrum, the transnational litigation of mass claims of Holocaust survivors against various European banks in the 1990s required massive diplomatic resources and was ultimately resolved only via an international treaty. "Aided by diplomatic initiatives by Germany and the United States, and by the vigorous support of many political figures and community organizations, Holocaust-related litigation in American courts against Swiss, German, Austrian, and French corporations over the past six years has resulted in the assemblage of a vast pool of assets valued in excess of $8 billion for distribution to Holocaust victims around the world."[245] The transaction costs of these à la carte interventions, in the absence of a permanent international institution to resolve such mass claims, is also self-evidently high.

Other foreign investors (usually MNCs) may also bear some of the costs of the missing forum and its consequences. Cross–border mass tort litigation has at times led to social unrest that caused the enactment of new, restrictive, and costly laws. (These are described in Chapter 4.)

In summary, no one wins under the current system. Victims have no access to justice. But MNCs must nonetheless defend themselves, often over and over again. Host countries and their citizens bear the majority of the costs, but home countries and MNCs also suffer from loss of political capital and a diminished investment climate. An ICCJ, conversely, would be a win for all involved, providing compensation and remediation to victims; reducing the direct and indirect costs of litigation for MNCs (as discussed in Chapters 4 and 5); protecting due process rights of all litigants; eliminating the moral hazard; decreasing pressure on national courts of both home and host states; defusing populist backlash against impunity; and preserving a healthy international investment climate.

3

The Problem of the Missing Forum

This chapter will present in detail the problem of the missing forum.[1] In summary, the courts of the United States and Europe, where most MNCs are based, will not hear most cross-border mass tort cases (albeit for different reasons). Plaintiffs are therefore forced into the courts of the low-income host states where the injuries occurred. While it might make some intuitive sense to sue where your injuries happened, the courts of host countries are ill equipped to handle such cases. Even when they attempt to do so their judgments are difficult to enforce in the home jurisdictions of the defendants, where most of their assets are found. The inability of plaintiffs to obtain final and enforceable judgments in either the home or host countries of MNCs is the crux of the problem of the missing forum. That state of affairs is unjust for plaintiffs and expensive for defendants. But there are also good reasons to be cautious when giving global effect to the decisions of courts that may lack capacity and may be compromised by corruption. At the same time, there are policy and normative reasons why the courts of the United States and/or Europe should decline the role of global arbiters of civil justice. On the policy level, there are reasons to doubt whether the taxpayers of MNCs' home states – far removed geographically, linguistically, and culturally from the places of injury – should bear the significant cost of judicial administration for large-scale trials of cross-border mass torts occurring elsewhere. Normatively, it is difficult to escape the specter of legal imperialism when making the domestic courts of any country the "court(s) of the world," and especially those of current hegemons or former colonizers.

Throughout this analysis, I pay particular attention to American MNCs and American law. The United States, through its MNCs, is responsible for nearly a quarter of the world's FDI flows.[2] Europe is the largest home base of nonfinancial MNCs and the second-largest generator of FDI.[3] Therefore, the chapter also explores in some detail why their courts are not, cannot, and should not be the solution for the global access-to-justice deficit created by the problem of the missing forum. International arbitration, which successfully deals with contract disputes but is ill suited for mass tort disputes, cannot fill the gap in transnational civil justice left by the unavailability and unsuitability of national courts, as explained next. The chapter will conclude with a discussion of existing proposals to solve the problem of the missing forum. These largely consist of recommendations to set up single-issue courts; to leave the problem in the hands of offending and potentially offending MNCs to solve through self-regulation; or to use alternative dispute resolution (ADR) mechanisms, including arbitration. The chapter will explain why an ICCJ is a better, and more politically viable solution than these existing proposals.

I MULTINATIONAL CORPORATIONS' HOME COURTS

Most plaintiffs injured in cross-border mass torts will first try to bring their claims in the courts of the MNCs' home states, usually without success. That initial decision is driven by a number of reasons, which certainly include the ease of enforcing a judgment against an MNC issued by the courts of its own country. Sue Union Carbide successfully in US courts, and it will almost certainly have to pay. Sue Chevron successfully in Ecuadorean court, and it will fight the judgment "until hell freezes over and then fight it out on the ice."[4] Plaintiff's considerations might also include how well developed the home courts' procedures are compared to those of the host courts, the probability of a fair trial, and the availability of increased recovery (e.g., through punitive damages). But claimants are rarely successful in their attempts to go to trial in MNCs' home states. In the United States they run afoul of resistance to making US courts available for settling overseas disputes. That resistance, historically expressed through the operation of the *forum non conveniens* doctrine, has been on the rise. Cases dismissed on *forum non conveniens* grounds usually end there. But, when they do reach a judgment in a foreign court, plaintiffs have difficulty enforcing that award in the United States. This interaction between *forum non conveniens* and the law governing the enforcement of foreign judgments results in "boomerang litigation." Separately, US courts are becoming generally more protective of businesses. Many of the features that have made US courts particularly attractive are increasingly seen by judges and lawmakers as too pro-plaintiff and therefore are being rolled back. It is worth exploring that rollback not only to explain the unavailability of US courts but also to set the stage for the argument, in Chapter 5, that the ICCJ should avoid those pitfalls and adopt procedures more reflective of the majority of the world's legal systems.

European courts are also very difficult for plaintiffs from the developing world to access, though for different reasons. On the one hand, Europe (through EU regulation) has a much more liberal jurisdictional default rule than the United States: European MNCs may be sued in the courts of their home state for conduct occurring anywhere in the world. European courts therefore have no *forum non conveniens* doctrine; a company's home court is always "convenient." Conversely, however, European courts are generally very conservative about extraterritoriality; if the conduct occurred overseas and the defendants or (in some circumstances) the plaintiffs are not from the country in question it will be very difficult to persuade that country's courts to hear the cases. Thus, the nationality of defendants becomes crucially important in cross-border mass tort cases. European courts will not impute the nationality of a parent corporation to its subsidiaries (except in extraordinary circumstances), so European MNCs can stay out of European court and evade liability by organizing and doing business through local subsidiaries. In the following sections I will explore in detail the legalities that make US and European courts unavailable, as well as the normative and policy reasons that would give us reason to question their suitability if they were available.

A US Courts and Foreign Plaintiffs

Foreign plaintiffs are whipsawed by the operation of liberal *forum non conveniens* rules and strict standards for the enforcement of judgments. Both *forum non conveniens* analysis and foreign judgment enforcement analysis in US courts are infused with the notion of comity. Comity is an amorphous concept that aims to capture the respect and deference that nations, inter alia through their courts, should afford to one another's laws and judicial decisions. In 1895, the Supreme Court of the United States described comity as "the recognition which one nation allows within its territory to the legislative, executive or judicial acts of another nation, having due regard both to international duty and convenience, and to the rights of its own citizens, or of other persons who are under the protection of its laws."[5] Comity is intended to prevent duplicative litigation while demonstrating respect for the laws and judicial systems of other nations. If a competent foreign court has already adjudicated a dispute, local courts may employ comity to justify deference to that foreign court's judgment. In addition, comity encourages countries to consider and understand how domestic adjudication affects foreign nations.[6] Comity is generally reciprocal, with courts of one country showing more deference to the courts of nations that afford it the same courtesy.

With these definitions in mind, let us return to the interplay between a US court's dismissing on the basis of *forum non conveniens* and deciding whether to enforce the judgment produced by the forum contemplated by the dismissing court. US courts use two different standards to determine the adequacy of foreign courts. Early in the process, when corporate defendants bring *forum non conveniens* motions to dismiss, courts apply a lax standard leading to high rates of dismissal. These cases are dismissed not to end them forever, but with the understanding that there is a more appropriate ('convenient') foreign court that can hear them. This can be seen in the fact that courts often condition the dismissal on a stipulation of the defendant that it will not object to the jurisdiction of the foreign courts. However convenient the foreign court might be for corporate defendants, though, "empirical data available demonstrate that less than four percent of cases dismissed under the doctrine of *forum non conveniens* ever reach trial in a foreign court."[7]

When litigants return to the United States to enforce a foreign judgment from the very jurisdiction found "adequate" in the early dismissal phase they are faced with a much stricter enforcement standard.[8] As little as a general discussion in a State Department report may lead a court to refuse to enforce a foreign judgment, on the basis that the judiciary of another country falls short of US standards.[9] This much stricter standard is used to deny enforcement of the foreign judgments in the United States, where the US corporations' assets are usually found. Some have argued that, at least at times, US courts' analyses of the legitimacy of foreign judicial systems betray a misunderstanding of the civil law conception of litigation, or an animus toward a certain regime, instead of identifying systemic failures of due process – or even due process deficiencies in the specific case resulting in the judgment the plaintiffs are seeking to enforce.[10]

The Second Circuit, hearing an appeal from an injunction issued by the US Court for the Southern District of New York purporting to enjoin the courts of all nations from enforcing the Ecuadorian judgment against Chevron, articulated the dual goals of laws governing the enforcement of foreign judgments. First, such laws seek "to provide a ready means for foreign judgment-creditors to secure routine enforcement of their rights [in the courts of New York], while reserving New York's right to decline to participate in the enforcement of fraudulent 'judgments' obtained in corrupt legal systems whose courts failed to provide the basic rudiments of fair adjudication."[11] Second, to enforce foreign judgments, where appropriate, is "to act as a responsible participant in an international system of justice."[12] The Second Circuit added an important caveat, that the legislature (the state legislature of New York, in this case) did not choose "to set up its courts as a transnational arbiter to dictate to the entire world which judgments are entitled to respect and which countries' courts are to be treated as international pariahs."[13]

It is tempting, as some scholars have done, to frame the collision between *forum non conveniens* outcomes and judgment enforcement outcomes as a problem of doctrinal incoherence that can be solved by judges cohering the law. That temptation, however, overlooks a very deep and broad ideological resistance to allowing foreigners to use the American court system to pursue justice, especially against MNCs. This resistance is the real barrier. It is worth unpacking, then, its roots: concerns about allocation of resources, separation of powers, the foreignness of the plaintiffs, and a uniquely American prioritization of free enterprise.

The main argument against enforcement of foreign judgments is the desire to protect American defendants from judicial processes tainted by corruption or otherwise not conforming to American notions of minimal due process.[14] Courts employ, as part of foreign judgment enforcement jurisprudence, the concept of "international due process" defined as requiring "that the foreign procedures are 'fundamentally fair' and do not offend against 'basic fairness'... [and is distinguished] from the complex concept that has emerged from American case law."[15] US courts are funded by US taxpayers, and juries are a limited resource as well. Many believe that conserving those public resources is a reason to restrict foreign access to US courts.

1 Declining to Act as Global Courts

Many constituencies both inside and outside the United States believe that US courts should be extremely cautious about assuming any kind of a global role. Within the United States, one central concern is that the judiciary will overstep its constitutional role and either interfere with or at least impermissibly and deleteriously affect the foreign relations prerogative of the executive branch. The worry is that by asserting jurisdiction over cases brought by foreigners, especially for harms occurring overseas, courts would be conducting judicial foreign policy. According to this view, Congress, not courts, is the proper branch of government to decide whether to apply American law to foreign activity and to engage in international lawmaking. The executive, meanwhile, is the proper locus of the power to conduct foreign relations. Such judicial restraint and deference reserve for the political branches the role of weighing the foreign policy consequences of subjecting conduct overseas to American laws and American courts. In so-called foreign cubed cases, in particular – where foreign plaintiffs sue a foreign defendant (often acting at the behest of a foreign government) over alleged wrongs committed overseas – it is indeed difficult to see why the United States is the natural forum to try and decide the case. Therefore, according to this view, *Kiobel* appropriately stems litigation that would embroil US courts in political relations with foreign nations.

Constituencies outside the United States also doubt whether US courts should judge the world. First, as discussed later, the preference for free enterprise over other values, such as the protection of the environment, international human rights, consumer and labor protection, is a reflection of American values. And while it is a perfectly legitimate exercise of sovereign will to enforce these values domestically, the same is not true on a global stage. This trade-off between free markets and other values, which is reflected in American jurisprudence on cross-border mass tort litigation, is not a universal truism but rather a political choice.

Next, the flip side of the American foreign policy and comity considerations reviewed previously is the difficulty of justifying, from the perspective of democratic legitimacy, a global governance regime in which the courts of any single country serve as *de facto* world courts. In the *Kiobel* proceedings, for example, the governments of the United Kingdom and the Netherlands filed a joint amicus brief urging the United States Supreme Court to instruct lower courts to refrain from exercising jurisdictions in "foreign cubed" cases. In their brief, the Governments of the United Kingdom and the Netherlands invoked the fundamental principle of sovereign equality – quoting the Supreme Court its own language – that "no principle of general law is more universally acknowledged[] than the perfect equality of nations."[16] They also invoked the principle according to which the traditional basis for jurisdiction under international law, as recognized by the United States Supreme Court, is that each nation regulates activity within its own territory. The principles of sovereign equality and territoriality help prevent the "serious risk of interference with a foreign nation's ability independently to regulate its own commercial affairs,"[17] they argued.

Instead of allowing US courts to exercise extraterritorial reach in violation of the principle of sovereign equality, the governments of the United Kingdom and the Netherlands argued that the proper methods of dealing with such cases include multilateral efforts such as those provided for in the Report of the Special Representative of the United Nations Secretary-General for Business and Human Rights (discussed later) and the associated UN Guiding Principles on Business and Human Rights as well as in international standards such as the OECD Guidelines for Multinational Enterprises.[18] What they emphatically objected to, however, is extraterritorial regulation by US courts:

> The Governments [of the United Kingdom and the Netherlands] continue to be committed to this process of multilateral dialogue… The Governments respectfully submit that it would be both inappropriate and undesirable for a domestic court to make a unilateral ruling, identifying a new rule of corporate liability based on customary international law. This would be particularly unfortunate if done now, when the question of how best to reduce the negative impacts of corporate activity on peoples' human rights, while ensuring the primary role of States for corporate regulation in their territory is maintained, is subject to ongoing multilateral deliberation.[19]

Germany also argued, in an amicus brief in *Kiobel*, that a strong presumption exists against allowing American courts to project American law into foreign countries just as there is "a presumption that Congress does not intend to extend U.S. law over conduct that occurs in foreign countries, a limitation that 'serves to protect against unintended clashes between our laws and those of other nations which could result in international discord.'"[20]

Citizens appear to agree with their governments on this issue. A multinational poll conducted by The Chicago Council on Global Affairs and WorldPublicOpinion. org in 2007 (before the financial crisis further diminished American global standing) found that "publics around the world reject the idea that the United States should play the role of preeminent world leader ... [and that] majorities in most countries want the United States to participate in international efforts to address world problems."[21]

Interestingly, the same poll found that "Americans largely agree with the rest of the world: most do not think the United States should remain the world's preeminent leader and prefer that it play a more cooperative role. They also believe that the United States plays the role of world policeman more than it should ... [and that] Americans match the French in their support for the United States doing its share together with other nations (75%), with small numbers favoring a preeminent role (10%) or isolationism (12%)."[22] (Similar, arguably surprising American views overwhelmingly favoring international courts are discussed in Chapter 1).

Further, in terms of legitimacy, it is important to mention the widespread perception (justified or not) among litigants, attorneys, and commentators that American courts, and in particular American juries, are biased against foreign parties.[23] Just as with MNCs' perception that foreign courts are corrupt, the global perception of antiforeign bias in US courts is an important data point in analyzing the suitability of those courts as a forum for resolving high-stakes cross-border disputes. There are some data supporting such fears and perceptions. One of the only empirical studies on the topic has found that "data validates concerns that American courts, and American juries in particular, exhibit xenophobic bias... [But that] there is no significant difference in win rate ... when judges adjudicate."[24]

The legitimacy concerns regarding American courts as world courts apply with extra force to state courts within the United States, rendering reform of state law as a reaction to *Kiobel*, as some scholars have advocated,[25] an inferior solution to the establishment of an ICCJ.

2 The Overall Decline of Access to Justice in US Courts

Just as it may be tempting to believe that an appeal to judicial coherence might fix the problem of boomerang litigation, some may believe that Congress or the courts will "correct" the result in *Kiobel* (which Congress could do by amending the ATS to allow extraterritorial application explicitly), and thereby provide foreign plaintiffs with a viable forum for litigating cross-border mass torts. But Congress and the courts are in the midst of a multidecade-long move to restrict access to the courts or, from a pro-business perspective, to limit excessive litigation and the costs it imposes on businesses.[26] The new trend is rooted in a long-standing suspicion of the role of states (via courts) in dispute resolution and a view that litigation is an imposition on business activities. These views have been on the ascent since the Reagan era. As the following paragraphs will demonstrate, this trend shows no signs of abating. To the contrary, it is evident in wide-ranging substantive and procedural legal developments that include, among other things, the restriction of civil rights litigation (especially "constitutional torts"), the restriction of class actions, the channeling of entire categories of disputes with corporations – e.g., consumer and employment – to arbitration, a return to more restrictive pleading standards, easier summary adjudication (avoiding juries), and limitation on the discovery of facts.

Constitutional torts are ideologically similar to alien human rights torts, and the demise of international human rights litigation in US federal courts parallels the demise of constitutional tort litigation. Constitutional torts are claims against state and local officials brought under Section 1983 of Title 42 of the United States Code (Section 1983)[27] or against federal officials brought under the doctrine articulated by the Supreme Court in *Bivens v. Six Unknown Federal Agents*.[28] Like the ATS, Section 1983 is an early provision that lay dormant for years. It had been enacted in 1871 as part of the Civil Rights Act, to allow civil damage actions to be brought against those "who, under color of state law,"[29] deprived others of constitutional rights. That statute remained in relative obscurity for ninety years until the 1961 Supreme Court ruling in *Monroe v. Pape*,[30] which held that a plaintiff whose constitutional rights had been infringed upon by one acting under color of state law could bring a federal cause of action under Section 1983 even when the state provided a remedy under its common law of tort. In the 1960s, federal courts used the newly invigorated statute to impose limitations on state actions that injure individual citizens. Many of the United States Supreme Court's most significant constitutional decisions, such as *Brown v. Board of Education*,[31] were brought under Section 1983.

The key concerns spurring the whittling away of Section 1983 parallel the concerns relating to the ATS and cross-border mass torts more generally: a fear of overburdening the federal courts, a belief that such claims are frivolous attempts to circumvent state law tort claims that should be brought in state courts (similar to the forum shopping concerns embodied in the statement that the United States should not be "uniquely hospitable" to foreign plaintiffs), and a "perceived tension between § 1983 and traditional values of American federalism. With increasing frequency, § 1983 actions are condemned as being inconsistent with the thesis that federal courts not interfere with state affairs unless absolutely necessary."[32] Formulated in that way, these concerns clearly parallel considerations of comity; simply substitute "foreign country" for "state" and the analysis is remarkably similar.

The Supreme Court has limited constitutional torts by progressively imposing more and more procedural restrictions such as standing and exhaustion of remedies and by advancing increasingly narrow statutory interpretations, so narrow that, according to Justice Blackmun, "The Court appears inclined to cut back on § 1983 in any way it can... The common theme of some of the recent decisions seems to me to be that § 1983 should be construed to minimize federal judicial intervention in state affairs whenever possible, regardless of the impact on the ability of federal courts to protect constitutional rights."[33] Justice Blackmun concluded his cautionary essay on the demise of civil rights litigation under Section 1983 in the hands of the United States Supreme Court with an observation that is similarly apt to human rights litigation under ATS and that relates to the difficulty to roll back doctrinal restrictions of a statute once they have taken hold:

> While we all can work to prevent a return to the judicial indifference and paralysis of the past, none of us can guarantee that the day will not return when a litigant who cannot vindicate his constitutional rights in federal court will not be able to vindicate them at all. If that day should come, it will be far harder to reconstruct a statutory remedy that has been judicially interred or legislatively undone in the meantime than it would be to resort to a remedy that has been intact and working in the intervening years. In short, once we restrict the role of federal courts in protecting constitutional rights, we may find ourselves hard pressed to recover what has been given up.[34]

The overall limitation of aggregate litigation in the United States in recent years provides further context to *Kiobel* and the closing of American courts' doors to foreign victims of American MNC-created mass torts. A systemic and broad view of contemporary congressional and federal courts' views on access to justice, or the protection of free enterprise, can be gleaned from the legislative history behind the 2005 Class Action Fairness Act (CAFA) and the class action jurisprudence that followed. CAFA is the last in a string of jurisdictional statutes[35] that greatly enlarged the jurisdictional reach of federal courts, at the expense of state courts, over class and mass actions in order to restrict the use of these devices. Specifically, CAFA removed class actions from "pro-plaintiff" state courts to "pro–corporate defendant" federal courts, clearly indicating that Congress itself perceives the federal courts to be "pro–corporate defendants." Just as CAFA pushed class actions from state into federal courts, the 2002 Multiparty Multiforum Trial Jurisdiction Act[36] vested federal courts with original jurisdiction over cases arising from accidents where seventy-five or more people died. With the removal to federal courts the door was open wide for further judicial restriction. In recent decades, both before and after CAFA, the Supreme Court has, for example, increased the evidentiary burden on plaintiffs and heightened its scrutiny of class action threshold requirements.

In a recent decision, *AT&T Mobility LLC v. Concepcion*, the United States Supreme Court held that the Federal Arbitration Act preempts state laws that prohibit contract provisions designed to avoid or eliminate classwide arbitration.[37]

Under such provisions, businesses contractually require consumers to bring claims only in individual arbitrations, rather than in court as part of a class action. This, of course, renders most consumer protection disputes impossible to pursue since many have a "negative value" – a value too low to justify litigation costs. One commentator described the *AT&T* decision as a "tsunami that is wiping out existing and potential consumer and employment class actions."[38]

The restriction of aggregate litigation is not the only context in which the protection of businesses is evident. The conjoined developments regarding the limitation of the constitutional right to a jury and the revisions to the Federal Rules of Civil Procedure are worth examining next. The constitutional right to a jury trial is a fundamental feature of American civil litigation. And the adoption of the Federal Rules of Civil Procedure (FRCP) in 1938 was the crowning achievement in an effort to liberalize procedure in order to facilitate access to the courts and allow disputes to be resolved on the merits (rather than on arcane technicalities). The FRCP achieved this result through a combination of interrelated changes: merging law and equity, simplifying pleadings, liberalizing joinder of parties and claims, and expanding of discovery – to name the major changes. In the 1980s Congress and the federal courts began to roll back this procedural revolution. These developments provide further support for the argument that we should be skeptical of the feasibility of "fixing" the law so that US courts become viable fora for foreign victims of cross-border mass torts.

In the mid-1980s a series of United States Supreme Court cases made it easier for judges to dismiss cases and harder for plaintiffs to get evidence in the possession of defendants. First, the Court made it easier to grant motions for summary judgments – a procedure whereby defendants can ask for a case to be dismissed through summary adjudication by a judge (rather than a jury) after at least some discovery or all discovery has taken place.[39] "Discovery" in this context means the stage of a lawsuit when the rules require the parties to turn over to one another relevant evidence in their possession. Part of the theory behind the famously liberal discovery rules in the United States is that evidence relevant to the determination of fault is most likely to be in the possession of the party whose conduct is at issue (think of a "smoking gun" email). Without discovery, that evidence might not come to light and plaintiffs would be less able to prove their case. The extent of discovery provided to plaintiffs in the United States has no parallel in Europe (about which more in Chapter 5) and is a major contributor to the direct costs of litigation (about which more in Chapter 4). The 1980s' push to facilitate early case dismissals by judges was accompanied by limitation of fact discovery by Congress itself. In 1983, the Federal Rules of Civil Procedures were changed to permit courts to limit discovery. A new rule of procedure[40] "encouraged judges to impose sanctions for discovery abuse and explicitly barred disproportionate discovery... Amendments to the federal rules expanded the role of judges early in litigation by requiring the approval of discovery plans. The 2000 amendments went even further to restrict the scope of discovery."[41]

Further restrictions were achieved by imposing sanctions on attorneys for abusing the discovery process. Some commentators regarded this as the most controversial civil procedure amendment that ever occurred.[42] For its proponents, the ability to impose sanctions is an important tool for reining in litigation abuses. For its opponents, it is a highly aggressive tool that reinforces limitations on the historically liberal pleadings and discovery standards by exposing attorneys to expensive and career-damaging sanctions merely for zealously representing the interests of their clients.

Limited discovery and the potential for early dismissal make it harder for plaintiffs to exercise their constitutional right to bring their case before a jury. This is by design. Juries are considered unpredictable and are generally regarded as "pro-plaintiff." Most recently, the Supreme Court, in *Bell Atl. Corp. v. Twombly* and *Ashcroft v. Iqbal*,[43] created new, heightened pleading standards for plaintiffs. These heightened standards require plaintiffs to develop a substantial factual record *before* discovery or face dismissal before a jury becomes involved.

The trend toward judicially created protections for corporations remains strong. During its 2012–2013 term, the United States Supreme Court sided with the US Chamber of Commerce, business' main lobbying group, 82 percent of the time.[44] For example, in addition to *Kiobel*, in *Daimler AG v. Bauman*,[45] the United States Supreme Court made it harder for US courts to exercise general jurisdiction over transnational corporations, by deciding that courts cannot assert personal jurisdiction over a corporation that is not headquartered or incorporated within its jurisdiction, even if the corporation does significant business there directly or through a subsidiary.

In summary, US courts are *de facto* unavailable to hear cases involving cross-border mass torts that took place in other countries, and there are strong reasons rooted in public policy and the norms of democratic legitimacy to resist efforts to "fix" the US system to make it more inviting for foreign plaintiffs. The next sections will examine why European courts offer no more hospitable a forum.

B *The Courts of Europe*

Since Europe is the largest home base of nonfinancial MNCs and the second-largest FDI exporter it is the obvious next stop in our quest for a viable existing forum.[46] While European courts meet standards of international due process, which means the courts of other nations are likely to enforce European judgments, Europe presents its own set of challenges to foreign (non-EU) plaintiffs seeking redress for cross-border mass torts.

Member states of the European Union have a system of parallel jurisdiction: EU member state courts assert jurisdiction over defendants domiciled within the EU on the basis of EU's rules of jurisdiction – the Brussels I Regulation (Recast) (BIR)[47] – whereas jurisdiction over defendants domiciled outside the EU – the defendants that interest us – is determined (with a few exceptions) according to the national procedural rules of the particular EU member state in which the plaintiffs bring their suit.[48] Therefore, European courts can easily be seized of jurisdiction in so-called foreign squared cases (foreign plaintiff and foreign locus of injury) against an EU-domiciled MNC. Under the BIR rules of jurisdiction, domicile provides an EU member state court general jurisdiction over a domiciliary that applies irrespective of where the cause of action arose. A tort claim (mass tort or otherwise) against an MNC domiciled in an EU member state could be adjudicated by courts of the member state where the defendant is domiciled, of the member state of the place where a "harmful event" occurred, or of any EU member state where a branch, agency, or other establishment of the EU-domiciled MNC is located (provided that the case concerns the conduct of that branch or office).[49] Under the BIR, *forum non conveniens* doctrines no longer apply in the EU. In *Owusu v. Jackson*,[50] the European Court of Justice held that the BIR is the exclusive, mandatory instrument for member state courts for the determination of jurisdiction and that the courts of member states could not decline "to exercise the jurisdiction conferred on it based on Article 2 of the Convention [now Article 4 of the Regulation] on the ground that a court of a non-Contracting State would be a more appropriate forum."[51] But while jurisdiction can be obtained over defendants domiciled in the EU, other hurdles, discussed later, remain.

First and foremost, the liberal BIR rule does not apply to subsidiaries of EU-domiciled MNCs where those subsidiaries are not, themselves, domiciled in the EU.[52] To unpack that a bit, consider the hypothetical example of Total France (a France-based MNC specializing in oil extraction); its joint venturer, British Petroleum; and its local subsidiary, Total Niger (organized under the laws of Niger and 100 percent operated there). BIR permits the courts of one member state to exercise jurisdiction over defendants domiciled in another member state if a) the courts of the first state already have jurisdiction (for instance, over a codefendant that is domiciled in that state); and b) it is the same matter (or one so closely related that it would be unfair to try them separately).[53] In that scenario, the courts of an EU member state (say, France) would have jurisdiction over Total France and BP, but not Total Niger. The BIR leaves the question of jurisdiction over non-EU-domiciled defendants up to national law. Some national legal systems would extend their existing jurisdiction to cover a non-EU-domiciled defendant.[54] In such countries, the court of a member state with jurisdiction over Total France could also have jurisdiction over BP and Total Niger (for the same matter). In those situations, however, claimants who sued the European parent company solely to obtain jurisdiction over injuries caused by the wholly independent actions of the subsidiary might be open to claims that they were abusing process.[55] Further because the extension of jurisdiction in that way is a matter of national law, the availability of European courts to plaintiffs from the developing countries injured by local subsidiaries of European MNCs is inconsistent (at best). And, of course, it would leave out victims of cross-border mass torts committed by a defendant with no connection to the EU.

Jurisdiction is harder to obtain in "foreign cubed" cases (foreign plaintiff, foreign defendant, foreign locus of injury) where there is no parent company to use (possibly) as the basis for BIR jurisdiction. In such cases the national rules of jurisdiction of each EU member state bar foreign-domiciled plaintiffs from pursuing a tort claim with a "foreign locus of injury" against a foreign-domiciled defendant. Even the most liberal jurisdictional rules – which, in principle at least, could allow a suit against a non-EU defendant where the cause of action also arose outside the EU – would preclude most foreign-cubed cases. For example, Article 14 of the French Civil Code permits "a French person [to] sue at home on any cause of action, whether or not the events in suit related to France and regardless of the defendant's connections and interests."[56] The BIR, furthermore, requires that Article 14 be extended to natural persons domiciled in France (and not just to nationals).[57] Thus only nationals or domiciliaries of France may make use of Article 14; this would likely bar a mass tort victim from a low-income country from bringing his or her claim in an EU member state court. Further, a treaty between the country of the defendant and the European country concerned may preclude application of such national rules of jurisdiction.[58]

Generally speaking, EU rules only apply where the defendant is domiciled in a member state. When a defendant is domiciled outside the EU, the member state's national jurisdictional law still applies in full force including, e.g. in the case of the United Kingdom, the doctrine of *forum non conveniens*. Therefore, member states with such laws on their books may still decline to hear mass tort claims against non-EU-domiciled MNCs.[59]

Another barrier to recovery in cross-border mass tort cases in the EU is imposed by the EU's choice of law regime. In 2007, all EU member states adopted Rome II on the Law Applicable to Non-Contractual Obligations[60] – an EU regulation that replaced national choice-of-law rules of each member state. ('Non-contractual obligations' in European law encompasses what is in America conceptualized as the law of torts). In tort actions, Rome II, with few exceptions,[61] dictates that EU member state courts must apply the law of the country in which the damage occurred.[62] Therefore, when victims of a mass tort committed outside the EU who succeed in bringing a non-EU MNC defendant – for instance, a US multinational corporation – into an EU member state court on the basis of the particular EU member state's national rules of jurisdiction, the EU member state court will still apply the law of the country in which the damage occurs. As discussed later, this often means courts will apply the underdeveloped tort law of a low-income nation, ill equipped to deal with modern torts generally and mass torts in particular. There is an exception to the application of the national law of the place of injury; EU law permits the courts of member states to make exceptions to mandatory rules on the basis of public policy.[63] But the Court of Justice of the European Union (CJEU) generally understands that to apply to "a manifest violation of a fundamental rule or right in the forum, including not only national values but also fundamental principles of EU law, especially the fundamental freedoms and the human rights as embodied in the Charter of Fundamental Rights of the European Union (EU Charter) and the European Convention on Human Rights (ECHR)."[64] Whether the presence or absence of tort or environmental laws covering certain types of harm rises to that level is, at best uncertain. That exception, therefore, would be a slender thread on which to hang the hopes of the world's victims of cross-border mass torts.

European enforcement law sets additional barriers to recovery. Even the most liberal members of the EU would refuse recognition and enforcement of judgments on public policy grounds (*Ordre public*) – a concept similar to the American due process concept. Therefore, foreign judgments perceived as tainted by corruption will likely face the same enforcement hurdles in Europe as they would in the United States. Enforcement may also be denied if the judgment-rendering court is deemed to have exercised jurisdiction without fair and reasonable basis to do so, as those concepts are understood in the jurisdiction where enforcement is sought.[65] One can therefore surmise, for example, that if the courts of a host state assert jurisdiction based on a retroactive statute tailor-made to allow litigation against a certain set of defendants for certain mass torts (these statutes are discussed in Chapter 4), European courts may refuse enforcement.

Further, practices regarding recognition and enforcement of non-EU member states' judgments are subject to national laws and vary considerably. While in Germany, Italy, and Greece enforcement of foreign judgments is fairly liberal, the Nordic countries (Denmark, Sweden, and Finland) generally do not enforce foreign judgments absent a treaty. Plaintiffs that prevailed in a non-EU court must relitigate the action if they seek enforcement against assets in those countries.[66] Austria enforces on the basis of reciprocity. But reciprocity requires a treaty or a proclamation of the Austrian government and since very few of these exist, *de facto* enforcement in Austria is almost as restrictive as in the Nordic nations.[67] Dutch law similarly requires reciprocity. However, Dutch courts have allowed recognition where the foreign judgment-rendering court exercised jurisdiction based on internationally recognized principles.[68] Even in the liberal jurisdictions (Germany, Italy, and Greece) courts will look to see whether the judgment was rendered under the same circumstances as where the enforcing court would have assumed jurisdiction. In England, a fairly liberal jurisdiction in terms of recognition and enforcement of EU member states' judgments, courts apply stricter standards to non-EU member states requiring that the defendant be present or resident in the judgment-rendering jurisdiction or express or implied submission to jurisdiction.[69] Neither condition is likely to obtain when the parent foreign MNC is sued in the host state.

Collective redress mechanisms, as aggregate litigation is referred to in Europe, are emerging on the Continent but are still in their infancy.[70] Only in 2013 did the EU Commission issue a nonbinding recommendation to member states to develop national collective redress mechanisms to improve EU citizens' access to justice.[71] As the American experience shows, the maturation of aggregate litigation can take decades. Where the class action does emerge in Europe, it is generally only public or quasi-public bodies that have standing to represent the interests of the plaintiffs.[72] In other words, there is no private cause of action. Experience shows, however, that private action has proven to be superior to public action in getting human rights cases brought.[73] It is no surprise, then, that EU's public enforcement entities do not currently and are not likely in the future to expend public (taxpayers') resources to police "foreign squared" and "foreign cubed" mass torts extraterritorially. The same policy considerations of conservation of public resources, sovereign equality, and separation of powers, discussed in the context of American courts, apply to enforcement by European public and quasi-public bodies. The exclusive reliance on public enforcement and the denial of a private right of action, are, therefore, barriers to the remediation of mass harms.

The contingency fee – a cornerstone of private enforcement of the law generally and of expensive aggregate litigation in particular in jurisdictions that permit it – is considered offensive to public policy in Europe.[74] Third-party funding, which has emerged as an alternative to the contingency fee in some jurisdictions, such as Australia, has been discouraged by the European Commission.[75] The combination of disallowing these two forms of litigation finance – attorney funding and third-party funding – leaves very little room actually to pursue class and mass action even if procedures for such cases exist on the books. (And, indeed, as discussed in Chapter 5, for this very reason while European countries have been adopting collective redress mechanisms those are rarely used.) Funding by nonprofit organizations or by governments – limited resources at best – are the only remaining finance options. (In addition to posing a barrier to litigation, limited funding gives superior bargaining power to large MNCs, who can afford an expensive legal defense, in the limited number of cases that are pursued with such public funding.)[76]

Punitive damages, another pillar of private enforcement, is similarly prohibited in Europe. Echoing existing national laws, it was also recently explicitly rejected by the European Commission.[77] The remedies allowed by the emergent class action regimes are often fines and these go to the state coffers. Like the contingency fee, punitive damages are viewed as incentivizing unnecessary litigation and as such are culturally repugnant to Europeans, who believe in regulation and public law enforcement rather than in privatization of law enforcement. Further, punitive damages – being a quasi-criminal sanction (as the word "punitive" suggests) – are also regarded as contrary to public policy in civil cases in which the burden of proof is preponderance of the evidence and are therefore grounds to refuse enforcement.

It is therefore not a coincidence that European lawyers – for reasons legal, ethical, economic, and cultural – cannot and will not bring the kind of cases that are pursued by the American plaintiffs' bar – a sociological, not institutional, concept. And, indeed, in terms of a sociology of the profession, a similar conception of a "French plaintiffs' bar" or a "German plaintiffs' bar" simply does not exist. The so-called entrepreneurial lawyer, who both seeks out and funds class and mass actions, is a distinctively American phenomenon.[78]

In addition, the "English rule" on fee shifts – the prevailing principle in the EU – according to which the loser pays the winner's legal expenses has, by design, a major chilling effect on bringing cases to court. The "English rule" is contrasted with the "American rule," according to which each side pays its own legal expenses irrespective of the outcome of the case, which was historically designed as a rejection of the English rules and devised to allow greater access to courts. As already hinted, these prohibitions are, in turn, rooted in a historical and cultural European preference for reliance on public intervention on behalf of private citizens. In essence, European civil procedure assumes a well-functioning regulatory-administrative state, embedded in a welfare state, that can and does regulate its corporations. However, such a well-functioning public enforcement system upon which European attitudes toward aggregate litigation are premised simply does not exist in the transnational context nor in the host states where mass torts often occur. This idea will be explored more fully in Chapter 5, where I suggest that – absent a global public order capable of shouldering the burdens described earlier – the ICCJ will need to incorporate some features of the entrepreneurial lawyering model (albeit in a more limited fashion than in the United States).

Normatively, the same objections to global adjudication, discussed previously in the context of the United States, apply with equal or greater force with respect to European courts. They may, indeed, apply with greater force as having former empires sit in judgment, as "world courts," over matters arising in their former colonies may be even more irksome than having US courts serve as world courts.

Victims of cross-border mass torts are then left with the courts of their own countries.

II LITIGATING IN COURTS OF THE JURISDICTION WHERE THE MASS INJURY OCCURRED

Once bounced out of US and European courts, victims of cross-border mass torts – at least the fortunate few who manage to refile their cases – must make do with the courts of the country where the injury occurred. The barriers to and difficulties in litigating complex mass tort cases in courts of low-income countries are many and, for example, are the reason behind the establishment of the World Bank's International Center for the Settlement of Investment Disputes (ICSID) and the broader investor-state dispute settlement (ISDS) system. Such courts often lack capacity and resources to prosecute even relatively simple civil cases. Adjudicating domestic mass tort litigation is a notoriously complex task. American courts are generally considered to be the gold standard for handling complex litigation, yet still they struggle mightily to administer such cases. Language and other technical barriers only fan the fire of inefficient transnational litigation in low-income countries.

Bias and corruption (whether real or perceived) may taint proceedings in the courts of host states, rendering judgments unenforceable (as already discussed), increasing the costs for both parties, and giving both plaintiffs and defendants reason to doubt the legitimacy of any verdict. Corruption is a real, well-documented problem:

> According to the 2013 "Corruption Perceptions Index" compiled by Transparency International, a global anti-corruption NGO and the leading source of corruption data, two-thirds of 177 nations studied scored below 50 on a 100-point scale of perceived corruption. In 2007, Transparency International produced a report focusing solely on judicial corruption. Among the findings recounted in that report, the following, based on a 2006 survey of almost 60,000 respondents in 62 countries, are particularly striking: first, "of the 8,263 people who had been in contact with the judicial system recently, 991, more than one in 10, had paid a bribe," second, "in 33 of the 62 countries polled, a majority of respondents described the judiciary/ legal system of their country as corrupt," and third, "in 35 countries, respondents singled out judges (from a list that also included: judge, police, prosecutor, lawyer, court staff, witness/jury and 'other') as the actors they most needed to bribe to obtain a 'fair' judgment."[79]

The substantive law of host states, which often fails to capture the type and scale of harms suffered, is another formidable barrier. "At present, the tort laws of many third world countries are not yet developed... [Therefore, when an American] court dismisses a case against a United States multinational corporation it often removes the most effective restraint on corporate misconduct."[80]

It seems, then, that national courts – whether of the home or host state, or of some other state taking on a kind of global role – do not and cannot offer plaintiffs in cross-border mass torts a forum that is consistently and predictably open and that can issue judgments that will be enforced against MNC defendants. Nor can those courts offer defendants global legal peace. But if not national courts, then perhaps some other existing mechanism? In the following sections I describe some of those mechanisms and discuss how they are inadequate solutions to the problem of the missing forum.

III INTERNATIONAL ARBITRATION

International investment arbitration and the institutions that support it are inapposite to the problem of the missing forum. [81] The broader term "investor-state dispute settlement" (ISDS) is used to describe the international investment arbitration regime that emerged in the second half of the twentieth century to replace gunboat diplomacy and to resolve disputes arising under international investment law. Institutionally, it encompasses international investment arbitration not only by ICSID but also at other institutions. International investment arbitrations are governed by bilateral investment treaties (BITs), which create protections for MNC foreign investors (but not their host countries). BITs further provide that disputes about the violations of those protections be submitted to international investment arbitration. Such arbitrations are usually administered by ICSID and thus are also governed by the ICSID Convention.[82] Proponents of the ISDS regime point to its role in supporting FDI, by virtue of its guarantee to foreign investors of a way to safeguard their investment against interference by host governments without being forced into those governments' own courts. However, that protection is asymmetrical. Neither host nations nor third parties (such as citizens injured by the foreign investors' (MNCs') activity) can bring any claims against investors. That asymmetry generates much of the considerable criticism directed at the ISDS regime.[83] Moreover, it means that plaintiffs in cross-border mass torts would be unable to access ISDS mechanisms – first, because they would not be parties to either a treaty or a contract granting authority to the arbitral body (a requirement of all arbitration) and, second, because ISDS protects foreign investors but not the victims of harms inflicted by those investors.

Some advocate that international commercial arbitration, and the institutions that administer such arbitration, assume the function of mass tort adjudication.[84] But there are strong practical, justice, and efficiency arguments against arbitration of mass torts that stem from the procedural nature of such adjudication. First, because parties must consent to arbitration for a tribunal to have jurisdiction, arbitration is ill suited for joinder generally and for mass aggregation, in particular. In a decision discussing the unsuitability of arbitration for class actions, the United States Supreme Court explained:

First, the switch from bilateral to class arbitration sacrifices the principal advantage of arbitration – its informality – and makes the process slower, more costly, and more likely to generate procedural morass than final judgment. "In bilateral arbitration, parties forgo the procedural rigor and appellate review of the courts in order to realize the benefits of private dispute resolution: lower costs, greater efficiency and speed, and the ability to choose expert adjudicators to resolve specialized disputes." But before an arbitrator may decide the merits of a claim in classwide procedures, he must first decide, for example, whether the class itself may be certified, whether the named parties are sufficiently representative and typical, and how discovery for the class should be conducted... Second, class arbitration *requires* procedural formality... And while parties can alter those procedures by contract, an alternative is not obvious. If procedures are too informal, absent class members would not be bound by the arbitration. For a class-action money judgment to bind absentees in litigation, class representatives must at all times adequately represent absent class members, and absent members must be afforded notice, an opportunity to be heard, and a right to opt out of the class. At least this amount of process would presumably be required for absent parties to be bound by the results of arbitration.[85]

There are additional reasons to reject arbitration as the appropriate method of mass tort adjudication. The basic argument against privatization of mass tort adjudication or, in other words, in favor of public adjudication of mass torts through a permanent court is a simple one, anchored in basic notions of democratic legitimacy. The adjudication of mass torts involves not only the resolution of liability between private parties but also the public interest in punishing and deterring such torts. The adjudicators of such disputes not only determine extremely high-stakes disputes between classes of victims and corporations, but they also provide persuasive interpretations of the law and, to the extent their decisions are regarded as having any precedential effect (even if only within the arbitral institution), they make the law as well. The fora in which such lawmaking and interpretation occur, therefore, fulfill the public function of law development as well as the enforcement of law that has public dimensions to it.

It is hard (so as not to say impossible) to think of a persuasive theory of democratic legitimacy that can support the notion that these functions should be entrusted to the hands of the invisible college of international arbitrators,[86] which is composed predominantly of litigators in prominent corporate law firms and which is largely devoid of popular participation, public accountability, or electoral supervision. In other words, the call to privatize the public function of adjudicating corporate atrocity torts is a call to entrust it to attorneys who compete for work provided by the pool of potential defendants in mass tort cases and who are (properly) immersed in the ethics of private practice and private gain rather than the ethos of public service. That approach would also ensure that adjudicators will be drawn exclusively from within the ranks of the world's richest members of society. The invisible college of international arbitrators is also notoriously unrepresentative:

> In 249 known investment treaty cases until May 2010... just 6.5% of all appointments [were of women]. Worse, of the 247 individuals appointed as arbitrators across all cases, only 10 were women. Women thus comprised 4% of those serving as arbitrators. The story is also almost entirely that of two women ... who together captured 75% of appointments of women... [In contrast], women made up 32% of European Court of Human Rights appointees ... and 19% of Appellate Body members ... in WTO history. Incidentally, on a perusal of the data, the system's record on racial and regional representation also appears poor.[87]

Private parties can in their contracts, usually *ex ante* before a breach occurs, opt out of any or all of the protections one normally associates with public adjudication. The principle of contract law that parties enjoy autonomy legitimates arbitration in contract disputes and is the foundation of arbitration law. But even if they were to find their way into arbitration, victims of torts should not be forced to forgo such protection *ex post*, after they have been injured. Simply stated, the private sector is not set up (nor should it be) to fulfill the public function of adjudicating tort disputes.

In sum, international arbitration is unlikely to provide a workable solution for complex mass torts, and even if it were, it would be normatively less desirable.

IV SINGLE-ISSUE INTERNATIONAL COURTS, ALTERNATIVE DISPUTE RESOLUTION, AND CORPORATE SOCIAL RESPONSIBILITY

Policy makers and commentators have offered various solutions aimed at addressing at least some aspects of the rule of law gap created by the problem of the missing forum. This section includes a nonexhaustive list of some of those suggestions and the limitations built into them, rendering an ICCJ a superior solution.

A solution exposed recently by the EU, France, and a few prominent American politicians is to replace the ISDS system with a permanent court of investment disputes. Prior to being adopted by politicians as a policy prescription the idea had been proposed by scholars. Professor Gus Van Harten, for example, argued for an international investment court to address the deficiencies of accountability, transparency, conflicts of interests, and incoherent jurisprudence. But recall that cross-border mass torts are private disputes between private parties: tortfeasors and their victims. Such disputes, as discussed, represent the "negative space," to borrow a term from the arts, created by the ISDS regime. This regime, as discussed, allows only for claims brought by foreign investors but precludes claims against foreign investors of the kind brought by the Indian, Ecuadorian and Nigerian plaintiffs of *Bhopal*, *Chevron–Ecuador*, and *Kiobel*. The new proposals relate exclusively to investment

IV Single-Issue International Courts

disputes under BITs and trade agreements, and do not contemplate opening the system up to any parties other than investors and states. Thus, while the new process, if it is ever put into place, may be a better version of ISDS, as far as the victims of cross-border mass torts are concerned it would offer no improvement over the current state of affairs.[88]

Another type of solution offered by some scholars and commentators consists of advocating for various single-issue tribunals with limited subject matters overlapping with the envisioned subject matter jurisdiction of the ICCJ. Examples include calls for the establishment of a global human rights court, an international court for environmental matters, and an international anticorruption court.[89] But each of those proposals only tackles part of the problem. And, as single-issue proposals, they are unlikely to garner enough support to be politically viable suggestions.

A different family of reform proposals involve recommendations to use various forms of alternative dispute resolution (ADR) to resolve mass human rights and environmental claims. While arbitration – the primary form of ADR – is, as discussed, currently irrelevant and normatively undesirable for cross-border mass torts, claims facilities are not. For example, Professor Burt Neuborne has proposed to solve the Chevron–Ecuador dispute by establishing a claims facility modeled on the Remembrance, Responsibility and the Future Foundation, which was set up to settle a series of class actions arising out of the Holocaust era and which is "the most successful use of the legal system, thus far, to provide relief to individuals harmed by allegedly unlawful transnational corporate behavior."[90] Such a proposal can be generalized into an argument that claims facilities may be useful in resolving cross-border mass claims. But claims facilities, and other forms of ADR, are properly understood as an alternative to courts. Beyond the fundamental fact that (global) rule of law requires courts – no advanced economy would exist if it provided only arbitration and no adjudication of disputes – there are additional problems with claims facilities that are not backed by the power of a court system. As a broad body of literature has argued and demonstrated, the shadow of in-court litigation is the source of claims facilities' appeal and success. Defendants agree to set up claims facilities when a viable threat of litigation hovers as the default. For example, the Gulf Coast Claims Facility (GCCF), which was set up by BP to compensate victims of its oil spill and has been largely successful in doling out expeditiously $20 billion, was set up because it afforded BP "global legal peace" in the form of dismissal of pending claims and the preclusion of future claims.[91] While ADR is an important counterpart of any form of dispute resolution and especially of highly complex mass tort litigation, as an inherently voluntary effort by its very nature, it can and should only supplement, not supplant, the rule of law that is nonvoluntary.

The same is true of self-regulation, another commonly prescribed remedy for the problem of the missing forum. A thoughtful and high-profile example of this school of thought is the Special Representative of the United Nations Secretary-General for Business and Human Rights' proposal that corporations "establish or participate in effective operational-level grievance mechanisms for individuals and communities" and that "industry, multi-stakeholder and other collaborative initiatives that are based on respect for human rights-related standards should ensure that effective grievance mechanisms are available."[92] This proposal is limited to human rights abuses (which are not coextensive with torts) and does not stand alone but rather is part of a larger remedial scheme that envisions self-regulation and ADR in the shadow of national courts. As we have already seen, national courts cannot, will not, and should not provide a forum for cross-border mass torts.

A particularly interesting attempt to regulate the behavior of MNCs, the OECD Guidelines for multinational enterprises (OECD Guidelines) occupies the space between voluntary self-governance and ADR. On the one hand, the OECD Guidelines are voluntary in the sense that no court or tribunal can issue a binding judgment or decision against an MNC that violates them. On the other hand, uniquely among similar initiatives, the OECD Guidelines provide for neutral third-party review of the conformity of MNCs' conduct with the content of the guidelines. This is particularly important since the guidelines include the requirements that MNCs abide by international human rights, humanitarian, and environmental laws; they also require businesses to take steps to ensure that those standards are followed throughout their entire supply chain. In the aftermath of the collapse of the Rana Plaza factory in Bangladesh, which killed more than a thousand people, for instance, the OECD launched an initiative to issue specific guidance for due diligence regarding supply chains in the garment and textile industries.[93] And several specific cases were filed with the OECD's oversight mechanism.[94] Some of these resulted in determinations that MNCs' conduct failed to meet their basic obligations under the Guidelines, for instance, in Denmark.[95] But the mechanism is, in the end, voluntary and has no way to require businesses to pay compensation to those they injure. To return to the Danish example, the company participated in mediation but reached no agreement, and even though the OECD process resulted in a determination that it violated its duties, it has not been required to pay compensation.[96] The OECD Guidelines are a source for the development of norms, but not for the law-based imposition of those norms on MNC defendants. For that, victims of cross-border mass torts need a court. They need an ICCJ.

V A BETTER SOLUTION: THE INTERNATIONAL COURT OF CIVIL JUSTICE

The following section will show how an ICCJ would be a better solution to the problem of the missing forum than the imperfect, impractical, or normatively undesirable alternatives discussed thus far.

V A Better Solution: The International Court of Civil Justice

Established by treaty, the ICCJ would be founded on the bedrock principle of sovereign equality. Host countries would choose to delegate their authority to adjudicate torts occurring on their territory to the ICCJ, and states participating in the enforcement regime would freely commit to honoring its decisions. The ICCJ would therefore derive its authority and legitimacy from the free exercise of sovereign authority, this, in contrast to concerns about comity and reciprocity that arise when national courts reach across borders and into the territory of other countries. Removing cross-border mass tort cases from the domestic to the international sphere would relieve pressure on national courts to balance giving plaintiffs their day in court and respecting the separation of powers or impermissibly wading into matters of foreign affairs.

The ICCJ, like all international courts and tribunals, would adhere to the rule of law. It would be neutral, in a way that national fora are not (or are not perceived to be). International courts and tribunals – whether those adjudicating public or private disputes – are subject to much scrutiny and critique. However, they are not generally charged with systemic bias against parties based on their nationality nor with corruption. Part of that neutrality would derive from the composition of the court; the ICCJ would be composed of professional judges on a permanent bench (not, as in international arbitration, selected ad hoc by the parties). As a "new style" international court (see Chapter 5) the ICCJ's jurisdiction would be compulsory and its judgments binding. That means that MNCs, plaintiffs, and both home and host governments participating in FDI would do so within the confines of the rule of law.

By providing its own applicable law – both substantive and procedural – the ICCJ would increase predictability for the parties, ensure that modern advances in tort law were incorporated, and further reduce concerns about legitimacy that might arise from privileging the law of one state or another. Thus, the ICCJ statute would set out the applicable substantive law, which I argue in Chapter 5 should be restricted to torts that cause physical injury (to a sufficient number of people to be considered "mass"). It would also incorporate procedural law that should be a hybrid of common-law and civil-law approaches. That hybridization is common in international courts and tribunals. And while many question the legitimacy of various aspects of their operation, they are not generally perceived as systemically lacking in international due process.[97] An ICCJ would, therefore, satisfy the due process concerns.

The ICCJ would be able to craft a model that draws on entrepreneurial lawyering to fill in for the absent global public authority, while reining in the worst excesses of that model as it exists in the United States. Thus, it would strike a balance between European and US sensibilities that favor, respectively, public versus private enforcement of law. So, for example, the statute of the court could permit conditional and contingency fees but subject them to judicial supervision. It could allow for punitive damages, but only if they were proven beyond a reasonable doubt. With that higher standard, and with bench trials only, punitive damages would be less common and less problematic than in the United States (where they need only be proved by a preponderance of the evidence and are issued by juries). In a similar vein, the ICCJ could adopt aggregate litigation procedures that have been developed in countries other than the United States, which reflect "lessons learned" from and improve upon the shortcomings of American practices. As a tabula rasa that would evolve in a system separate from the American – or any other national – system, an ICCJ could offer specialized and cutting-edge solutions that might be politically impractical in national courts no matter how desirable.

Establishing an international court to adjudicate cross-border mass torts would avoid imposing either resource or doctrinal constraints on national court systems. An ICCJ would in all likelihood be funded by assessing costs from the parties; states parties would only need to contribute if there were a shortfall (see Chapter 5). This means that no single country would bear a disproportionate portion of the cost of providing justice – thus eliminating the resource implications of making American courts "a uniquely hospitable forum" for tort victims the world over. In addition, because decisions of international courts have no precedential value domestically (though they may, of course, serve as persuasive authority) an ICCJ can proceed in ways that might be contrary to existing national laws without impacting those laws. For example, it may be the case that the only way to serve justice is to pierce the corporate veil in order to assert jurisdiction over a parent company for the actions of its subsidiary. There may be a legitimate concern that allowing this domestically may overly erode the principle of limited liability so fundamental to business law. But limiting the change to the jurisprudence of an ICCJ would prevent spillage, allowing for such a piercing only when it was used abusively transnationally.

I have endeavored to show in this chapter that the problem of the missing forum cannot and should not be addressed by adjudication in national courts, arbitration, corporate social responsibility, or through single-issue international courts – all of which pose some combination of practical, policy, and normative problems. The ICCJ could solve those problems. But would it really be feasible? Would MNCs and their political representatives support the creation of an ICCJ, which could, in the end, issue enforceable judgments against them? I offered part of the answer to that question in Chapter 1, where I explored the conditions under which new (and often improbable) international courts come into being. In the Chapter 4, I present an economic analysis of the business case for an ICCJ. This analysis serves as a counterargument to a knee-jerk reaction that American (and other) MNCs are likely to object to an ICCJ. Then, in Chapter 5, I suggest institutional and procedural design choices for the court that would, among other things, result in cost savings over the steep costs of the existing transnational litigationscape.

4

The Business Case for the ICCJ

There are strong reasons to believe that informed MNCs would support the creation of an ICCJ. Certainly, it makes intuitive sense that a proposal to create a new international tribunal for cross-border mass torts would meet with insurmountable objections from corporations willing to use their political clout and lobbying power to ensure the proposal's demise. Underlying this notion is an outdated belief that corporations benefit from forum shopping under the status quo. Historically, the conventional analysis of corporate defendants' choice between US courts and foreign ones has been simple:

> Defendants use transnational avoidance doctrines often and aggressively. There are a few interrelated assumptions that explain this behavior. First, U.S. litigation is seen as the most expensive and plaintiff-friendly in the world. U.S. courts boast several attractions, including permissive personal jurisdiction rules, contingent attorney fees, lack of fee-shifting, onerous discovery rules, trial by jury, and the potential for large money judgments... Second, it was often assumed that dismissal from a U.S. federal court would effectively end litigation. Third, most took for granted that no foreign forum offered plaintiffs anything remotely approaching a viable alternative.[1]

But this approach is decreasingly viable.

Businesses are beginning to realize that the "good old days" when they could count on *forum non conveniens* dismissals as the end of a case are ending. In a 2010 article titled "Forum Shopper's Remorse,"[2] a reporter for *Corporate Counsel* magazine concluded that, after seeing the Chevron–Ecuador and Dole litigations unfold,[3] fewer corporations would seek dismissals from US courts in favor of foreign ones. The reporter quoted an attorney from Gibson Dunn, the firm that represented both corporations, stating, "I think you're going to see a lot fewer U.S. companies voluntarily going to other jurisdictions... We're already seeing fewer forum non motions in my practice."[4]

Chevron's experience in Ecuador is illustrative of the new uncertainties facing corporate defendants in cross-border mass tort litigation. After prevailing on its *forum non conveniens* motion, it encountered several unpleasant surprises in Ecuador. Chevron expected, at most, to battle a few dozen small medical claims. But instead the plaintiffs were able to take advantage of a recently passed law to advance multibillion-dollar claims for environmental harm. The 1999 Environmental Management Act allowed individuals to file claims based on harms to the environment. It applied retroactively. The law appears to have been the result of successful lobbying efforts by the plaintiffs' lawyers.[5] Nor were the plaintiffs, as they might have been in the past, unequipped to pursue complex and expensive environmental claims. As of 2006, plaintiffs' new lead lawyer was a New York–based highly entrepreneurial attorney, Steven Donziger. Among other things, Donziger obtained for the plaintiffs additional breathing room and litigation stamina by availing them of litigation finance, not generally available before the first decade of the twenty-first century.[6]

Chevron's attorneys were dissatisfied with their experience in Ecuador (to understate the point), but not so much that they were willing to accede to jurisdiction in the United States "If I knew all these shenanigans would happen," Chevron's in-house attorney told the reporter, "yeah, most likely, we'd do something different [than move the case to Ecuador]."[7] However, the report immediately proceeded to quote Chevron's general counsel, who clarified, "I'm not trying to promote the idea that the U.S. should open its doors as a world court."[8] In short, neither foreign courts nor American ones appear agreeable to the defendant in one of the most expansive and expensive cross-border mass tort cases in history. Indeed, the corporate counsel's report concludes with an observation by Chevron's general counsel that "one lesson of Chevron's saga ... is that companies ought to be supportive of rule of law and anticorruption activities."[9]

The experiences of Chevron and Dole in Ecuador and Nicaragua, respectively, may seem to be perfect storms but, as will be explained later, they were not.[10] Rather, those companies encountered what I call the "new transnational litigationscape," which is much more challenging for MNCs than that which characterized the second half of the twentieth century. Among other things, the plaintiff-friendly features of this new transnational litigationscape mean that Chevron's general counsel's conclusion – that corporations benefit from rule of law and anticorruption activities – is more true now than ever.

More and more states are adopting litigation-enabling features such as favorable jurisdictional statutes, class action procedures, and requests for security of costs. In addition to more pro-plaintiff legal environments, defendants are facing the specter of pro-claimant corruption in some courts, where there used to be only pro-defendant corruption. Corruption, real or perceived, distorts legal processes, increases the costs of litigation, and ups the stakes. These changes make the magnitude of potentially bad outcomes for MNC defendants much larger; that would not be terribly alarming if the chance of the actual occurrence of catastrophic outcomes remained small (as it has traditionally been). But those chances are higher today than they were and are poised to grow.

The advent and growth of global litigation finance over the last two decades have largely erased the traditional resource advantage of MNC defendants in transnational litigation. Litigation finance levels the playing field by providing resources to traditionally poor plaintiffs. Plaintiffs now have the financial wherewithal to withstand long and expensive trials. It also means that plaintiffs' attorneys, and the institutional investors backing them, have strong financial incentives to seek out potentially profitable claims.

The new transnational litigationscape imposes significant and unnecessary costs on corporate defendants. Yet for all these changes, most of those costs (so far at least) arise from the conduct of litigation and not from paying out awards or settlements. Plaintiffs still lose, but winning has become very, very expensive for corporate defendants.

An ICCJ would ameliorate the costs and reduce uncertainty for corporate defendants in cross-border mass tort cases. The ICCJ would adopt institutional features that combine the best of common law and civil law traditions. These would include reduced discovery (compared to the United States), streamlined early-stage dismissal, limited punitive damages, and no juries. It would provide a neutral and independent forum, with judges applying a single body of law. Finally, the ICCJ would offer global preclusion and finality. Streamlined procedures would cost less. Early dismissals would reduce the ability of plaintiffs' lawyers to hold even blameless corporate defendants' hostage for settlements. Neutral judges and published law would prevent surprises of the kind Chevron encountered in Ecuador (see later discussion). Global preclusion and finality would eliminate boomerang, parallel, and sequential litigation; allow corporations to get litigation off their balance sheets; and reduce the diminution in firm value that can result from the various indirect costs of large-scale litigation. In other words, the ICCJ would be a tremendous benefit for corporate defendants in the kinds of transnational litigation that cost the most and impose the most risk.

In this chapter I will illustrate how the current climate is increasingly unfavorable for corporate defendants (without being much better for plaintiffs). First, I will detail the direct costs of litigating transnational claims, emphasizing costs that are specific to cross-border mass tort cases. Then, I will explore the indirect, often hidden costs of litigation. These can exceed the already-significant direct costs. I will demonstrate that either real or perceived corruption exacerbates transnational litigation's direct and indirect costs in foreign courts. At the same time, corporate defendants' traditional assumption that plaintiffs bounced out of US courts by a *forum non conveniens* motion will give up the fight, find themselves short of funding to continue, be disadvantaged by distinctively plaintiff-unfriendly procedures back home, or experience some combination of those outcomes no longer holds true. Supporting a solution for the problem of the missing forum makes sense for corporations, economically, therefore; doing so would also help fulfill a desire to participate in socially conscious corporate practices, a desire increasingly held by some corporate managers, employees, investors, and consumers. All of the foregoing reasons for MNCs and governments to favor an ICCJ are bolstered by developments in the broader global economic context in which these entities operate.

I RISING DIRECT LITIGATION COSTS

The direct costs of transnational litigation can be immense; an ICCJ would help to reduce them. Several examples illustrate how cross-border litigation that traverses multiple legal systems can be significantly more expensive than single-jurisdiction litigation. According to the leading corporate lobbying group:

> Chiquita Brands International, in defending against an ATS suit, recovered over $8 million for defense costs from just one of its five insurers... And in the Unocal ATS litigation, the company's legal bill ran to $15 million – and that case was not even a class action... Where plaintiffs and defendants are more numerous than in Unocal, and the challenged conduct more complex, the costs of litigation might make the $15 million Unocal reportedly spent look like a bargain.[11]

Shell paid out about as much in attorneys' fees as it had to obtain a pretrial settlement in the *Kiobel*-related Wiwa litigation.[12]

These high direct costs are due in part to the normal (and expensive) conduct of litigation, but also in part to the unique – and uniquely expensive – requirements of transnational litigation. "Direct costs," generally, are the ones normally associated with litigation, such as legal fees. Other direct costs include paying external vendors such as discovery service providers, service processors, and the like. In addition to those usual costs of any litigation, cross-border litigation has its own unique and expensive procedures. These include forum shopping procedures such as *forum non conveniens* motions, parallel and sequential litigation in multiple international fora, antisuit injunctions aimed at eliminating parallel and sequential litigation, and procedures challenging the enforcement of foreign awards.

Although the following sections focus on the cross-border-specific procedures, it is worth noting that direct costs also include international, and therefore presumably more expensive, versions of general litigation costs. Examples include international evidence-gathering specialists, international service processors, and international collection specialists. In transnational litigation, the gathering of evidence may need to take place in both the home and host states. Attorneys, investigators, and other personnel must be flown to and accommodated in the foreign country. Documents and testimony must be translated. Evidence could be located in remote areas that are difficult to access. In addition to these more expensive versions of the standard fare, corporate defendants may need to pay for cross-border-specific procedures such as obtaining or dissolving injunctions issued by foreign courts, litigating the same issues in multiple national fora in parallel, and potentially navigating irreconcilable discovery regimes as a threshold to obtaining evidence. These are discussed next.

A *Forum Shopping, Parallel and Sequential Litigation*

As we have seen, cross-border mass tort litigation often involves forum shopping. These preemptive practices themselves can be expensive. *Forum non conveniens* motions alone can require lengthy proceedings involving extensive and expensive discovery, expert testimony, and evidentiary hearings. Recall that in the Chevron–Ecuador case, the *forum non conveniens* proceedings alone lasted nine years.

Forum non conveniens motions and other preemptive procedural challenges – expensive as they are – do not always herald the end of pretrial maneuvering. A decision on jurisdiction in one court system does not bind another court considering its own authority. Defendants, therefore, remain open to additional attempts to establish jurisdiction, even as national courts in country after country decline jurisdiction. Thus, before reaching the merits of a case – indeed, even if a trial on the merits never happens – as a result of international forum shopping a case may bounce around the world as the plaintiffs seek a court that will hear their claim.

Because plaintiffs have so many fora to choose from, a decision favorable to the defendant MNC on the merits does not necessarily end all litigation – just as a successful *forum non conveniens* is not necessarily the end of pretrial jurisdictional maneuvering. Even beyond appeals, under the current patchwork system, parties can relitigate their claim in multiple fora. Courts in one jurisdiction, say Canada, are not obligated to decline to hear a case because a similar litigation is pending in, for example, Chinese courts or because American courts have decided to reject similar claims by similar plaintiffs. And, as we have seen in Chapter 2, international arbitration tribunals are increasingly assuming the role of supreme courts of appeal over the decisions of national courts. Thus, transnationally, the same case can proceed in two or more jurisdictions at once or sequentially. It is even possible that two or more jurisdictions would reach the opposite outcomes in the same case, leading to glaring unfairness.

These kinds of parallel and sequential proceedings are perhaps the highest direct costs of cross-border litigation (as Section II, The Indirect Costs of Litigation, will show, indirect costs can dwarf even the highest direct costs). In "parallel litigation" the same or very similar cases proceed in different fora simultaneously. Examples include the factually similar lawsuits concerning the Bhopal disaster that proceeded at the same time in India and the United States and litigation regarding the corruption that tainted the Ecuadorian judgment in the United States and international arbitration in the Chevron lawsuits. "Sequential litigation" refers to the litigation of the same or very similar cases in sequence in the same or in multiple fora. Examples of sequential litigation include the claims Mrs. Kiobel filed against Shell in the Netherlands after the dismissal of similar claims in the United States, and the claims the Bhopal victims filed in the United States in Texas state courts in 1990 and subsequently filing claims in New York federal courts in 1999.[13]

Parallel and sequential litigation of similar claims appears to be on the rise:

> Increasingly, courts in numerous jurisdictions encounter litigation arising out of the same facts and proceedings worldwide – in courts with a variety of class and aggregate procedures – and judges will need to grapple with the question whether their citizens are bound by class settlements arrived at elsewhere. This may lead to some surprising turns of events.[14]

Creating an ICCJ will significantly lower the direct costs of transnational litigation by eliminating or reducing forum shopping and parallel and sequential litigation. Some costs will remain, of course: lawyers, translators, and experts will still charge fees; witnesses and others will still incur travel costs; investigation and evidence gathering will still require time and money. But giving an ICCJ exclusive jurisdiction over cross-border mass tort claims would mean that those costs would be incurred only once – not over and over again. Even giving the ICCJ complementary jurisdiction – though less effective – would reduce costs. I discuss exclusive and complementary jurisdiction extensively in Chapter 5, but in short summary the former takes the national courts of host states completely out of the picture while the latter gives defendants the ability to opt into national courts both willing and able to hear the case. "Complementary jurisdiction" would mean that defendants select either the ICCJ or a national court with jurisdiction that is both willing and able to adjudicate the case and meet international due process standards.[15]

II THE INDIRECT COSTS OF LITIGATION

Astonishingly, researchers have found that "the cost of litigation to established defendants significantly exceeds the sum of the expected transfers to the plaintiff and the expected attorneys' fees."[16] In other words, being a defendant in a major lawsuit can decrease the value of a firm by more than the value of transfers in the form of legal fees and settlements. This section explores the indirect costs of litigation that help explain this value diminishment and the ways in which they may be amplified in the transnational mass tort context. First, a key indirect cost is the uncertainty about the corporation's long-term viability that large-scale litigation may cause. Such uncertainty may impose restraints on the ability of a firm to undertake business activities, disrupt its operations and finances, and prevent it from creating value that it otherwise would. Second, litigation distracts managers and employees. Such distraction is most acute when managers and employees find themselves at the center of criminal investigations and prosecutions, tools that host government sometimes employ as leverage. Third, a corporation's reputation and goodwill can be negatively affected by litigation generally; transnational litigation – especially with sympathetic plaintiffs – may exacerbate that loss. Fourth, unredressed mass harms can contribute to a change in the investment environment that is detrimental for the foreign investor firm's long-term business interests in the region.

A Uncertainty and the Restraint on Business Activities

Uncertainty is one of corporations' biggest foes. Among other things, uncertainty generated by litigation – which, depending on the size of the case could include uncertainty about whether the company will survive – can create financial distress. That distress may be pronounced, even without the prospect of bankruptcy. It can, for example, generate hesitance among lenders, hamper the firm's ability to obtain credit, and, more generally, affect the cost of capital. Uncertainty can also generate hesitance among suppliers and business partners.[17] Even if only a handful of plaintiffs choose to continue litigating after a settlement has been reached with a majority of a class's members, the additional negative publicity, regulatory attention, and obstacle to accessing capital markets can be significant.[18]

For example, in the Texaco–Pennzoil litigation, the court ordered Texaco to post a multibillion-dollar bond.[19] Texaco submitted an affidavit explaining the negative repercussions of the bond, arguing that it caused some suppliers to demand cash payments or insist on secured forms of repayment, while others halted or cancelled crude shipments. Banks refused to enter into exchange-rate futures contracts, or restricted Texaco's use of them. Texaco had to forgo certain business opportunities.[20] These impediments "made it more and more difficult, with each passing day ... to continue to finance and operate [Texaco's] business."[21] Texaco further projected in the affidavit that "as normal supply sources become inaccessible and other financing is unavailable, Texaco's operations will begin to grind to a halt. In fact, Texaco is already having to consider the prospect of shutting down one of its largest domestic refineries because of its growing inability to acquire crude and feedstock."[22]

The uncertainty generated by litigation can also affect the litigating corporation's stock price by diminishing the confidence of investors. Depressed stock price leads to diminishing value for stockholders.[23] While the effects of filing an action or of negative developments in a litigation on stock price can be short-lasting and not, overall, suggestive of a loss of value, research has shown that some stock price fluctuations lead to longer-lasting effects. These effects can be quite consequential. Such lasting effects on stock price can suggest a diminishment of the value of the corporation ("wealth leakage"). Cutler and Summers, for instance, found that the extensive takeover-related Texaco–Pennzoil litigation in the 1980s led to enormous "leakages" in value. The ongoing litigation reduced the value of the companies by a combined "$3.4 billion, [or] over 30% of the joint value of the two companies before the dispute arose" during the litigation.[24] Subsequently, "a large fraction of the losses in combined value was restored when the case was settled."[25] In the end, Texaco's shareholders gained forty cents to every dollar lost by Pennzoil shareholder.[26] Importantly, among the affected shareholders are the corporations' executives, who are often partially compensated with stocks and stock options. (In other words, corporate executives may have a personal incentive to support an institution that can reduce this effect on their compensation, though this incentive, alone, should not be exaggerated.)

Pending litigation can also have unfavorable accounting implications.[27] Conversely, settling a mass claim enables a corporation to eliminate contingent liabilities – funds that must be set aside and not be put to more productive use in order to meet regulatory requirements of capital sufficiency. Carrying litigation on a corporation's books can also have negative tax consequences.[28]

Hence in addition to the financial stress described, litigation can cause operational stress. Put simply, the uncertainty of litigation and its effect on balance sheets, capital requirements, investors, lenders, vendors, and potential partners may restrain a firm from undertaking business activities that it would have absent the litigation. The court hearing the claim may also directly impose such restraint, especially when plaintiffs seek preliminary injunctions or other assurances that the corporate defendant will satisfy any eventual judgment. Other deviations from normal operations may result from the reactions of corporate managers and third parties to the risks posed by the litigation. In addition, when defendants faced the possibility of permanent injunctions at the end of the process that would require a change of business practices going forward, a judgment could permanently increase the costs of doing business. Research has shown that the concern defendants might have over potential prohibition of profitable business practices may be greater than their concern over damages. The former affects stock prices, whereas the latter may not. Indeed, even the threat of treble monetary damages has been shown to be less of a concern to defendants, and stock markets, than the threat of the potential loss of ability to engage in certain kinds of profitable business practices.[29] This research is in the area of antitrust, where threats to defendants' core business model may be more common than in other areas. But, as the Bhopal and Chevron–Ecuador cases show, such concerns are hardly limited to antitrust.

To take an example of court-imposed restraints, in the Bhopal litigation the Government of India sought and won a sweeping preliminary injunction against Union Carbide. Although the injunction was lifted in relatively short order upon agreement of the parties (discussed later), it provides an example of the potential scope of the disruption of business activities that could result from transnational litigation. After the decision by Judge Keenan of the Southern District of New York that the case would be more properly tried in India, the Government of India sued Union Carbide in the District Court of Bhopal. Very quickly the government asked the court to issue an injunction preventing Union Carbide from shifting any assets in any part of its business. According to a statement issued by the advocate general of Madhya Pradesh State: "In view of the magnitude of the disaster and human suffering and the decree which is likely to be passed for damages, it is essential that the defendant should not be allowed to alienate or dispose of its assets."[30] In arguments to the Second Circuit Court of Appeals, counsel for Union Carbide described the Indian court's interim injunction as "restrain[ing] [the company] from creating any change in their assets, directly or indirectly, until the application for an interim injunction is decided"[31] and, specifically, "from paying dividends to its shareholders."[32]

This injunction came at a particularly inconvenient time for Union Carbide. It was in the process of a significant restructuring[33] and had already declared a dividend for its stockholders. The injunction spurred concerns from Union Carbide about the fairness of Indian courts (the very courts it had argued were the proper forum for the case): "Nobody, I think, anticipates or could anticipate that as a price, a price of getting your day in court you have to pay, that you have to stop functioning. That you have to, in short, be restrained from creating any change in assets, directly or indirectly. That is a price that makes a mockery of due process."[34] Eventually, the Government of India and Union Carbide agreed on the creation of a $3 billion fund to pay out any judgments. That agreement allowed Union Carbide to proceed with its restructuring and to continue business unencumbered.[35]

Pending cross-border mass tort cases can also restrain business activities even without court intervention. For instance, litigation can, in uncommon but important situations, cause difficulties engaging in large, strategic transactions such as mergers and acquisitions. "Importantly, when litigation causes difficulties in entering into mergers or acquisitions, transacting into large equity infusion, or affects the cost of capital, the hidden costs can dwarf the expense of pursuing a claim."[36]

In the Chevron–Ecuador dispute, the plaintiffs' plan to seek enforcement of a fraudulently obtained[37] Ecuadorian judgment led Chevron to urge the District Court for the Southern District of New York to issue a worldwide injunction

II The Indirect Costs of Litigation

blocking its enforcement. (To recall, Chevron had successfully resisted that court's jurisdiction over the case itself.) Chevron explained in a court filing the irreparable harm that would be caused to its operations if the enforcement attempts were not blocked. The district court obliged, finding that

> absent a preliminary injunction, Chevron would be forced to defend itself and litigate the enforceability of the Ecuadorian judgment in multiple proceedings. There is a significant risk that assets would be seized or attached, thus disrupting Chevron's supply chain, causing it to miss critical deliveries to business partners, damaging Chevron's business reputation as a reliable supplier and harm the valuable customer goodwill Chevron has developed over the past 130 years, and causing injury to Chevron's business reputation and business relationships.[38]

In granting this request, the court went on to emphasize the amplified nature of the harm given the transnational nature of the dispute (and of Chevron's business):

> First, [enforcement of the potentially fraudulent foreign judgment] would be subjected to the coercive effect of multiple proceedings and the risk of asset seizures and attachments that might occur, some without even advance notice. Second... Chevron would be put to the cost, distractions and other burdens of defending itself in multiple fora, probably simultaneously... Finally, to whatever extent that the [Lago Agrio plaintiffs] collect on the judgment before its validity ultimately is determined, Chevron would be unable to recover the money if it ultimately prevailed.[39]

However, because the District Court for the Southern District of New York is not a global court, the Court of Appeals for the Second Circuit vacated the so-called global injunction that the district court in New York purported to impose.[40] A global court could solve this problem.

B *Distracted Management and Criminal Prosecution*

Another well-understood indirect cost of litigation is the distraction that it causes to managers and employees. "Internal costs may represent a large portion of a party's total costs when in-house counsel, managers, experts and other staff take a proactive role before and during [litigation]."[41]

Employees need to collect evidence and conduct other factual research and managers need to analyze the suit to make informed decisions on how to direct counsel and the litigation. Depending on the scope of the case, a company may appoint a staff member designated to manage the case full-time. Such staff assignment may be in addition to the work conducted by in-house counsel. A corporation may also need to retain outside technical expertise. A particular source of distraction and stress for managers and employees is the need to prepare for, travel to, and submit to depositions and testimony.[42]

The problem of distracted managers reaches its extreme manifestation when corporate personnel in the host state find themselves subjected to criminal prosecution as a consequence of their involvement in the business operations of the allegedly offending MNC. In Chapter 2, for example, we encountered the successful criminal prosecution of Bhopal executives. Similarly, in 2008, Ecuador's President Correa called for indictments of all who signed off on Texaco's cleanup a decade earlier, following demands by protesters. Days later, Ecuador's attorney general indicted two Chevron lawyers who negotiated and signed the settlement and release. The criminal charges were ultimately dropped.[43] Dole faced a similar fate upon succeeding in removing its case, based on *forum non convenien*, to Nicaragua. Defense lawyers are increasingly perceiving that what these and other examples "show is that the politicization and outright bias that can plague foreign courts are many orders of magnitude greater than we can imagine."[44]

C Harms to Reputation and Goodwill

Litigation can harm a corporation's reputation. In *Kiobel*, the US Chamber of Commerce took the position that "complaints asserting ATS claims impose a severe social stigma that may scuttle stock values or destroy debt ratings."[45] When the alleged tort involves moral turpitude, in particular, as when plaintiffs accuse manufacturers of using child or forced labor, reputational harm can be significant and lasting. Violations of human rights, such as forced labor or displacement of peoples, which carry a heightened negative stigma, are more likely in the context of operations in the developing world.

> In the *Doe* case, press releases and demonstrations just before Halloween and Valentine's Day urged parents and children to refuse to purchase chocolate candy from the defendant corporations because it was allegedly the product of "child slavery" – with the pending ATS action cited as support for that claim... And in a case against Coca-Cola based on the alleged activities of its subsidiaries in Colombia, the plaintiffs and their lawyers launched protests at the company's shareholder meetings. The news that the company was being accused of murder and torture prompted some shareholders to quickly dump Coca-Cola stock, even though the case ultimately was dismissed. That sort of reputational harm is different in kind from the publicity accompanying a run-of-the-mill commercial or tort suit.[46]

Reputational harm can also take forms other than customer perceptions of a brand.

Third parties – suppliers, distributors, investors, and employees – may no longer trust the corporation's "implicit promises," or noncontractual notions that a business would continue to produce products or services and provide jobs to its employees.[47] When a company faces a major lawsuit, the cost of establishing and maintaining implicit contracts rises. For example, counterparties who fear that a large award may leave the defendant short for cash may worry that the defendant will cut corners,[48] and employees may presume their employment is no longer secure. Consequently, when significant litigation is launched, some implicit promises need to be replaced with costly written contracts. These explicit contracts must become more elaborate to counter new concerns that third parties may now have.

In additional to reputational harm, litigation can harm the goodwill a company has built over time[49] and it can reveal unfavorable information about the corporation's prospects that would not otherwise become public.[50] It is a principle of accounting that a company's goodwill, intangible as it is, is considered an asset that can be accounted for on its books. While a corporation is not required to offset goodwill by any ill will it may have generated, ill will is a liability. For example, for Chevron in Ecuador, "these days the only Chevron employees who visit the former oil fields, in a region where resentment against the company runs high, do so escorted by bodyguards toting guns ... in a country where American corporations once wielded strong influence but are now treated with discourtesy, if not contempt."[51]

D Change in Investment Climate

The most influential corporations and those whose harms are most extensive may be most easily able to make strategic use of forum shopping, but they are also the ones who are most likely to find themselves at the receiving end of populist rage. In extreme circumstances, outrage at unredressed and unredressable harms contributes to a change in the investment climate, including change of regime from pro-FDI to one hostile to it. Latin American countries, for example, have elected regimes that openly resist MNCs. Examples include the regimes of Hugo Chavez in Venezuela, former Sandinista Daniel Ortega in Nicaragua, and Evo Morales in Bolivia.[52] Similarly, after many years of criticism, some countries are withdrawing from the global system for protecting foreign investors. Venezuela, Bolivia, and Ecuador withdrew from the ICSID convention. In 2014 Indonesia announced its intention to allow all its bilateral investment treaties to expire, and since then has, in fact, allowed several to do so (perhaps as a prelude to concluding new BITs on better terms).[53]

The opportunity costs – the lost business opportunities caused by hostility toward foreign investing MNCs – are another incalculable but likely high cost to which a reality of *de facto* impunity contributes. And at the extreme end of the spectrum, MNCs can find themselves the target of expropriation, which is a devastating loss of value.[54]

There are additional ways in which the indirect costs are compounded in the transnational sphere. The refusal to enforce foreign judgments issued in cases that have been dismissed on *forum non conveniens* grounds and the actual and alleged torts committed that are not remedied create a host of backlash effects that take the form of statutes aimed at frustrating successful prosecution of *forum non conveniens* and that, in turn, exacerbate the problem of boomerang litigation. They also take the form of legislation aimed at enabling litigation of specific mass torts against specific defendants. And they coincide with a rise in legislation enabling class actions, including by global classes of litigants, in foreign courts.

By providing a forum that can reach the merits of the case, ICCJ proceedings can minimize anger and backlash in nations and regions where the defendant may wish to continue doing business. Here, an analogy is apt to the transitional justice context, where international courts' function is understood to be, in part, providing a forum in which victims' voices are heard, historical records that recognize past suffering are created, and closure can be attained. The result is that victims and victimizers can move forward and have better chances of avoiding lapsing back into hostilities.[55] By analogy, a forum that actually reaches the merits of mass torts, especially those that stem from mass human rights violations, can contribute to the creation of an environment that is more conducive to foreign investment both by the tortfeasor MNC as well as by other foreign investors. This, in turn, reduces the risk of retaliatory legislation, expropriations, populist criminal prosecutions, and other forms of retribution.

These issues are discussed in more detail later. Before we examine them, however, we should first take a look at an accelerant of all of the foregoing costs, direct and indirect: corruption.

III THE COST OF CORRUPTION AND THE VALUE OF THE RULE OF LAW

Corruption is immoral and the rule of law, which corruption undermines, is underpinned by a host of values that have nothing to do with maximizing profits for corporations. These include ensuring that the law applies equally to all members of society – especially to the rulers and the ruled – and providing transparency and predictability about the norms governing conduct. The focus here, however, is on the value that the rule of law represents for corporations engaged in international business dealings (particularly FDI) and, conversely, the costs corruption imposes on those same activities. Unsurprisingly, researchers have found that conducting business in the absence of corruption benefits corporations and that the availability of well-functioning courts increase, corporate profitability and that exposure to courts highly ranked by the business sector, furthermore, increases firm value.[56] Firms in industries with high operational legal risk appear to derive the most value from such courts.[57] Of corporate lawyers surveyed by the US Chamber of Commerce 75 percent stated that "the quality of a state's court system was likely to impact specific business decisions, such as where to conduct business."[58] Yet, MNCs do not have the luxury of operating only in countries with a strong rule of law. In fact, MNCs claim they often find themselves in corrupt forums facing due process violations and there is evidence to support this contention.[59]

Corruption exacerbates both the direct and indirect costs detailed in the preceding sections. Corruption, generally speaking, is a violation of the rule of law, which can take one of two forms. "Tainting corruption" refers to a situation "where an individual or institution becomes corrupted by an external influence that disrupts [its] decision-making process."[60] Examples of tainting corruption might be a judiciary beholden to its political or military benefactors rather than to the law, or courts conscious of the economic effects of their decisions and more concerned with those than with fidelity to the law. In contrast, "disloyalty corruption" refers to situations when an individual sells his loyalty to some third party "rather than directing it at those to whom loyalty is owed."[61] Accepting a bribe is a paradigmatic example of disloyalty corruption. Both kinds of corruption can be in play at any given time, and both kinds inform the analysis of the effects of corruption and, importantly, the perception of corruption on the prospects for the fair and effective adjudication of transnational harms.

Direct costs will be increased by the amount of any payments over and above the cost of an honest litigation to secure disloyalty corruption and by additional costs required to combat the corruption secured by the other party. Indirect costs will be increased as well, for example, in the form of payments to secure tainting corruption (e.g., paying lobbyists' fees) and the criminal and civil liability to which both disloyalty corruption and training corruption give rise. Even unproven rumors of corruption could increase uncertainty about a firm's prospects, further depressing stock value and increasing the cost of capital, services, and supplies. Finally, the perception that a corporation engaged in corruption would do further harm to its reputation and diminish its goodwill. Unfortunately, because the effects of corruption are produced by structural features and driven by perceptions, there is no easy escape from them in the current system of transnational litigation before national courts.

In contrast to the win–win solution of an ICCJ, the prevalence of corruption in courts of low-income nations poses a particular lose–lose situation: it creates a "prisoner's dilemma" according to which it is rational to engage in preemptive corruption when litigating in their courts.[62] Where parties to a dispute know, or genuinely believe, that the courts hearing the dispute are tainted corrupt and/or that their judge is disloyal corrupt it is rational (albeit immoral) for each party to engage in corruption first to secure a favorable outcome before the other party does so corruptly. Arguing that corruption is rational does not mean it is normatively preferred. In fact, given the extra cost of corruption and its distorting effects on the rule of law over time, both parties to a given dispute may well prefer honest litigation. However, under current circumstances, the decision-making process of the parties when litigating in a corrupt forum takes the form of a prisoner's dilemma.

A prisoner's dilemma is a game-theoretical term for a type of situation wherein two players must decide – without knowing the other's choice – whether to cooperate or defect. Mutual cooperation (i.e., refraining from corruption) benefits both players more than mutual defection (i.e., both parties engaging in corruption). But if only one player defects (acts corruptly) while the other cooperates (acts honestly), the defecting (corrupt) player gains a higher advantage than she would from mutual cooperation (honesty). Meanwhile, the sole cooperating player does worse than she would from either mutual cooperation or mutual defection. Hence, the sole cooperating player assumes the worst position. The upshot of the prisoner's dilemma is that it is rational to defect to avoid the possibility of occupying that worst spot.

Applied to transnational litigation, each party has a choice: litigate honestly or engage in corruption. However, the perception of corruption – such as when a party perceives, rightly or wrongly, that a judicial system is tainted corrupt – is enough to create an incentive to act corruptly first. And once one party engages in corruption or is perceived to be doing so, then the other party gains a reason to balance the scales with corruption of its own. In other words, perception of tainting corruption of a judiciary alone would suffice to incentivize a vicious cycle of actual corruption. "In such a situation, the litigants will prefer mutual honesty to mutual corruption, but the conjunction of their strictly dominant strategies will lead them to, e.g., pay bribes and waste their money all while imposing the negative externalities caused by supporting a corrupt legal system."[63] In other words, real or perceived corruption begets corruption.

Understanding corruption as a prisoner's dilemma poses two significant challenges for those seeking a forum for the fair and effective adjudication of transnational harms. First, it highlights that the problem of corruption is structural rather than individual and is self-reinforcing. Any given bad corporate actor, greedy judge, or cowboy plaintiffs' attorney – however prevalent and pernicious, or not, those actors may be – is only part of the problem. That means that solutions that focus on holding bad actors accountable – punishing individuals who litigate a case corruptly – will not suffice when the underlying problem is structural. Second, the description of transnational litigation as a prisoner's dilemma shines a light on the deleterious effects of parties' perceptions that many countries' courts are corrupt. Hence, it does not depend on the existence of actual corruption and would not be affected by incremental efforts of individual countries to curb corruption. In other words, structural reforms that target bad actors – litigants, lawyers, or judges – will have only limited effect, and perceptual reforms that target bad judicial actors or systems will be similarly limited in their effect.

Another complicating factor is the elusive nature of court and government reform in developing countries. "Experience has shown reform to be both difficult and slow, especially where the independence and integrity of the judiciary are in question."[64] While the existence of properly functioning courts is a necessary, albeit insufficient, condition for economic development and "badly performing courts are a burden not only for litigants, but nations as a whole,"[65] reforming underperforming courts has proved difficult to achieve. It is reasonable to surmise that establishing a new international body, while itself a significant undertaking, is nonetheless a more attainable goal for the first part of the twenty-first century than is the successful reformation of the majority of the world's judicial systems.

Historically, MNCs may have been confident in their ability to avoid litigation in foreign courts after a dismissal in their home courts on *forum non conveniens* grounds and thereby to avoid many of the direct and indirect costs, exacerbated by corruption, described previously. But changes in the transnational litigationscape, including the rise of a global class of entrepreneurial lawyers, the advent of litigation funding, and the accelerated emergence of pro-plaintiff features in host countries, mean that plaintiffs will increasingly have their day in court – perhaps many days, in many courts. One effect of all those changes is that they will make global legal peace for corporate defendants even more valuable – and even more difficult to obtain. That reality, in turn, will drive up settlement prices. The value of global legal peace and the features of the new transnational litigationscape are discussed in Sections IV and V.

IV THE GLOBAL PEACE PREMIUM

Global legal peace (meaning a final end to all litigation) in the context of cross-border mass torts is of fundamental importance to MNCs but – in light of the features described in the foregoing sections – unnecessarily difficult and costly to acquire. Scholars have shown, and courts have recognized, that finality is, literally, at a premium for corporate defendants in mass claim cases. Without it, defendants exposed to numerous suits "may be motivated to pay class members a premium and achieve a global settlement in order to avoid additional lawsuits."[66] But finality is hard to come by in transnational litigation, where many bites at the apple are afforded to plaintiffs at every stage of the litigation. Taken together, all those costs and multipliers drastically increase the cost of finality for defendants. It is important to note that in the current system of transnational litigation, characterized by parallel and sequential litigation, and where national courts' final judgments do not bind one another, courts do not offer a meaningful route to finality. Settlement is the surest way to achieve global legal peace. All those factors together increase what is known as the "peace premium" in the transnational litigation context. And that premium is at its very highest in the context of cross-border mass torts.

The following examples explain why and how corporate defendants pay a premium for finality. After the Deepwater Horizon spill, BP was willing to pay higher settlements to victims who brought their claims through the more expensive class action process than to those who claimed through the less expensive Gulf Coast Claims Facility (the GCCF).[67] This runs counter to basic economic theory, which would predict that when transaction costs are lowered both parties benefit from distributing the surplus generated by the savings. The statute governing the spill, the Oil Pollution Act of 1990 (OPA), provided for strict liability and the GCCF provided a simplified claims procedure that enabled claimants to proceed on their own, without paying for counsel. This significantly reduced the costs for BP and for claimants. But claimants received higher payouts by BP, sometimes significantly so, through the more expensive court process because that process enabled them to offer BP something of value: finality. In exchange, defendants paid a "peace premium."[68]

In the World Trade Center Disaster Site litigation,[69] which followed the September 11, 2001, terrorist attacks, the City of New York was also willing to pay a peace premium. In that case, more than ten thousand first responders and cleanup workers sued the City of New York for illnesses developed after working in Ground Zero. The city agreed to pay $625 million as long as 95 percent of the plaintiffs accepted the settlement. But if 100 percent of the plaintiffs signed on, it was willing to increase the settlement amount to $712.5 million. Namely, to induce the last 5 percent of plaintiffs to agree to the settlement, thereby providing complete peace, the city was willing to pay a premium of more than twice the per-claimant amount for the first 95 percent.[70] The corollary to such "bonus payments" for full participation are "walk-away" provisions that allow defendants to walk away from a global settlement if too few plaintiffs sign on. Such provisions are common in aggregate litigation and like the bonus payment they are evidence of the peace premium.

The value of global peace is the reason that, in economic terms, settlements of mass claims are a discontinuous function. Simply put, this means aggregation of claims is not merely additive but rather has a compounding savings effect:

> The peace premium is a reflection that there may be thresholds that are critical to defendants. Such thresholds may include complete peace, the settlement of the claims held by major aggregators on the plaintiffs' side, the specifics of regulatory compliance, or other potential case-specific factors. The premium comes from the realization of whichever threshold is of enhanced value to the defendant such that each individual plaintiff does not add very much to the value of the potential settlement until a sufficient number of claims have been aggregated.[71]

Put another way, getting finality for just some of the claims but leaving others to be litigated (or relitigated) does little or nothing to mitigate consideartions such as falling shareholder confidence, distraction of employees and officers, or diminished reputation. Only something close to complete finality will work.

Domestically, courts can provide that finality. They can, for instance, avoid or reduce parallel and sequential litigation by using their power to transfer and consolidate cases. Further, the law governing such areas as claim and issue preclusion, recognition of the decisions of sister states, and other legal principles eliminate otherwise endless and duplicative litigation. Clear and finite lines of appeal also provide corporate defendants with predictability and a foreseeable end to the litigation. These measures provide defendants with the peace of mind that comes with knowing that, win or lose, a case is over once it has gone through the trial and appellate levels of the jurisdiction. None of these preclusive, finality-producing effects are available in transnational litigation.

Even a final judgment against the plaintiffs, on the merits, in the highest court of a national jurisdiction does not necessarily end the story.[72] This issue has been explored in the context of class actions in the United States, where the putative class has included foreign plaintiffs. Corporate defendants have typically resisted motions to certify classes that include foreign plaintiffs on the ground that "transnational class actions provide no assurance of finality for a defendant because it will always be possible for a non-U.S. class member to initiate subsequent proceedings in a foreign court."[73] Defendants claim that foreign plaintiffs "get 'two bites at the apple' at defendants' expense: once in a US court in the original class proceeding and once in a foreign court that refuses to give effect to the resultant U.S. class judgment."[74] One commentator has observed that this gives foreign members of classes in the United States a "litigation option."[75] Recent scholarship calls into question whether it is possible to know, *ex ante*, whether foreign courts will enforce foreign judgments. Thus, the only way for a corporate defendant in transnational mass tort litigation to obtain completely certain finality is to secure a settlement in which the plaintiffs agree to forbear from all further claims in any forum.

This skews the incentives in transnational litigation and makes settlements more expensive than they would be if a single institution could issue judgments that bound all relevant jurisdictions. In the absence of harmonization and cooperation, the parties are, in effect, bargaining outside the law. The bargaining position of the plaintiffs is not bounded by the likely result in a given court, but rather by the extent of their resources to relitigate the case in multiple courts. Given sufficiently resourced plaintiffs, then, one would expect the price of a settlement to increase to include the value of the additional bites at the apple they would be forgoing.

An ICCJ would offer defendants global legal peace at a significantly lower cost. Its decisions would have global preclusive effect. Thus, an ICCJ would eliminate the specter of boomerang, parallel, and sequential litigation. Also, global preclusive effect means that finality could result through judicial decision (such as a dismissal) and not just through settlement. The parties would once again be bargaining in the shadow of the law. And that law would be applied by neutral judges on a court that adhered to the norms of the rule of law; the actuality or perception of corruption would no longer distort the process or exacerbate costs. The ICCJ would develop coherent, and therefore predictable, jurisprudence, enhancing predictability to foreign investors and thereby lowering the cost of FDI.

That is not to say that an ICCJ would eliminate all direct and indirect costs. Litigation would still be expensive and distracting. A company defending mass torts claims might still lose the confidence of shareholders and others; its reputation could still suffer. But the direct expenses would only be incurred once, and the indirect effects would be time-bound instead of stretching off long into the future. Aggregation of claims, one of the hallmarks of the ICCJ, would also provide economies of scale: decreasing the number of actions would eliminate duplication and thereby lower transaction costs. Enabling global settlements could create additional efficiencies for defendants. Global settlements facilitate lump sum payments, thereby eliminating the expense of valuing and negotiating individual claims.[76]

To recap, litigating transnational mass tort claims causes corporate defendants to pay for expensive pretrial procedures, such as *forum non conveniens* motions. Defendants potentially have to pay for such motions practice more than once as plaintiffs search for a hospitable forum. Also, they may have to pay significantly higher trial expenses in the event that the plaintiffs find a hospitable forum. And they may have to pay those higher trial costs over and over again as the lack of global preclusion allows for parallel and sequential litigation. For the duration of those trials and retrials corporate defendants may suffer from distracted officers and employees; loss in the confidence of shareholders, investors, and vendors; loss in firm value (some of which may be permanent); and diminished reputation and goodwill. In order to prevent these collateral costs, defendants pay a premium for a settlement that confers global legal peace. In the past, corporate defendants may have been able to rest easy in the knowledge that whatever the magnitude of the potential bad litigation outcome, the chance that catastrophe would actually strike was low. But recent changes in the transnational litigationscape, including litigation funders and a growing cadre of global entrepreneurial lawyers (discussed later), mean that those chances have increased. These new players have every financial incentive to seek out claims and pursue them in every possible forum, and they are aided in that endeavor by a growing body of pro-plaintiff legislation in both developed and developing countries. These changes are the subject of Section V.

V BACKLASH AND THE NEW TRANSNATIONAL LITIGTIONSCAPE

Transnational litigation of cross-border mass torts is currently in a liminal state between the days when corporations were largely safe from litigation in developing countries' courts and a new era when the risk of large judgments from such litigation is no longer trivial. I say "liminal" because the current state of affairs retains the worst of the previous era for plaintiffs and the worst of the new for corporate defendants. MNCs now have to contest claim after claim in forum after forum; as Section IV demonstrated the direct and indirect costs of parallel and sequential litigation, especially involving cross-border-specific procedures, can be exorbitant. Yet plaintiffs, for all the bites at the apple they currently enjoy, frequently find themselves – at the end of the day – either without a forum that will hear the merits of their claims or, in the rare event they secure a judgment, unable to enforce it.

It is possible for this liminal state to continue indefinitely. Sympathetic victims will always have sizable claims that will attract committed attorneys and investors interested in adding a high-risk, high-reward investments to their portfolio. And corporations can perhaps continue to fight those same claims, over and over, in forum after forum, "successfully" spending vast amounts money, reputation, and firm value to avoid judgment. But the shape of the emerging transnational litigationscape should cause corporate defendants concern. Retaliatory pro-plaintiff legislation in developing countries, coupled with the emergence of a global cadre of entrepreneurial lawyers backed by a new industry of global legal finance, means that some cases here and there proceed through all the way to enforcement. That does not mean that plaintiffs' problems will all be solved and that they will suddenly find open fora; ultimately, most will face all the same problems plaintiffs face today. But it does mean that corporations conducting business overseas will start to have to calculate whether their bet-the-firm case will be the one that makes it all the way.

The most dramatic and systemic change in the ability to fund cases is seen in the emergence and rapid growth of a global litigation finance industry. This development is explored next.

A *The Rise of Litigation Finance*

Litigation finance, also called "litigation funding" or "third-party funding," dramatically changes the nature of the relationship between MNCs and plaintiffs from developing countries by providing them with financial resources they have traditionally lacked and – perhaps more importantly – converting one-shotters into repeat players.[77] Litigation finance is the provision of funding by a nonparty to a party in return for a share of the litigation proceeds, if any are paid through judgment or settlement. Traditionally, participating in litigation finance has been a crime, a tort, and an ethical violation. It was barred in the common law world by means of the doctrine of "champerty" and through other mechanisms in other legal systems. But, in recent years, funding of large commercial claims, international arbitration, and class actions has become increasingly acceptable and available in many common law and civil law jurisdictions.

The modern practice of litigation finance began when Australia authorized it, followed in short order by the United Kingdom and the United States. In addition, third-party funding of litigation or arbitration is now permitted and available – in different forms, subject to a variety of restrictions and regulations – in France, Germany, the Netherlands, and Singapore. In Switzerland, third-party funding of international arbitrations exists and is increasing.[78] Hong Kong allows third-party funding in narrow cases, including cases in which access to justice is at stake,[79] and, in 2016, the Hong Kong Law Reform Commission released a report recommending expanding the use of funding in arbitration.[80] In 2017, the Singapore Parliament passed a bill endorsing the use of third-party finance in arbitration.[81] Korea has no prohibition against litigation funding, and a budding interest in litigation funding, which is expanding in the region, has been reported.[82] Litigation finance is also being offered in South Africa.[83]

The business model of litigation finance means that cross-border mass torts will be particularly attractive investments. It is important to emphasize that the litigation finance industry is large and growing. Although not yet fully mature, it has passed well beyond the startup phase to become diversified and stratified. The largest players are publicly traded and have billions of dollars under management.[84] As of mid-2016, four of the largest litigation finance firms had $1.8 billion invested in litigation in the United States and abroad. Many litigation financiers invest in any global jurisdiction where third-party funding is permissible. For example, one funder with offices in London and Hong Kong has financed cases in twelve international jurisdictions and four arbitral forums. Two of the largest litigation funders have invested in lawsuits against Volkswagen in the wake of its diesel emissions scandal – including a shareholder class action with damages exceeding $1 billion.[85] Cross-border mass torts are expensive to prosecute but offer the prospect of large verdicts and, consequently, put immense pressure on defendants to settle. This makes them precisely the kind of investment litigation funders seek out. As more and more firms, seeking to invest more and more capital, join the ranks of litigation funders, defendants will face well-resourced, repeat players on the other side.

B *The Rise of the Global Entrepreneurial Lawyer*

Litigation finance has been embraced by, among others, global firms and other lawyers whose practice crosses national boundaries. The legal profession's globalization since the mid-1980s has been colorfully described in the following terms:

Like the drummers, messengers and concubines that accompanied ancient armies on the march, professional-service firms followed their industrial clients as they expanded around the world in the 1980s and 1990s. Wherever western multinationals went to set up or buy a new business, there too went their accountants, bankers, consultants and lawyers ... to advise on what deals to do, how to finance them, how to compute their consequences and how to tie up all the messy loose ends.[86]

What is true of the defense bar is also true of the plaintiffs' bar; it too has gone global. Examples, specifically, of American entrepreneurial lawyers abound. "Entrepreneurial lawyers" denote the type of lawyering characteristic in American class or mass actions context when lawyers initiate, finance, litigate, and assume *de facto* control of the litigation.[87] The rise in mass injuries by MNCs in host nations is not the only force that drives the increased role American lawyers are taking in initiating and facilitating class actions abroad. Commentators describe a rise in American plaintiff firms' "creative legal engineering" by operating in Europe and Asia. These firms collaborate with local firms – using "synthetic class actions" (described later) – to overcome the closing of American courts to securities class actions.[88]

In addition to American representation of Indian, Ecuadorian, and Nigerian plaintiffs in, respectively, Bhopal, the Chevron–Ecuador dispute, and *Kiobel*, American lawyers have more recently represented classes in the Netherlands, Germany, and Japan – to name but just a few examples.[89] By way of background, in 2005, Germany passed the Capital Markets Model Case Law (the "KapMuG law") authorizing "test case" litigation, which can resolve common questions and bind class members who opt into the litigation. The Netherlands passed the Dutch Act on Collective Settlement of Mass Claims (the "WCAM") authorizing global class settlements in 2005.[90] Specifically, WCAM allows an existing or specially created association representing claimants and defendants to negotiate a settlement and then jointly petition the Amsterdam Court of Appeals to approve it. This court approval is binding on all class members who do not opt out. The Dutch law only allows for global class settlements, not class actions, so plaintiffs' bargaining power under its scheme is limited.[91] At the time of this writing, however, legislation is pending in the Netherlands to allow class actions.[92]

In an example of a so-called synthetic class action, a group of plaintiffs obtained a $1.337 billon settlement against Fortis, an international bank, in 2016. The plaintiffs recovered despite an American court's dismissal of their case. The [European] investors retained American law firms, who formed associations to which the claims were transferred. This gave the plaintiffs the protection of limited liability and protected them from a fee shift. The associations then turned to third-party funders to finance their case and obtained insurance against a "loser pays" fee shift.[93] The result was a record settlement for European securities litigation.[94] Similar successful aggregate securities settlements, organized by American law firms, followed in Germany and Japan.[95] In another case, institutional investors from around the world used the German KapMuG with the expectation of later using the Dutch WCAM, which allowed converting the consolidated German proceedings into a *de facto* opt-out class, to sue Volkswagen.[96] American plaintiffs' firms also fared well obtaining a settlement for a global class of shareholders in the Netherlands against Shell Petroleum, a Netherlands-based corporation, for a securities case. In this case, investors alleged material misrepresentations by Shell.[97] The Dutch court assumed jurisdiction over foreign shareholders as well as Dutch ones. Here, too, claims were transferred to a foundation, which retained American lawyers on contingency, in accordance with the fee rules of their home jurisdiction rather than that of the Netherlands.[98]

The Dutch collective settlement negotiations and the US litigation[99] proceeded in parallel, leading to conflicts and clashes. After much wrangling, the non-US claims were dismissed from federal court in light of the remedy provided by the Dutch WCAM mechanism. The US lead plaintiffs and Shell settled the US action for $82.85 million and the WCAM action settled for $353.56 million.[100]

In sum, the growing global supply of institutional investors in claims has aligned sophisticated and moneyed repeat players (litigation funders and international law firms) with unsophisticated, impecunious "one-shotters" (plaintiffs in developing countries). The effect is an increasing leveling of the playing field between MNCs and indigenous plaintiffs.[101] The resulting new aggregate actions are played out in a patchwork of inconsistent national regimes. This results in increased forum shopping, enforcement problems, and sequential litigation. These problems will become more frequent and complex as courts being asked to enforce foreign judgments are called on to assess whether defendants were provided with due process. In addition to being expensive and unpredictable, this unintended system is also susceptible to legitimacy charges, as courts increasingly pass judgment on their counterparts in other nations, and as national laws are used with extraterritorial effects.

C Blocking Statutes and Other Pro-Plaintiff Legislation

Litigation funders and global lawyers are aided by different kinds of pro-plaintiff legislation passed by a growing number of countries. As we have seen in Chapter 2, host governments often have conflicts of interest with the plaintiffs. If nothing else, they are often the coventurers of the foreign investors. But MNCs may also face local governments with interests conflicting to their own. It has been reported, for example, that Ecuador was set to receive 90 percent of the damages that plaintiffs would have received from Chevron for remediation.[102] Such governments have a legislative pen that gives their interests effect in the real world. In the transnational mass litigation context, this has, in some cases, led to controversial, pro-plaintiff or, at least, pro-litigation legislation. Increasingly, legal systems outside the United States are adopting features of the American legal system that are considered to be pro-plaintiff such as mechanisms for claim aggregation and punitive damages.[103] Courts in foreign jurisdictions are asserting jurisdiction over US companies[104] and are "more likely to grant relief to plaintiffs and to do so in larger amounts than they previously were."[105]

1 Blocking Statutes and Litigation-Enabling Legislation

In reaction to the refusal of US courts to assert jurisdiction on convenience grounds, discussed in Chapter 3, several Latin American countries – including Costa Rica, Guatemala, Ecuador, the Dominican Republic, and Nicaragua – have enacted or drafted "blocking statutes." Blocking statutes prohibit the courts of such jurisdictions from hearing claims first brought in the United States.[106] As such, they are meant to block the application of American *forum non conveniens* jurisprudence by eliminating the alternative forum required by the doctrine as a condition for dismissal.

Blocking statutes and litigation-enabling legislation facilitate litigation against foreign MNCs in other ways, as well. These include requiring nonrefundable deposits and the posting of bonds at amounts exceeding the expected damages, imposition of strict liability for foreign defendants, allowing punitive damages, requiring that the amount of compensatory damages be determined under the same standards used by US courts, setting minimum compensation, providing that the blocking statutes operate retroactively, targeting specific defendants, setting truncated procedural processes, allowing certain forms of proof such as irrebuttable presumption of causation, and guaranteeing legal assistance to impecunious plaintiffs.[107]

Our case studies showed that states can respond to mass torts by passing litigation-enabling legislation. To recall, the Government of India, for instance, enacted the Bhopal Gas Leak Disaster (Processing of Claims) Act (the "Bhopal Act") in 1985, granting the Government of India the right to represent Indian plaintiffs in India and elsewhere. It was pursuant to this act that the Government of India filed a complaint in the Southern District of New York, on behalf of the victims of the Bhopal disaster. Similarly, as we have also seen, in 1999, Ecuador enacted the Environmental Management Act in anticipation of a dismissal in New York. This legislation served as the basis for the second round of litigation, in Ecuador – the Lago Agrio litigation. The Second Circuit described this legislative development and its significance:

[One of the plaintiffs' lawyers] indicated that "his team" had "worked with Ecuadorian lawyers to draft [the Environmental Management Act]" ... and that those efforts were in preparation "for a possible move from U.S. courts" ... They did so because they feared losing the forum non conveniens motion in New York and being remitted to Ecuador, which had no class actions and thus no vehicle for the sort of giant toxic tort and other litigations common in the United States. They intended the EMA to provide a basis for suing in Ecuador to recover billions in damages in the absence of any other vehicle for doing so.[108]

Similarly, in 2000, Nicaragua enacted Law No. 364,[109] tailored to allow aggregate litigation of a specific mass tort by enabling workers in banana plantations allegedly harmed by exposure to DCBP to sue a specific set of defendants – the manufacturers of DBCP – for damages allegedly caused by exposure to the pesticide. According to the US Chamber of Commerce, the law was passed after pressure from the plaintiffs' lawyers.[110] The new statute applied only to companies that have been sued in American courts and obtained a dismissal on *forum non conveniens* grounds. It set a minimum compensation of $100,000 per plaintiff regardless of the degree of actual damage. It also provided that civil and criminal claims relating to the use of DBCP were not subject to a statute of limitations. The new statute required defendants to deposit $100,000 for each claim as a condition for participating in the proceedings. A firm that refused to provide the deposit was required to submit unconditionally to the jurisdiction of US courts and waive *forum non conveniens* claims. Defendants were also required to deposit approximately $15 million to guarantee the payment of compensation to workers. Claims were to be resolved by summary proceedings. Finally, all these measures were to apply not only prospectively but also retroactively to disputes already on going when the new statute came into force.[111] In the wake of the enactment of Law 364, more than ten thousand Nicaraguan plaintiffs filed more than two hundred lawsuits in Nicaragua. They obtained an aggregate of more than $2 billion in Nicaraguan judgments against Dole and other defendants.[112] American courts refused to enforce the judgments.[113]

Latin America is not the only region evolving to adopt American features considered pro-plaintiff. Incremental steps toward punitive damages are evident in jurisdictions traditionally hostile to such damages. In 2005, an EU Commission Green Paper contemplated allowing doubling of damages in antitrust actions.[114] German courts have commenced awarding punitive damages in some civil actions. In France, proposed revisions to the Civil Code have been contemplated that, if adopted, would similarly allow punitive damages in some civil cases. An Italian court awarded punitive damages in two cases. Argentina amended its Consumer Law to allow punitive damages. Also, Thailand now allows punitive damages more broadly.[115]

2 Class Action Goes Global

Class actions are also on the rise, a fundamental shift in litigation risk for MNCs in emerging and other markets. Globalization and the expansion of MNCs have increased the chance of mass injuries resulting from negligence or violations of private contracts or public law.[116] The consequence has been the worldwide spread of the class action. Until the 1990s, the United States stood alone in allowing class actions.[117] But just as the United States has been mounting obstacles to bringing and prevailing on aggregated claims, legislatures around the world have adopted legislation that opened their doors to (domestic) aggregate litigation. Now, some form of class action is available in more than three dozen countries. Importantly, civil law systems in Europe, South America, and Asia now provide class actions. As of 2017, twenty-one of the world's twenty-five largest economies had adopted a class action procedure. In North America, Canada and Mexico both have joined the United States in affording procedures for claim aggregation. In Europe and the Middle East, Belgium, Bulgaria, Denmark, Finland, France, Israel, Italy, Lithuania, the Netherlands, Norway, Poland, Portugal, Spain, and Sweden all have some form of collective redress mechanisms.[118] In 2005 Germany adopted the Capital Markets Model Case Law, which allows for bellwether trials on common issues and binds class members who opted into the litigation.[119] In the United Kingdom, the Consumer Rights Act now allows citizens to bring opt-out class action suits against corporations for anticompetition activities.[120] The Netherlands is also poised to pass a general opt-out class action procedure that allows private lawyers to initiate class actions (in contrast to the more common European requirement that specially designated associations initiate suits). In Asia and Australasia, Australia, China, Indonesia, Japan, South Korea, Taiwan, and Thailand have all joined the global class action wave with their own versions of the procedure. In Latin America, Argentina, Bolivia, Brazil, Chile, Colombia, Costa Rica, Ecuador, Panama, Peru, Uruguay, and Venezuela have put in place claim aggregation procedures.[121] In Africa, South Africa is pioneering the adoption of the class action.[122]

Thus, while traditionally the class action was an American invention and a distinctive feature of that system, civil law nations have adopted the device to deal with mass injuries. The need for and increasing acceptance of claim aggregation transcend more than just national boundaries. The jurisdictions that have adopted class actions "include countries on every continent, civil law as well as common law countries, and countries with authoritarian as well as liberal democratic traditions."[123] The European Union recommended "that all Member States should have collective redress systems at national level that follow the same basic principles throughout the Union."[124] Accordingly, the class action is poised for further growth.

As the class action spreads, features that enable the class action are also gaining ground across the globe. Fee regimes are changing specifically, restrictions on contingency fees are on the decline, and one-way fee shifting is on the rise.[125] Thus, while the European commission qualified its recommendations on collective redress recommending that "elements such as punitive damages, intrusive pre-trial discovery procedures and jury awards, most of which are foreign to the legal traditions of most Member States, should be avoided as a general rule,"[126] some nations are taking tentative steps toward contingency and conditional fees. The Netherlands allows the use of contingency fees (though actual usage is rare).[127] In 2006, Germany's Constitutional Court recognized an exception to the general prohibition against contingency and conditional fee arrangements.[128] Israel now allows contingent fees and fee shifts.[129] In England, where conditional fees have long been allowed but where the English rule on fee shifts got its name, the Jackson Report[130] examined comprehensive reforms to facilitate access to civil justice and reduce litigation costs. It endorsed both contingency fees and third-party financing. Japan permits contingent fees and has authorized insurance against fee shifting, which is already in use in the United Kingdom. (Such insurance eliminates the "loser-pay" risk to the insured plaintiffs.) In Canada, Ontario has gone a step further and set up a class action fund that finances class actions.[131] Some see this example as a model. The Jackson Report, for example, recommended experimentation with a public financing scheme, funded by a tax on successful class actions, on the model of the Ontario fund.[132]

VI BUSINESS ETHICS

Arguments that corporate executives are never motivated by ethics or by the notion that profit seeking should be bounded by morality support, rather than undermine, the need to impose external constraints on such executives' decision making. Happily, however, we know that corporate executives are multidimensional human beings; they operate on the basis of multiple motivations that include both profit-seeking as well as other forms of welfare maximization. Employees, too, prefer working for socially minded businesses. "Survey data show that workers – especially young ones – want to work for socially conscious companies, and will take less compensation in exchange for a greater sense of purpose."[133]

More importantly, many consumers are willing to pay a premium for socially conscious goods. The success of the fair-trade movement, socially responsible investment funds and strategies, and the proliferation of environmentally sound products demonstrate consumers' interest in socially conscious goods and services:

> The classical economic analysis of the corporation assumes that shareholders are interested only in maximizing the present value of their dividend streams. That

this is an imperfect description of the real world can be found in the popularity of socially responsible investment funds, which avoid companies that, for example, invest in Sudan or produce tobacco. In 2005 these funds had $2.3 trillion in assets, 10% of all U.S. assets under management. These funds average a return 35 basis points less than comparable nonfiltered funds, meaning that investors put a value of at least $84 billion per year on steering capital to firms that do good.[134]

A belief that businesses have a social role beyond maximizing shareholder value has a long history in capitalist thought:

> A century ago, industrial magnates played a central role in the Progressive movement, working with unions, supporting workmen's compensation laws and laws against child labor, and often pushing for more government regulation. This wasn't altruism; as a classic analysis by the historian James Weinstein showed, the reforms were intended to co-opt public pressure and avert more radical measures. Still, they materially improved the lives of ordinary workers. And they sprang from a pragmatic belief that the robustness of capitalism as a whole depended on wide distribution of the fruits of the system. Similar attitudes prevailed in the postwar era ... [when] "At the very top, corporate leaders were much more moderate and pragmatic..." Corporations supported policies that might have been costly in the short term in order to strengthen the system as a whole.[135]

Part of the support stemmed from a desire to contain populist anger, which all but disappeared in the 1970s. (Following that logic, the populist agitation that led to the election of Donald Trump to the US presidency bodes well, not poorly, for the possibility of renewed interest from corporate America in the welfare of the middle and working classes.)

The emergence of a new type of business entity, the benefit corporation (B-corp), is another example of the desire to engage in bounded profit seeking. Benefit corporations are for-profit businesses that pledge and legally bind themselves in their corporate charters to pursue social goals as well as business ones. They focus on "the three P's" – profits, people, and planet.[136]

The rise and expansion of corporate social responsibility and the associated movement are yet other indications that many, including in the corporate world, see goals other than profit and shareholder value maximization for corporations. Although corporate social responsibility has its roots in eighteenth-century movements to ameliorate the harms of the British and American factory systems,[137] modern conceptions of corporate social responsibility began to emerge in the late 1940s before taking root in the 1950s.[138] In 1946, *Fortune* magazine polled business executives, asking "whether they were responsible for the consequences of their actions in a sphere wider than that covered by their profit-and-loss statements. Specifically, the question was 'do you think that businessmen should recognize such responsibilities and do their best to fulfill them?' Of those polled, 93.5% said 'yes.'"[139] In its early phases in the 1950s, corporate social responsibility was, broadly speaking, a form of philanthropy.[140] During this time, the understanding of corporate managers as pure profit maximizers was tempered with a new understanding of their role as trustees, with recognition of the need for corporations to balance shareholder demands against other claims – including public claims – on their resources, and with the growing acceptance of corporate philanthropy, which had previously been considered in many jurisdictions to be unlawful.[141] Notably, in these earlier conceptions, the link between a corporation's social responsibility and the direct consequences of its own activities was diffuse at best.

In the 1960s and 1970s, the idea that corporations could and should serve a public function in addition to private ones continued to gain traction. In an influential paper published in 1971, the Committee for Economic Development – a group composed of representatives of businesses as well as prominent academics – described the evolving conception of corporate social responsibility: "Business is being asked to assume broader responsibilities to society than ever before and to serve a wider range of human values. Business enterprises, in effect, are being asked to contribute more to the quality of American life than just supplying quantities of goods and services. Inasmuch as business exists to serve society, its future will depend on the quality of management's response to the changing expectations of the public."[142] Around the same time, some commentators began to express misgivings about the imprecision of corporate social responsibility and the lack of concrete obligations for businesses.[143]

In subsequent decades, two important trends influenced the direction of corporate social responsibility. First, economic globalization was accompanied by the globalization of concern about the impact of increasingly powerful global corporations. Second, corporate social responsibility became increasingly institutionalized as civil society, business, and international organizations adopted (frequently overlapping) guidelines. In the 2000s, corporate social responsibility, which had not previously been much discussed in Europe, became a significant issue. The Organization for Economic Cooperation in Europe, for instance, released a study in 2001 that documented corporate social responsibility's increasing popularity and touted its many benefits for businesses.[144] The OECD's Guidelines for Multinational Enterprises were adopted in 1976, but in 2000 the organization strengthened its procedures for dealing with complaints. Importantly, in 2011, the guidelines were revised to include a chapter on business's obligations to respect human rights.[145] Meanwhile, the United Nations created the Global Compact in 2000. The Global Compact is a set of ten principles covering human rights, labor, the environment, and anticorruption. To date, more than twelve thousand companies have signed on to the Global Compact in 170 countries, making it the largest corporate social responsibility organization in the world.[146]

It is important not to overstate the significance of corporate social responsibility, which has attracted significant criticism from constituencies that view it as less an expression of genuine concerns and more a public relations tool. Critics of the Global Compact, for instance, coined the term "bluewashing" to convey the idea of corporations "wrapping themselves in the UN flag as a way to enhance their image as ethically responsible members of the global community."[147] In the present context it is enough to note that corporate social responsibility is the current manifestation of a current (or at least an eddy) of thinking about the broader role of corporations that stretches back decades.

VII GLOBAL GROWTH AS THE TIDE THAT LIFTS ALL BOATS

An ICCJ would serve the interests of MNCs and nations on both sides of FDI flows. Ensuring that transnational business activities are governed by the rule of law and conducted according to international norms boosts profits, spurs economic growth, and fosters social development. Economic studies have shown that respect for civil liberties and human rights are associated with improved economic performance. One study, for example, examined the performance of World Bank–financed projects in countries with strong versus weaker civil liberties. The study found that economic returns were systematically higher in countries that had higher scores on indices of human rights and civil liberties.[148] Another study concluded that human rights protection demonstrates "political stability and predictability within a host country and reduced corporate vulnerability to outcries by a socially conscious consumer public."[149] Accordingly, availability and receptive judicial fora for human rights litigation "facilitate an environment conducive to the development of human capital, with foreign investors increasingly attracted to countries where they can draw upon high-skilled labor."[150]

Typically, the counterargument to that assertion is that enforcing such norms would cause MNCs to divest from enforcing nations. Joseph Stiglitz, the Nobel Laureate in economics, responded to that argument, in part, by noting the difference between short-term and long-term benefits. He explained that any short-term divestments would be more than offset by the long-term improvement in developing host states' economic and social climate, which international norms encourage. This improvement, ultimately, benefits MNCs.[151] Conversely, he argued that "no support for the argument that such litigation would be a significant deterrent to welfare-enhancing investments can be found in economic theory."[152] This makes sense because the decision whether to invest is derived by a much more complex analysis that includes considerations that make up an overall business climate. This complex set of consideration includes access to infrastructure, capital, labor, and natural resources; governmental attitudes towards business; and broader social and political stability. The risk of civil liability, of any type, is just one among many cost considerations that corporations evaluate in assessing the likely return on any investment.[153]

If, combined, these considerations are favorable, profit-seeking enterprises will not forgo profitable investment opportunities because of fear of possible litigation for unrelated conduct.

Indeed, evidence points in the other direction. The governments of South Africa and the United States both expressed concern that the *Balintulo v. Daimler AG* litigation – in which plaintiffs alleged that two corporations, Daimler and Barclays, were complicit in apartheid – would deter FDI and economic growth in South Africa. In fact, FDI flows into South Africa increased from less than $1 billion on average annually in the period 1990–2000 to nearly more than $9 billion in 2008. In 2007 alone, after the Second Circuit permitted the litigation to proceed, FDI flows to South Africa increased dramatically. Indeed, Barclays National Bank Ltd, a defendant in that case, made the then-largest single FDI investment in South Africa during the pendency of the litigation.[154]

Stiglitz argues that enforcement of norms such as international human rights "foster[s] stability and long-term economic development and attract[s] foreign direct investment."[155] It is therefore, in the long term, a net positive. Specifically, he makes the case for private enforcement of international human rights law and imposition of tort liability. He explained, in support of the *Kiobel* plaintiffs, that ATS-like corporate liability reduces the transaction costs associated with enforcing the relevant norms (customary international law prohibiting the most egregious human rights violations in the case of *Kiobel*) and enhances the efficiency of economic activity for at least two reasons: the victims are the ones with the most information about the harm and MNCs are in the best position to monitor their own compliance.[156]

The value of the distinction between good businesses and the bad businesses they compete with is also worth emphasizing. Most MNCs disavow engaging in human rights violations and similar practices. This is true especially of publicly listed firms that are subject to public scrutiny. For such responsible firms, liability for mass infringement of human rights and similar violations should be welcomed because they will not have to change their behavior. Rather they gain a competitive advantage against firms that do engage in injurious behavior but escape scrutiny under the current system. Such good actors need not make any changes, or incur associated costs, to comply with the law. Thus, liability for violating such norms is "bad for bad businesses, but it is good for good businesses."[157]

> This long-term net gain is demonstrated by U.S. experience with the Foreign Corrupt Practices Act ... At least one study has demonstrated that U.S. business

in some bribery-prone countries fell sharply following the implementation of the FCPA.... However, few would suggest that the U.S. should have abandoned its strong anti-bribery stance to avoid the decline in U.S. corporate investment in countries with a history of corruption. Rather, U.S. efforts were directed at ensuring that others adopted similar standards.[158]

Such efforts were promoted multilaterally, through the OECD, and those efforts have set the new standard. As a consequence, good businesses are now facing an improved investment climate. Specifically, American businesses that do not engage in corrupt practices have been the main beneficiaries of the new, internationalized anticorruption standards. In addition to an improved business environment such firms garner a reputational premium because they are regarded as good corporate actors.[159]

MNCs located in jurisdictions that have acceded to the jurisdiction of an ICCJ are likely to enjoy the same reputation- and competition-enhancing effects that membership in anti-corruption regimes provide. By supporting an ICCJ, good businesses can distinguish themselves from bad ones and enjoy the various benefits that engagement in social responsibility produces to businesses as entities and to their managers and employees as individuals. (Anecdotally, the author has repeatedly heard from business executives and corporate defense lawyers that corporations do not object to paying for harms; rather, their opposition is to overpaying because of faulty courts, faulty procedures, or abusive practices.)

In the new transnational litigationscape, transnational mass tort litigation is likely to rise not fall. The closing of American courts means further diffusion and decentralization of litigation and an absence of coordination and cohesion. *Forum non conveniens* dismissals, far from being the silver bullet they once were, are increasingly becoming a be-careful-what-you-wish-for scenario. Defendants would be better off in a single professional specialized court with streamlined processes and a global reach than they are in the current system and the evolutionary trajectory it is currently on.

In addition to the advantages mentioned in the foregoing sections, an ICCJ would streamline processes such as evidence gathering and international collection efforts; give rise to specialized industry of private providers of services such as international service processors, discovery vendors, and collection experts; and develop a specialized bar. All those things would lead to greater efficiencies and therefore lower costs.

But the greatest impact of the ICCJ would be in the way it fundamentally changed the value proposition of transnational mass tort litigation. By its very existence it would eliminate boomerang, parallel, and sequential litigation, as well as the pernicious effects of real and perceived corruption. It would avoid or soften many of the more controversial procedures characteristic of American civil litigation (discussed at length in Chapter 5). These include overly extensive discovery, the "battle of the experts," juries, class procedures, and punitive damages (which would still be available but made much more difficult).

An ICCJ would help defendants avoid unnecessarily destabilizing effects of litigation by keeping them away from national courts that might otherwise issue orders that place severe operational, financial, and reputational strain. Offering support to the ICCJ gives MNCs the opportunity to enhance their reputation as good global players and to benefit from the healthier investment environment. That support would also, crucially, give them access to global legal peace. As we have gleaned from the arguments made by UCC and Chevron in their pleadings to the District Court of the Southern District of New York, corporations seem to yearn for a forum that can provide true finality. I will explore just exactly how the ICCJ will do all of these things in Chapter 5.

In sum, the ICCJ would enhance the global rule of law and provide a competitive advantage to ethical businesses and would benefit their managers and employees, investors and customers. Since business and rule of law are not inherently antithetical, quite the contrary, fair-minded executives and good corporate citizens should, for all of the foregoing reasons, support, rather than object to, an ICCJ.

5

Institutional and Procedural Features of an ICCJ

This chapter describes possible institutional and procedural design choices for an ICCJ. The ICCJ's actual features would be set out in a treaty (or, as suggested later, a set of two treaties), which, in turn, would be the outcome of years of multilateral diplomatic negotiations. The suggestions in this chapter are, therefore, a theorist's thought exercise on how such a court might be structured and what its features could be.[1] In some cases, the suggested features constitute part of the explanation for why internationalizing and coordinating the resolution of cross-border mass tort litigation are desirable for plaintiffs, defendants, host states, and home states and are therefore politically viable. In other parts of the discussion, the suggestions take the form of advocacy, setting out what I believe is the best way to advance justice and efficiency. And in yet other parts, I offer a menu of options that represent different but overall comparable sets of trade-offs, and discuss the pros and cons of each.

In its design, the ICCJ should not try to reinvent the wheel, but rather should build on and, where feasible, improve upon the existing global institutional and procedural infrastructure of transnational and aggregate litigation. As a preliminary matter, then, the project will involve some measure of integration of civil and common law approaches.[2] International law, after all, has long been regarded as a "mixed jurisdiction": a legal system that draws from two or more legal traditions.[3] Two brief sentences of explanation for nonspecialists: common law legal systems are those found in the United States, the United Kingdom, and the latter's former colonies; while civil law systems are found in Continental Europe and in the former colonies of Continental European states. The two systems are generally understood to have very different ideas about the roles of judges and lawyers, among other things. It is important, however, not to overstate the difference between civil and common law systems. I discuss this in more detail later, but in short summary one can observe increasing convergence of the two approaches – especially in the area of mass claims. In dealing with mass claims, even common law jurisdictions tend to favor mechanisms where the judge plays an active role in ascertaining the facts of the case (called the "inquisitorial mode" and usually associated with the civil law tradition), while even in civil law jurisdictions we see growing acceptance of the need to adopt collective redress measures, traditionally a feature of the common law. These two aspects of convergence form the foundation upon which the ICCJ should be designed.

International law, as already noted, has always been a "mixed jurisdiction." As such it is not dissimilar to national mixed jurisdictions such as Quebec, Louisiana, Scotland, South Africa, Israel, and, arguably, the EU, which brought together diverse national systems (including civil law and common law) under a single legislature.[4] Because of the overwhelming dominance of the civil law and common law systems, in terms of both their geographical spread and the fact that one version or another of them characterizes the democracies of the West, they tend to be the strongest influences in international courts and tribunals.[5] As a function of international law as a mixed jurisdiction, the international judiciary is a hybrid of the two traditions. The Statute of the International Court of Justice, for instance, specifically provides that its bench will include judges representative of the principal legal systems of the world. Specifically, the envisioned legal systems are civil and common law.[6] International judges are often dual-trained.[7]

Even in the context of domestic systems, the dichotomy was always a caricature. It is, rightly, a constant refrain of comparativists that positing a dichotomy between the common law and the civil law traditions must be understood as a necessary evil – an oversimplification required for the enterprise of comparing, which one must accept with the caveat that, in reality, the distinctions between the two are not as stark as the need for a taxonomy might suggest.[8] So, for example, while the civil law is generally understood to have specialized courts and judges while the common law has general courts and generalist judges, in reality the United States has specialized courts including family courts, patent courts, juvenile courts, tax courts, drug courts, and the US Court of International Trade. Similarly, civil law systems have no juries at all (and many civil law jurists are horrified by the idea); yet "lay judges" are sometimes used to introduce a nonlegal perspective (e.g., on labor relations). In contrast, a right to a jury (even in civil trials) is a constitutional guarantee in the US. Nonetheless, US courts have found ways to curtail the roles of juries, for example by creating and then expanding procedures such as summary judgment, where judges can decide cases on their own, before submitting them to juries. That is not to say, however, that the systems are identical. There are significant differences, although in some important areas such differences are eroding as practices converge.

Perhaps the most important convergence for our purposes is the judicial management of mass claims. There is an emerging international consensus on the "best practices" for dealing with mass claims. One such best practice – "managerial judging" – consists of increased judicial control over the pretrial process aimed at limiting duplication, confusion, and waste. Managerial judging techniques include judge-driven pretrial conferences to identify and sharpen key issues, judicial management and limitation of discovery, and active judicial promotion of settlement.[9] Such techniques are well known in civil law systems but have typically been disfavored in the common law. Yet US federal courts have adopted managerial judging as a reaction to the rise of complex multiparty litigation. It has proven to be so much of a necessity that, as early as the mid-1980s, it was observed that "the Manual for Complex Litigation [which was created to deal with complex multiparty cases] is infused with notions of judicial management of fact-gathering for the multi-party Big Case."[10]

Collective redress is another area of convergence, at least on the question of whether such mechanisms should be permitted. Much disagreement remains, however, about the best way to design those mechanisms (these disagreements are discussed in more detail in the section III "Procedural Features"). As discussed at length in Chapter 4, although resistance to the class action, the fullest form of aggregation, remains strong in some quarters, especially in Europe, various forms of collective redress (including class actions, albeit in a modified form compared to the American model) have been introduced by all of the EU member states. Indeed, the EU Commission recently affirmed that "the possibility of joining claims and pursuing them collectively may constitute a better means of access to justice, in particular when the cost of individual actions would deter the harmed individuals from going to court."[11]

In this chapter I will therefore, as a general matter, draw on both common and civil law systems in recognition of their long hybridization in international law and international judicial mechanisms. International arbitration, for instance, is based on hybrid, relatively homogeneous procedures and is generally considered highly functional.[12] I will also look to contemporary mass claims facilities, most of which integrate one or another of the features of both systems. Importantly, lawmakers and regulators have embraced this convergence even in domestic claims facilities within the United States by adopting inquisitorial judicial functions in the Continental style.[13] Returning briefly to the discussion in the Introduction, such transnational claims facilities have a long history dating back at least to the commissions established by the Jay Treaty in 1794.[14] Notwithstanding these sources of inspiration, I envision the ICCJ primarily as a court, albeit one that offers nonjudicial options as well. But in contrast to, for instance, ad hoc arbitral panels, the ICCJ should have judges serving on a permanent bench and applying law set down prior to any given dispute.

The Rome Statute will be another important source of inspiration. The International Criminal Court (ICC) and the ICCJ share several important features. Under the Rome Statute, for instance, states parties delegate to an international body jurisdiction over private individuals who would otherwise be under those states' jurisdiction. Few international courts and tribunals have jurisdiction over private defendants (private plaintiffs are more common), making the ICC a particularly useful case study for the ICCJ. In addition, the states parties under the Rome Statute delegate to the ICC the power to decide matters of law that overlap with the applicable law within those states – bringing up the thorny issue of the proper balance between national and international jurisdictions, which is less central to classical interstate disputes governed by public international law.

After dispensing with some preliminary matters regarding the ICCJ's institutional relationships, the Chapter unpacks the two most consequential features of the court: one is its jurisdiction – a legal concept that describes the power granted to a court to hear certain kinds of disputes. Included in that is the concept of subject matter jurisdiction, which addresses the law to be applied by the court. Second is admissibility, which describes the conditions under which a court may refuse to exercise its power to hear a case.[15] In the context of international courts in particular, an important aspect of admissibility is the relationship of the international court with any national courts that might also be empowered to hear the case.

With this foundation in place, the chapter then proceeds to discuss key procedural issues. These include which kinds of plaintiffs would be allowed to bring claims (standing); absence of juries and limitation of punitive damages; early case management including fact finding (discovery) and case dismissals; claim aggregation on a class and nonclass basis; making sure poor claimants will still be able to make use of the court (access to justice); and, finally, the all-important issues of recognition and enforcement of judgments. Next, the chapter examines additional institutional features such as the need for appellate review (in the form of an appellate chamber); of in-house alternative dispute resolution (ADR) facilities; and of a mechanism for settlement funds administration. The financing of the operation of the court and a few miscellaneous features, such as outreach programs, conclude the chapter.

A few themes run throughout the chapter. One, discussed earlier, relates to the effects of hybridizing common law and civil law procedures of civil litigation. Another, related, theme is the need for inquisitorial-managerial judging to deal with the complexities of cross-border mass claims. A third theme, implied in the exercise of envisioning a new and international court, relates to the benefits that flow from having an institution unshackled from traditions and path-dependent domestic legal and institutional arrangements. The fact that an ICCJ will be designed from scratch and that its applicable law, procedures, and decisions will be cabined within it, means that it will neither require changes to domestic law, nor set a precedent applicable domestically. That separation will enable its architects to choose arrangements that may be superior for cross-border mass torts specifically but may exact too heavy a cost if applied domestically and generally.

I INSTITUTIONAL RELATIONSHIPS

A *With States Parties*

1 The Two-Tiered Structure of an ICCJ and Its Effect on Institutional Arrangements

Capital importing countries may worry that by being the first, or among the first, to become parties to the ICCJ they would drive FDI away and into states that have not joined.[16] Similarly, corporations influencing the policy of their capital exporting states may be concerned that an undersubscribed ICCJ would be unable to offer the global legal peace that is the lynchpin of corporate buy-in because fewer members would mean fewer legal systems bound to respect the decisions of the ICCJ. That, in turn, could mean more, rather than less, litigation. Finally, one might wonder whether it might be impossible to attract states such as China, notoriously wary of delegating sovereignty to international organizations, into the ICCJ and what the effect of the nonparticipation of such a global economic power might be.

While all of these problems are, to some extent, transformations of the question of the effect of low initial membership on the incentives of different groups to join the ICCJ, not all of the groups are responding to the same incentives. For capital importing countries the driving desire would be to provide their citizens with access to redress for certain categories of harms. Capital exporting countries, on the other hand, might be less concerned about their citizens, reasoning that their domestic courts are more than capable of handling mass torts that occur on their territory. Furthermore, it may be difficult to convince, say, the United States to delegate some of the powers of its federal courts to provide relief to its own citizens-plaintiffs to an international body. Rather, the interest of the United States and other capital exporting countries, other than a desire to support the international rule of law, is in providing their MNCs with global legal peace while minimizing their competitive disadvantage.

The solution to these problems is to provide for a two-tiered membership in the ICCJ, via two separate treaties. The first treaty would, inter alia, create the court and establish its jurisdiction in the territory of states parties (hereinafter: the ICCJ statute). The Rome Statute provides a useful example. It established the ICC; delimited its relationship with the United Nations; set out, inter alia, its jurisdiction; defined the crimes it would adjudicate; adopted as law certain general principles of criminal law; determined the composition and administration of the court; outlined pretrial, trial, and appellate procedures; laid out an international cooperation and judicial assistance scheme, enforcement procedures, and obligations; and set out financing provisions.[17]

The second treaty (hereinafter: the ICCJ enforcement treaty) would be an enforcement treaty along the lines of the Convention on the Recognition and Enforcement of Foreign Arbitral Awards, known as the New York Convention.[18] Recognition and enforcement[19] are the lynchpins of binding dispute resolution, and, as noted throughout, the difficulty plaintiffs encounter in obtaining enforceable judgments is the motivating problem behind the proposal to set up an ICCJ. Similarly, the value of finality is a core benefit of an ICCJ for defendants. The New York Convention requires courts of contracting states to recognize and enforce arbitration awards made in other contracting states and is generally considered one of the most successful international treaties in the area of commercial law.[20] To balance the need for reliable enforcement of awards issued by arbitral tribunals with the requirements of due process and the rule of law, the New York Convention lays out a narrow and exhaustive list of exceptions to recognition and enforcement. Importantly, the New York Convention does not permit courts to review the arbitral tribunal's decision. They may not refuse to enforce arbitral decisions on the basis of errors in law or fact, or on procedural grounds (other than due process). And this principle has been accepted and, indeed, "unanimously confirmed in the case law [of Contracting States] and commentary on the New York Convention."[21] In other words, as a practical matter, "courts in the Contracting States have generally construed the grounds for refusal under the Convention narrowly, and have exercised their discretion to refuse recognition and enforcement of foreign arbitral awards under the New York Convention in exceptional cases only."[22]

The ICCJ enforcement treaty would not give the ICCJ jurisdiction in the territory of states parties, but would require states parties to recognize and enforce the ICCJ's decisions and judgments. States parties to the ICCJ statute would automatically become states parties to the enforcement convention, but not vice versa. The court's statute would not enter into force until the enforcement treaty did, while the latter, crucially, would set a high numerical threshold for entering into force and would ensure that the minimum threshold included a sufficiently large group of capital exporting countries.[23]

The two-tiered participation in the court and sequencing the creation of the ICCJ via the two treaties in this way would allay the fears of capital importing countries by giving them the assurance that their decision to join the ICCJ regime would not alienate investors – because it would only become operative when the investors' home states (or some substantial number of them), along with a substantial number of other capital importing states, were on board. Similarly, sufficiently broad participation would assure capital exporting states that their MNCs could reasonably expect to receive the promised global legal peace and would not be at a competitive disadvantage vis-à-vis their counterparts in other states since a substantial number of those states would also be participating. Finally, this process would significantly lessen the impact of holdouts such as China (assuming that China would choose to hold out). As will be discussed later, the ICCJ should have the power (jurisdiction) to hear cases based on the territory where the harm occurred. That would mean that Chinese companies operating on the territory of any state party would be subject to being sued in the ICCJ. Furthermore, the ICCJ's judgments would be enforced against the assets of the Chinese enterprise in any state party to the enforcement agreement. So, given broad participation, Chinese companies (to continue with the hypothetical of a reluctant China) would have to subject themselves to the jurisdiction of the ICCJ by virtue of operating in the territory of states parties or else forgo significant economic opportunity in order to confine their operations to the territory of non–states parties.

2 Dependent or Independent?

Wherever possible, the design choices suggested herein are geared toward creating an independent court. Some scholars have strongly argued for the position that dependent tribunals – institutions closely controlled by the states that created them – are more effective than independent ones.[24] Others have just as strongly advanced the opposite view.[25] The strongest case for dependent courts relates to interstate disputes, where the interests of the states that created the forum are most in danger of being constrained by its decisions. The interests of states are considerably more weakly implicated, however, in the adjudication of disputes between private parties. Indeed, the lack of independence and impartiality – real or perceived – of national courts is one of the key factors that contribute to the problem of the missing forum, discussed earlier in the book. When a choice presents itself, therefore, on issues such as composition of the court, compulsory jurisdiction, applicable law and procedure, and fact-finding capacity it is best to resolve that choice in favor of independence.

3 Composition of the Court

The ICCJ statute should provide for the qualifications of the judges and the nature of their appointment (both the process and the terms). The statute should also, in all its provisions, ensure the independence and impartiality of its judges.[26] Regarding qualifications, the commonly used formulations are that the nominees should be "persons of high moral character, who possess the qualifications required in their respective countries for appointment to the highest judicial offices, or are jurisconsults of recognized competence in international law."[27] Other courts soften that requirement, requiring that nominees be qualified for "high" judicial office (rather than the highest).[28]

As is the common practice in international courts and tribunals, the judges of the ICCJ should be elected by the states parties.[29] The designers of the ICCJ, however, will have to consider whether to restrict voting to states parties to the ICCJ statute or whether to open it up to members of the ICCJ enforcement treaty as well. The latter option may give more confidence to the courts of states parties to the enforcement treaty – which would, after all, be called upon to ensure the execution of the ICCJ's judgments – since national judges' own governments would have had a voice in selecting the members of the international court. Potential defendants may have more confidence as well, for similar reasons. On the other hand, restricting the right to elect judges to the states parties to the ICCJ statute would perhaps conform more to the principle of sovereign equality by more closely aligning the consent of sovereign states, on the one hand, to the application of the law of the ICCJ in their territory with, on the other hand, the power to elect the judges applying that law.

Questions about the overall composition of the bench, however, can be dealt with explicitly in the ICCJ statute and need not rest solely on the question of which states are entitled to vote. Most international courts and tribunals permit, but do not require, that states nominate judges of their own nationality. Some, such as the ICJ, specifically require states to nominate a judge not of their nationality.[30] In addition, the ICJ statute includes a soft requirement that "the electors shall bear in mind not only that the persons to be elected should individually possess the qualifications required, but also that in the body as a whole the representation of the main forms of civilization and of the principal legal systems of the world should be assured."[31] The ICC has the same requirement, stated in stronger language ("shall ... take into account").[32] At the Inter-American Court of Human Rights (IACtHR) and ICC, no two judges may be of the same nationality.[33] The ICC permits states parties to nominate judges of any nationality, provided that they are nationals of a state party.[34]

Drafters will also need to consider how to balance the terms of the judges' appointment in order, on the one hand, to attract the most distinguished jurists to the ICCJ while, on the other, maximizing the stability and stature of the bench. That will be particularly true in addressing the question of whether to permit extra-judicial activities or to make appointment to the ICCJ a full-time endeavor. That concern is reflected in the provision regarding extrajudicial activities in the Burgh House Principles on the Independence of the International Judiciary promulgated by a Study Group of the International Law Association, which provides that "judges shall not engage in any extra-judicial activity that is incompatible with their judicial function or the efficient and timely functioning of the court of which they are members, or that may affect or may reasonably appear to affect their independence or impartiality."[35] Different international courts and tribunals require different levels of time commitment; some prohibit all extrajudicial activity while others are explicitly part-time.[36] In order to maintain a permanent judiciary while attracting the most distinguished jurists, the ICCJ could permit extrajudicial activities while maintaining a sizable bench and allowing for chambers of three or five judges to hear a case.

B With Other International Organizations

As a preliminary matter, an ICCJ should be a stand-alone institution, unattached to an existing multilateral body. The alternative would be to create a new organ of an existing body, such as the United Nations. Another candidate parent might be the World Bank, which is the parent organization of the International Centre for Settlement of Investment Disputes (ICSID). Generally speaking, affiliating an ICCJ with an existing institution carries the benefits of availing it of an existing infrastructure and institutional knowledge and lending it the credibility of the existing institution. It is not clear that either the UN or the World Bank would yield significant benefits to the ICCJ given the differences in their missions. And the credibility-enhancing effect discussed earlier can be a double-edged sword: any legitimacy deficits the parent organization suffers may attach to the ICCJ as well.

Once again, the ICC provides a potentially useful example. In the early stages of the negotiation of the Rome Statute, preliminary drafters and delegates considered several versions of the relationship between the court and the UN.[37] On one end of the spectrum were calls to make the court an organ of the UN. On the other end of the spectrum, countries such as France and Switzerland advocated for an independent court established as an entity entirely separate from the UN. Those in favor of the UN approach pointed to the credibility and effectiveness that such an affiliation would confer on the new court, as well as the practical efficiencies of being a part of the UN's existing budgetary, personnel, and infrastructure systems.[38] Proponents of the separate entity approach argued that separation was an important component of independence, and therefore of legitimacy, and also that creating the court under the auspices of the UN would likely require an amendment of the charter – a very high procedural bar that would pose an unnecessarily difficult challenge for the court. By the time of the Rome Conference, the delegates had come to a high degree of consensus on establishing the Court as a separate entity.[39]

The drafters of the Rome Statute did, however, recognize the practical benefits of an ICC able to avail itself of the existing UN infrastructure. Hence, they included an article providing that the court and the UN "shall" reach an agreement establishing that relationship. That agreement touches, among other things, on issues such as office space, human resources, privileges and immunities (the judges at the ICC enjoy diplomatic status conferred by the UN through the agreement), and other forms of institutional cooperation. It is possible that the ICCJ could benefit from a similarly cooperative arrangement with an existing institution whose mission is closely aligned with that of the court. The Permanent Court of Arbitration, for example, could offer the ICCJ the benefit of providing infrastructure – e.g., an existing secretariat and existing facilities – from an institution similarly tasked with resolving private-law disputes.[40]

II JURISDICTION AND ADMISSIBILITY

The potentially most important and contentious set of design choices for the ICCJ relates to the court's jurisdiction. It is important to emphasize again the distinction between jurisdiction and admissibility. Every court – whether international, national, or local – is granted power by its constitutive document (treaty, constitution, legislation) to hear certain kinds of cases. This is the court's jurisdiction. Normally, a court may not refuse to hear cases that fall within its enumerated powers because it is in the nature of a court, as a public body, to be open to all members of the polity. Admissibility, then, deals with the limited situations in which a court may decline to hear cases that otherwise fall within its jurisdiction. Sections A–C deal with jurisdiction, or the ICCJ's power; Section D deals with important questions of admissibility, or limitations the drafters may choose to place on the ICCJ's powers.

Classically, courts and commentators have broken down jurisdiction into the subsets *ratione temporis* (temporal), *ratione personae* (personal), and *ratione materiae* (subject matter). Roughly speaking, these categories of jurisdiction are driven by bedrock questions about the court's authority to entertain certain claims. First, did those claims arise at a time that is within the court's mandate (*ratione temporis*)? The ICC, for instance, cannot prosecute where the conduct at issue occurred prior to the moment when the relevant state joined the Rome Statute. Second, does the court have the power to decide cases with respect to the specific parties before it (*ratione personae*)? Only states may appear before the ICJ; for example, the court would have no power to decide a contentious case brought by, for instance, the United Nations. Finally, what kinds of disputes does the court have the power to decide (*ratione materiae*)? This can refer to almost any features of the claims that seem relevant to the drafters of a given court's statute, commonly including, on the international plane, geographical provenance and applicable law. The Iran–United States Claims Tribunal, for example, despite being empowered to hear cases involving nationalization and appropriation, would be unable to hear a claim on that subject from Argentina because its jurisdiction *ratione materiae* is restricted to Iran and the United States. Nor would it be able to hear a slip-and-fall case against a poorly maintained supermarket in Tehran, because it can only hear claims related to the conduct of the Iranian or US government. Each of these axes – temporal, personal, and subject matter – admits of several possible approaches. Generally speaking, courts have the power to interpret the scope of their own jurisdiction – someone has to, and unless the court in question does it, that court would be giving away a very large chunk of its independence. The principle is called "compétence de la compétence," and the ICCJ statute should explicitly include it.

A *Temporal Jurisdiction*

Of the three categories, temporal jurisdiction is the most straightforward but it is still not without complications. On the one hand, it seems uncontroversial to provide that the ICCJ's jurisdiction begins on the date its statute enters into force with respect to the relevant state party (Sections B and C deal with the question of which states parties might be relevant). That was the choice made by the drafters of the Rome Statute.[41] To make the ICCJ's jurisdiction retroactive would be counter-intuitive and potentially unjust, in the sense that as a matter of the rule of law we would normally expect those to whom a law applies to have had notice of the law when planning their conduct. It would also be potentially unlawful, as the rule-of-law norm is embodied in the rule of customary international law prohibiting the retroactive application of treaties.[42]

The more difficult question is how the ICCJ will deal with what is referred to in the literature as "continuing circumstances"[43] – when acts, omissions, facts, or harms originate before the "magic date" but persist afterward. Imagine, for instance, that a chemical spill takes place before the relevant date, but the chemicals persist in the soil and continue to damage the environment after the date. There is no easy way to address this at the level of the treaty, since the difficulty arises from the nature of the facts underlying the claim and not from the precision or imprecision of the grant of temporal jurisdiction. In other words, anytime there are continuing circumstances judges will encounter problems of interpretation. Public international courts, human rights bodies, and even investor-state arbitral tribunals have all applied some version of an interpretation of jurisdiction *ratione temporis* that permits parties to bring cases based on continuing circumstances. Such permissiveness, however, must be balanced against the potential disincentive for states to subject their corporate citizens to the uncertain and potentially expansionist jurisdiction of an ICCJ. This will, ultimately, be an issue for the judges on the ICCJ and not the drafters of the statute. A full analysis of the question is therefore outside the scope of this chapter. In any case, the ICCJ should follow common practice and set its temporal jurisdiction to begin on or at some predetermined time after the statute enters into force with respect to the relevant state.

B Subject Matter Jurisdiction

1 Mass Claims and Mass Torts

At the heart of this book is the argument that the world needs a court to hear cross-border mass tort cases. Each of these terms – "cross-border," "mass," and "tort" – requires definition. First, however, it is important to draw a distinction between mass claims and mass torts. That distinction will then inform the discussion of the numerosity requirement (what constitutes "mass") that immediately follows, and many of the procedural features suggested in Section III Procedural Features. Although the adjudication of mass claims – including, but not limited to mass tort claims – overlaps in many significant ways with aggregate litigation and class actions, they are not precisely the same things. Since all of them are important in designing the ICCJ it is worth taking some time to elaborate on the difference among the three models. As mentioned in the Introduction, transnational mass claims commissions have a long history dating back at least to the end of the eighteenth century. "Mass claims" in this context means large numbers of separate claims against the same respondent (or group of respondents) for the same conduct or the same general pattern of conduct. Two elements of this definition distinguish mass claims from aggregate litigation and from class actions. First, the claimants are not aggregated together in the sense of being merged into a single action. Rather, the collective aspect of mass claims facilities comes in because the large numbers of individual claimants are (collectively) routed out of the normal court system and into the specialized claims facility. But in that facility, claims are adjudicated or processed individually. To understand this distinction, consider the Iran–United States Claims Tribunal (IUSCT). It is collective in the sense that all claims against Iran or the United States were taken out of the Iranian and US courts – where many such cases had already been filed. But the tribunal adjudicated all of the more than four thousand cases individually; it did not permit claimants to join together.

The second important distinction is that mass claims facilities can deal with more than one type of injury caused by different activities undertaken by the same defendant(s). By contrast, aggregate litigation and class actions encompass damages caused by a single activity or tightly related group of activities. Consider the scope of the United States–Mexico Special Claims Commission. It was empowered to decide on claims stemming from "losses of life or property suffered ... as the result of acts of military forces of the various de facto or de jure governments of the period in Mexico, or of various revolutionary or insurrectionary forces ..., or of mobs or bandits or general insurrectionary forces, as to which the Mexican authorities showed lenity."[44] The only connections between those broad categories of injuries are that they occurred in roughly the same time and place and that responsibility for them could, ultimately, be placed with Mexico. No court would permit claims with such a tenuous relationship to one another to proceed in a single litigation. Although the precise standard varies, most court systems apply some version of a limiting principle that restricts the scope of defendant conduct that can be reached in a single case.

I discuss the differences between aggregate litigation and class actions in some detail in Section III on procedural features. But to summarize: mass claims are loosely related cases tried individually; aggregate or collective litigation is the partial consolidation of some, but not all, aspects of a trial. Importantly, in aggregate litigation all the plaintiffs are named. Finally, class or representative actions are the complete consolidation of the trial on behalf of plaintiffs who may not be named or even known.

With that out of the way, "mass" becomes the easiest term to define. The goal of both mass and aggregate claims resolution is to promote efficiency of adjudication where common issues of facts or law predominate. The ICCJ statute can select a numerical threshold, such as seventy-five claimants.[45] This approach has the downside shared by all arbitrary line drawing, namely, there could be cases when a lower number of claimants creates similar inefficiencies if adjudicated individually yet such cases would be excluded. Alternatively, the statute can select a more flexible numerosity test akin to that of Rule 23 of the Federal Rules of Civil Procedure, which lists as one of the conditions for class certification that "the class is so numerous that joinder of all members is impracticable."[46] The downside of this approach is that it opens up the question of numerosity to costly and time-consuming litigation.

2 "Cross-Border" Claims and Enterprise Liability

"Cross-border" should mean cases where at least a certain nontrivial percentage of plaintiffs and at least one defendant are from different countries. In the United States, this form of jurisdiction is called "diversity jurisdiction," meaning the power federal courts have to hear cases involving parties with diverse citizenship (i.e., they are citizens of different states or a non-American party is involved). Undoubtedly, the ICCJ would be required to develop a nuanced jurisprudence on the complex questions that arise when parties are required to be diverse. This would probably include tackling questions such as the time at which diversity is determined and whether to allow supplemental jurisdiction (the authority to hear additional claims substantially related to the original claim even though the court would otherwise lack jurisdiction to hear the additional claims).[47]

Premising the jurisdiction of the ICCJ on diversity of nationality between the plaintiffs and defendants will raise the difficult question of how to treat a situation in which the claim arose from the activities of a local subsidiary of an MNC – a subsidiary, in other words, of the same nationality as the plaintiffs. Recall that the pollution in the Chevron–Ecuador case was alleged to have been caused by the extraction activities of TexPet, a joint venture of Ecuador and Texaco established under Ecuadorian law. In *Kiobel*, the operations in southern Nigeria were undertaken by the Shell Petroleum Development Company of Nigeria (a Nigerian entity). Of course, it makes perfect sense for a variety of legitimate business reasons – including tax, accounting, and employment law – to establish and do business through local entities. But that common practice leaves the ICCJ with the question of how to treat local claims against (or including) local subsidiaries of foreign-based MNCs.

Thus, for the purpose of deciding on diversity the ICCJ statute should explicitly empower it to consider the entire multinational enterprise against which a claim is brought. This is the procedural corollary of the idea discussed previously that the ICCJ should adopt a broad theory of enterprise liability. To be specific, if an entity working in one state is owned or controlled by an entity that is a national of another state, the cross-border criterion will be met.[48] This, in turn, brings up the question of what constitutes control and citizenship. In the United States, securities regulations provide that, in certain circumstances, ownership of 10 percent of an entity is evidence of control.[49] That may be a good guidepost, or at least a starting point. "Citizenship," for the sole purpose of ICCJ jurisdiction, should be determined by either the place of incorporation, the place where the MNC is headquartered, or the place where business is conducted. So an MNC incorporated in Delaware, with headquarters in New York and with operations in fifteen different countries, would be considered by the ICCJ to be a "citizen" of the United States and of each of the fifteen countries where it works.

This is a significant departure from the way MNCs are normally treated, so it bears emphasis, again, that these considerations would only apply to the question of jurisdiction and only in the ICCJ. Given that the ICCJ's jurisprudence has no binding effect outside the ICCJ, such broad definitions of "enterprise" and "citizenship" would not undermine limited liability for businesses in any other area of law and would not bind national courts in any context.

3 Applicable Law

The ICCJ statute should grant the court jurisdiction over the most serious kinds of torts and over environmental claims. From the perspective of plaintiffs, this list covers the most severe kinds of harms – the kinds in which people lose their lives, limbs, and livelihoods. The term "torts" means, in simple terms, "an act or omission that gives rise to ... harm to another and amounts to a civil wrong for which courts impose liability."[50] The term comes from the common law, but most legal systems of the world provide relief for such harms in one version or another.[51] For the sake of convenience, torts can be divided into intentional torts, negligence, and strict liability, although those labels have no particular legal significance. The former two categories are based on some notion of fault, whereas the latter is a no-fault category (and as such controversial). From the perspective of corporate defendants, the most serious torts and environmental claims are the highest-liability, most expensive to defend, and most potentially reputation-damaging types of claims they could face. In that sense, they are also the cases most in danger of attracting funding and spiraling out of control in the current "wild west" of boomerang, parallel, and sequential litigation. Thus if MNCs agree at all that it is worth it for them to pay a "peace premium" (see Chapter 4) then these are precisely the kinds of claims that would justify that premium.

Within the very large category of torts, the ICCJ's jurisdiction should cover intentional torts and negligence that results in physical injury. This jurisdictional grant would encompass intentional conduct of the kind that was alleged in *Kiobel*, industrial accidents like Bhopal, and pollution of the kind alleged in Chevron–Ecuador – in other words, the kinds of claims most in need of a forum and the kinds of plaintiffs most in need of justice. Intentional torts in the United States, for instance, include false imprisonment – which would cover slavery and human trafficking; battery (beating and torture); wrongful death; conversion (stealing); trespass to land (land grabbing); and deceit (fraud and misrepresentation). Negligence does not require intention, but rather covers injuries to person or property sustained as the result of actions or omissions that fall short of accepted standards. In the ICCJ, claims for negligence should be restricted to those based on bodily injury, in keeping with the emphasis on providing redress for the most serious harms and on the pragmatic need not to overburden the court via overly broad jurisdiction.

But the ICCJ need not, and should not, be bound by the definitions of torts in one or another legal system. The drafters of the ICCJ statute should take the opportunity to do what the drafters of the Rome Statute did: update the definitions and elements of the laws it will apply. For instance, injuries to person or property from modern toxic pollution notoriously resist easy application of classical tort models.[52] And harm to the environment qua environment may be provided for by statute but is not part of tort law. The ICCJ statute need not be hampered by those defects.

It follows from the preceding that the ICCJ should define its own applicable law in the ICCJ statute.[53] The alternative would be to apply national law (for instance, of the locus of the harm). Doing that would undermine the ability of the ICCJ to handle many of the very harms it is intended to address. Where national law, for instance, does not provide for recovery of damages for environmental harm, then the ICCJ would be forced to dismiss pollution cases. Applying national law could also have the effect of shifting the legal "field of battle" from the domestic courts of host states to their legislatures. The problem of corruption (and the perception thereof), discussed in Chapter 4, would still apply; litigants would have all the same incentives to game local legislatures as they would to game local courts. The example of Chevron/Ecuador highlights this danger: it was, after all, a change in Ecuadorian legislation that paved the way for the plaintiffs' multibillion-dollar judgment. Chevron alleges that the plaintiffs' counsel illegitimately elicited the change in law. Finally, requiring the judges of the ICCJ to apply the different laws of the many different states parties to the ICCJ statute would place an immense burden on the bench and raise litigation costs for the litigants. The difficulty of applying foreign law is a key reason judges dismiss in *forum non conveniens* cases.

The drafters of the ICCJ statute could, of course, make other choices about the scope of the applicable law, but most of those would make the court considerably less efficient and, to understate the case, would decrease buy-in from MNCs and states. Certainly, a broader mandate could create economies of both scope and scale. ("Economies of scope" are "efficiencies wrought by variety, not volume" while efficiencies created by volume are "economies of scale.")[54] To illustrate the former, if the ICCJ heard both mass torts arising from FDI and investor claims arising from FDI, the court would develop more well-rounded expertise and greater depth of understanding in both. That expanded expertise is a benefit in itself, but it could have the additional benefit of increasing legitimacy in the eyes of MNC defendants who would know their case was before judges who see all the sides of FDI and understand the realities and complexities of conducting transnational business operations. Importantly, as discussed in Chapter 3 there is already a movement afoot calling for the establishment of a permanent court for investment disputes to replace the existing system of arbitration. Therefore, bundling both can serve additional perceived needs. To illustrate the latter (economies of scale), the broader the applicable law, the higher the number of claims that would fall under the ICCJ's jurisdiction, which means that for similar fixed costs more cases could be heard.

Even taking into account those potential benefits, however, granting the ICCJ a broad mandate would likely doom the institution from the outset. It seems extremely unlikely that countries would accede to a court with such a breathtaking jurisdictional scope. Such a court would essentially remove from national jurisdiction all private claims once they had a transnational dimension. While this would suffice to render such a proposal moot, it is also worth noting that such jurisdictional scope would overwhelm an ICCJ. It would also limit the ability of the judges to become specialists. All in all, such jurisdiction is neither likely nor desirable. These problems hold true for any broad jurisdictional grant – making the ICCJ a general claims court, for instance, or permitting it to adjudicate all cross-border torts (whether mass or not, and whether involving physical harm or not).

C *Personal Jurisdiction*

The ICCJ should be a "new-style" international court with compulsory jurisdiction. Traditionally, consent to international jurisdiction has been a two-stage process. The personal jurisdiction of the ICJ, for instance, extends only to states that are parties to its statute or to jurisdiction-conferring treaties. But joining the statute alone is not enough; each state participating in a given case must separately accept the court's jurisdiction. That acceptance can be general or limited to a specific dispute or category of disputes.[55] In the case of a jurisdiction-conferring treaty, joining the treaty constitutes the requisite acts of affirmative consent.[56] In more recent decades, that attenuated, two-step acceptance of jurisdiction has given way. "Following the increased success of some international courts in attracting a critical mass of ex ante acceptances of their jurisdiction ... and with the rise of international courts endowed with compulsory jurisdiction ... the centrality of consent as a jurisdictional condition has declined."[57] Thus in most contemporary international courts and tribunals, to join the court is to accept its jurisdiction.[58] The ICCJ should adopt the contemporary practice of providing for compulsory jurisdiction.

The personal jurisdiction of the ICCJ should extend to all persons, natural or corporate, within the territory of a state party to the ICCJ statute (but not, as mentioned previously, the enforcement treaty). For plaintiffs, that would mean that any citizens, permanent residents, even tourists (all in sufficient numbers) harmed (in a manner covered by the statute) by cross-border activities within the territory of a state party would be able to bring a claim, without regard to whether the state of which they were nationals was a state party. This conception of the territorial nexus of the ICCJ's jurisdiction flows from the sovereign power of a state to regulate activities taking place within its territory. It is straightforward that a state – say, Peru – would have the power to adjudicate a tort case in Peruvian domestic court against an MNC operating in its territory. It therefore follows that Peru could delegate the exercise of that sovereign power to an international court. It is also straightforward to say that Peru's sovereign power to adjudicate (or to delegate the adjudication) of disputes that arise on its territory exists independently of the nationality of the disputing parties. Thus, if Peru joins the ICCJ statute, a (sufficiently large) group of German tourists injured in a boating accident in the Peruvian Amazon caused by a Brazilian touring company would be able to bring a claim in the ICCJ. So, too, would Chinese workers injured in an accident at a mining project run by a Chinese company in Peru be able to bring a claim against their employer – even though both the plaintiffs and defendant in that case would be nationals of a non–state party.

It may be tempting, in order to provide access to justice for as many plaintiffs as possible and to create more nearly universally applicable standards for the behavior of MNCs, to provide the ICCJ with jurisdiction over MNCs that are nationals of states parties to the ICCJ statute wherever they operate. Such a decision would be misguided, however. First, it would do nothing at all to achieve global legal peace because MNCs operating in the territory of a non–state party would still be subject to local laws, even with a provision in the ICCJ statute conferring jurisdiction over the worldwide activities of MNCs that are nationals of states parties. That would follow because the local courts of the non–state party would not be bound by the terms of the treaty and would therefore be free to exercise their own jurisdiction in favor of the ICCJ's. And if the non–state party did exercise its jurisdiction, then the courts of a state party would have to enforce that judgment, subject to their normal laws regarding the enforcement of foreign judgments. Thus it seems that nationals of non–state parties would, whatever the ICCJ's stance regarding the effect of defendants' nationality on jurisdiction, retain their ability to forum shop and to engage in the kind of parallel and sequential litigation the ICCJ is aimed at ending. Furthermore, premising jurisdiction on the defendants' nationality could incentivize host states to hold out (i.e., not join the ICCJ) because their citizens would benefit from having a forum when injured by such MNCs even without the state's participation in the ICCJ. Better, then, to arrange the incentives in such a way as to encourage more host states to join.

D Admissibility – Relationship of the ICCJ to National Courts

Admissibility potentially covers many features of a case; common criteria for admissibility include compliance with any applicable statute of limitations, compliance with pleading requirements, and use of proper language.[59] In the context of admissibility, the most important and complex issue by far is the effect of national jurisdictions on the ability of the ICCJ to admit a case. The following paragraphs will examine the suitability for the ICCJ of several models of admissibility rules covering the interaction between national and international courts.

There are, conceptually speaking, four common types of rules that govern admissibility when national and international courts share the power to hear a case: exclusivity, complementarity, exhaustion of domestic remedies, and, *electa una via* (choose one course).[60] Exclusivity means that the international court is the only one with the power to hear the case. Complementarity means that both national and international courts would have the power to hear the case, with rules regulating the circumstances under which one must defer to the other. Exhaustion of domestic remedies is a prominent feature of admissibility in human rights bodies; it requires claimants to have taken advantage of every possible legal avenue within the state to address their claim before bringing it to the international level. Finally, *electa una via* offers parties the free choice of international or national jurisdictions, but requires them to forgo all other options upon making that choice. Of these, the best choice for the ICCJ is exclusive jurisdiction.

II Jurisdiction and Admissibility

Exclusivity, as the name suggests, means that no court other than the court in question can hear a given case. In much of this book I try to offer different aspects of the argument for why national courts – whether of capital exporting or importing countries – are not and, perhaps, should not be, normatively, adjudicators of cross-border mass torts. All of those arguments in support of the creation of the ICCJ also support granting it exclusivity vis-à-vis national courts. To the extent that adjudicating cross-border mass torts is beyond the capacity of a given court system, or raises the specter of real or perceived corruption, or risks elevating the courts of a single nation to the status of "courts of the world," or lands plaintiffs and defendants in the morass of parallel and sequential litigation, it would follow that cross-border mass tort cases should be removed from such courts and instead routed to a forum cured of those defects – the ICCJ.

Furthermore, anything other than exclusivity will create unnecessary and expensive layers of litigation, as well as decrease predictability for MNCs managing their operations. The ICCJ is ultimately intended to provide defendants with a simplified and streamlined process for deciding cross-border mass tort claims, and to provide plaintiffs with a reliably open forum, capable of producing enforceable judgments, in which to bring those claims. An ICCJ with exclusive jurisdiction is the simplest and most streamlined way to accomplish that because it removes all consideration of competing jurisdictional claims. Exclusivity thus eliminates the costly and time-consuming stage of litigating the question of whether the ICCJ is the proper place to litigate. It offers the most predictability as well, since MNCs would only have to take a single body of law into account in making decisions about their operations in the territory of states parties. For plaintiffs, guaranteed access to the ICCJ through exclusive jurisdiction would mean confidence that they could avoid the prospect of the no-man's-land of *forum non conveniens* motions, boomerang litigation, and fighting out enforcement on the ice after hell freezes over.[61]

The remaining models of regulating admissibility at the ICCJ vis-à-vis national courts would be either impracticable or distinctly inferior. Requiring the exhaustion of domestic remedies, for instance, should be discarded as normatively undesirable and as inefficient: normatively undesirable because it would place the ICCJ in a coordinately superior hierarchical role to national courts, effectively turning it into a court of appeal reviewing domestic decisions. The point of the ICCJ is to play a universalizing and harmonizing role, to augment national jurisdictions through delegation – not to judge their deficiencies. Furthermore, by establishing the ICCJ as a *de facto* appeals court the exhaustion model would do nothing more than add time and expense to the process of adjudicating cross-border mass tort claims, thereby creating inefficiency. The model of *electa una via* is designed to prevent forum shopping by restricting plaintiffs to whichever choice of forum they made first. It is therefore irrelevant if the ICCJ has exclusivity. If the ICCJ has complementarity (discussed in more detail in the following), then defendants moving to transfer a case from the ICCJ to a national jurisdiction should be required to stipulate to their consent to jurisdiction and their intention to abide by the decision made by the national court they chose. In either case (exclusivity or complementarity), then, *electa una via* could not have a meaningful role in the ICCJ's rules on admissibility.

Complementarity, while viable, dilutes each of the advantages of exclusive jurisdiction. Developed in the negotiations of the Rome Statute, the principle provides that the ICC must determine that a case is inadmissible, and decline to hear it, if the relevant national system is willing and able to take it up.[62] It is important to note at the outset that the version of complementarity adopted by the drafters of the Rome Statute would be inapplicable to the ICCJ. At the ICC, the principle focuses on the activities of the prosecuting authorities at the national level. If national prosecuting authorities have investigated, initiated a prosecution, or completed a prosecution, the case is inadmissible before the ICC. In the context of the ICCJ, the party responsible for "prosecuting" the claim is the same at the international and national levels – the plaintiffs. A direct application of complementarity would, therefore, translate into expanding forum shopping by permitting plaintiffs to choose whether to bring the case before national courts or the ICCJ. Instead, complementarity at the ICCJ would have to be defendant-focused, permitting defendants to make a motion to move the case from the ICCJ to a national jurisdiction or from a national jurisdiction to the ICCJ. The benefit of such a structure would be to encourage developed nations to join the ICCJ statute because they would be providing their potential defendants the opportunity to enjoy the benefits of the ICCJ (primarily, global preclusion) without eliminating the option to remain in the home or host jurisdiction's courts. The downside, however, is that the ICCJ, like the ICC, should not be required to defer to national systems that cannot or will not offer due process.

If the complementarity route is taken, "able" in this context should mean, at a minimum, that a court has the capacity to handle complex mass torts and is not corrupt. This may entail a judicial determination as to the ability of the national courts. While this is certainly possible, even without deep expertise about the system in question,[63] it is a distinct drawback for the complementarity model because it places the ICCJ in a hierarchical relationship with national jurisdictions by requiring it to make determinations about the competence, honesty, and/or capacity of national systems. States parties would therefore be giving the ICCJ the power to pronounce on the strength of the rule of law in their countries. That is very different from a grant of exclusivity, which would say nothing more than that the states parties made an all-things-considered judgment that delegation was in their best interests.

"Willing" to adjudicate would mean that a court has accepted jurisdiction over the case. "Willingness" may only be subject to determination after challenges to jurisdiction – such as lack of personal jurisdiction or *forum non conveniens* – have either been waived by the defendants or determined by a national court. At that point, the decision for the ICCJ should be quite technical. Importantly, complementarity should make accepting the jurisdiction of the national courts of a developed home state, when plaintiffs file their action in such a court, an appealing option for defending MNCs. Since persuading a court to decline a case would no longer mean impunity, some firms may be more likely to accept jurisdiction at home rather than litigate at the ICCJ. This would mean fewer procedural hurdles in these types of cases, in which, currently, jurisdictional battles abound. The converse may also be true: a defendant may wish to stipulate to the ICCJ's jurisdiction rather than, say, stand trial back home if it believes the procedures or jurisprudence of the ICCJ are preferable.

All that said, as noted previously, any version of complementarity will, at a minimum, require MNCs to consider two legal regimes in managing their operations. It also has the potential to increase forum shopping and, with that, raises again the specter of parallel and sequential litigation that the ICCJ is intended to combat. An ICCJ decision that an "able" forum exists would not require the courts of third countries to enforce the judgments of the courts the ICCJ deemed suitable. Hence boomerang litigation may once more ensue. Complementarity, in other words, although a workable compromise, is in most respects a second best to exclusive jurisdiction.

III PROCEDURAL FEATURES

Mass torts involve claims of actionable misconduct that affects large numbers of dispersed individuals. The alleged victims complain of injuries that may be latent for many years but once they emerge, present a limited set of factual variations. The numerosity, geographic and temporal dispersion, and factual similarities among the claims pose considerable challenges for tort systems designed originally for present-day injuries adjudicated through one-on-one litigation. Judiciaries, legislatures, and defendants have developed several answers to those challenges: consolidating parts of the litigation process in the court system, representative litigation, and creating claims facilities separate from the court system. Even within those three models there is significant variation. The best way of thinking about that variation is as a continuum of coordination and aggregation. At one end of the spectrum are mass claims. I discussed the distinction between mass claims and mass torts in Section II.B, but to recap: Mass claims are large numbers of separate claims against the same defendant (or group of defendants) for the same conduct or the same general pattern of conduct. Although there are many of them, and they are somewhat related, mass claims proceed individually. In instances of low overlap, courts might choose to conduct only certain procedures jointly – for example, considering a single motion affecting an entire group of cases that would otherwise proceed individually. In instances of significant overlap, courts might conduct more (but still not all) of the process jointly, for instance, by consolidating the entire pretrial phase. I refer to these types of procedural mechanisms as "aggregate litigation" or "collective action." Their distinguishing characteristics are that some, but not all, parts of the litigation are consolidated or at least coordinated and that all the parties are named.

This continuum culminates in the class action, also called the "representative action."[64] Class actions enable one or more representatives of a group to sue on behalf of all plaintiffs, who are unnamed and, generally, do not participate in the litigation. The entire class is then bound by the result of the case. Judges make a preliminary decision which cases can proceed as representative actions; for a group to proceed as such there must be a sufficient commonality of factual and legal questions.[65] Certifying a group of claimants and allowing representatives to sue on their behalf are meant to eliminate duplicative litigation of the same legal or factual issues. If certification as a class is not possible, judicial management techniques are necessary to coordinate the cases and eliminate inconsistent rulings.[66] Representative actions also serve the interests of justice, by making it possible for claimants who might otherwise lack sufficient resources to have their claim heard; by offering the possibility of compensation even for injuries too small to pursue on an individual basis economically; and, in the view of some at least, by deterring similar conduct.

To deal with the complexity of cross-border mass tort cases properly, the ICCJ should offer claimants and defendants a range of procedures and mechanisms for adjudicating and amicably resolving their disputes as well as administer settlements where necessary. In particular, the ICCJ should have a flexible approach with respect to joinder, consolidation, and coordination – aggregating all or parts of the process of adjudicating similar claims as appropriate. Judges should be empowered to act as active managers, reflecting the global convergence on managerial judging in the context of mass claims discussed previously. It is important to acknowledge, however, that there is no such convergence in respect of representative litigation. My suggestions – both the overall design and the resolution of conflicts between comparative procedures – are animated by the following normative and political commitments. First, the problem of the missing forum deserves to be solved because people who are injured by the activities of MNCs deserve to have access to justice. This starting point means that features that make it easier for claimants to access the ICCJ will have more weight than those that would tend to exclude cases easily. Second, MNCs deserve to have claims against them fully and finally resolved by a neutral forum. This, in turn, will lower the cost of doing business internationally, thereby contributing to the improvement of the global marketplace. Hence, procedures that make global legal peace more easily achieved are favored over those that do not. Third, in order to realize the first two aims the ICCJ must become a practical reality and not just an academic proposal. That will inevitably involve tough choices and compromise. That will be especially true in the design of representative actions, about which there is much unresolved controversy both within national legal systems and comparatively across national boundaries and legal traditions.

I will begin, in the following, with a brief comparison of the main features of common law and civil law systems, in order to orient the reader to the kinds of choices that must be made in designing the ICCJ. I will then discuss, in turn, each of the several dispute settlement mechanisms and key procedures that should be offered by the ICCJ. The first of these is judicial screening and routing whereby a "concierge" judge (or small chamber) may keep claims out of the ICCJ, route the remaining claims to the proper mechanism, decide whether and what form of aggregation to use, and recommend or require ADR. I will next discuss ADR mechanisms, nonrepresentative aggregation procedures, and representative aggregation procedures that I believe the ICCJ should adopt. Supervision and administration of aggregate settlement are next. The section concludes with a discussion of the financing of the court.

A *Civil Law–Common Law Hybrids*

The two most prevalent families into which legal systems are generally grouped are the adversarial Anglo-American (common law) tradition and the inquisitorial Continental (civil law) tradition.[67] Where colonizers went, they took their legal systems with them, and almost without exception those remained as the foundations of the legal systems of the former colonies once they gained independence. Those systems have since developed on their own, leading to a dizzying array of procedural and substantive law. By necessity, therefore, the discussion herein generalizes, simplifies, and focuses on the two leading families of legal systems, common law and civil law, only.

The monikers "adversarial" and "inquisitorial" that are used to describe the common law and the civil law, respectively, relate to what is perhaps the most fundamental difference between the two traditions – the role of judges versus that of parties and their lawyers in truth finding. "The adversarial mode of proceeding takes its shape from a contest or a dispute: it unfolds as an engagement of two adversaries before a relatively passive decision maker whose principal duty is to reach a verdict. The non-adversarial mode is structured as an official inquiry. Under the first system, the two adversaries take charge of most procedural action; under the second, officials perform most activities."[68] Another fundamental difference between the two traditions is the existence of a civil jury in the common law versus its absence in other traditions.

In practical terms, the difference between the inquisitorial and the adversarial mode manifests in features such as the presence or absence of discovery, the existence and role of a trial, the ease of dismissing or otherwise concluding a case in whole or in part without a trial, and the strictness or laxity of evidentiary rules. Civil law systems generally do not have discovery, and in most cases do not hold a trial. "Instead, a civil-law civil action is a continuing series of meetings, hearings, and written communications through which evidence is introduced and evaluated, testimony is taken, and motions are made and decided."[69] All of that takes place mostly in writing, and under the careful and close management of the judge. Judges can also dismiss all or part of a case at any point, without a requirement to bring factual determinations to a jury, at a trial, at the end of a long process.

Importantly, civil litigation in the inquisitorial system tends to be cheaper and more predictable than in the adversarial one.[70] The level of litigation costs is driven, universally, by work conducted by nonparty actors, namely, lawyers, experts, and judges.[71] These are significantly higher for the lawyer-driven common law trials than in judge-driven civil law actions.[72]

The foregoing comparative primer notwithstanding, the history of the evolution of the legal response to the rise in mass harms and mass legal claims, in the United States and transnationally, has been to shift from a torts paradigm, which evolved historically to deal with individual cases, to an administration paradigm.[73] This administrative nature is the reason that even in the United States claims facilities use an inquisitorial model. Therefore, the recommendation to empower ICCJ judges to hew toward the inquisitorial model is consistent with the trajectory of the development of mass litigation in the United States and other common law jurisdictions. Further, the main upshot of the administrative nature of mass tort litigation is that, with rare exceptions, mass torts are resolved by way of aggregate settlements, not trials, with defendants seeking the most comprehensive peace for the litigation as a whole.[74] The quasi-administrative procedure, therefore, is designed with this end game in mind.

With this short overview of the divergent legal procedure traditions that the framers of the ICCJ can draw from and must hybridize, we can now examine procedural design features that can contribute to more efficient and effective dispute resolution in the new forum.

B *Claim Screening and Routing*

Claimants' first stop at the ICCJ should be a judge, or a small chamber of judges, whose role is to dismiss claims that can easily be identified as unqualifying. This type of initial screening, discussed in more detail later, is done in some claims facilities and is also a service provided by arbitral institutions before a tribunal is empaneled.

The judge/chamber should then route the qualifying claims to the appropriate mechanism(s) within the ICCJ. A danger of class actions in the United States is that corporate defendants can be forced to settle even claims that are without merit because of the expense of defending against large lawsuits and also because of the risk of extremely large liability if an unpredictable jury finds for the plaintiff. Those concerns could be further addressed if judges were able to assess and dismiss cases early in the process. Because of the constitutional requirement to afford a jury trial, the ability of judges in the United States to do so is much more limited than that of their European counterparts.

Hence the first function of the screening should be to exclude claims that raise jurisdictional problems, that are inadmissible, that are very clearly unlikely to succeed on the merits, or that otherwise fail to confirm to the ICCJ's requirements. If a group were to bring a claim based on conduct that occurred on the territory of a nonmember state, for instance, the case would be dismissed for lack of subject matter jurisdiction. Or if the ICCJ operated on the principle of complementarity and national courts were already dealing with the case, it would be inadmissible in the ICCJ. These are fairly straightforward reasons for refusing to hear a case; more difficult questions arise in deciding whether to dismiss a case because the claimants are unlikely to prevail. Clearly this should be, at such a preliminary stage, a high bar, but where, for instance, the plaintiffs bring an otherwise procedurally perfect complaint – right territory, right law, right defendant(s) – but are unable to provide any evidence of their claimed injuries, it should be within a judge's discretion to dismiss the case.

Given the importance of the decision to dismiss early on, these decisions should be subject to appeal. This (as well as other reasons discussed later) would require the ICCJ to have an appellate chamber. While appeals prolong the litigation process and, therefore, also increase costs, they serve two core functions that, in the case of mass tort adjudication, trump these downsides: appeals serve to correct (and deter) mistakes and to ensure that decisions are consistent so that like cases are treated alike. Given the complexity of cross-border mass torts, the risk of mistakes and inconsistencies is heightened and therefore an appellate chamber is especially important. An appellate chamber can render the jurisprudence of a court internally consistent by deciding any splits between the trial chambers and clarifying the jurisprudence of the court. Such coherence can, over time, lead to more predictability for the parties. Predictability is valuable generally and especially to uncertainty-adverse corporations. And when mass claims are concerned, equal treatment of all claimants through consistent decisions is a primary goal. In permitting appeals, the ICCJ would not be breaking new ground. The WTO Appellate Body is generally recognized as having contributed significantly to the legitimacy of the dispute settlement system.[75] The International Criminal Tribunal for the Former Yugoslavia

(ICTY), International Criminal Tribunal for Rwanda (ICTR), and ICC all provide for appeals.

Additional functions of the screening and routing chamber should be to decide whether and in what form claims should be aggregated; if proceeding as a representative case whether the case should be classified as "opt in" or as "opt out"; appoint attorneys to leadership committees (a coordination function); and recommend or require ADR (all discussed in the following).

C Alternative Dispute Resolution

There is a general consensus that ADR procedures are a key component to the settlement of mass claims. The EU, for example, concluded that ADR mechanisms should always be available on a voluntary basis alongside judicial collective redress.[76] There are many possible ADR mechanisms. At the center of most ADR schemes is mediation (sometimes referred to, in the international courts context, as "conciliation"). Mediation is facilitated negotiation, and many domestic and international courts offer, or even compel the usage of, mediation services that can be employed both before and during a lawsuit.[77] Similarly, ICCJ judges should be empowered either to recommend or to require it, at their discretion. Mediation can be evaluative as well as facilitative. Namely, mediators with relevant expertise – for example, doctors who may be able to assess the medical aspects of personal injury claims or scientists who may be able to assess environmental harm claims – can provide the parties a nonbinding evaluation of the claims and defenses being advanced. Such mediation can serve as a "reality check" that can move parties closer together, thus making a settlement more likely and more speedy. In the transnational mass tort context, diplomacy is also, at times, employed, and as an international organization the ICCJ can facilitate that as well.

D Nonrepresentative Collective Litigation

Even when representative action (discussed next) is inappropriate, efficiency can be enhanced through consolidation and coordination of parts of the litigation process when one or more common questions of fact are present, upon determination by the presiding judge that such measures "will be for the convenience of parties and witnesses and will promote the just and efficient conduct of such actions."[78] Any and all parts of the process – e.g., discovery, motions to dismiss, hearing of expert or fact testimony – can be coordinated or even consolidated when overlap exists. Another source of efficiency is use of uniform methods for the assessment and valuation of evidence in similar cases with common factual foundation.[79] Increasingly, statistical sampling and modeling are used to calculate and extrapolate damage calculations from individual cases to the entire population of cases. Statistical analysis allows "extrapolat[ing] the results of certain decisions – such as a decision to use evidentiary presumptions – [] on the basis of a representative random sample, to all the remaining claims in the population from which the sample was taken."[80] Algorithms based on sampling have also been used by claims facilities to develop damage calculation schemes.

An additional technique used by claims facilities that should be available to the judges is "to provide a choice to individual claimants to select a payment option that has more relaxed criteria with a correspondingly lower payment."[81] Relatively popular in claims resolution facilities is the method of developing a payment grid based on anywhere between three and twenty variables. "Once eligible, a claimant is placed on a grid depending upon the evidence on the limited number of axes and awarded the designated amount."[82]

E *Representative Actions*

In deciding on which procedural features to adopt, the designers of the ICCJ will be able to draw on a wealth of knowledge generated by the previous experience of other international courts and tribunals and other transnational claims facilities and the work of comparative proceduralists. None of those sources of information and inspiration, however, offers easy or uniform answers. Many of the procedural issues at the heart of any mechanism intended to adjudicate large-scale claims are sources of controversy – with competing conceptions of justice and of the proper role of the state versus the free markets underlying them – with different jurisdictions arriving at answers that are in tension with one another.

Much of that tension stems from disagreement about the best way to structure representative action, known in the United States as "class action." The distinctive feature of the representative action is that a representative plaintiff brings the action in the name of a group of unnamed plaintiffs (the class). The membership in the class may be unknown, unknowable, or too large and dispersed to contact and consult. This means that individuals may be parties to an action without knowing so and, by implication, without being consulted about the conduct of the litigation or, crucially, the terms of its settlement. As some critics note, this, *de facto* (though not legally or ethically), reverses the natural order of things with the class attorneys as the *de facto* principals who are the ones deciding to commence an action, steering it strategically, and deciding when and for how much to settle. When the principal–agent relation is thus turned on its head, conflicts of interest between the attorneys and their clients proliferate and are enhanced.

Until fairly recently, while the United States and other common law jurisdictions permitted class actions, many other countries disfavored representative actions in any form. That is changing, however, as discussed in Chapter 4. Many European countries have recognized that representative actions promote both access to justice and efficiency, and so have authorized them in one form or another. But, as European countries try to decide how to govern such actions, "the debate ... is dominated by the concern that, whatever the new procedure looks like, it should *not* be an 'American-style' class action."[83] Wherever possible, the procedures I suggest for the ICCJ will be, as discussed at the beginning of the chapter, a hybrid of the procedures prevalent in the common law and civil law traditions. But where that is not possible, where those procedures are in tension with one another, I suggest approaches designed to maximize access to justice, global preclusion, and the probability of attracting a consensus sufficiently broad to bring the ICCJ into being.

This section will focus on the most controversial questions about the procedure governing representative actions. Will representative actions require claimants to opt into the group ("opt-in") or to opt out of it ("opt-out")? Who has standing to bring a claim? How will attorneys be compensated, and will they be permitted to share winnings with successful claimants? The first question goes to the extent to which the legal rights of potential claimants can or should be settled or adjudicated without their consent. The last two questions go to the extent to which the procedures of the ICCJ will facilitate entrepreneurial lawyering, including the question of whether to permit punitive damages. And all questions are connected in that the unifying theme is the question of whether and to what degree to incentivize the bringing of claims to the ICCJ. This, in turn, hinges on political philosophy: whether and to what degree to encourage private enforcement of tort law in the transnational sphere by empowering so-called private attorney generals.[84]

The ICCJ need not resolve the question of whether opt-in or opt-out procedures are the superior option; rather, it should follow the lead of a few European countries in permitting both and allowing judges to make the determination of which is appropriate in a given case. This is because the concerns about justice that drive European jurisdictions to favor opt-in actions vary on the basis of factors that judges should be able to ascertain easily. The primary objection raised to opt-out representative actions is that the final decision in such cases binds all members of the group, whether or not they were even aware the litigation existed. This offends notions of due process, which require that "a person who was not heard in court could not be bound by the outcome of the procedure."[85] And indeed, in the United States – the global exemplar of opt-out representative actions – it is frequently documented that putative group members are bound by a settlement or final decision in a class action that they never even knew existed.[86] That is especially true for those who place a premium on the role of voice in evaluating the legitimacy of judicial proceedings; to the extent that opt-out representative actions purport to bind parties who had no voice in the proceedings – either through ignorance or apathy – they run afoul of some understandings of the requirements of justice.

Defenders of the opt-out model, on the other hand, argue that it is the best way to ensure preclusion, which, in turn, bears on defendants' willingness to participate and courts' ability to provide efficiency, compensation, and deterrence. Further, they point out that due process is satisfied by a combination of notice and close judicial supervision. In addition, opt-in leads to significantly smaller classes, which reduce plaintiffs' leverage (which may be either a good or bad thing depending on whether you ask plaintiffs or defendants). This is particularly a problem with "negative value" suits – suits that are much more expensive to bring individually than the potential recovery each plaintiffs stands to obtain (for example, when millions of people have been harmed but the value of the harm is one hundred dollars per victim). Only a large class would make it worthwhile to pursue such claims, and large classes, realistically, are only likely under an opt-out regime.

A small and possibly growing number of jurisdictions in Europe have adopted *both* opt-in and opt-out procedures, letting judges decide which is appropriate. In England, for instance, the Rules of the Competition Appeals Tribunal (CAT) provide that "in determining whether collective proceedings should be opt-in or opt-out proceedings, the Tribunal may take into account all matters it thinks fit."[87] The rules go on to list factors that might influence the CAT's decision, including the strength of the claims and the estimated amount of damages. Belgium's limited representative action, established in 2014, also leaves to the discretion of the judge whether to proceed on an opt-in or opt-out basis (although class members who reside outside Belgium must opt-in, and an action that "aims for restoration of physical or moral collective damage" must be opt-in).[88] Denmark requires opt-in classes in most circumstances, but allows opt-out classes for low-value claims brought by the public consumer authority.[89] Legislation was recently proposed to the Parliament of the Netherlands to establish opt-out representative actions for damages.[90]

The case for allowing judges to decide between opt-in and opt-out gains support if we consider that the due process concerns about the opt-out model are not uniform across all potential groups. They vary depending on a number of factors, which, at a minimum, would include, on the plaintiff side the geographic proximity of group members and/or their ability to share information easily with one another. On the other side, the ability of a defendant to identify the members of a group would influence the potential prejudice of an opt-out scheme. Where a group consisted of every landowner whose property abutted a toxic waste dump, for instance, one might reasonably conclude that nearly every potential group member would have heard about the suit and that the likelihood of prejudice from an opt-out scheme would therefore be low. In contrast, members of a group that consisted of every downstream user of a polluted river or every person who consumed tainted food would be much less likely to hear about any pending litigation and the possibility of prejudice would be higher. Where the potential group members included, for example, all current and former employees of a factory that used unreasonably dangerous chemicals in the manufacturing process, the potential claimants could presumably be located using the defendants' employment records. Indeed, France's system – although in most respects a paradigmatic example of the European collective action as a contrast to the US class actions – provides for something approaching an opt-out class action in limited situations when the identity and number of the potential claimants are known; otherwise, in the majority of cases, the law requires opt-in actions.[91] The foregoing is meant to illustrate the kinds of factors that might influence the decision of which model to adopt, not to be exhaustive or determinative. The ICCJ should follow the example of England, Belgium, and Denmark and not unduly burden the judges' discretion in this regard.

Whichever scheme the court chooses, opt-in or opt-out, the question arises, What will become of claimants who opt out or decline to opt in? This is a crucial question because it goes directly to the ability of the ICCJ to remove cross-border mass tort litigation from the "wild west" of transnational litigation in the courts of home and host states. For all the reasons discussed at length in Chapters 3 and 4, the ICCJ must retain jurisdiction over all nonparticipating claimants. Whether the ICCJ is premised on exclusive or complementary jurisdiction, by the time the question of participation in the group comes up the relevant national system(s) will no longer have jurisdiction – either as a matter of course, in the exclusivity model, or because of the inability or unwillingness of the national courts in the complementarity model. Either way, letting nonparticipating claimants bring their claims outside the ICCJ gives them the opportunity to forum shop and exposes defendants (and claimants) to the pernicious effects of real and perceived corruption and parallel, sequential, and boomerang litigation. Processing the claims of nonparticipating claimants individually (as would happen domestically as well) would certainly be a burden on the ICCJ, but it is the only way to ensure that its mission is not undermined by gamesmanship.

Because of the lack of state (or statelike) institutions at the international level, the questions about standing and attorney compensation should be resolved in favor of more entrepreneurial lawyering and less centralized decision making. As an initial take, it might seem that those questions are more difficult to grapple with than the choice between opt-in and opt-out, since they implicate the fundamental tension between the private powers of parties and counsel and the public function of the state. And that is certainly true for states that are debating whether and how to enable representative litigation: every additional prospect for private action is necessarily a diminution of state control; compromise is difficult. In the context of transnational litigation, however, and especially of cross-border mass torts, the absence of strong state or statelike institutions makes the public option less attractive and clarifies the need for procedures that incentivize entrepreneurial lawyering.

Many states that previously resisted collective litigation now recognize the need for it, but most continue to resist the US version of the system, which privatizes the control over when, where, and on whose behalf to bring such litigation. One reason for that resistance is the common view that the profit-motivated attorney-driven US model encourages frivolous litigation, incentivizes extortionate settlements, enriches lawyers at the expense of their clients, and creates conflicts of interest between the former and the latter.[92] On a deeper level, the model of entrepreneurial lawyering challenges bedrock-level commitments about the proper role of government in regulation and law enforcement. As one commentator notes, aggregate litigation is, at its heart, a mechanism to overcome collective action problems. But "the simple fact is that all societies already possess an institution designed to overcome collective action barriers to common security and the proper allocation of burdens and resources: the state, in its most basic Hobbesian functions."[93] Many countries view any decision by the state to delegate its oversight of public goods (which include access to justice) to private lawyers and claimants as abdicating essential state functions in favor of unelected actors with neither democratic legitimacy nor democratic accountability.

The typical response to such concerns has been to restrict standing in representative actions to government bodies or to specifically identified associations (nonprofit organizations), to prohibit contingency fees, and to prohibit monetary damages in general and/or punitive damages in particular.[94] France's representative action system is a useful example of this model. Created in 2014, and updated in 2016, the system permits representative actions in the areas of consumer protection, health care, environment, and data privacy. The law governs the type of remedies. For data privacy actions, no monetary damages are available. For consumer actions, the law only permits damages for pecuniary loss, although in health care actions plaintiffs may claim damages for personal injuries. French law prohibits contingency fees; lawyer fees are based on a predetermined rate. Absent a judicial ruling to the contrary, the losing party pays the legal fees of the winning party.[95]

Whatever the comparative merits of the entrepreneurial model of the United States and the public or quasi-public European model, public/private concerns apply with less force in the context of the ICCJ because there are no transnational public or quasi-public institutions capable of shouldering the burden. Similarly, no existing intergovernmental organization has the mandate or the ability to regulate transnational business activity. States' unwillingness and intergovernmental organizations' inability to regulate the conduct of MNCs *ex ante* translates directly into the absence of public entities able or willing to play the role of public managers of representative litigation in the European mode.

One might respond that the ICCJ itself could play that role, but there are practical, policy, and conceptual difficulties with that approach. On the practical level such an approach would have the effect of limiting actions brought to the ICCJ since any entity – whether the ICCJ itself or certain nominated organizations – would of necessity have to make choices about how to invest limited resources among competing potential claims. Private attorneys, running portfolios of cases that in the aggregate must be profitable for their law firms to survive, suffer no such limitation. At the policy level, entrusting the same institution to decide which claims are appropriate to bring and to adjudicate those claims is problematic. For one thing, unpopular decisions about how to allocate resources among competing claims could undermine the legitimacy of the institution as a whole. We have seen this with the ICC, which has suffered immensely from the perceived geopolitical bias in the selection of cases it has pursued to date. And in domestic systems it is the legislature that makes decisions about standing and claim selection, not the court system. Giving the choice of which claims to bring to private attorneys and their clients would absolve the ICCJ of any perceived bias or conflict of interest, as the body that then adjudicates the cases it selected. There is also the policy question of how best to allocate the cost of acquiring information about potential claims. The public model assumes that the relevant public bodies are able to know which claims exist in order to make an informed choice about which one(s) to bring. And in a single country that is perhaps possible for little or no cost – especially for a body already mandated (and funded) to monitor a particular sector. But on a global scale the cost of acquiring information about the universe of potential cross-border mass torts would be immense. Private attorneys, on the other hand, would serve as a global "search function."

That is not to say that entrepreneurial lawyering is without its problems. Understood as a search function, entrepreneurial lawyering may produce overinclusive results, meaning nonmeritorious claims. But that is mostly problematic in the US context in combination with its procedural restrictions on early dismissal; where, as discussed previously, ICCJ judges have robust powers to end a case early if it appears to be nonmeritorious, such concerns have less force. Another problem is that entrepreneurial lawyering will tend to weight the discovery of "paying" claims – especially those with the potential for punitive or exemplary damages – over meritorious but less lucrative ones such as where plaintiffs may be more interested in injunctive relief than in damages. Having said that, establishing certain minimum pay scales could bring into the "ICCJ bar" a broader array of attorneys than the high-value class action plaintiffs' bar of the United States. The case of one hundred workers injured (but not killed) in a factory fire in Malaysia, for instance, might not be of interest to the class action giants in the United States. But perhaps it would be of interest to a boutique litigation firm or NGO who were assured a certain minimum fee.

III Procedural Features

Thus the ICCJ should adopt procedures that facilitate entrepreneurial lawyering while curbing its worst excesses. "There is an inextricable connection between the architecture of the procedure and the cost rules. The rules were designed with the costs rules in mind, and vice versa."[96] The decision about whether to bring a claim should rest with claimants and their attorneys, not with the ICCJ itself or with NGOs (although NGOs could, of course, bring claims as attorneys for claimants). Private attorneys should have a profit incentive sufficient to encourage them to seek out meritorious claims but not so expansive as to promote frivolous claims designed to extract settlements. To that end, the ICCJ should have a minimum fee schedule applicable in every case and should avoid the practice of fee shifting. Often called "the English Rule," fee shifting means that the losing party bears the winning party's legal costs (see Chapter 3). While fee shifting has its benefits, including discouraging frivolous litigation, it also deters impecunious claimants (such as tort victims from the developing world) who may be unable to pay those costs in the event they lose. In order to prevent discouraging the very claimants it seeks to attract, the ICCJ should avoid fee shifting. But it need not eliminate the practice altogether; judges could exercise discretion in instances when the rule would not operate to the detriment of the claimants – for instance, if they were backed by litigation finance.

The ICCJ should also maintain an access to justice fund for impecunious claimants to secure representation and to enable cases where injunctive relief rather than monetary compensation is sought. Many international courts and tribunals provide financial assistance to parties. The secretary general of the UN, for instance, maintains a trust fund for states seeking to make use of the ICJ.[97] The WTO established the Advisory Centre on WTO Law, which, among other services, provides least-developed countries with legal assistance in preparing for and conducting hearings before dispute settlement panels.[98] The Inter-American Commission on Human Rights (IACHR) maintains a fund that covers, among other thing, the expenses derived from "gathering and sending documentary evidence."[99] Such funds are funded by voluntary contributions of states, NGOs, intergovernmental organizations, individuals, and corporations.[100] In addition to the minimum fee schedule, the ICCJ should permit contingency and conditional fees, subject to judicial approval.[101] Representative actions outside the United States are rarely utilized because such procedures were "dropped into … legal financing regime[s] that prohibit[] or limit[] conditional or contingent fee arrangements, provide[] no mechanism for cost sharing among members of an opt-out class, and require[] fee shifting… In these jurisdictions, there is a class action procedure 'on the books,' [only]."[102] Conversely, in the United States, almost all tort litigation is paid for on a contingency fee basis and, increasingly, with the use of third-party funding.[103] In the United States, however, attorneys' fee arrangements are subject to little scrutiny, leading to charges that some attorneys exploit their clients and walk away with a too-high percentage of the recovery.

The ICCJ statute should explicitly permit litigation finance. Litigation finance introduces competition into the market for litigation, previously monopolized by attorneys (in jurisdictions that permitted lawyer financing of suits through the contingent or conditional fee). It therefore has the potential of reducing the cost of financing to plaintiffs, leaving them with more of the recovery. Further, given the complexity, and therefore costs, of transnational mass tort litigation it is best to allow for as many financing sources as possible, including the potential for collaboration and syndication between multiple public and private funding sources.

A major point of divergence between the common law, especially the United States, and the civil law is the availability of discovery. The term "discovery" refers to a group of fact-gathering tools afforded to parties in adversarial systems. Exchanges of documents and physical evidence between adversaries and pretrial deposition of witnesses are among the most commonly used discovery tools. Such party-led discovery can be very effective at truth finding but is notoriously expensive. Conversely, in the inquisitorial systems of the civil law, it is up to the judge to find the truth, and in order to do so she can utilize such methods "as ordering documents, interviewing witnesses, [and] inspecting sites."[104] A hybrid approach that privatizes some of the truth finding by allowing some, limited discovery, as has become acceptable in international arbitration, but that also grants judges the powerful and efficient inquisitorial tools is probably the best approach to fact finding the ICCJ.

F *Supervision and Administration of Aggregate Settlement*

As already noted, the end game of virtually all mass tort litigation is aggregate settlements. An aggregate settlement is an "all-or-nothing total settlement of a single sum of money for all claims pending for a group of plaintiffs."[105] While there is no one-size-fits-all solution to mass tort settlements, scholars have identified recurring structures for the process that results in such settlements.[106] In addition to requiring a lump sum, the terms of aggregate settlements generally include terms for the allocation of amounts among the plaintiffs and the conditions under which settlements are voidable by defendants for failure to obtain releases from a sufficient percentage of plaintiffs.

Because lawyers who control portfolios of cases, not clients who are concerned with their individual cases, negotiate the settlement terms, the process through which these settlements come into being is rife with conflicts of interests.[107] The main way to control and minimize such conflicts is to subject aggregate settlements to court supervision. Such supervision may include a requirement of informed consent following full disclosure regarding the key terms of the settlement. Often, regulation of other aggregate settlements happens not through courts but rather through the rules of ethics for attorneys. In the transnational context, where lawyers from one jurisdiction (possibly in a developed economy) may represent clients from another, likely underdeveloped jurisdiction, the likelihood that such clients would file complaints with bar associations in foreign lands is vanishingly small. Therefore, court supervision, through review and approval of settlements and of attorneys' compensation, is doubly important, whether cases proceed as representative action or otherwise.

Arriving at a settlement agreement is not necessarily the end of the story. Often, it can be the beginning of a new, decades-long phase characterized by the challenge of administering the funds equitably and efficiently, with an eye toward preserving the rights of victims whose injuries may not yet be known. Claims facilities and bankruptcy courts have developed procedures to administer future distribution of funds, and an ICCJ would be more attractive if it provided this service. To achieve that, a separate unit should be set up and a trusteelike appointee and governance structure should be put in place to govern the distribution of the funds.[108]

G *Remedies*

In considering remedies, it is important to start with first principles: the goals of tort law. These depend in large part on one's theory of tort law – in particular, whether that theory is rooted in conceptions of justice or economics – but by most accounts they include compensation, deterrence, risk allocation, restoration, or prevention of future harm (in the context of injunctions or other forward-looking equitable remedies). Further, torts generally and mass torts in particular have a strong public interest dimension – the public's interest in the environment, in the protection of fundamental human rights, and in consumer protection, for example. This interest is heightened in the international context, where no regulators exist, and in the transnational context, where mass torts often occur where governmental structures may be weak and corrupt. In these situations, litigation often will not be a complement to public enforcement but rather the only form of enforcement. And litigation is only likely when it is incentivized monetarily. Therefore, monetary compensation should be available in addition to declaratory and injunctive relief.

Beyond monetary compensation, historically, relief "provided by transnational claims facilities is limited only by the imagination of [their] creators."[109] Examples of relief granted by such bodies in the past include medical treatment, repair of property, removal of a hazardous or defective product, and the provision of psychological or other counseling.[110] Notably, these types of remedies conceptually overlap with corporate social responsibility initiatives. This means that in addition to resolving outstanding claims, the relief provided through an ICCJ can help MNCs generate goodwill in the host state and, realistically, may be used by MNCs for promotional purposes. While the latter may be distasteful to some, it does mean that the broader array of remedies may be viewed as more legitimate and beneficial by MNCs than may be initially intuitive.

When considering remedies, it is important to note that interim relief, as we have seen in the Chapter 4, can be as consequential as final relief, and so an ICCJ should be properly empowered to grant it. Interim relief, also known variously as "preliminary," "provisional," or "conservatory" relief, relates to measures that protect the status quo or that ensure the final relief is meaningful and not vacuous. To meet the needs of claimants, an ICCJ should, for example, be able to freeze assets and enjoin harmful activities. To meet the needs of defendants, an ICCJ should, for example, be granted the power to enjoin parallel proceeding in the courts of states parties to both the ICCJ statute and the ICCJ enforcement treaty and to impose security of costs when such a measure may be warranted.[111]

As explained in Chapter 4, punitive damages are a key component of private enforcement of law in jurisdictions that favor that modality. In the transnational context, where plaintiffs are likely to be among the world's poorest, one might also point out that without punitive damages plaintiffs may only be awarded very low compensatory damages, which may diminish the deterrence effects of tort litigation. But punitive damages are considered objectionable in many legal systems because they are viewed as overincentivizing litigation and because, being a quasi-criminal sanction, awarding them without proof that meets the criminal burden of proof is viewed as unjust. The ICCJ should strike a balance by allowing punitive damages when the plaintiffs establish beyond a reasonable doubt (i.e., meet the criminal burden of proof) that the tortious conduct was of so reprehensible a nature as to warrant the punitive measure. At a minimum, fines (in the European tradition) should be allowed.

H Appellate Review

When considering precedent, it is worth noting that as *stare decisis* (binding precedent) is a common law principle, not a universal one, decisions of international courts are not binding precedent on other international courts nor, of course, on national ones. Nor, generally speaking, are previous decisions of international courts binding on those courts in their future decisions. However, it is common practice for international courts to refer to their previous decisions – in order to maintain consistency in their judgments – and to refer from time to time to decisions of other international courts and tribunals where similar issues arise.[112] At the ICTY and ICTR, decisions of the appellate chambers were binding on future trial chambers although at the WTO they are not.[113] To achieve the desired consistency and predictability, the ICCJ's appellate chamber's decisions should be binding on the trial chambers.

IV FINANCING THE OPERATION OF THE COURT

The ICCJ should, to the extent practicable, finance its activities by assessing fees to be paid by the parties. This would make the ICCJ more efficient from the perspective of the states parties in the sense that it would be cost-neutral (to the extent possible), and also more independent since the court would not have to depend on any outside entity for its funding. Because substantial sums of money would be at stake in ICCJ cases, and because those cases would often involve well-funded parties, the ICCJ in the context of financing is more analogous to ICSID than to the ICC. The latter, as a criminal court, must of necessity be funded from external sources. This creates a tension between the control that inevitably rests in the exercise of the "power of the purse" and the independence of the court.[114] To be clear, this is not to say that international organizations or their member states attempt to interfere in cases, or to suggest that international judges act with anything other than integrity or exercise anything other than their best legal judgment. Rather, it is to note that the ability of judges to exercise their judicial function is related to the financial capacity of the institution to which they belong.

To take but one illustration, the budget of the ICC, approved annually by the Assembly of States Parties, is often less than the court maintains it needs to accomplish its tasks. In November 2016, a group of states parties moved to restrict the court's funding further, prompting Amnesty International to observe that the move was "part of a damaging long-term effort by the biggest financial contributors to the court to curtail the ICC's growth, citing the global financial crisis and inefficiencies in the court. [That] effort ignore[d] the recommendations of an independent expert body that additional funding is needed. It also ignores the devastating impact that reductions of resources requested by the Court in previous years have had on the court's capacity to conduct investigations and keep pace with crimes committed at alarming rates in new situations."[115] Of course, the global economic crisis is very real, and states parties are free to reconsider their financial commitments for any reason – certainly including real or perceived inefficiency, or declining legitimacy based on some high-profile defections.[116] Indeed, that is precisely the point of the example – to illustrate the tension between the entirely reasonable financial and political calculations of states parties and the equally reasonable desire for the court they fund to have adequate resources to carry out its functions.

The ICCJ need not recreate that tension, and can instead adopt ICSID's approach. The ICSID Convention provides that the Centre is funded by a two-tier system. First, the parties to any dispute contribute to the costs. In the event that the costs of operating the Centre exceed parties' contributions, states parties cover the excess.[117] In practice, ICSID recovers costs from the parties in two ways. First, each party is required to deposit an advance payment to cover the costs of the proceeding, most of which goes to cover the fees of the members of the tribunal, commission, or committee convened to hear the dispute.[118] Second, ICSID assesses a flat fee per case per year to cover the organization's expenses (such as legal and administrative staff). The ICCJ could follow suit, and could, similarly, provide that expenses in excess of collected fees would be covered by the states parties of both the ICCJ statute and the enforcement treaty. If a claimant qualified for assistance from the access to justice fund discussed earlier, part of the assistance could include covering the court and administration fees (or the fees could be waived). This would require the ICCJ to develop financial regulations. While such regulations are outside the scope of this chapter, which deals with the questions to be addressed at the treaty level, it is worth noting that there is no shortage of existing systems – including ICSID's – that could be readily adapted to serve the ICCJ.

Conclusion

This premise of this book is that the ICCJ is both desirable and feasible. Therefore, I aim to open academic and policy discussions about how to design an ICCJ and make it a reality. In Chapter 1, I discussed research that suggests that such a wide-ranging debate is a necessary (albeit insufficient) condition for the establishment of a new court. While the complex and serendipitous confluence of global forces necessary for the creation of a new international court cannot be socially engineered, I nonetheless hope that scholars, practitioners, activists, diplomats, and politicians can take action to increase the likelihood and pace of the establishment of the ICCJ.

As I argued throughout the book, I believe that many of the geopolitical factors that presage international institutional change can be found in the context of international civil justice, particularly as it relates to transnational mass torts. Perhaps the most prominent among these is what I call the new transnational litigationscape. MNCs have historically been able to minimize the risk that they would face a trial for cross-border mass torts, much less several trials, a judgment on the merits, or the enforcement of that judgment. That is less true today than it was even a few years ago, and will be even less so a few years from now. One major driver of this change is the increased adoption of collective redress in many jurisdictions coupled with backlash legislation opening up courts in host nations – two very different ways of inviting mass tort litigation into courts of nations that in the past did not have the legal infrastructure to facilitate it. Another is the rise of litigation finance. Litigation funders turn unsophisticated, impecunious one-shotters into sophisticated and well-resourced repeat players. They have deep pockets, an appetite for risk, assets under management that must be deployed, and every incentive to continue to seek out more and more cross-border mass torts. Since litigation financiers build portfolios of cases in order to diversify their risk, there will always be a market for the kind of high-risk/high-reward investment characteristic of cross-border mass torts. The combination of litigation finance, the global expansion of pro-litigation features, the global rise of the class action, and the existence of a global cadre of experienced entrepreneurial lawyers ought to give MNCs pause about the suitability of maintaining the current state of affairs.

Other, broader factors also lead to the conclusion that the time is right for an ICCJ. States' discontent with the current investor-state dispute settlement system is leading to calls for reform. Although that does not bear directly on the question of a forum for cross-border mass torts, it does signal a change in the perceived desirability of investor-only protection that was an acceptable cornerstone of the legal regime governing FDI in the second half of the twentieth century. Increasing populist backlash against FDI has resulted in regimes hostile to MNCs, and even, in some cases, to nationalization. Meanwhile, the discourse on corporate social responsibility has also globalized; it has transformed from a domestic issue to a global one garnering more attention and galvanizing broader audiences.

Despite these incentives, much work remains to be done in order to create the template of a court. The engagement of international civil society will be indispensable. The project of an ICCJ is but one in a whole range of initiatives being pursued by a strong international coalition interested in advancing international civil justice and accountability for MNCs. How the institutional proposal for an ICCJ will interact with substantive proposals being developed is an open and complex question. For instance, what would be the relationship of the effort under way at the UN to "elaborat[e] ... an international legally binding instrument on Transnational Corporations and Other Business Enterprises with respect to human rights"[1] to the law applied by the ICCJ? How would, and how should, the ICCJ integrate with existing efforts to improve business practices such as the Global Compact and the Respect, Protect, and Remedy framework? What specific forms of advocacy would be effective, or ineffective? Which constituencies are crucial to enlist (some, such as victims' groups and coalitions, are obvious candidates; others will be less obvious)? International civil society has the experience and the capacity to help to answer those questions (and others).

Diplomats and politicians, meanwhile, have the capacity to marshal the support of the states they represent. Representatives of government should be involved from an early stage. Participation in the design of a new court has been shown to be linked to the likelihood that states would join it. By participating in the design stages, states are able to develop features of the court that are familiar to them from their own domestic systems (this is part of the reason why international courts, as creatures of multilateral negotiations, have always been "mixed jurisdictions").

> States have several incentives to create international courts in their own legal image to reduce uncertainty in future bargaining situations. Similarly, states that join standing international courts look to the court's rules and procedures in order to assess the ability of the court to be fair and unbiased. The design put into place

by the originators of a new international court influences the level of state support for the court, the design of states' commitments to the court, as well as the ultimate influence of the court on members' behavior.[2]

Uncertainty about how a court will rule in individual cases "is mitigated if the court's rules and procedures are familiar. Furthermore, if states have the ability to forum shop in the process of dispute settlement, then the negotiators of a new court have incentives to lock in an institutional design that will benefit their state in the future."[3] In particular, a concerted effort should be made actively to include representatives of potential holdouts, such as China and the United States.

Much academic work is needed, as well, to flesh out the ideas that underpin the ICCJ and that will inform its design. There are no empirical data on the type and prevalence of cross-border mass torts, either in absolute numbers or in terms of the number of cases filed. More comparative research is needed on forms of aggregate litigation and how different approaches might play out in an international court. The same is true of emerging forms of representative litigation. I have discussed in broad terms the convergence in some areas, and the divergence in others, in the procedures for dealing with group claims. And much literature is devoted to a comparative analysis of those procedures. That literature, however, takes as its starting point the constraints of existing national systems. Research is needed into the related but different questions of precisely how best, given a tabula rasa, to integrate and harmonize those approaches. Similar questions arise when considering the substantive law the ICCJ would apply. Neither the goals of tort law nor its content are universally agreed upon. Which tort concepts would be sticking points in negotiating an ICCJ? Among which constituencies? What is the nature of the disagreements and could they be bridged? Setting aside the nonideal question of achievable agreement, which tort norms *should* an ICCJ incorporate? All these require further examination for viable templates of an ICCJ statute to be developed, circulated, and debated. The academic questions are not only for legal scholars. Scholars of political science and international relations will have much to say. Area specialists, in particular, could contribute nuanced analyses of the likely attitudes of states to this proposal and ways to influence those attitudes. And scholars of institutional design can help illuminate the details of which institutional design features might contribute to an institution that would be most attractive for nations to join as well as most likely to contribute to successful execution of the mission of the ICCJ once established.

The ICCJ will of course not happen tomorrow. Or even the next day. It is nonetheless my hope that the arguments in this book will galvanize a critical mass of readers into thinking it is *possible*. History tells us that when that happens even international courts previously thought implausible can become a reality.

Notes

INTRODUCTION

1 Gwynne L. Skinner, "Beyond Kiobel: Providing Access to Judicial Remedies for Violations of International Human Rights Norms by Transnational Business in a New (Post-Kiobel) World" (2014) 46 *Columbia Human Rights Law Review* 158, 168.
2 Brian Roach, "Corporate Power in a Global Economy" (2007) *Global Development and Environment Institute*, 1, 3–5.
3 See Elisabetta Silvestri, "Cultural Dimensions of Group Litigation: Italy" (2012) Remarks at the International Association of Procedural Law Moscow Conference, p. 3. See also EU Commission, Recommendation of 11 June 2013 on Common Principles for Injunctive and Compensatory Collective Redress Mechanisms in the Member States Concerning Violations of Rights Granted under Union Law (2013/396/EU) Official Journal of the European Union L201/60, explaining the growing need to address mass harm situations.
4 Francesco Francioni, "Access to Justice, Denial of Justice and International Investment Law," in *Human Rights in International Investment Law and Arbitration* (Oxford: Oxford University Press, 2009), p. 63–81.
5 See, e.g., Alexandra Lahav, "Bellwether Trials" (2008) 76 *George Washington Law Review* 576, 577.
6 The three cases are explored at length in Chapter 2.
7 Alien Tort Statute, 28 U.S.C. § 1350 (1789).
8 Michael J. Saks, "Do We Really Know Anything about the Behavior of the Tort Litigation System – and Why Not?" (1992) 140 *University of Pennsylvania Law Review* 1147, 1149.
9 I use the terms "home state" and "host state" as they are used in the international investment literature: "home state" is the (capital exporting) country where the MNC is based; "host state" is the (capital importing) state in which the MNC is engaged in FDI and where most of the mass torts contemplated in this book occur.
10 United Nations Conference on Trade and Development, 24 June 2015, "FDI Outflows, by region and economy," 1990–2014 (the United States accounts for 24.9 percent of FDI outflows).
11 The narrowing of access to justice in the United States, as well as reasons why other fora are not available, is the subject of Chapter 3.

184   Notes to Pages 8–17

12 See Project on International Courts and Tribunals at www.pict-pcti.org/. An international court has the following features: it 1) is established by treaty; 2) applies international law; 3) establishes, *ex ante*, its rules of procedure; 4) has independent judges; 5) hears cases where at least one party is a state or international organization; 6) issues binding judgments; and 7) is a standing (permanent) body. See Cesare Romano, "A Taxonomy of International Rule of Law Institutions" (2011) 2 *Journal of International Dispute Settlement* 241, 261–262, n. 33 and accompanying text. The ICCJ, which will be the first international court that adjudicates private disputes between private parties, will deviate from the fifth criterion.
13 Gary Born, *International Commercial Arbitration* (2nd ed., Alphen aan den Rijn, Netherlands: Kluwer Law International, 2001), p. 7.
14 The Treaty of Amity, Commerce, and Navigation, between His Britannic Majesty and the United States of America (The Jay Treaty), London, Nov. 19, 1794, in force Feb. 29, 1796.
15 For a discussion of these mass claims mechanisms, see generally Lea Brilmayer et al. (eds.), *International Claims Commissions: Righting Wrongs after Conflict* (Cheltenham, UK: Edgar Elgar Publishing, 2017); Howard M. Holtzmann & Edda Kristjánsdóttir (eds.), *International Mass Claims Processes: Legal and Practical Perspectives* (Oxford: Oxford University Press, 2007); and Permanent Court of Arbitration (eds.), *Redressing Injustices through Mass Claims Processes: Innovative Responses to Unique Challenges* (Oxford: Oxford University Press, 2006).
16 Karen J. Alter, *The New Terrain of International Law: Courts, Politics, Rights* (Princeton, NJ: Princeton University Press, 2014), p. 170–171.
17 Convention on the Recognition and Enforcement of Foreign Arbitral Awards, New York, June 10, 1958 in force June 7, 1959.
18 Legal Information Institute, Torts, Wex Legal Dictionary, www.law.cornell.edu/wex/tort. See also American Law Institute, Restatement (Second) of Torts §7.

1 HOW NEW INTERNATIONAL COURTS COME INTO BEING

1 See generally, Karen J. Alter, *The New Terrain of International Law: Courts, Politics, Rights* (Princeton, NJ: Princeton University Press, 2014).
2 The term was coined by Bruce Ackerman to describe changes in American constitutional law. In a history-of-ideas analysis, he explained that major constitutional shifts occur "by crucial historical events which provoke popular efforts to modify, sometimes radically, preexisting starting points: the war for independence or the war between the states or the struggle between capital and labor or the struggle against Nazism and Communism or the struggle for racial equality" are all examples. Bruce Ackerman, "A Generation of Betrayal?" (1997) 65 *Fordham Law Review* 1519, 1519. Shifts "depend[] on the capacity of a political movement to impress its diagnosis of 'the public and its problems' on the ongoing-debate." Ackerman, "A Generation of Betrayal?" p. 1519. The rise of a constitutional moment is a discontinuous event, with each success "preceded by a long period during which movement-activists are hard at work developing their critique of the existing system and organizing their political forces." Ackerman, "A Generation of Betrayal?" p. 1520.
3 Alter, *New Terrain*, p. 22.
4 The Conclusion of the book then offers the outline of such an action plan.
5 Project on International Courts and Tribunals, available at www.pict-pcti.org/.

6 Oona A. Hathaway & Ariel N. Lavinbuk, "Rationalism and Revisionism in International Law" (2006) 119 *Harvard Law Review*, 1404, 1432–1434 and, generally, Harold Hongju Koh, "Why Do Nations Obey International Law?" (1997) 106 *Yale Law Journal*, 2599.
7 See, e.g., G. John Ikenberry, *After Victory: Institutions, Strategic Restraint, and the Rebuilding of Order after Major Wars* (Princeton, NJ: Princeton University Press, 2001); Douglas Lemke, *Regions of War and Peace* (Cambridge: Cambridge University Press, 2002); Eric A. Posner & John C. Yoo, "Judicial Independence in International Tribunals" (2005) 93 *California Law Review*, 1; Jack L. Goldsmith & Eric A. Posner, *The Limits of International Law* (Oxford: Oxford University Press, 2005).
8 Sara McLaughlin Mitchell & Emilia Justyna Powell, *Domestic Law Goes Global: Legal Traditions and International Courts* (Cambridge: Cambridge University Press, 2011), p. 4, referencing Nico Krisch, "International Law in Times of Hegemony: Unequal Power and the Shaping of the International Legal Order" (2005) 16 *European Journal of International Law*, 369.
9 Posner & Yoo, "Judicial Independence in International Tribunals," p. 14.
10 Mitchell & Powell, *Domestic Law Goes Global*, p. 10.
11 Paul K. Huth & Todd L. Allee, *The Democratic Peace and Territorial Conflict in the Twentieth Century* (Cambridge: Cambridge University Press, 2002), p. 164 (blame deflection); Beth A. Simmons, "Capacity, Commitment, and Compliance: International Institutions and Territorial Disputes" (2002) 46 *Journal of Conflict Resolution*, 829, 829–831; and Beth A. Simmons, "Trade and Territorial Conflict in Latin America: International Borders as Institutions," in Miles Kahler & Barbara F. Walter, *Territoriality and Conflict in an Era of Globalization* (Cambridge: Cambridge University Press; 2006) p. 251–287 (economic benefits for delegation of territorial disputes; quantitative evidence); Christina L. Davis, *Why Adjudicate? Enforcing Trade Rules in the WTO* (Princeton, NJ: Princeton University Press, 2012), p. 3. (domestic benefits and economic benefits to the United States from initiating WTO litigation).
12 Mitchell & Powell, *Domestic Law Goes Global*, give the following example: "The British and American governments were extremely reluctant in their support for the creation of the [Permanent Court of International Justice] in comparison to their French and German counterparts," and go on to note that "interestingly, however, the British and American negotiators ... were much more in favor of a court with compulsory jurisdiction." Mitchell & Powell, *Domestic Law Goes Global*, p. 5.
13 Mitchell & Powell, *Domestic Law Goes Global*, p. 5 (referencing Article 220 of the Treaty Establishing the European Community); World Trade Organization Dispute Settlement Understanding, Annex 2, Art. 3(1), p. 354, available at www.wto.org/english/docs_e/legal_e/28-dsu.pdf; General Agreement on Tariffs and Trade, Text of the General Agreement, Geneva, July 1986, available at www.wto.org/english/docs_e/legal_e/gatt47_e.pdf.
14 Alter, *New Terrain*, p. 167–170.
15 Andrew Moravcsik, "The Origins of Human Rights Regimes: Democratic Delegation in Postwar Europe" (2000) 54 *International Organization*, 217, synopsis.
16 See Fernando R. Tesón, "The Kantian Theory of International Law" (1992) 92 *Columbia Law Review*, 53, 75–77; Bruce Russett & John R. Oneal, *Triangulating Peace: Democracy, Interdependence, and International Organizations* (New York: W. W. Norton, 2001); and Anne-Marie Slaughter, "International Law in a World of Liberal States" (1995) 6 *European Journal of International Law*, 503, 503–504.

17 Mitchell & Powell, *Domestic Law Goes Global*, p. 9, referencing Firew Kebede Tiba, "What Caused the Multiplicity of International Courts and Tribunals?" (2006) 10 *Gonzaga Journal of International Law*, 202.
18 Benjamin N. Schiff, *Building the International Criminal Court* (Cambridge: Cambridge University Press, 2008), p. 14–15, citing Martha Finnemore & Kathryn Sikkink, "International Norm Dynamics and Political Change" (1998) 52 *International Organization at Fifty: Exploration and Contestation in the Study of World Politics*, 887. The development of the ICC was marked by "international legal currents [that] were shaped at least partly by conscious efforts of legal practitioners, scholars, politicians, decision makers, and civil society advocates"; Schiff, *Building the International Criminal Court*, p. 14–15, citing Finnemore & Sikkink, "International Norms Dynamics and Political Change," p. 887.
19 Nico Krisch, "International Law in Times of Hegemony: Unequal Power and the Shaping of the International Legal Order" (2005) 16 *European Journal of International Law*, 369, synopsis.
20 Andrew T. Guzman, *How International Law Works: A Rational Choice Theory* (Oxford: Oxford University Press, 2008), p. 41; Beth A. Simmons & Allison Danner, "Credible Commitments and the International Criminal Court" (2010) 64 *International Organization*, 225, 225–256 (seeking to explain why "the states that are both the least and the most vulnerable to the possibility of an ICC case affecting their citizens [] committed most readily to the ICC" by applying credible commitments theory); Laurence R. Helfer & Anne-Marie Slaughter, "Why States Create International Tribunals: A Response to Professors Posner and Yoo" (2005) 93 *California Law Review*, 899, 901 (arguing a "theory of 'constrained independence' in which states establish independent international tribunals to enhance the credibility of their commitments in specific multilateral settings").
21 Andrew Moravcsik, "The Origins of Human Rights Regimes: Democratic Delegation in Postwar Europe" (2000) 54 *International Organization*, 217, 217–220 (empirically testing why, in deviation from Westphalian notions of sovereignty and from liberal ideals of direct democratic legitimacy, nations empower individuals to bring human rights actions against them in supranational (European) courts and concluding that governments of newly established democracies predominantly bind themselves in this way to lock in and consolidate democratic gains. This form of self-binding is most beneficial for newly established democracies who wish to establish the new democratic status quo against nondemocratic threats).
22 Harold Hongju Koh, "Why Do Nations Obey International Law?" (1997) 106 *Yale Law Journal*, 2599, 2364.
23 G. John Ikenberry, *After Victory: Institutions, Strategic Restraint, and the Rebuilding of Order after Major Wars* (Princeton, NJ: Princeton University Press, 2001), p. 244.
24 John C. Coffee Jr., "Class Wars: The Dilemma of the Mass Tort Class Action" (1995) 95 *Columbia Law Review*, 1343, 1344. Going on to note that "recent developments in class action practice bear witness to this phenomenon," and citing evolutionary theory which explains evolution "as characterized by 'punctuated equilibria': long periods of stasis interrupted by events causing rapid change." Coffee, "Class Wars," p. 1344.
25 See generally Alter, *New Terrain* (classifying and characterizing international courts as "old style" versus "new style" and explaining the contemporary shift from the former to the latter). The old style courts are voluntary interstate dispute settlement courts.
26 Alter, *New Terrain*, p. 154.

27 Alter, *New Terrain*, p. 154.
28 Alter, *New Terrain*, p. 155.
29 Alter, *New Terrain*, p. 155; see also John Williamson, "A Short History of the Washington Consensus" (2009) 15 *Law & Business Review of the America*, 7; Rome Statute of the International Criminal Court, Rome (July 17, 1998); and United Nations, "Millennium Developmental Goals and Beyond 2015" available at www.un.org/millenniumgoals/.
30 Alter, *New Terrain*, p. 156.
31 Alter, *New Terrain*, p. 157.
32 As discussed later, pinpointing the moment an idea "first" emerged is a matter of debate and a few "first moments" can be selected when describing the emergence of the idea of international criminal court(s). On the history of the establishment of the ICC see, e.g., John P. Cerone, "Dynamic Equilibrium: The Evolution of U.S. Attitudes toward International Criminal Courts and Tribunals" (2007) 18 *European Journal of International Law*, 277; Cesare P. R. Romano (ed.), *The Sword and the Scales: The United States and International Courts and Tribunals* (Cambridge: Cambridge University Press, 2009); William A. Schabas, *An Introduction to the International Criminal Court* (Cambridge: Cambridge University Press, 2011); Mark J. Osiel, "The Demise of International Criminal Law," (2014) *Humanity Journal*; Schiff, *Building the International Criminal Court*.
33 Rome Statute.
34 Schiff, *Building the International Criminal Court*, p. 89.
35 Schiff, *Building the International Criminal Court*, pp. 89–90 (noting that realist explanations for the creation of new international organizations tend to be circular: "If states get together to sign a treaty creating a new organization, by definition it must be in their interests to do so").
36 See Convention for the Creation of an International Criminal Court, opened for signature 16 November 1937, available at http://biblio-archive.unog.ch/Dateien/CouncilMSD/C-547(1)-M-384(1)-1937-V_BI.pdf. Many excellent histories of international humanitarian law, the law of war, and international law of war exist. Among them are John Carey, et al., *International Humanitarian Law: Prospects* (Leiden: Brill, 2006); Peter H. Maguire, *Law & War: International Law and American History* (New York: Columbia University Press, 2010). Unless otherwise noted, the historical account herein in based on Schiff, *Building the International Criminal Court*.
37 Schiff, *Building the International Criminal Court*, p. 24.
38 See UN Secretary General, "Historical Survey of the Question of International Criminal Jurisdiction," UN General Assembly Law Commission, New York, 1949.
39 See R. John Pritchard, *The Tokyo Major War Crimes Trial: The Transcripts of the Court Proceedings of the International Military Tribunal for the Far East* (Lewiston, NY: Mellen Press, 1998).
40 William Schabas, *An Introduction to the International Criminal Court* (Cambridge: Cambridge University Press, 2001), p. 27.
41 Cesare P. R. Romano, et al. (eds.), *Internationalized Criminal Courts: Sierra Leone, East Timor, Kosovo, and Cambodia* (Oxford: Oxford University Press, 2004), pp. 15–16.
42 Ruti G. Teitel, "Transitional Justice Genealogy (Symposium: Human Rights in Transition)" (2003) 16 *Harvard Human Rights Journal*, 69.
43 Schiff, *Building the International Criminal Court*, p. 39. For an elaborate, step-by-step account of the development of the Rome Statute drafts, see Schiff, *Building the International Criminal Court*, pp. 68–72.

44 Schiff, *Building the International Court*, p. 29. See also Schabas, *An Introduction to the International Criminal Court*, pp. 10–16.
45 Antonio Cassese, "On the Current Trends towards Criminal Prosecution and Punishment of Breaches of International Humanitarian Law" (1998) 9 *European Journal of International Law*, 2.
46 Robert E. Hudec, "GATT Dispute Settlement after the Tokyo Round: An Unfinished Business" (1980) 13 *Cornell International Law Journal*, 145, 151–152.
47 Robert E. Hudec, "GATT Dispute Settlement," p. 151.
48 William J. Davey, "John Jackson and WTO Dispute Settlement," (2016) 15(3) *World Trade Review*, 404, 404.
49 Joel P. Trachtman (ed.), *Developing Countries in the GATT/WTO Legal System*, 'Biographical Note' (Aldershot: Gower, 1987), p. 8, available at http://law-prdweb.law.umn.edu/uploads/hy/Jz/hyJzgIiHRF7Q3VUx-XRBZQ/wto-trachtman.pdf.
50 Trachtman, Developing Countries in the GATT/WTO Legal System, p. 8. See also Daniel L.M. Kennedy & James D. Southwick (eds.), *The Political Economy of International Trade Law: Essays in Honor of Robert E. Hudec* (Cambridge: Cambridge University Press, 2002); Ricardo Ramirez, "Professor Hudec and the Appellate Body" (2011) 20 *Minnesota Journal of International Law*, 265; John H. Jackson, et al., "Tribute to Robert Hudec" (2003) 6 *Journal of International Economic Law*, 729.
51 Charles N. Brower & Jason D. Brueschke, *The Iran–United States Claims Tribunal* (The Hague: Martinus Nijhoff, 1998), p. 4.
52 See United States Department of State, "U.S. Relations with Iran" Fact Sheet (April 28, 2017), available at www.state.gov/r/pa/ei/bgn/5314.htm.
53 Brower & Brueschke, *Iran–United States Claims Tribunal*, pp. 4–5.
54 See Executive Order No. 12,170 (Nov. 14, 1979) reprinted in 44 Federal Register 65,729 (1979); Iranian Assets Control Regulations, 31 C.F.R. § 535.201 (1980).
55 Brower & Brueschke, *Iran–United States Claims Tribunal*, p. 6 (quoting 31 C.F.R. § 535.504(a), (b)(1) (1980).
56 Brower & Brueschke, *Iran–United States Claims Tribunal*, p. 6.
57 The asset freeze was effectuated by the president exercising powers authorized under the International Emergency Economic Powers Act (IEEPA) Pub. L. No. 95–223, 91 Stat. 1626 (1977) (codified at 50 U.S.C. § 1701 (Supp. III 1979), and the National Emergencies Act, Pub. L. No. 94–412, 90 Stat. 1225 (1976) ((codified as 50 U.S.C. § 1601 (1976)).
58 The Algiers Accords comprised two "Declarations" by the Government of Algeria and five "Technical Agreements." Respectively, the Declaration of the Government of the Democratic and Popular Republic of Algeria (19 Jan. 1981) [hereinafter: the "General Declaration"] (providing for the release of the hostages in return for various actions and undertakings by the U.S. including the nullification of the judicial attachment orders and the return of the frozen assets) and the Declaration of the Government of the Democratic and Popular Republic of Algeria Concerning the Settlement of Claims by the Government of the United States of America and the Government of the Islamic Republic of Iran (19 Jan. 1981) [hereinafter: the "Claims Settlement Declaration"].
59 Executive Order No. 12,294 (Feb. 24, 1981), 14 Fed. Reg. 14, 111 (1981). Implementing regulations were published at 46 Fed. Reg. 14,330–337 (Feb. 1981) codified at 30 1 C.F.R. Part 535.
60 Brower & Brueschke, *Iran–United States Claims Tribunal*, pp. 7–8.
61 See Claims Settlement Declaration, Art. II; and General Declaration, para. 2.

62 See General Declaration, paras. 6–7.
63 Rudolf Dolzer, "Mixed Claims Commissions," in *Max Planck Encyclopedia of Public International Law* (Oxford: Oxford University Press, 2011), para. 1.
64 Rudolf Dozer, "Mixed Claims Commissions," para. 6 (citing Alexander Marie Stuyt, *Survey of International Arbitrations, 1794–1989* [The Hague: Martinus Nijhoff, 1990]).
65 Claims Convention, Art. 6, México, Jan. 30, 1843, in force March 29, 1843, available at www.loc.gov/law/help/us-treaties/bevans/b-mx-ust000009-0788.pdf.
66 Treaty Guadalupe Hidalgo, Art. XV (2 Feb. 1848), available at http://avalon.law.yale.edu/19th_century/guadhida.asp.
67 McLane–Ocampo Treaty, Art. X (1859). See "Our Relations with Mexico: Text of the McLane–Ocampo Treaty," *New York Times* (15 Feb. 1860).
68 Claims Convention, Washington D.C., 4 July 1868, in force Feb. 1, 1869, Preamble, available at www.loc.gov/law/help/us-treaties/bevans/b-mx-ust000009-0826.pdf.
69 General Claims Convention, Washington D.C., 8 Sept. 1923 in force March 1, 1924, available at www.loc.gov/law/help/us-treaties/bevans/b-mx-ust000009-0935.pdf.
70 Special Claims Convention, Art. 1, México, 10 Sept. 1923, in force 19 Feb. 1924, available at www.loc.gov/law/help/us-treaties/bevans/b-mx-ust000009-0941.pdf.
71 See Louis W. McKernan, "Special Mexican Claims" (1938) 32 *American Journal of International Law*, 457, 457.
72 See Final Settlement of Certain Claims Convention, Washington D.C., 19 Nov. 1941, in force April 2, 1942, available at www.loc.gov/law/help/us-treaties/bevans/b-mx-ust000009-1059.pdf.
73 Dolzer, "Mixed Claims Commissions"; United Nations, "Reports of International Arbitral Awards" (2006) available at http://legal.un.org/riaa/cases/vol_VII/1–391.pdf.
74 Burns H. Weston et al. (eds.), *International Claims: Their Settlement by Lump Sum Agreements, 1975–1995* (Leiden: Brill, 1999), p. vii.
75 David D. Caron, "International Claims and Compensation Bodies," in *The Oxford Handbook of International Adjudication* (Oxford: Oxford University Press, 2013), n. 16 (citing Brower & Brueschke, *Iran–United States Claims Tribunal*, p. 669; David D. Caron & John R. Crook (eds.), *The Iran–United States Claims Tribunal and the Process of International Claims* (Ardsley, NY: Transnational 2000), p. 363.
76 *Dames & Moore v. Reagan*, 453 U.S. 654 (1981).
77 Justices Burger, Brennan, Stewart, White, Marshall, and Blackmun joining and Justices Powell and Stevens joined in pertinent part.
78 *Dames & Moore*, 453 U.S. 654, 673 (1981) (internal quotation marks omitted) citing *Propper v. Clark*, 337 U.S. 472, 493 (1949).
79 *Dames & Moore*, 453 U.S. 654, 674 (1981) (*quoting Youngstown Sheet & Tube Co. v. Sawyer*, 343 U.S. 579, 637 (1952)).
80 *Dames & Moore*, 453 U.S. 654, 687 (1981) (going on to note that "although being overly sanguine about the chances of United States claimants before the Claims Tribunal would require a degree of naiveté which should not be demanded even of judges").
81 Rahmatullah Khan, *The Iran–United States Claims Tribunals: Controversies, Cases and Contribution* (The Hague: Martinus Nijhoff, 1990).
82 Some believed that the Algiers Accords were illegal, having been procured through the use of force. "I really don't know of any civilized nation that honours an agreement to pay hostage-taker or kidnapper for release of hostages." Professor Hans Smit quoted in Khan, *Iran–United States Claims Tribunals*, p. 24.

83 Khan, *Iran–United States Claims Tribunal*, p. 41.
84 9 May 2016 Communiqué regarding the work of the Tribunal, IUSCT official website, available at www.iusct.net/General%20Documents/Communique%2016.1%20(9%20May%202016).pdf.
85 This episode, which presented the greatest practical and legitimacy-based challenge for the tribunal, is recounted from an American perspective by Judge Brower, Brower & Brueschke, *Iran–United States Claims Tribunal*, p. 662, and from an Iranian perspective by Khan, *Iran–United States Claims Tribunals*, pp. 61–77.
86 Brower & Brueschke, *Iran–United States Claims Tribunal*, p. 657.
87 See discussion of the Gulf Coast Claims Facility in the introduction, p. [5–4].
88 Tamar Meshel, "The Jerusalem Arbitration Center – a New Form of Dispute Resolution in the Middle East," *Young Canadian Arbitration Practitioners Newsletter*, 2012.
89 I was an adviser to the founders of the JAC and was appointed as one of nine members of the inaugural bench of its court. The account herein is based on my personal observations. The Rules of the JAC are available at www.jac-adr.com/rules-of-arbitration.html and its mission is described at www.jac-adr.com/about-us.html.
90 The writing on the histories and ideologies of both are legion and impossible to survey fully here. Examples include the following: Oona A. Hathaway & Harold Hongju Koh (eds.), *Foundations of International Law and Politics* (Durham, NC: Carolina Academic Press, 2005) (providing an overview of the leading theories of international law and politics). The seminal realist texts include Hans J. Morgenthau, *Politics among Nations: The Struggle for Power and Peace* (2nd ed., New York: Knopf, 1954); Thomas C. Schelling, *The Strategy of Conflict* (Cambridge, MA: Harvard University Press, 1960), p. 960; Kenneth N. Waltz, *Theory of International Politics* (New York: McGraw-Hill, 1979). The origins of institutionalism can be traced back to the writings of Immanuel Kant, *Perpetual Peace: A Philosophical Essay*, M. Campbell Smith (trans.) & A. Robert Caponigri (ed.) (New York: Liberal Arts Press, 1948). Contemporary writings include Robert O. Keohane, *After Hegemony: Cooperation and Discord in the World Political Economy* (Princeton, NJ: Princeton University Press, 1984); Thomas M. Franck & Jerome M. Lehrman, "Messianism and Chauvinism in America's Commitment to Peace through Law," in Lori F. Damrosch (ed.), *The International Court of Justice at a Crossroads* (Dobbs Ferry, NY: Transnational, 1987), p. 3.
91 Romano, *Sword and the Scales*, p. xviii.
92 Romano, *Sword and the Scales*, pp. xiii–xiv. See also Mary Ellen O'Connell, "Arbitration and Avoidance of War: The Nineteenth-Century American Vision," in Romano, *Sword and the Scales*, p. 30 (describing American attitudes toward international arbitration from 1776 to the early twentieth century. Also describing how with the rise of American power in the early twentieth century, support for international arbitration gave way to support for other forms of peaceful dispute resolution including the United Nations and the ICJ).
93 Romano, *Sword and the Scales*, p. xiv.
94 Alter, *New Terrain*, p. 158.
95 See Steven Kull & Clay Ramsay, "American Public Opinion on International Courts and Tribunals," in Romano, *Sword and the Scales*, pp. 20–27.
96 Kull & Ramsay, "American Public Opinion," pp. 13, 20–27 (reviewing public opinion polls taken since the 1940s and reporting their original findings from "the most comprehensive examination ever conducted of American public attitudes toward international tribunals").

97 Kull & Ramsay, "American Public Opinion," pp. 13, 19–20.
98 Kull & Ramsay, "American Public Opinion," p. 16.
99 Kull & Ramsay, "American Public Opinion," p. 20. Respondents were presented with a general question on international adjudication as well as with eight hypotheticals relating to specific types of disputes. And respondents were presented with pros and cons for each before responding. Kull & Ramsay, "American Public Opinion," pp. 20–24.
100 Kull & Ramsay, "American Public Opinion," p. 21. (The one case where support fell below 64 percent related to preferential trade treatment. The authors noted generally that "arguments against international adjudication, however, held some sway, which suggests that Americans acknowledge there are some costs and risks associated with it." Kull & Ramsay, "American Public Opinion," p. 20. Other relevant findings include the findings that 87 percent of Republicans and 92 percent of Democrats supported the United States' being part of "treaties that establish standards for protecting the human rights of their citizens," Kull & Ramsay, "American Public Opinion," p. 21; that 85 percent found convincing the argument that "it is much easier for the U.S. to pursue its interests if the world is a place where countries are resolving disputes peacefully in accordance with international law," Kull & Ramsay, "American Public Opinion," pp. 21–22; 78 percent concurred that it is "better for the U.S. to generally use international courts to resolve its disputes with other countries than to allow some disputes to escalate to destructive levels" even if it may "lose a case from time to time," Kull & Ramsay, "American Public Opinion," p. 22. The weakest argument, which met with only 48 percent approval, was the exceptionalist argument that "because the United States is the most powerful country in the world, it has the means to get its way in international disputes [and therefore] it has nothing to gain from submitting to the jurisdiction of international courts, where its arguments are put on the same footing as those of weaker countries," Kull & Ramsay, "American Public Opinion," pp. 22–23.
101 Simon Chesterman, "Asia's Ambivalence about International Law and Institutions: Past, Present and Futures" (2016) 27 *European Journal of International Law*, 945, 957–960.
102 Of the ninety-eight Chinese companies on *Fortune*'s Global 500 list for 2015, only twenty-two were private. Scott Cendrowski, "China's Global 500 Companies Are Bigger Than Ever – and Mostly State-Owned," (July 22, 2015), available at www.fortune.com/2015/07/22/china-global-500-government-owned/.
103 Regarding China's outbound direct investment, see Ministry of Commerce, National Bureau of Statistics, State Administration of Foreign Exchange, China's Foreign Direct Investment Statistics for 2015 (Sept. 22, 2016) (in the original Chinese, translated with Google Translate), available at http://fec.mofcom.gov.cn/article/tjsj/tjgb/201609/20160901399223.shtml. Regarding the comparison with inbound FDI, see KPMG, GCP News Alert: "China ODI Exceeded FDI in 2015 for the First Time, Led by the Private Sector," (29 Sept. 2016) available at (https://assets.kpmg.com/content/dam/kpmg/cn/pdf/en/2016/09/china-odi-exceeded-fdi-2015-private-sector.pdf).
104 The Bank of Finland Institute for Economies in Transition, FDI spending of Chinese firms hit record in 2016 (Feb. 17, 2017), available at www.bofit.fi/en/monitoring/weekly/2017/vw201707_4/.
105 Don Weinland, "China Trade Flows Threatened by Capital Flight Battle," *Financial Times* (Jan. 24, 2017).

106 Xiaohong Xia, "Implementation of the New York Convention in China," (2011) 1 *International Commercial Arbitration Brief*, pp. 20–24, available at http://digitalcommons.wcl.american.edu/cgi/viewcontent.cgi?article=1009&context=ab
107 International Centre for Settlement of Investment Disputes, Washington, DC, Convention Art. 54(1) (1965).
108 United Nations Conference on Trade and Development, 2005, "Investor-State Disputes Arising from Investment Treaties: A Review" pp. 4–5; Julie A. Kim, "A Standard Public Order Treaty Carve-Out as a Means for Balancing Regulatory Interests in International Investment Agreements," *Seoul National University* (Feb. 2017), p. 21.
109 *Ansung Housing Co, Ltd v. People's Republic of China* (ICSID Case No. ARB/14/25).
110 *Ekran Berhad v. People's Republic of China* (ICSID Case No. ARB/11/15).
111 Ann Kent, "China's Participation in International Organisations," in Yongjin Zhang and Greg Austin (eds.), *Power and Responsibility in Chinese Foreign Policy* (Acton: ANU Press 2014), p. 141.
112 Gus Van Harten, *Investment Treaty Arbitration and Public Law* (Oxford Scholarship Online 2008), pp. 4–5.
113 See Attila Tanzi, et al. (eds.), *International Investment Law in Latin America: Problems and Prospects* (Leiden: Brill, 2016), p. 97; See also Catharine Titi, "Investment Arbitration in Latin America: The Uncertain Veracity of Preconceived Ideas," 30 *Arbitration International*, 357 (2014).
114 On the initiative of the European Commission to create a Multilateral Investment Court to replace the existing ad hoc system (but that would not, in its current version, permit host state nationals to bring claims against investors) see Athina Fouchard Papaefstratiou, "TTIP: The French Proposal for a Permanent European Court for Investment Arbitration," Kluwer Arbitration Blog (July 22, 2015), available at www.kluwerarbitrationblog.com/2015/07/22/ttip-the-french-proposal-for-a-permanent-european-court-for-investment-arbitration/. See also Elizabeth Warren, "The Trans-Pacific Partnership Clause Everyone Should Oppose," *Washington Post* (Feb. 25, 2015).
115 European Commission, Consumer Affairs, "Collective Redress Studies," (Dec. 4, 2013), available at www.ec.europa.eu/consumers/archive/redress_cons/collective_redress_en.htm#Studies
116 Deborah Hensler, "The Globalization of Class Actions," *The Annals of the American Academy of Political and Social Science* (2009), p. 10; Deborah R. Hensler, Christopher Hodges, and Ianika Tzankova (eds.), *Class Actions in Context: How Culture, Economics, and Politics Shape Collective Litigation* (Cheltenham: Edward Elgar, 2016).
117 See United Nations Human Rights Council, Resolution A/HRC/RES/26/9 (calling for the creation of a working group to develop binding international law governing the conduct of Multinational Enterprises); see also United Nations Human Rights Council, "Open-Ended Intergovernmental Working Group on Transnational Corporations and Other Business Enterprises with Respect to Human Rights," available at www.ohchr.org/EN/HRBodies/HRC/WGTransCorp/Pages/IGWGOnTNC.aspx.
118 See Chapter 3; Kevin T. Jackson,"A Cosmopolitan Court for Transnational Corporate Wrongdoing: Why Its Time Has Come" (1998) 17 *Journal of Business Ethics*, 757. Stuart Bruce, "The Project for an International Environmental Court," in Christian Tomuschat, Riccardo Pisillo Mazzeschi, and Daniel Thürer (eds.), *Conciliation in International Law* (Leiden: Brill, 2017), pp. 133–136.

119 Mark L. Wolf, "The Case for an International Anti-Corruption Court," *Brookings Institution* (July 2014), available at www.brookings.edu/wp-content/uploads/2016/06/AntiCorruptionCourtWolfFinal.pdf.
120 Tom Lantos, "Human Rights Commission Briefing: An International Anti-Corruption Court (IACC) to Mitigate Grand Corruption and Human Rights Abuses," *Human Rights Watch* (Nov. 13, 2014), available at www.hrw.org/news/2014/11/13/tom-lantos-human-rights-commission-briefing-international-anti-corruption-court-iacc.
121 Kateryna Kapliuk, "Experts Call for International Cooperation in Fighting Corruption,"*International Anti-Corruption Conference* (Dec. 3, 2016), available at www.iaccseries.org/blog/experts-call-for-international-cooperation-in-fighting-corruption/.

2 THE HUMAN TOLL

1 The absence of systemic data about transnational mass tort is, in turn, similar to the absence of data about torts more generally. "Much of what we think we know about the behavior of the tort litigation system is untrue, unknown, or unknowable… Students of legal policy face an intellectual challenge comparable to that encountered by paleontologists and archaeologists. On the evidence of a few bones, a whole dinosaur must be extrapolated." Michael J. Saks, "Do We Really Know Anything about the Behavior of the Tort Litigation System – and Why Not?" (1992) 140 *University of Pennsylvania Law Review*, 1147, 1149.
2 An overview of the empirical literature examining the underclaiming thesis was first proposed by Richard L. Abel, "The Real Tort Crisis – Too Few Claims" (1987) 48 *Ohio State Law Journal*, 443, discussed in Nora Freeman Engstrom's review of David M. Engel, "The Myth of the Litigious Society: Why We Don't Sue" (2017), available at https://torts.jotwell.com/iso-the-missing-plaintiff/. ("Using a number of methodologies, these researchers have, again and again, confirmed Abel's basic empirical premise. In most areas of the tort law ecosystem, only a small fraction of Americans seek compensation, even following negligently inflicted injury.") A classic law and economics analysis of the suboptimal levels of litigation is Steven Shavell's "The Fundamental Divergence between the Private and the Social Motive to Use the Legal System" (1997) 26 *Journal of Legal Studies*, 575.
3 Eric Helland, Jonathan Klick, & Alexander Tabarrok, "Data Watch: Tort-uring the Data" (2005) 19(2) *Journal of Economic Perspectives*, 207, 207–208 ("We know very little about the number of incidents that give rise to torts… We know something about cases that are filed, but very little about the cases that are dropped and very little about cases that are settled… Most of the data on torts has not been collected for research purposes and so analysis often requires cobbling together information from several incomplete sources").
4 See "Final Decisions in Alien Tort Statute Cases Pending at Time of Kiobel Decision," *Institute for Legal Reform* (Feb. 2016), available at www.instituteforlegalreform.com/uploads/sites/1/Chart_of_Final_Decisions_in_Alien_Tort_Statute_Cases_Pending_at_Time_of_Kiobel_Decision.pdf.
5 See Roger P. Alford, "The Future of Human Rights Litigation after Kiobel" (2014) 89 *Notre Dame Law Review*, 1749, 1751–52.
6 Case Database, *OECD Watch*, available at www.oecdwatch.org/cases.
7 Respectively, *Friends of the Earth Japan and WALHI vs. Marubeni and JERA* (23 May 2017); *European Center for Constitutional and Human Rights vs. TÜV Rheinland AG*

(2 May 2016); *Equitable Cambodia and Inclusive Development International vs. Australia and New Zealand Banking Group* (6 Oct. 2014).
8. Deborah R. Hensler & Mark A. Peterson, "Understanding Mass Personal Injury Litigation: A Socio-Legal Analysis" (1995) 59 *Brooklyn Law Review*, 961, 965 (listing an interdependence of claim value as a third characteristic of mass torts).
9. These are discussed in more detail in Chapter 5.
10. Amended and Consolidated Complaint, *In re Union Carbide Corp. Gas Plant Disaster at Bhopal, India in Dec., 1984*, 634 F. Supp. 842, 852 (S.D.N.Y. 1986), aff'd as modified, 809 F.2d 195 (2d Cir. 1987) at para. 16, reproduced in Baxi & Paul, *Mass Disasters and Multinational Liability*, p. 151; Pico Iyer, "India's Night of Death," *Time Magazine* (Dec. 17, 1984), available at http://content.time.com/time/magazine/article/0,9171,923797,00.html.
11. Amrit Dhillon, "Forgotten but Not Gone," *Jerusalem Post* (Dec. 27, 2002).
12. Dhillon, "Forgotten but Not Gone."
13. Dhillon, "Forgotten but Not Gone."
14. Sanjoy Hazarika, "As Death Toll Climbs, India Now Fears Epidemic," *New York Times* (6 Dec. 1984).
15. Iyer, "India's Night of Death."
16. Iyer, "India's Night of Death."
17. Iyer, "India's Night of Death."
18. Dhillon, "Forgotten but Not Gone."
19. Iyer, "India's Night of Death."
20. *In re Union Carbide Corp.*, 634 F. Supp. 842, 844 (S.D.N.Y. 1986).
21. Lydia Polgreen & Hari Kumar, "8 Former Executives Guilty in '84 Bhopal Chemical Leak," *New York Times* (7 June 2010). The official Government of India numbers are more than 3,000 initial deaths between December 3 and 6, 1984, and 15,000 deaths and nearly 600,000 affected as of 2010. (It appears that the Government of India has not updated the estimates since 2010.) See "Bhopal: India Wants Compensation Doubled," *BBC News* (3 Dec. 2010).
22. Dinesh C. Sharma, "Bhopal: 20 Years On," *Lancet* (8 Jan. 2005)."
23. Government of Madhya Pradesh, Bhopal Gas Tragedy Relief and Rehabilitation Department, "Facts & Figures," available at http://archive.is/LbtR.
24. Amended and Consolidated Complaint, para. 45, reproduced in Upendra Baxi & Thomas Paul, *Mass Disasters and Multinational Liability: The Bhopal Case* (New Delhi: Indian Law Institute, 1986), p. 155; Edward Broughton, "The Bhopal Disaster and Its Aftermath: A Review," Environmental Health: A Global Access Science Source (10 May 2005), available at www.ncbi.nlm.nih.gov/pmc/articles/PMC1142333/; Dhillon, "Forgotten but Not Gone."
25. Baxi & Paul, *Mass Disasters and Multinational Liability*, p. ii, n.4 (citing approximately $4 billion USD in economic loss and $10–15 billion USD in noneconomic loss, respectively, more than $9 billion USD and $24–35 billion USD in today's dollars); James B. Stewart, "Legal Liability: Why Suits for Damages Such as Bhopal Claims Are Very Rare in India," *Wall Street Journal* (23 Jan. 1985) ("seeking billions of dollars"); in an early-filed suit in Charleston, West Virginia, American lawyers claimed $15 billion USD ($35 billion USD in today's dollars), according to Iyer, "India's Night of Death."
26. Broughton, "Bhopal Disaster and Its Aftermath."
27. Upendra Baxi & Amita Dhanda, *Valiant Victims and Lethal Litigation* (New Delhi: Indian Law Institute, 1990), p. xii.

28 Ingrid Eckerman, *The Bhopal Saga: Causes and Consequences of the World's Largest Industrial Disaster* (India: Universities Press, 2005), p. 39.
29 Iyer, "India's Night of Death."
30 *In re Union Carbide Corp. Gas Plant Disaster at Bhopal, India in Dec.*, 1984, 809 F.2d 195, 200 (2d Cir. 1987).
31 Union of India Complaint, *In re Union Carbide Corp.*, 634 F. Supp. 842, 852 (S.D.N.Y. 1986), at paras. 30, 34, reproduced in Baxi & Paul, *Mass Disasters and Multinational Liability*, pp. 6–7 (as well as nuisance and ultrahazardous activity). See id. at paras. 20, 22 reproduced in Baxi & Paul, *Mass Disasters and Multinational Liability*, pp. 4–5.
32 Union of India Complaint, paras. 10–11, reproduced in Baxi & Paul, *Mass Disasters and Multinational Liability*, p. 3–6; see also Baxi & Dhanda, *Valiant Victims*, p. 4.
33 Union of India Complaint, para. 29, reproduced in Baxi & Paul, *Mass Disasters and Multinational Liability*, p. 6.
34 Dhillon, "Forgotten but Not Gone."
35 Bhopal Gas Leak Disaster (Processing of Claims) Act 1985 (21 of 1985); Baxi & Paul, *Mass Disasters and Multinational Liability*, p. ii.
36 *In re Union Carbide Corp.*, 634 F. Supp. 842, 845 (S.D.N.Y. 1986).
37 *In re Union Carbide Corp.*, 809 F.2d 195, 198 (2d Cir. 1987).
38 *In re Air Crash Disaster Near Bombay*, 531 F. Supp. 1175, 1176 (1982).
39 *In re Air Crash Disaster*, 531 F. Supp. 1175, 1181 (the other reason for the unavailability of Indian courts was that under Indian law the relevant statute of limitations would have run).
40 *In re Union Carbide Corp.*, 634 F. Supp. 842, 848 (S.D.N.Y. 1986) (internal quotation marks and citations omitted).
41 *In re Union Carbide Corp.*, 634 F. Supp. 842, 852 (S.D.N.Y. 1986).
42 *In re Union Carbide Corp.*, 634 F. Supp. 842, 867 (S.D.N.Y. 1986).
43 *In re Union Carbide Corp.*, 809 F.2d 195, 201 (2d Cir. 1987).
44 *In re Union Carbide Corp.*, 809 F.2d 195, 201–202 (2d Cir. 1987).
45 *In re Union Carbide Corp.*, 809 F.2d 195, 202–06 (2d Cir. 1987).
46 In describing *forum non conveniens*, the Union Carbide court recapped the two leading cases: *Gulf Oil Corp. v. Gilbert*, 330 U.S. 501 (1947) and *Piper Aircraft Co. v. Reyno*, 454 U.S. 235 (1981).
47 *In re Union Carbide Corp.*, 634 F. Supp. 842, 846 (S.D.N.Y. 1986) (quoting *Piper Aircraft Co.*, 454 U.S. 235, 264 (1981)).
48 *In re Union Carbide Corp.*, 634 F. Supp. 842, 846 (S.D.N.Y. 1986) (quoting *Piper Aircraft Co.*, 454 U.S. 235, 264 (1981)).
49 See generally *Gulf Oil Corp.*, 330 U.S. 501, 508 (1947); *Piper Aircraft Co.*, 454 U.S. 235 (1981).
50 *In re Union Carbide Corp.*, 634 F. Supp. 842, 847–851 (S.D.N.Y. 1986) (citing Marc Galanter's Affidavit). Galanter is an Indian law scholar. See generally, Marc Galanter, "Bhopal's Past and Present: The Changing Legal Response to Mass Disaster" (1990) 10 *Windsor Yearbook of Access to Justice*, 151; Marc Galanter, "The Transnational Traffic in Legal Remedies," in Sheila Jasanoff (ed.), *Learning from Disaster: Risk Management after Bhopal* (Philadelphia: University of Pennsylvania Press, 1994), pp.133–157.
51 James B. Stewart, "Legal Liability: Why Suits for Damages Such as Bhopal Claims are Very Rare in India," *Wall Street Journal* (23 Jan. 1985).
52 Stewart, "Legal Liability."

53 Stewart, "Legal Liability" (internal quotation marks omitted).
54 Stewart, "Legal Liability."
55 Baxi & Paul, *Mass Disasters and Multinational Liability*, pp. iii–iv (the authors detail, inter alia, the different views of Indian jurists supporting and opposing litigation in the United States).
56 Stewart, "Legal Liability."
57 Stewart, "Legal Liability."
58 *In re Union Carbide Corp.*, 634 F. Supp. 842, 849 (S.D.N.Y. 1986).
59 *In re Union Carbide Corp.*, 634 F. Supp. 842, 849 (S.D.N.Y. 1986).
60 Stewart, "Legal Liability."
61 Ironically, "the delay stems in part from the Indian reverence for due process. An unlimited number of issues may be appealed at almost any point in a proceeding. Judges routinely grant lawyers' requests for delays, for fear of denying litigants their rights. Oral arguments, subject to strict time limits in the U.S., often continue for days; Mr. Chandrachud says he is currently hearing an argument that has already taken three months. Elaborately written opinions, 1,500 pages in a recent important case, sometimes appear years after an argument." Stewart, "Legal Liability."
62 Stewart, "Legal Liability." For a general discussion of contemporary corruption in courts of low-income nations, see Chapter 4.
63 *In re Union Carbide Corp.*, 634 F. Supp. 842, 851 (S.D.N.Y. 1986).
64 *In re Union Carbide Corp.*, 634 F. Supp. 842, 852 (S.D.N.Y. 1986).
65 *In re Union Carbide Corp.*, 809 F.2d 195, 202 (2d Cir. 1987).
66 *In re Union Carbide Corp.*, 809 F.2d 195, 205 (2d Cir. 1987).
67 *In re Union Carbide Corp.*, 809 F.2d 195, 205 (2d Cir. 1987).
68 Baxi & Dhanda, *Valiant Victims*, pp. 527–529.
69 Supreme Court of India Settlement Order 15 Feb. 1989 in Baxi & Dhanda, *Valiant Victims*, p. 529.
70 State of Alaska, 'Details about the Accident', available at www.evostc.state.ak.us/index.cfm?FA=facts.details; State of Alaska, 'Settlement', available at www.evostc.state.ak.us/index.cfm?FA=facts.settlement.
71 Dhillon, "Forgotten but Not Gone."
72 See Dhillon, "Forgotten but Not Gone."
73 Broughton, "Bhopal Disaster and Its Aftermath."
74 Baxi & Dhanda, *Valiant Victims*, p. lv.
75 Government of Madhya Pradesh, Bhopal Gas Tragedy Relief and Rehabilitation Department, "Facts and Figures," available at http://archive.is/LbtR.
76 Plaintiffs' Memorandum of law in opposition to Union Carbide Corp.'s motion to dismiss these actions on the grounds of Forum Non Conveniens, reproduced in Baxi & Paul, *Mass Disasters and Multinational Liability*, p. 80.
77 Baxi & Paul, *Mass Disasters and Multinational Liability*, p. viii.
78 *In re Union Carbide Corp.*, 634 F. Supp. 842, 866 (S.D.N.Y. 1986).
79 *In re Union Carbide Corp.*, 634 F. Supp. 842, 867 (S.D.N.Y. 1986).
80 Kate Miles, *The Origins of International Investment Law: Empire, Environment and the Safeguarding of Capital* (Cambridge: Cambridge University Press, 2013), pp. 153–154.
81 Stewart, "Legal Liability."
82 *In re Union Carbide Corp.*, 634 F. Supp. 842, 201 (S.D.N.Y. 1986).

Notes to Pages 59–61

83 *In re Union Carbide Corp.*, 809 F.2d 195, 198 (2d Cir. 1987).
84 Vladimir R. Rossman & Morton Moskin, *Commercial Contracts: Strategies for Drafting and Negotiating* § 18.03 (Aspen Publishers Online, 2016) (identifying the ability to limit liability as a main reason to form a joint venture); Gwynne L. Skinner, "Rethinking Limited Liability of Parent Corporations for Foreign Subsidiaries' Violations of International Human Rights Law" (2015) 72 *Washington & Lee Law Review* 1769, 1777 (stating foreign subsidiaries "externalize the risks of their operations through their subsidiaries – such as environmental risks and violations of international human rights law – and avoid liability, leaving victims with no remedy").
85 *In re Union Carbide Corp.*, 809 F.2d 195, 197 (2d Cir. 1987). The remainder of the stock was held by approximately 23,500 Indian citizens and was publicly traded on the Bombay Stock Exchange.
86 Baxi & Paul, *Mass Disasters and Multinational Liability*, p. iv.
87 Union of India Complaint, para. 12, reproduced in Baxi & Paul, *Mass Disasters and Multinational Liability*, p. 4.
88 Plaintiffs' Memorandum of Law in Opposition to Union Carbide Corp.'s Motion to Dismiss These Actions on the Grounds of Forum Non Conveniens, s. II(A) reproduced in Baxi and Paul, *Mass Disasters and Multinational Liability*, pp. 62–64.
89 Plaintiffs' Memorandum of Law in Opposition to Union Carbide Corp.'s Motion to Dismiss these Actions on the Grounds of Forum Non Conveniens, s. II(B) reproduced in Baxi and Paul, *Mass Disasters and Multinational Liability*, pp. 65–74.
90 Plaintiffs' Memorandum of Law in Opposition to Union Carbide Corp.'s Motion to Dismiss these Actions on the Grounds of Forum Non Conveniens, s. II(B) reproduced in Baxi and Paul, *Mass Disasters and Multinational Liability*, p. 74.
91 Memorandum of Law in Support of Union Carbide Corporation's motion to dismiss these actions on the grounds of Forum Non Conveniens, 'Background and Prior Proceedings', reproduced in Baxi & Paul, *Mass Disasters and Multinational Liability*, p. 27.
92 *In re Union Carbide Corp.*, 809 F.2d 195, 200 (2d Cir. 1987); *In re Union Carbide Corp.*, 634 F. Supp. 842, 853–858 (S.D.N.Y. 1986).
93 *In re Union Carbide Corp. Gas Plant Disaster*, 1992 WL 36135, at *2 (S.D.N.Y. 1992); *Bi v. Union Carbide Chems. & Plastics Co.*, 984 F.2d 582, 584 (2d Cir. 1993).
94 *Bi*, 984 F.2d 582, 584 (2d Cir. 1993).
95 *Bi*, 984 F.2d 582, 584 (2d Cir. 1993).
96 *Bi*, 984 F.2d 582, 584 (2d Cir. 1993).
97 *Bi*, 984 F.2d 582, 587 (2d Cir. 1993).
98 *Bi*, 984 F.2d 582, 586 (2d Cir. 1993).
99 *Bano v. Union Carbide Corp.*, 2000 WL 1225789, at *5 (S.D.N.Y. 2000), aff'd in part, vacated in part, 273 F.3d 120 (2d Cir. 2001).
100 *Bano*, 2000 WL 1225789, at *5 (S.D.N.Y. 2000).
101 *Bano*, 2000 WL 1225789, at *13 (S.D.N.Y. 2000).
102 *Bano v. Union Carbide Corp.*, 198 F. App'x 32, 34 (2d Cir. 2006).
103 *Sahu v. Union Carbide Corp.*, 528 F. App'x 96, 104 (2d Cir. 2013); *Sahu v. Union Carbide Corp.*, 2014 WL 3765556, at *1 (S.D.N.Y. 2014), aff'd sub nom. *Sahu v. Union Carbide Corp.*, 2016 WL 2990941 (2d Cir. 2016).
104 "Bhopal: India Wants Compensation Doubled," *BBC News* (Dec. 3, 2010) (citing Indian Supreme Court, Madhya Pradesh Government, Indian Council of Medical Research).

105 BBC News, "Bhopal: India Wants Compensation Doubled."
106 Utkarsh Anand, "Bhopal Gas Tragedy: No Private Party Can Claim Damages, Union Carbide Tells SC," *Indian Express* (10 Aug. 2016).
107 Marcus Williamson, "Warren Anderson: Chief Executive of Union Carbide at the Time of the Catastrophic Gas Leak at Their Plant in Bhopal, India" (31 Oct. 2014), available at www.independent.co.uk/news/obituaries/warren-anderson-chief-executive-of-union-carbide-at-the-time-of-the-catastrophic-gas-leak-at-their-9832080.html. See also Dhillon, "Forgotten but Not Gone" ("The federal government in New Delhi, eager to attract foreign investment and improve relations with the U.S., was taken aback. Within 24 hours Anderson was freed on bail").
108 Douglas Martin, "Warren Anderson, 92, Dies; Faced India Plant Disaster," *New York Times* (30 Oct. 2014).
109 Polgreen & Kumar, "8 Former Executives Guilty."
110 Polgreen & Kumar, "8 Former Executives Guilty."
111 Martin, "Warren Anderson."
112 *Chevron Corp. v. Naranjo*, 667 F.3d 232, 235 (2d Cir. 2012).
113 Judith Kimerling, et al., in Susan S. Henriksen (ed.), *Amazon Crude* (Charlottesville: University of Virginia Press, 1991), p. 33 (internal quotation marks omitted).
114 Kimerling, "Disregarding Environmental Law," p. 849.
115 Counter-Memorial on the Merits of the Republic of Ecuador, *Chevron Corp. and Texaco Petroleum Co. v. The Republic of Ecuador*, para. 28, available at www.italaw.com/sites/default/files/case-documents/italaw1426.pdf (hereinafter Ecuador's Counter-Memorial).
116 'Chevron's Chernobyl in the Amazon', Amazon Watch, available at www.amazonwatch.org/work/chevron.
117 Ecuador's Counter-Memorial, para. 39.
118 Ecuador's Counter-Memorial, para. 54–55.
119 Ecuador's Counter-Memorial, para. 115.
120 Ecuador's Counter-Memorial, para. 35, 68–69.
121 Ecuador's Counter-Memorial, para. 68.
122 Ecuador Lawsuit – Background, Chevron, available at www.chevron.com/ecuador/background/#.
123 *Naranjo*, 667 F.3d 232, 234 (2d Cir. 2012). The description and analysis of the Chevron–Ecuador litigation contained in this section was first developed in Maya Steinitz & Paul Gowder, "Transnational Litigation as Prisoner's Dilemma" (2016) 94 *North Carolina Law Review* 751, 779–797.
124 See Patrick Radden Keefe presentation at the Stanford Journal of Complex Litigation symposium, Patrick Radden Keefe, "Reversal of Fortune: The Lago Agrio Litigation" (2013) 1 *Stanford Journal of Complex Litigation*, 199 (Chevron's litigation costs exceeded a billion, at the time). See also Patrick Radden Keefe, "Reversal of Fortune," *New Yorker* (9 Jan. 2012) (estimating Chevron's legal costs at approximately $140 million a year).
125 Petition for Writ of Mandamus, *In re Hugo Gerardo Camacho Naranjo*, No. 11-cv-0691-LAK (S.D.N.Y. June 6, 2011), n. 8.
126 Petition for Writ of Mandamus, *In re Hugo Gerardo Camacho Naranjo*, n. 8.
127 *Aguinda v. Texaco, Inc.*, 303 F.3d 470, 473 (2d Cir. 2002) (The consortium was originally equally owned by Texaco and Gulf Oil Corporation. In 1974, the Ecuadorian

Notes to Pages 64–66

128 *Aguinda*, 303 F.3d 470, 473 (2d Cir. 2002).
129 Ecuador's Counter-Memorial, para. 29.
130 Claimant's Notice of Arbitration, *Chevron Corp. v. Republic of Ecuador*, UNCITRAL Arb., PCA Case No. 2009–23 (Sept. 23, 2009), paras. 1–2, available at www.italaw.com/sites/default/files/case-documents/ita0155_0.pdf. [hereinafter, Chevron's Notice of Arbitration].
131 Chevron's Notice of Arbitration, *Chevron Corp. v. Republic of Ecuador*, at para. 26; *Naranjo*, 667 F.3d 232, 235 (the release became final three years later, after certain conditions had been met).
132 Chevron's Notice of Arbitration, *Chevron Corp. v. Republic of Ecuador*, at para 2.
133 Simon Romero and Clifford Krauss, "In Ecuador, Resentment of an Oil Company Oozes," *New York Times* (14 May 2009).
134 Romero and Krauss, "In Ecuador, Resentment of an Oil Company Oozes."
135 *Aguinda*, 303 F.3d 470, 473 (2d Cir. 2002).
136 *Aguinda*, 303 F.3d 470, 473–474 (2d Cir. 2002); Ecuador's Counter-Memorial, para. 123. ATCA was not the only legal theory asserted. Others included negligence, public nuisance, and violations of international law.
137 Ecuador's Counter-Memorial, para. 130; *Aguinda v. Texaco Inc.*, 142 F. Supp. 2d 534, 542 (S.D.N.Y. 2001) (specific affidavits below).
138 Ecuador's Counter-Memorial, at para. 130 (internal quotation marks omitted) quoting affidavit of Dr. Enrique Ponce y Carbo (4 Feb. 2000), paras.5, 7; R-32, Affidavit of Dr. Alejandro Ponce Martinez (9 Feb. 2000), paras. 5, 7; Exhibit R-33, Affidavit of Dr. Sebastian Perez-Arteta (7 Feb. 2000), paras. 4, 7; R-34, Affidavit of Rodrigo Pérez Pallares (4 Feb. 2000), paras. 3–4, 6; R-35, Supplemental Affidavit of Dr. Alejandro Ponce Martinez (4 Apr. 2000), paras. 1–2; R-36, Affidavit of Jaime Espinoza Ramírez (28 Feb. 2000), paras. 2–6; R-37, Affidavit of Ricardo Vaca Andrade (Mar. 30, 2000), paras. 4–7; R-38, Declaration of Ramon Jimenez Carbo (5 Apr. 2000), para. 1; R-39, Affidavit of Dr. Jose Maria Perez-Arteta (Apr. 7, 2000), para. 2.
139 Plaintiff's Memorandum of Law in Opposition to Defendant's Motion to Dismiss Based upon Forum Non Conveniens, s. I(A), (B), (C), *Aguinda v. Texaco Inc.*, 1994 WL 16188155 No. 93 Civ. 7527 (S.D.N.Y. 1994).
140 Plaintiff's Memorandum of Law in Opposition to Defendant's Motion to Dismiss Based upon Forum Non Conveniens, s. II(B), *Aguinda*, 1994 WL 16188155 No. 93 Civ. 7527 (S.D.N.Y. 1994).
141 *Aguinda*, 142 F. Supp. 2d 534, 537 (S.D.N.Y. 2001).
142 *Jota v. Texaco, Inc.*, 157 F.3d 153, 155 (2d Cir. 1998).
143 *Aguinda*, 142 F. Supp. 2d 534, 537 (S.D.N.Y. 2001).
144 *Aguinda v. Texaco Inc.*, 2000 WL 122143, at *1 (S.D.N.Y. 2000).
145 Ecuador's Counter-Memorial, para. 128. The right to challenge a foreign award on due process ground is enshrined in New York's Uniform Foreign Country Money-Judgments Recognition Act, N.Y. C.P.L.R. § 5304(a)(1) (McKinney, 2013), which provides that enforcement of a foreign money judgment may be challenged if "the judgment was rendered under a system which does not provide impartial tribunals or procedures compatible with the requirements of due process of law."
146 *Aguinda*, 303 F.3d 470, 478 (2d Cir. 2002).

147 Ecuador's Counter-Memorial, para. 129.
148 See *Dow Chemical Co. v. Alfaro*, 786 S.W.2d 674, 683 (Tex. 1990) (Doggett J., concurring). See also Christopher A. Whytock, "The Evolving Forum Shopping System" (2011) 96 *Cornell Law Review* 481, 504 (discussing dismissal rates for foreign plaintiffs and providing empirical data on topic). Other jurisdictions, such as the United Kingdom and Canada, also adopted the *forum non conveniens* doctrine, and it appears to have a similar effect on foreigners' mass tort claims. See, e.g., James Yap, "Bil'in and Yassin v. Green Park International Ltd.: Quebec Court Acknowledges War Crimes as Potential Basis for Civil Liability, Claim Ultimately Fails on Forum Non Conveniens" (14 Oct. 2009), available at www.thecourt.ca/bilin-and-yassin-v-green-park-international-ltd-quebec-court-acknowledges-war-crimes-as-potential-basis-for-civil-liability-claim-ultimately-fails-on-forum-non-conveniens/ (noting that "the doctrine of forum non conveniens has long been a staunch ally to Canadian corporations beset by human rights claims launched from abroad"); Alexander Reus, "Judicial Discretion: A Comparative View of the Doctrine of Forum Non Conveniens in the United States, the United Kingdom, and Germany" (1994) 16 *Loyola Los Angeles International & Comparative Law Review* 455, 478–480; Ellen L. Hayes, "Forum Non Conveniens in England, Australia and Japan: The Allocation of Jurisdiction in Transnational Litigation" (1992) 26 *University of British Columbia Law Review* 41, 46–48.
149 Ecuador's Counter-Memorial, para. 129.
150 See *Aguinda v. Chevron Corp.*, No. 002-2003 (Superior Court of Nueva Loja, 14 Feb., 14, 2011) (Ecuador) aff'd in part, rev'd in part, Corte Nacional de Justicia, 12 Nov. 2013, Wilson Andino Reinoso, Juicio No. 174–2012, available at http://chevrontoxico.com/assets/docs/2011-02-14-Aguinda-v-ChevronTexaco-judgement-English.pdf (reversing the punitive damages, but otherwise affirming the judgment). The litigation is known as the "Lago Agrio litigation" after the oil field in which the claimed injuries took place.
151 Texaco's Memorandum of Law in Support to Renew Motion to Dismiss, p. 16 (11 Jan. 1999), available at www.texaco.com/ecuador/docs/motions_to_dismiss.pdf. See 2/25/2011 Peters Decl., D.E. 141, Exhibit 28, pp. 16–17.
152 See Draggan Mihailovich, "Amazon Crude," 60 Minutes Interview (3 May 2009), available at www.chevrontoxico.com/news-and-multimedia/2009/0503-60-minutes-amazon-crude.
153 The Cheveron–Ecuador litigation and its significance was the subject of the first symposium issue of the *Stanford Journal of Complex Litigation*, "Lessons from Chevron."
154 See *Aguinda v. Chevron Corp.*, No. 174–2012, pp. 176–184 (Corte Nacional de Justicia [National Court of Justice], 12 Nov. 2013) (Ecuador), 27, available at http://chevrontoxico.com/assets/docs/2013-11-12-final-sentence-from-cnj-de-ecuador-spanish.pdf.
155 See generally, Patton Boggs, "Path Forward: Securing and Enforcing Judgment and Reaching Settlement" (also known as "Invictus Memo"), available at www.earthrights.org/sites/default/files/documents/Invictus-memo.pdf.
156 See Manuel A. Gómez, "The Global Chase: Seeking the Recognition and Enforcement of the Lago Agrio Judgment Outside of Ecuador" (2013) 1 *Stanford Journal of Complex Litigation*, 429, 430. See, e.g., Application for the Recognition of Foreign Judgment, *Yaiguaje v. Chevron Corp.*, No. CV-12-454778 (May 31, 2012).
157 *Chevron Corp. v. Donziger*, 768 F. Supp. 2d 581, 616, 634 (S.D.N.Y. 2011). See generally, Chevron's Notice of Arbitration, *Chevron Corp. v. Republic of Ecuador*; Claimants' Memorial on the Merits, *Chevron Corp. and Texaco Petroleum Co. v. Republic of Ecuador*, Arbitration under UN Commission on International Trade Law Rules,

Notes to Pages 68–69

available at www.italaw.com/sites/default/files/case-documents/itao164.pdf; Claimants' Memorial on the Merits, *Chevron Corp. v. Republic of Ecuador*, UNCITRAL Arb., PCA Case No. 2009-23, available at www.italaw.com/sites/default/files/case-documents/itao164.pdf; Chevron's web site, available at www.chevron.com/ecuador/. Legally, the aforesaid alleged facts constitute, according to Chevron, multiple violations of Ecuador's obligations under its bilateral investment treaty with the United States. Specifically, it argues that Ecuador violated its obligation to provide Chevron, as a foreign investor, with effective means of asserting claims and enforcing rights; that Ecuador failed to treat Chevron's investments fairly and equitably; that Ecuador violated its obligations to provide full protection and security to Chevron's investments; and that Ecuador engaged in arbitrary and discriminatory measures to impair Chevron's investment.

158 New York Uniform Foreign Country Money-Judgments Recognition Act, N.Y. C.P.L.R. ss.§§ 5301–09 (McKinney, 2013).
159 *Donziger*, 768 F. Supp. 2d 581, 634 (S.D.N.Y. 2011). It then went on to hold that there was "ample evidence of fraud in the Ecuadorian proceedings," id. at 636. But cf. Neubrone's retort: "Unlike the United States, where politics simply never affects judicial nominations or the outcome of litigation, I am shocked to learn that President Correa has been charged with seeking to exercise undue influence over the Ecuadorian judiciary by asserting the power to appoint friendly judges." Burt Neuborne, "A Plague on Both Their Houses: A Modest Proposal for Ending the Ecuadorian Rainforest Wars" (2013) 1 *Stanford Journal of Complex Litigation*, 509, 509 (n. 1).
160 *Donziger*, 768 F. Supp. 2d 581 (S.D.N.Y. 2011).
161 *Naranjo*, 667 F.3d 232, 238 (2d Cir. 2012) (noting that the finding relied heavily on a single declaration by an avowed political opponent of President Correa).
162 *Naranjo*, 667 F.3d 232, 239 (2d Cir. 2012).
163 *Naranjo*, 667 F.3d 232, 240 (2d Cir. 2012).
164 *Chevron Corp. v. Republic of Ecuador*, UNCITRAL Arb., PCA Case No. 2009-23, available at www.italaw.com/cases/257.
165 Chevron's Notice of Arbitration, *Chevron Corp. v. Republic of Ecuador*, paras. 3, 4, 69.
166 Chevron's Amended Complaint, *Chevron v. Donziger*, 2011 WL 1805313 (S.D.N.Y. 2011), paras. 87, 139, 165, and 189; Chevron's Notice of Arbitration, *Chevron Corp. v. Republic of Ecuador*, para. 43.
167 Chevron's Notice of Arbitration, *Chevron Corp. v. Republic of Ecuador*, para. 76.
168 *Naranjo*, 667 F.3d 232, 242 (2d Cir. 2012).
169 First Interim Award on Interim Measures, *Chevron Corp. v. Republic of Ecuador*, UNCITRAL Arb., PCA Case No. 2009-23 (Jan. 25, 2012), available at www.italaw.com/sites/default/files/case-documents/itao173.pdf.
170 *Chevron Corp. v. Donziger*, 974 F. Supp. 2d 362 (S.D.N.Y. 2014) (hereinafter: "The RICO Decision").
171 See generally, The RICO Decision, 974 F. Supp. 2d 362 (S.D.N.Y. 2014).
172 See generally, The RICO Decision, 974 F. Supp. 2d 362 (S.D.N.Y. 2014).
173 The RICO Decision, 974 F. Supp. 2d 362, 385 (S.D.N.Y. 2014).
174 *Chevron Corp. v. Donziger*, 833 F.3d 74, 81 (2d Cir. 2016).
175 See, Shannon A. Thomas, Email dated 4/20/2007, available at https://d1cwxpo5pwteg2.cloudfront.net/C05446126.pdf. These and other documents were obtained by Ted Folkman, a Massachusetts-based attorney and manager of a legal blog, pursuant to a Freedom of Information Act Request. See generally, Ted Folkman, "Letters Blogatory

Sues the Government under FOIA" (March 18, 2013), available at www.lettersblogatory.com/2013/03/18/letters-blogatory-foia/.

176 "In Ecuador, Resentment of an Oil Company Ooze," *New York Times* (May 14, 2009). See also Chapter 4 for a lengthier discussion of the effects of transnational litigation on defendants and for examples of the use of political and diplomatic efforts on behalf of both plaintiffs and defendants.

177 Ecuador's Counter-Memorial, para. 126.

178 Bronwen Manby, "The Price of Oil: Corporate Responsibility and Human Rights Violations in Nigeria's Oil Producing Communities" (1999) *Human Rights Watch*, 9, available at www.hrw.org/reports/1999/nigeria/nigeria0199.pdf.

179 Manby, "The Price of Oil" at p. 7.

180 Statement by Dr. G. B. Leton, president of the Movement for the Survival of Ogoni People (Dec. 24, 1991), available at www.nigerianlawresources.com/2014/01/30/ogoni-bill-of-rights-mosop-movement-for-the-survival-of-ogoni-people/.

181 Michael L. Ross, "Does Oil Hinder Democracy?" (April 2001), 53 *World Politics*, 325, 325–361; Michael L. Ross, "What Have We Learned about the Resource Curse?" (2015) 18 *Annual Review of Political Science*, 239, 241–243.

182 Ed Ayres, "The Hidden Shame of the Global Industrial Economy," *Worldwatch* (2016), available at www.worldwatch.org/node/543.

183 Staff of Senate Committee on Foreign Relations, 110th Congress, "The Petroleum and Poverty Paradox: Assessing U.S. and International Community Efforts to Fight the Resource Curse" (Commercial Print, 2008), available at www.gpo.gov/fdsys/pkg/CPRT-110SPRT44727/pdf/CPRT-110SPRT44727.pdf.

184 See Press Release, Office of Public Affairs, Department of Justice, "U.S. Freezes More than $458 Million Stolen by Former Nigerian Dictator in Largest Kleptocracy Forfeiture Action Ever Brought in the U.S." (March 5, 2014), available at www.justice.gov/opa/pr/us-freezes-more-458-million-stolen-former-nigerian-dictator-largest-kleptocracy-forfeiture.

185 *Kiobel v. Royal Dutch Petroleum Co.*, 569 U.S. 108, 113 (2013).

186 Manby, "The Price of Oil," p. 9.

187 Plaintiffs' Amended Complaint, *Kiobel v. Royal Dutch Petroleum Co.*, 2004 WL 708112 (S.D.N.Y. 2004), para. 2.

188 Plaintiffs' Amended Complaint, *Kiobel v. Royal Dutch Shell*, para. 1.

189 Plaintiffs' Amended Complaint, *Kiobel v. Royal Dutch Shell*, para 54.

190 *Kiobel*, 569 U.S. 108, 113 (2013).

191 Plaintiffs' Amended Complaint, *Kiobel v. Royal Dutch Shell*, paras. 3, 6(b).

192 Memorandum of Law in Support of the Petition of Esther Kiobel, Pursuant to 28 U.S.C. § 1782, for Leave to Issue Subpoenas to Cravath, Swaine & Moore LLP for the Production of Documents for Use in a Foreign Proceeding, *Kiobel v. Cravath, Swaine & Moore, LLP*, Case No. 1:16-cv-07992 at 4 (Oct. 18, 2016), available at https://earthrights.org/wp-content/uploads/District-court-_-Kiobel-memorandum-of-law-in-support-of-petition-_-filed-2016-10-18.pdf.

193 *Kiobel*, 569 U.S. 108, 113.

194 28 U.S.C. § 1350.

195 Center for Constitutional Rights, "Filartiga v. Pena-Irala," Historical Cases, available at www.ccrjustice.org/home/what-we-do/our-cases/fil-rtiga-v-pe-irala.

196 Center for Constitutional Rights, "Filartiga v. Pena-Irala."

197 Center for Constitutional Rights, "Filartiga v. Pena-Irala"; see also *Filartiga v. Pena-Irala*, 630 F.2d 876, 885 (2d Cir. 1980).
198 Center for Constitutional Rights, "Filartiga v. Pena-Irala."
199 Donald Earl Childress III, "The Alien Tort Statute, Federalism, and the Next Wave of Transnational Litigation" (2012) 100 *Georgetown Law Journal*, 709, 713 (citing Julian G. Ku, "The Curious Case of Corporate Liability under the Alien Tort Statute: A Flawed System of Judicial Lawmaking" (2011) 51 *Virginia Journal of International Law*, 353, 357.
200 *Doe v. Unocal Corp.*, 963 F. Supp. 880 (C.D. Cal. 1997), aff'd in part and rev'd in part, 395 F.3d 932 (9th Cir. 2002).
201 Rachel Chambers, "The *Unocal* Settlement: Implications for the Developing Law on Corporate Complicity in Human Rights Abuses" (2005) 13 *Human Rights Brief*, 14, 14–15.
202 Respectively, *Abdullahi v. Pfizer, Inc.*, 562 F.3d 163 (2d Cir. 2009); *Sinaltrainal v. Coca-Cola Co.*, 578 F.3d 1252 (11th Cir. 2009); and *Balintulo v. Daimler AG*, 727 F.3d 174 (2d Cir. 2013).
203 *Kiobel v. Royal Dutch Petroleum Co.*, 456 F. Supp. 2d 457, 459 (S.D.N.Y. 2006).
204 *Sosa v. Alvarez-Machain*, 542 U.S. 692, 732 (2004).
205 *Kiobel*, 456 F. Supp. 2d 457, 459 (S.D.N.Y. 2006).
206 *Kiobel*, 456 F. Supp. 2d 457, 465–467 (S.D.N.Y. 2006).
207 *Kiobel*, 456 F. Supp. 2d 457, 464–465 (S.D.N.Y. 2006).
208 *Kiobel*, 456 F. Supp. 2d 457, 467–468 (S.D.N.Y. 2006).
209 Brief for the Petitioner, *Kiobel v. Royal Dutch Shell*, 2011 WL 6396550 (2011), p. *4.
210 Brief for the Petitioner, 2011 WL 6396550, p. *4; see *Kiobel v. Royal Dutch Petroleum*, 621 F.3d 111, 145 (2d Cir. 2010).
211 *Kiobel*, 621 F.3d 111, 118 (2d Cir. 2010).
212 *Kiobel*, 621 F.3d 111, 118 (2d Cir. 2010) (emphasis omitted).
213 *Kiobel*, 621 F.3d 111, 120 (2d Cir. 2010).
214 *Kiobel*, 621 F.3d 111, 149–150 (2d Cir. 2010).
215 *Kiobel*, 621 F.3d 111, 150 (2d Cir. 2010).
216 *Kiobel*, 621 F.3d 111, 151 (2d Cir. 2010).
217 See *Doe v. Exxon Mobil Corp.*, 654 F.3d 11, 39–57 (D.C. Cir. 2011); *Flomo v. Firestone Nat'l Rubber Co.*, 643 F.3d 1013, 1017–1021 (7th Cir. 2011); *Sarei v. Rio Tinto, PLC*, 671 F3d 736, 747–748 (9th Cir. 2011).
218 Petition for Writ of Certiorari, *Kiobel*, 569 U.S. 108 (No. 10–1491), p. i, available at https://ccrjustice.org/sites/default/files/assets/2011.06.06%20Kiobel%20Cert%20Petition.pdf.
219 See, e.g., In Support of the Plaintiffs: Brief for International Law Scholars as Amici Curiae Supporting Petitioners, *Kiobel*, 569 U.S. 108 (2013), 2011 WL 6780141; Brief for Former U.S. Senator Arlen Specter, Human Rights First, and the Anti-Defamation League as Amicus Curiae Supporting Petitioners, *Kiobel*, 569 U.S. 108 (2013), 2011 WL 6813568; Brief for Nuremberg Historians and International Lawyers as Amicus Curiae, *Kiobel*, 569 U.S. 108 (2013), 2011 WL 6813573; Brief for Navi Pillay, The United Nations High Commissioner for Human Rights as Amicus Curiae Supporting Petitioners, *Kiobel*, 569 U.S. 108 (2013), 2011 WL 6780142. In Support of Defendants see, e.g., Brief for the Chamber of Commerce of The United States of America as Amicus Curiae Supporting Respondents, *Kiobel*, 569 U.S. 108 (2013), 2012 WL 392540.
220 Order in Pending Case, *Kiobel v. Royal Dutch Petroleum*, No. 10–1491 (Mar. 5, 2012), available at http://sblog.s3.amazonaws.com/wp-content/uploads/2012/03/10-1491-order-rearg-3-5-12.pdf; see also Lyle Denniston, "Kiobel to Be Expanded and Reargued,"

SCOTUSblog (Mar. 5, 2012), available at www.scotusblog.com/2012/03/kiobel-to-be-reargued/.
221 Center for Constitutional Rights, "Kiobel v. Royal Dutch Petroleum Co. (Amicus): Case Timeline," available at www.ccrjustice.org/home/what-we-do/our-cases/kiobel-v-royal-dutch-petroleum-co-amicus (quoting *Kiobel*, 569 U.S. 108, 125 (2013)).
222 *Kiobel*, 569 U.S. 108 (2013) (quoting *Morrison v. National Australia Bank Ltd.*, 561 U.S. 247, 248 (2010)).
223 *Kiobel*, 569 U.S. 108, 124–125.
224 *Kiobel*, 569 U.S. 108, 117–124.
225 *Kiobel*, 569 U.S. 108, 115 (quoting *Microsoft Corp. v. AT&T Corp.*, 550 U.S. 437, 454 (2007)).
226 *Kiobel*, 569 U.S. 108 (quoting *EEOC v. Arabian American Oil Co.* 499 U.S. 244, 248 (1991)).
227 *Kiobel*, 133 569 U.S. 108, 123 (quoting *United States v. The La Jeune Eugenie*, 26 F. Cas. 832, 847 (No. 15,551) (CC. Mass. 1822)).
228 *Kiobel*, 569 U.S. 108, 124–125.
229 Press release, Center for Constitutional Rights, "Kiobel Decision: Supreme Court Limits U.S. Courts Ability to Use Human Rights Law to Address Human Rights Abuses Committed Abroad" (7 April 2013), available at www.ccrjustice.org/home/press-center/press-releases/kiobel-decision-supreme-court-limits-us-courts-ability-use-human.
230 "Ogoni Widows File Civil Writ Accusing Shell of Complicity in Nigeria Killings," *The Guardian* (27 June 2017).
231 *Kiobel v. Cravath*, case number 1:16-cv-07992, in the U.S. District Court for the Southern District of New York. The District Court ordered Cravath, which represents Shell, to turn over the documents, but the Second Circuit Court of Appeals has stayed that order pending Cravath's appeal.
232 M. Ryan Casey & Barrett Ristroph, "Boomerang Litigation: How Convenient Is Forum Non Conveniens in Transnational Litigation?" (2007) 4 *Brigham Young University International Law & Management Review*, 21, 21–22; See also Cassandra Burke Robertson, "Transnational Litigation and Institutional Choice" (2010) 51 *Boston College Law Review*, 1081, 1093 (2010) (discussing the access-to-justice gap created by the incompatible standards for *forum non conveniens* versus foreign judgment enforcement and "forum shopper's remorse"); Christopher A. Whytock & Cassandra Burke Robertson, "Forum Non Conveniens and the Enforcement of Foreign Judgments" (2011) 111 *Columbia Law Review*, 1444, 1451; Michael D. Goldhaber, "Forum Shopper's Remorse," *Corporate Counsel* (April, 1, 2010).
233 RICO litigation (and boomerang litigation) was similarly used in the notorious Nicaraguan Banana cases whereby Nicaraguan workers sought compensation for harms caused by exposure to chemicals supplied by Dow and used by Dole. See *Osorio v. Dole Food Co.*, 665 F. Supp. 2d 1307, 1311–1314 (S.D. Fla. 2009), aff'd sub nom. *Osorio v. Dow Chem. Co.*, 635 F.3d 1277 (11th Cir. 2011); *Franco v. Dow Chem. Co.*, No. CV 03-5094 NM, 2003 WL 24288299, at *1 (C.D. Cal. 2003).
234 *Donziger*, 768 F. Supp. 2d 581, 626–628 (S.D.N.Y. 2011) (internal quotation marks omitted).
235 Henry Hansmann & Reinier Kraakman, "Toward Unlimited Shareholder Liability for Corporate Torts" (1991) 100 *Yale Law Journal*, 1879, 1920 (arguing that for involuntary creditors, limited liability prevents tort law from fulfilling the function of allocating costs

among actors). See also Janet Cooper Alexander, "Unlimited Shareholder Liability through a Procedural Lens" (1992) 106 *Harvard Law Review*, 387, 391 ("Limited liability ... threatens the animating principles of tort law").

236 Gwynne Skinner, "Rethinking Limited Liability of Parent Corporations for Foreign Subsidiaries' Violations of International Human Rights Law" (2015) 72 *Washington & Lee Law Review*, 1769, 1769–1770, 1775 (discussing the "three primary solutions various authors and practitioners have advocated thus far to address the problem – the enterprise liability approach, the due diligence approach, and the direct parental duty-of-care approach").

237 John. A. Nyman, "American Health Policy: Cracks in the Foundation" (2008) 32 *Journal of Health Politics, Policy and Law*, 759 (emphasis in the original).

238 Jorn Madslien & Ben Richardson, "Bhopal's Economy Was Stalled by the 1984 Gas Leak," *BBC News* (Nov. 29, 2009), news.bbc.co.uk/2/hi/business/8380243.stm.

239 Purnima Menon, Anil Deolalikar, & Anjor Bhaskar, "India State Hunger Index: Comparisons of Hunger across States," *International Food Policy Research Institute* (Feb. 2009), p. 5, available at http://ebrary.ifpri.org/utils/getfile/collection/p15738coll2/id/13891/filename/13892.pdf.

240 Casey & Ristroph, *Boomerang Litigation*, p. 35.

241 Cesare P. R. Romano (ed.), *The Sword and the Scales: The United States and International Court and Tribunals* (Cambridge: Cambridge University Press, 2009), p. xxi.

242 "Extracting Natural Resources: Responsibility and the Law: Hearing before the Subcomm. on Human Rights and the Law of the H. Comm. on the Judiciary," 110th Cong. 1 (2008) (statement of Sen. Dick Durbin, Chairman, S. Comm. on Human Rights and the Law), available at http://congressional.proquest.com.proxy.lib.uiowa.edu/congressional/docview/t39.d40.c30c6a5d00029036?accountid=14663.

243 Suzanne Goldenberg, "Barack Obama's Pound of Flesh: $20bn Compensation and No BP Dividends," *Guardian* (June 16, 2010).

244 Suzanne Goldberg, "Barack Obama's Pound of Flesh."

245 Burt Neuborne, "Preliminary Reflections on Aspects of Holocaust-Era Litigation in American Courts" (2002) 80 *Washington University Law Quarterly*, 795, 795.

3 THE PROBLEM OF THE MISSING FORUM

1 This chapter (particularly the discussions of corruption and the Chevron–Ecuador litigation), draws heavily from Maya Steinitz, "The Case for an International Court of Civil Justice" (2014) 67 *Stanford Law Review Online*, 75, 76 and Maya Steinitz & Paul Gowder, "Transnational Litigation as a Prisoner's Dilemma" (2016) 94 *North Carolina Law Review* 751, 759. The argument regarding the undesirability of arbitration was first fleshed out in Maya Steinitz, "Back to the Basics: Public Adjudication of Corporate Atrocities Torts" (2016) 57 *Harvard International Law Journal*, 70 and has been expanded and updated for this book.

2 United Nations Conference on Trade and Development, June 24, 2015, "FDI Outflows, by Region and Economy, 1990–2014" (the United States accounts for 23.3 percent of FDI outflows).

3 United Nations Conference on Trade and Development, 31 March 2014, *100 Largest Non-Financial Transnational Corporations*.

4 Petition for Writ of Mandamus, *In re Hugo Gerardo Camacho Naranjo*, No. 11-cv-0691-LAK (S.D.N.Y. 2011), n. 8.

5 *Hilton v. Guyot*, 159 U.S. 113, 164 (1895).
6 American Law Institute, Restatement (Third) of Foreign Relations Law § 403 cmt. A (1987).
7 See *Dow Chemical Comp. v. Alfaro*, 786 S.W.2d 674, 683 (Tex. 1990) (Doggett J., concurring).
8 See Christopher A. Whytock & Cassandra Burke Robertson, "Forum Non Conveniens and the Enforcement of Foreign Judgments" (2011) 111 *Columbia Law Review*, 1444, 1490.
9 See *Soc'y of Lloyd's v. Ashenden*, 233 F.3d 473, 476–477 (7th Cir. 2000) (discussing the international due process standard); see also Montré D. Carodine, "Political Judging: When Due Process Goes International" (2007) 48 *William & Mary Law Review*, 1159, 1182–1188.
10 Brief for Defendants-Appellants, *Chevron v. Naranjo*, 2014 WL 3402507, at 57–58 (C.A.2, July 1, 2014); Carodine, "Political Judging," p. 1160.
11 *Chevron Corp. v. Naranjo*, 667 F.3d 232, 242 (2d Cir. 2012).
12 *Naranjo*, 667 F.3d 232, 242 (2d Cir. 2012).
13 *Naranjo*, 667 F.3d 232, 242 (2d Cir. 2012).
14 *Ashenden*, 233 F.3d 473, 476 (7th Cir. 2000).
15 See *Ashenden*, 233 F.3d 473, 476–477 (7th Cir. 2000).
16 Brief of the Governments of the Kingdom of the Netherlands and the United Kingdom of Great Britain and Northern Ireland as Amici Curia in Support of the Respondent, *Kiobel v. Royal Dutch Petroleum Co.*, 2012 WL 2312825 (2012) (No. 10–1491) at 7 (hereinafter *U.K. and the Netherlands*) (quoting *The Antelope*, 23 U.S. 66, 122 (1825)).
17 *U.K. and the Netherlands*, p. 31 (quoting *F. Hoffmann-La Roche Ltd. v. Empagran S.A.*, 542 U.S. 155 (2004)).
18 *U.K. and the Netherlands* referencing John Ruggie, "Report of the Special Representative of the Secretary-General on the Issue of Human Rights and Transnational Corporations and Other Business Enterprises," 29 *Netherlands Quarterly of Human Rights*, 224, 236–246 (2011) and Organization for Economic Co-Operation and Development, OECD Guidelines for Multinational Enterprises (2008), available at www.oecd.org/corporate/mne/.
19 *U.K. and the Netherlands*, p. 27.
20 Brief of the Federal Republic of Germany as Amici Curia in Support of the Respondents, *Kiobel v. Royal Dutch Petroleum Co.*, 2012 WL 2312825 (2012) (No. 10–1491) at 15 (quoting and citing *EEOC v. Arabian Am. Oil Co.*, 499 U.S. 244, 248 (1991) and *Morrison v. Nat'l Austl. Bank Ltd.*, 130 S. Ct. 2869, 2881).
21 Eric Weiner, "Should America Be the World's Policeman?" *NPR* (20 Feb. 2008), www.npr.org/2008/02/20/19180589/should-america-be-the-worlds-policeman; Program on International Policy Attitudes, "World Publics Reject U.S. Role as the World Leader," *World Public Opinion* (17 Apr. 2007), p.1 (emphasis added) (going on to note that this poll "reinforces the conclusions of other recent global surveys, which have found that the United States' image abroad is bad and growing worse"); see also Michael Cohen, "Americans Are No Longer Interested in Policing the World, Mr. Obama," *Guardian* (Sept. 8, 2013).
22 "World Publics Reject U.S. Role as the World Leader," *World Public Opinion* (17 Apr. 2007), p. 3., p. 1, 3.
23 Kimberly A. Moore, "Xenophobia in American Courts" (2003) 97 *Northwestern University Law Review*, 1497, 1497–1499 especially n. 1 & 8 providing literature review. See also Kevin M. Clermont & Theodore Eisenberg, "Xenophilia in American Courts" (1996) 109

Harvard Law Review, 1120 ("Many people believe that litigants have much to fear in courts foreign to them. In particular, non-Americans fare badly in American courts. Foreigners believe this. Even Americans believe this").
24 Moore, "Xenophobia in American Courts," p. 1504.
25 See, e.g., Nathan J. Miller, "Human Rights Abuses as Tort Harms: Losses in Translation" (2016) 46 *Seton Hall Law Review*, 505; Roger P. Alford, "The Future of Human Rights Litigation after Kiobel" (2014) 89 *Notre Dame Law Review*, 1749, 1769.
26 A similar argument has been advanced in Pamela K. Bookman, "Litigation Isolationism" (2015) 67 *Stanford Law Review*, 1081, 1081.
27 42 U.S. Code § 1983.
28 *Bivens v. Six Unknown Named Agents of Federal Bureau of Narcotics*, 403 U.S. 388 (1971).
29 *Bivens*, 403 U.S. 388 (1971).
30 *Monroe v. Pape*, 365 U.S. 167 (1961).
31 *Brown v. Bd. of Educ.*, 347 U.S. 483 (1954).
32 Harry A. Blackmun, "Section 1983 and Federal Protection of Individual Rights–Will the Statute Remain Alive or Fade Away?" (1985) 60 *New York University Law Review*, 1, 2.
33 Blackmun, "Section 1983 and Federal Protection of Individual Rights," p. 23–24.
34 Blackmun, "Section 1983 and Federal Protection of Individual Rights," p. 28.
35 CAFA was preceded by the Private Securities Litigation Reform Act (1995) (PSRLA), which in addition to expanding federal original jurisdiction in securities class, also reformed pleading standards, discovery, liability, class representation, and awards of fees and expenses in a business-friendly fashion and by the Multiparty Multiforum Trial Jurisdiction Act.
36 The Multiparty Multiforum Trial Jurisdiction Act, 28 U.S.C. § 1369 (2002) (MMTJA).
37 *AT&T Mobility LLC v. Concepcion*, 563 U.S. 333, 352 (2011).
38 Jean R. Sternlight, "Tsunami: *AT&T Mobility LLC v. Concepcion* Impedes Access to Justice" (2012) 90 *Oregon Law Review*, 703, 704.
39 *Celotex Corporation v. Catrett*, 477 U.S. 317 (1986); *Anderson v. Liberty Lobby, Inc.*, 477 U.S. 242 (1986); *Matsushita Elec. Indus. Comp. v. Zenith Radio Corp.*, 475 U.S. 574 (1986).
40 Federal Rules of Civil Procedure 26(g).
41 Seymour Moskowitz, "Discovering Discovery: Non-Party Access to Pretrial Information in the Federal Courts 1938–2006" (2007) 78 *University of Colorado Law Review*, 817, 832–833.
42 Carl Tobias, "Reconsidering Rule 11" (1992) 46 *University of Miami Law Review*, 855, 855–856.
43 *Bell Atl. Corp. v. Twombly*, 550 U.S. 544 (2007); *Ashcroft v. Iqbal*, 556 U.S. 662 (2009).
44 Lauren Carasik, "The Uphill Battle to Hold U.S. Corporations Accountable for Abuses Abroad," *Al Jazeera* (8 Aug. 2014) (citing the Corporate Accountability Coalition yearly report card that measures congressional efforts to protect people by promoting corporate transparency and accountability).
45 *Daimler AG v. Bauman*, 134 S. Ct. 746, 748–749 (2014).
46 United Nations Conference on Trade and Development, 31 March 2014, *100 Largest Non-Financial Transnational Corporations*.
47 Regulation 1215/2012 of the European Parliament and of the Council of 12 Dec. 2012 on Jurisdiction and the Recognition and Enforcement of Judgments in Civil and Commercial Matters (recast), art. 4–6, 2012 O.J. (L 351/13) (hereinafter BIR); Peter Stone, *EU Private International Law* (3rd ed., Cheltenham: Edward Elgar, 2014), p. 52.

48 BIR, art. 6. There are three important exceptions, according to which jurisdiction over defendants domiciled *outside* the EU is *not* determined by national law, but by the BIR: Exclusive Jurisdiction, art. 24 (1); Choice of Court Agreements, art. 25; and where another member state already had jurisdiction over the same case between the same parties, arts. 29–32. See also Trevor C. Hartley, *International Commercial Litigation: Text, Cases and Materials on Private International Law* (2nd ed., 2015), p. 29.
49 Hartley, *International Commercial Litigation*, p. 29, 44, 65, 74–75.
50 Case C-281/02, *Owusu v. Jackson*, 2005 E.C.R. I 1453–54.
51 *Owusu*, 2005 E.C.R. I, 1462. See also Stone, *EU Private International Law*, p. 55–57.
52 Marios Koutsais, "Corporate Domicile and Residence," in Peter Stone & Youseph Farah, eds., *Research Handbook on EU Private International Law* (Cheltenham: Edward Elgar, 2015), p. 346–354. This picture is somewhat complicated by the fact that the national law of each member state determines whether or not parents and subsidiaries will be treated together such that a lawsuit against a subsidiary of a parent domiciled in a member state would trigger the BIR. Hence the outcome may be different in the United Kingdom than it would be in Germany. Marios Koutsais, "Corporate Domicile and Residence," p. 346–354.
53 BIR Art. 8. ("A person domiciled in a Member State may also be sued ... where he is one of a number of defendants, in the courts for the place where any one of them is domiciled, provided the claims are so closely connected that it is expedient to hear and determine them together to avoid the risk of irreconcilable judgments resulting from separate proceedings").
54 *Akpan v. Royal Dutch Shell PLC*, District Court of The Hague, 30 Jan. 2013, Case No. C/09/337050/HA ZA 099-1580. (decision of Jan. 30, 2013).
55 Shell raised that defense in *Akpan*. *Akpan*, District Court of The Hague, Case No. C/09/337050/HA ZA 099-1580 (2013). While Shell was ultimately unsuccessful, the defense remains viable under Dutch law. It is not, therefore, a given that Dutch courts will always have jurisdiction over subsidiaries not domiciled in the EU.
56 Kevin M. Claremont & John R.B. Palmer, "French Article 14 Jurisdiction, Viewed from the United States" (2004) *Cornell Faculty Law Publication*, Paper No. 04-011, available at http://scholarship.law.cornell.edu/cgi/viewcontent.cgi?article=1012&context=lsrp_papers; see also Hartley, *International Commercial Litigation*, p. 23; BIR art. 6(1), 6 (2), which extends the right, under French law, of a French citizen to sue "anyone in the world in France," to foreigners domiciled in France.
57 Hartley, *International Commercial Litigation*, p. 22–23.
58 BIR Art. 72. BIR permits application of such agreements if they were concluded prior to 2000, but "the door is closed to future agreements. As far as is known, the only two such agreements still in existence were concluded by the United Kingdom, one with Canada and one with Australia." Hartley, *International Commercial Litigation*, p. 24.
59 Hartley, *International Commercial Litigation*, p. 16, 22, 270.
60 Regulation 864/2007, of the European Parliament and of the Council of 11 July 2007 on the Law Applicable to Non-Contractual Obligations (Rome II), 2007 O.J. (L199/44) (hereinafter Rome II).
61 Stone, *EU Private International Law*, p. 374 ("the general rule ... is definite in content, and probably rather firm in effect. In contrast the exception ... is vague or flexible in content, but probably rather limited in scope").
62 Rome II, Art. 4 (1).

63 This exception appears in various places in EU law. See Susanne Lillian Gössl, "Private International Law and International Civil Procedure: The Public Policy Exception in the European Civil Justice System" (2016) 4 *European Legal Forum*, 85, available at www.jura.uni-bonn.de/fileadmin/Fachbereich_Rechtswissenschaft/Einrichtungen/Institute/Familienrecht/Dokumente/Goessl__The_public_policy_exception_in_the_European_civil_justice_system.European_Legal_Forum_4-2016__S._85-92.pdf (citing Article 45 Brussels I.a Regulation; Article 22 Brussels II.a Regulation; Article 21 Rome I Regulation; Article 26 Rome II Regulation, Article 12 Rome III Regulation).
64 Gössl, "Private International Law," p. 86–87 (citing, inter alia, CJEU, 28.3.2000 – C-7/98 – *Krombach v. Bamberski*, unalex EU- 101 para. 37).
65 Joseph Lookofsky & Ketilbjørn Hertz, *EU-PIL: European Union Private International Law in Contract and Tort* (JurisNet, LLC, 2009), p. 136.
66 Lookofsky & Hertz, *EU-PIL: European Union Private International Law*, p. 137–138.
67 Lookofsky & Hertz, *EU-PIL: European Union Private International Law*, p.138.
68 Lookofsky & Hertz, *EU-PIL: European Union Private International Law*, p. 138 (as well as based on forum selection clauses, which are relevant in contract cases).
69 Lookofsky & Hertz, *EU-PIL: European Union Private International Law*, p. 139. See also Lookofsky & Hertz, *EU-PIL: European Union Private International Law*, p. 140–141 for a discussion of restrictions on enforcement of foreign judgments in France and Portugal.
70 S. I. Strong, "Regulatory Litigation in the European Union: Does the U.S. Class Action Have a New Analogue?" (2012) 88 *Notre Dame Law Review*, 899, 903–904.
71 EU Commission, Recommendation of 11 June 2013 on Common Principles for Injunctive and Compensatory Collective Redress Mechanisms in the Member States Concerning Violations of Rights Granted under Union Law (2013/396/EU) Official Journal of the European Union L201/60 (hereinafter EU Commission Recommendation).
72 Belgium's 2014 law on class action serves as an illustrative example. Notably, the Belgium law sets out that judicial proceedings can only be initiated by "(i) an established organisation protecting consumer interests …; (ii) other specialised organisations with at least three years legal personality and a core business that is linked to the harm suffered by the consumer group; or (iii) the Federal Ombudsman for consumers … whose role [is] limited to the negotiation phase." Van Bael Bellis, "Adoption of Belgian Law on Collective Redress Procedure," *Mondaq* (19 May 2014).
73 Mark Gibney, "On the Need for an International Civil Court" (2002) 26 *The Fletcher Forum of World Affairs*, 47, 51 (demonstrating in the human rights context that individuals "have shown a far greater interest in seeing that justice is served than states have"); Karen J. Alter, *The New Terrain of International Law: Courts, Politics, Rights* (Princeton, NJ: Princeton University Press, 2014), p. 7.
74 EU Commission Recommendation, paras. 29–30.
75 EU Commission Recommendation, para. 32.
76 See generally, Maya Steinitz, "Whose Claim Is This Anyway? Third-Party Litigation Funding" (2011) 95 *Minnesota Law Review* 1268, 1271–1275.
77 EU Commission Recommendation, para. 31.
78 John C. Coffee, *Entrepreneurial Litigation: Its Rise, Fall, and Future* (Cambridge, MA: Harvard University Press, 2016), p. 9–17.
79 Maya Steinitz and Paul Gowder, "Transnational Litigation as a Prisoner's Dilemma" (2016) 94 *North Carolina Law Review* 751, 763 (quoting Mary Noel Pepys, "Corruption within the Judiciary: Causes and Remedies," p. 3, 12). See also Global Corruption Report

2007: Corruption in Judicial Systems, *Transparency International* (2007), p. 12, available at http://files.transparency.org/content/download/173/695/file/2007_GCR_EN.pdf;

80 *Alfaro*, 786 S.W.2d 674, 689 (Tex. 1990).

81 This section is an edited and updated version of Maya Steinitz, "Back to the Basics: Public Adjudication of Corporate Atrocities Torts" (2016) *Harvard International Law Journal Online*, available at www.harvardilj.org/2016/07/back-to-the-basics-public-adjudication-of-corporate-atrocities-torts/.

82 1965 Convention on the Settlement of Investment Disputes between States and Nationals of Other States, part II, Mar. 18, 1965, 575 U.N.T.S. 159.

83 See generally, Gus Van Harten, *Investment Treaty Arbitration and Public Law* (Oxford: Oxford University Press, 2007), p. 5.

84 See e.g., S. I. Strong, "Class and Collective Relief in the Cross-Border Context: A Possible Role for the Permanent Court of Arbitration" (2010) 23 *Hague Yearbook of International Law*; S. I. Strong, *Class, Mass and Collective Arbitration in National and International Law* (Oxford: Oxford University Press, 2013).

85 *Concepcion*, 563 U.S. 333 (2011) (internal citations omitted) (quoting *Stolt-Nielsen S.A. v. AnimalFeeds Int'l Corp.*, 559 U.S. 662, 685 (2010)). The US Supreme Court went on to note that class arbitration greatly increases risks to defendants because the absence of appellate review makes it more likely that errors will go uncorrected. Such risk is acceptable to defendants, according to the US Supreme Court, when their impact is limited by the size of individual disputes and, therefore, probably outweighed by the savings defendant incur by avoiding the courts. The same is not true in what may be bet-the-company class and mass actions.

86 Alluding to Oscar Schachter's famous identification of an 'invisible college of international lawyers.' See Oscar Schachter, "The Invisible College of International Lawyers" (1977) 72 *Northwestern University Law Review*, 217, 217. See also Santiago Villalpando, "The 'Invisible College of International Lawyers' Forty Years Later" (ESIL 2013 5th Research Forum: International Law as a Profession Conference Paper No 5/2013), available at www.ssrn.com/abstract=2363640; Susan D. Franck, et al., "The Diversity Challenge: Exploring the 'Invisible College' of International Arbitration" (2015) 53 *Columbia Journal of Transnational Law* 429.

87 See e.g., Gus van Harten, "The (Lack of) Women Arbitrators in Investment Treaty Arbitration" (2012) 59 *Columbia FDI Perspectives*.

88 See generally Gus Van Harten, *Investment Treaty Arbitration and Public Law*.

89 See, e.g., Claes Cronstedt & Robert C. Thompson, "A Proposal for an International Tribunal on Business and Human Rights" (2016) *Harvard International Law Journal Online*; Luis Gallegos & Daniel Uribe, "The Next Step against Corporate Impunity: A World Court on Business and Human Rights?" (2016) *Harvard International Law Journal Online*, available at www.harvardilj.org/2016/07/the-next-step-against-corporate-impunity-a-world-court-on-business-and-human-rights/; Julia Kozma, Manfred Nowak & Martin Scheinin, *A World Court of Human Rights: Consolidated Statute and Commentary* (Neuer Wissenschaftlicher Verlag, 2010); Mark Gibney, "On the Need for an International Civil Court"; Amedeo Postiglione, "A More Efficient International Law on the Environment and Setting Up an International Court for the Environment within the United Nations" (1990) 20 *Environmental Law*, 321; Audra Dehan, "An International Environmental Court: Should There Be One?" (1992) 3 *Touro Journal of Transnational Law*, 31; Robin L. Juni, "The United Nations Compensation Commission as a Model for an International Environmental Court" (2000) 7 *Environmental Law*, 53; Mark

L. Wolf, "The Case for an International Anti-Corruption Court," *Governance Studies at Brookings* (July 2014).
90 Burt Neuborne, "A Plague on Both Their Houses: A Modest Proposal for Ending the Ecuadorian Rainforest Wars" (2013) 1 *Stanford Journal Complex Litigation*, 509, 512.
91 Samuel Issacharoff & D. Theodore Rave, "The BP Oil Spill Settlement and the Paradox of Public Litigation" (2014) 74 *Louisiana Law Review*, 397, 404–405.
92 The report of the Special Representative of the United Nations Secretary-General on the Issue of Human Rights and Transnational Corporations and Other Business Enterprises: A/HRC/17/31, para. 29–30.
93 Jim Yardley, "Report on Deadly Factory Collapse in Bangladesh Finds Widespread Blame," *New York Times* (22 May 2013); "New OECD Due Diligence Guidance Targets the Garment and Footwear Sector," *OECD Guidelines for Multinational Enterprises* (Aug. 8, 2017), available at http://mneguidelines.oecd.org/new-oecd-due-diligence-guidance-targets-the-garment-and-footwear-sector.htm; Full text of guidance: OECD Due Diligence Guidance for Responsible Supply Chains in the Garment and Footwear Sector, OECD, available at https://mneguidelines.oecd.org/OECD-Due-Diligence-Guidance-Garment-Footwear.pdf
94 See, e.g., *ECCHR et al vs. TÜV Rheinland AG*, German NCP(2016), available at www.oecdwatch.org/cases/Case_461; *PWT Group's role in the Rana Plaza collapse*, Danish Business Authority Erhvervsstyrelsen (2014), available at www.oecdwatch.org/cases/Case_467.
95 Danish National Contact Point to the OECD, Specific instance notified by Clean Clothes Campaign Denmark and Active Consumers regarding the activities of PWT Group (Oct. 17, 2016), available at www.oecdwatch.org/cases/Case_467/1587/at_download/file.
96 Danish National Contact Point to the OECD, Specific instance notified by Clean Clothes Campaign Denmark and Active Consumers regarding the activities of PWT Group (Oct. 17, 2016), available at www.oecdwatch.org/cases/Case_467/1587/at_download/file; see also Karin Buhmann, "Lost in Translation or Learning to Walk? On CSR and Risk-Based Due Diligence in Ship Recycling and Textile Sector Supply Chain Management,"*Business of Society blog: Copenhagen Business School* (Oct. 28, 2016), available at www.oecdwatch.org/cases/Case_467/1588/at_download/file.
97 The point here is that international courts and tribunals, while imperfect institutions and therefore the subjects of critique, are not more imperfect than their domestic counterparts in democracies. For example, the critiques of the ICC, plagued with "childhood illnesses" and leaving much to be desired, are not incomparable to critique of the American judiciary when it comes to, e.g., the racial injustices of criminal adjudication. This is in contrast to intractable, fundamental problems such as systemic judicial bribe taking in many low-income nations' courts.

4 THE BUSINESS CASE FOR THE ICCJ

1 Paul B. Stephan (ed.), *Foreign Court Judgments and the United States Legal System* (Boston: Brill Nijhoff, 2014), p. 40.
2 Michael D. Goldhaber, "Forum Shopper's Remorse," (April 2010) *Corporate Counsel*, p. 63; see also Christopher A. Whytock & Cassandra Burke Robertson, "Forum Non Conveniens and the Enforcement of Foreign Judgments" (2011) 111 *Columbia Law Review* 1444, 1447; Simon Baughen, *Human Rights and Corporate Wrongs: Closing the Governance Gap* (Cheltenham: Edward Elgar, 2015), p.82–90.

3 Both cases are described in Chapter 2
4 Goldhaber, "Forum Shopper's Remorse," p. 63 (internal quotation marks omitted).
5 Goldhaber, "Forum Shopper's Remorse," p. 63 (internal quotation marks omitted).
6 Maya Steinitz, "The Litigation Finance Contract" (2012) 54 *William & Mary Law Review* 455, 467–468 (discussing, specifically, the funding of the postjudgment phase in the Chevron–Ecuador dispute). As discussed in Chapter 2, Danziger was found liable for corruptly procuring the judgment. Confronted with allegations of corruption, the funders withdrew their funding after the first of three funding tranches. See Maya Steinitz and Paul Gowder, "Transnational Litigation as a Prisoner's Dilemma" (2016) 94 *North Carolina Law Review* 751, 782–784.
7 Goldhaber, "Forum Shopper's Remorse," p. 63 (internal quotation marks omitted).
8 Goldhaber, "Forum Shopper's Remorse," p. 63 (internal quotation marks omitted).
9 Goldhaber, "Forum Shopper's Remorse," p. 63 (internal quotation marks omitted).
10 Dole faced a similar pattern: "Like Chevron, Dole won dismissal in the U.S. on forum non conveniens, only to enter a Latin American nightmare. The U.S. plaintiffs lawyers refiled against Dole in Nicaragua and lobbied for a new law that changed the game; the American company became the butt of local protests and indictments, and lost a series of large judgments that it attributed to a conspiracy of bribery and fraud by the plaintiffs." See Goldhaber, "Forum Shopper's Remorse," p. 63.
11 See Brief for the Chamber of Commerce of the United States of America as Amici Curiae in Support of Respondents, *Kiobel v. Royal Dutch Petroleum Co.*, 2012 WL 392540 (2012) (No. 10–1491).
12 Michael D. Goldhaber, "Corporate Human Rights Litigation in Non-U.S. Courts: A Comparative Scorecard" (2013) 3 *University of California Irvine Law Review* 127, 129.
13 See Chapter 3.
14 Deborah R. Hensler, "The Future of Mass Litigation: Global Class Actions and Third-Party Litigation Financing" (2011) 79 *George Washington Law Review* 306, 310.
15 Geoffrey Miller makes an analogous argument with respect to the American legal system with its fifty states and federal judiciary. See Geoffrey P. Miller, "A New Procedure for State Court Personal Jurisdiction" (2013) *New York University School of Law, Public Law & Legal Theory Research Paper Series Working paper* No. 13-12, 1 (arguing that both the fairness and the efficiency of the American civil justice system would be improved if instead of the current system of diffused jurisdiction at the state and federal levels, federal district courts were granted the "full judicial power authorized by the Constitution coupled with discretion to dismiss, transfer or remand cases when it appears that some other forum is more adequate for resolving the controversy").
16 Kathleen Engelmann & Bradford Cornell, "Measuring the Cost of Corporate Litigation: Five Case Studies" (1988) 17 *Journal of Legal Studies* 377, 395. The authors analyzed business-to-business disputes but there is no reason to think the same is not true in mass tort cases. In that context, they found that litigation "events that increase the probability that the plaintiff will be victorious cause the dollar value of the defendant company to drop up to 100 times more than the value of the plaintiff company rises." *Id.* at 398. Similar asymmetric wealth effects were found by Sanjai Bhagat, James A. Brickley & Jeffrey Link Coles, *The Wealth Effects of Interfirm Lawsuits: An Empirical Investigation* (Chicago: University of Chicago Press, 1988), p. 1; and by John M. Bizjak & Jeffrey L. Coles, "The Effect of Private Antitrust Litigation on the Stock-Market Valuation of the

Firm" (1995) 85 *American Economic Review* 436, 436–437 (finding that in inter-firm antitrust cases "defendants experience significant wealth losses that are [significantly] larger than the wealth gains of plaintiffs"; "the average wealth loss for defendants is approximately 0.6 percent of the firm's equity value... on average the defendant loses more than the plaintiff gains").

17 David M. Cutler & Lawrence H. Summers, "The Costs of Conflict Resolution and Financial Distress: Evidence from the Texaco-Pennzoil Litigation" (1988) 19 *RAND Journal of Economics* 157, 167–168.

18 D. Theodore Rave, "Settlement, ADR, and Class Action Superiority" (2012) 5 *Journal of Tort Law* 91, 119–120.

19 See *Pennzoil Co. v. Texaco Inc.*, 481 U.S. 1, 5 (1987) (stating Texaco submitted a $13 billion bond).

20 Cutler & Summers, "Costs of Conflict Resolution," p. 168 (lost business opportunity).

21 Cutler & Summers, "Costs of Conflict Resolution," p. 168.

22 Cutler & Summers, "Costs of Conflict Resolution," p. 168.

23 Engelmann & Cornell, "Measuring the Cost of Corporate Litigation," p. 377; Bhagat, Brickley & Coles, *The Wealth Effects of Interfirm Lawsuits*, p. 1 (emphasizing financial distress costs and finding about 1 percent decline in the combined equity value of opposing firms in a large sample of interfirm lawsuits); Sanjai Bhagat, James A. Brickley & Jeffrey L. Coles, "The Costs of Inefficient Bargaining and Financial Distress: Evidence from Corporate Lawsuits" (1994) 35 *Journal of Financial Economics* 221; Bizjak & Coles, "Effect of Private Antitrust Litigation," p. 436.

24 Cutler & Summers, "Costs of Conflict Resolution," p. 158.

25 Cutler & Summers, "Costs of Conflict Resolution," p. 158.

26 Cutler & Summers, "Costs of Conflict Resolution," p. 158.

27 Maya Steinitz, "Incorporating Legal Claims" (2015) 90 *Notre Dame Law Review* 1155, 1172.

28 Cutler & Summers, "Costs of Conflict Resolution," p. 166 (explaining the possible tax consequences of the Texaco–Pennzoil litigation).

29 Bizjak & Coles, "Effect of Private Antitrust Litigation," p. 437.

30 Sanjoy Hazarika, "India Fighting Sales of Union Carbide Assets," *New York Times* (Nov. 2, 1986) (internal quotation marks omitted).

31 Order governing the maintenance of status quo until interlocutory applications filed by the plaintiff are finally heard and decided, *Union of India v. Union Carbide Corporation*, 11-24-1986, p. 22 para. 13, available at http://14.139.60.114:8080/jspui/bitstream/123456789/699/14/Ad-Interim%20Injunction%20Order%20dated%2017.11.86.pdf.

32 Order governing the maintenance of status quo until interlocutory applications filed by the plaintiff are finally heard and decided, *Union of India v. Union Carbide Corporation*, 11-24-1986, p. 22 para. 13.

33 Eric Schmitt, "Major Refinancing Planned for Carbide," *New York Times* (Nov. 5, 1986).

34 Oral argument transcript, *Union of India v. Union Carbide Corporation*, 11-24-1986, p. 35 lines 1–8.

35 Sanjoy Hazarika, "India and Carbide in Pact on Assets," *New York Times* (Nov. 30, 1986). Shell faced a similar predicament after succeeding in moving its case to Nicaragua. "On January 13, 2006, the same Nicaraguan judge who handed down the $489 million judgment against the defendant-corporations ordered an embargo against various Shell enterprises in punishment for its lack of compliance." See M. Ryan Casey & Barrett

Ristroph, "Boomerang Litigation: How Convenient Is Forum Non Conveniens in Transnational Litigation?" (2007) 4 *Brigham Young University International Law & Management Review* 21, 37.

36 Maya Steinitz, "Incorporating Legal Claims" (2015) 90 *Notre Dame Law Review* 1155, 1172. See also Jonathan T. Molot, "A Market in Litigation Risk" (2009) 76 *University of Chicago Law Review* 367, 374–375.
37 At the time the injunction was sought, and granted, fraud was alleged but not yet found by a court of law. By the time of this writing, the New York District Court, in a judgment affirmed by the Second Circuit, has made a finding of fraud and other forms of corruption. *Chevron Corp. v. Donziger*, 974 F. Supp. 2d 362, 384 (S.D.N.Y. 2014).
38 *Chevron Corp. v. Donziger*, 768 F. Supp. 2d 581, 627 (S.D.N.Y. 2011) (internal quotation marks omitted).
39 *Donziger*, 768 F. Supp. 2d 581, 627 (S.D.N.Y. 2011).
40 See detailed discussion in Chapter 3.
41 ICC Commission Report: Decision on Costs in International Arbitration, para. 72.
42 Daniel Bent, "Game Theory Explains How Mediation Can Trump Litigation," *Mondaq* (June 1, 2001), available at www.mondaq.com/unitedstates/x/11840/Game+Theory+Explains+How+Mediation+Can+Trump+Litigation (stating corporations "los[e] thousands of person-hours of its most important executives and managers" because of depositions).
43 Lawrence Hurley, "Dropped Charges in Ecuador Could Affect Chevron Racketeering Case," *New York Times* (June 3, 2011), available at www.nytimes.com/gwire/2011/06/03/03greenwire-dropped-charges-in-ecuador-could-affect-chevro-90134.html
44 Goldhaber, "Forum Shopper's remorse," p. 63. (quoting defense firm Gibson, Dunn partner Scott Edelman (internal quotation marks omitted)). Goldhaber goes on to opine bluntly that "the real problem is that Texaco's tactic [of filing for *forum non conveniens* dismissal] was stupid. Everyone knew that the courts were politicized. And there was no guarantee that Ecuador's politics would remain friendly to U.S. corporations." *Id*. He quotes Professor John Knox's view that firms like Chevron and Dole "should hardly be surprised if the courts that they begged to get into are corrupt or marginally competent. The idea that these countries could become more populist was entirely predictable").
45 Brief for the Chamber of Commerce of the United States of America as Amici Curiae in Support of Respondents, *Kiobel*, 2012 WL 392540 (2012), p. 4.
46 Brief for the Chamber of Commerce of the United States of America as Amici Curiae in Support of Respondents, *Kiobel*, 2012 WL 392540 (2012), p. 16 (internal citations omitted). An extreme example of reputational harm is the example of the accounting firm Andersen, which was complicit in Enron's fraud – a corporate scandal that rattled the corporate world in the early 2000s. "Although the indictment [of Andersen] charged only a relatively minor offense (the government claimed that Andersen had obstructed justice when it destroyed Enron-related records), the firm could not withstand the reputational effects of the indictment and quickly closed its doors"). See Geoffrey P. Miller, *The Law of Governance, Risk Management and Compliance* (Aspen Casebook Series, 2014), p. 139.
47 Engelmann & Cornell, "Measuring the Cost of Corporate Litigation," p. 381; Bradford Cornell & Alan C. Shapiro, "Corporate Stakeholders and Corporate Finance" (1987) 16 *Financial Management Association* 5, 6–7.
48 Engelmann & Cornell, "Measuring the Cost of Corporate Litigation," p. 382.
49 Engelmann & Cornell, "Measuring the Cost of Corporate Litigation," p. 380–381.
50 Bhagat, Brickley & Coles, "Wealth Effects of Interfirm Lawsuits," p. 1, para. 1 sec. 5.

51 Simon Romero & Clifford Krauss, "In Ecuador, Resentment of an Oil Company Oozes," *New York Times* (May 14, 2009).
52 Casey & Ristroph, "Boomerang Litigation," p. 21 (n. 1).
53 Denunciation of the ICSID Convention and BITS: Impact on Investor-State Claims, United Nations UNCTAD (Dec. 2010), available at http://unctad.org/en/Docs/webdiaeia20106_en.pdf (Ecuador and Bolivia); José Torrealba, Fernando Peláez & Gonzalo Capriles, Venezuela Officially Withdraws From the International Centre for the Settlement of Investment Disputes, *Mondaq Business Briefing* (April 12, 2012) (Venezuela); and Indonesia–2-Bilateral Investment Agreements, available at www.export.gov/article?id=Indonesia-bilateral-investment-agreements (Indonesia).
54 Quan Li, "Democracy, Autocracy, and Expropriation of Foreign Direct Investment" (2009) 42 *Comparative Political Studies* 1098, 1098–1127.
55 Mark Osiel, *Mass Atrocity, Collective Memory, and the Law* (New Brunswick, NJ: Transaction, 1997), p. 5.
56 Stefano Colonnello & Christoph Herpfer, "Do Courts Matter for Firm Value? Evidence from the U.S. Court System" (2016) Paris Finance Meeting EUROFIDAI – AFFI (all references are to the March 14, 2016 draft), available at https://papers.ssrn.com/sol3/Papers.cfm?abstract_id=2686621.
57 Colonnello & Herpfer, "Do Courts Matter for Firm Value?" p. 2.
58 See Colonnello & Herpfer, "Do Courts Matter for Firm Value?" p. 1 (n. 1) (citing 2015 Lawsuit Climate Survey, available at www.instituteforlegalreform.com/uploads/sites/1/ILR15077-HarrisReport_BF2.pdf).
59 See Robert Kossick, "The Rule of Law and Development in Mexico," (2004) 21 *Arizona Journal of International and Comparative Law* 715, 717 (corruption in Mexican courts); Kenneth W. Dam, "China as a Test Case: Is the Rule of Law Essential for Economic Growth?" (2006) *University of Chicago Law School, John M. Olin Law and Economics*, Working Paper Series No. 275, 18–23 (corruption and lack of judicial independence in China); Ethan S. Burger, "Corruption in the Russian Arbitrazh Courts: Will There Be Significant Progress in the Near Term?" (2004) 38 *International Lawyer* 15, 22 (corruption in Russian courts).
60 Steinitz & Gowder, "Transnational Litigation as a Prisoner's Dilemma," p. 761 (citing Paul Gowder, "Institutional Corruption and the Rule of Law" (2014) 9 *Les Ateliers De L'ethique/The Ethics Forum* 84, 94–96). See also Paul Gowder, *The Rule of Law in the Real World* (Cambridge: Cambridge University Press, 2016) p. 244.
61 Steinitz & Gowder, "Transnational Litigation as a Prisoner's Dilemma," p. 761.
62 For an extensive explanation and formal modeling of this prisoner's dilemma, as well as how it in fact unfolded in the Chevron–Ecuador litigation, see Steinitz & Gowder, "Transnational Litigation as a Prisoner's Dilemma," p. 751.
63 Steinitz & Gowder, "Transnational Litigation as a Prisoner's Dilemma," pp. 768–769.
64 Jens Dammann & Henry Hansmann, "Globalizing Commercial Litigation" (2008) 94 *Cornell Law Review* 1, 3. See also Damman & Hansmann, "Globalizing Commercial Litigation," pp. 7–9 for a review of empirical literature on the topic.
65 Damman & Hansmann, "Globalizing Commercial Litigation," p. 3.
66 Samuel Issacharoff & D. Theodore Rave, "The BP Oil Spill Settlement and the Paradox of Public Litigation," (2014) 74 *Louisiana Law Review* 397, 413 (quoting *Sullivan v. DB Invs., Inc.*, 667 F.3d 273, 311, 339 (3d Cir. 2011) (Scirica, J., concurring)).
67 Issacharoff & Rave, "BP Oil Spill Settlement," p. 402.

68 Issacharoff & Rave, "BP Oil Spill Settlement," p. 403.
69 See *In re World Trade Center Disaster Site Litigation*, 834 F. Supp. 2d 184 (S.D.N.Y. 2011).
70 D. Theodore Rave, "Governing the Anticommons in Aggregate Litigation," (2013) 66 *Vanderbilt Law Review* 1183, 1195.
71 Issacharoff & Rave, "BP Oil Spill Settlement," pp. 415–416. The notion of threshold means that there is not a need for a 100 percent participation for the defendant to achieve significant gains. "It is not necessary for all the claims to be assembled for there to be any surplus, but the value of settling each additional claim approaching a certain threshold may be disproportionately high." Rave, "Governing the Anticommons," p. 1197 (citing Lee Anne Fennell's "Common Interest Tragedies," in explaining that aggregate settlements are 'step good'. "A step good ... delivers no benefits at all until a certain contribution threshold is reached; it then delivers all of the benefits in a single lump upon reaching that threshold, and delivers no additional benefits beyond that point." Lee Anne Fennell's "Common Interest Tragedies" (2004) 98 *Northwestern University Law Review* 907, 957–961, 971–978). "Thus, the defendant may be willing to pay something to settle an incomplete aggregation but would be willing to pay a considerable peace premium for a settlement that includes the claims at the threshold." Rave, "Governing the Anticommons," p. 1197.
72 Tanya J. Monestier, "Transnational Class Actions and the Illusory Search for *Res Judicata*" (2011) 86 *Tulane Law Review* 1, 31, 5.
73 Monestier, "Transnational Class Actions," p. 5.
74 Monestier, "Transnational Class Actions," p. 5.
75 Zachary D. Clopton, "Transnational Class Actions in the Shadow of Preclusion," (2015) 90 *Indiana Law Journal* 1387, 1388–1389. (Since US class judgments are not uniformly enforceable through any international law of preclusion, many foreign courts do not treat these judgments as binding on passive plaintiffs, thus resulting in "an asymmetry between defendants bound by a judgment versus some passive plaintiffs with the option to bring a new suit in a foreign forum if they are unsatisfied with the first result." These plaintiffs are said to have a litigation option.)
76 See Rave, "Governing the Anticommons," p. 1186.
77 See Marc Galanter's analysis of "repeat players" vs. "one shotters" in the classical article, Marc Galanter, "Why the 'Haves' Come Out Ahead: Speculations on the Limits of Legal Change," (1974) 9 *Law & Society Review* 95.
78 "Third Party Funding: Snapshots from around the Globe," *Global Arbitration Review* (March 5, 2012), www.wongpartnership.com/index.php/files/download/1101.
79 "Third Party Funding: Snapshots from around the Globe" (citing *Siegfried Adalbert Unruh v. Hans-Joerg Seeberger*, Civil Appeal No. 298/2004, Oct. 7, 2005).
80 The Law Reform Commission of Hong Kong (HKLRC), "Consultation Paper on Third Party Funding for Arbitration," Third Party Funding for Arbitration Sub-Committee of the Law Reform Commission (Oct. 19, 2015), pp. 93–96, available at www.hkreform.gov.hk/en/publications/tpf.htm.
81 Civil Law (Amendment) Bill, 38/2016, Singapore Parliament, 7 Nov. 2016 (on third-party funding).
82 HKLRC, "Consultation Paper on Third Party Funding," p. 91–92.
83 Taurus Capital, "Challenges in Litigation" (March 9, 2017), available at tauruscapital.co.za/litigation-funding.

84 Ben Hancock, "Who Rules the World of Litigation Funding?" *American Lawyer* (March 30, 2017).
85 John C. Coffee Jr., "Securities Litigation Goes Global," 256 *New York Law Journal* 5, 5–7 (2016).
86 "Home Torts from Abroad," *Economist* (Feb. 26, 2004). Among those chronicling and analyzing the globalization of the legal profession are Marc Galanter & Thomas Palay, *Tournament of Lawyers: The Transformation of the Big Law Firm* (Chicago: University of Chicago Press, 1991); Yves Dezalay & David Sugarman (eds.), *Professional Competition and Professional Power: Lawyers, Accountants and the Social Construction of Markets* (London: Routledge, 1995); and Laura Empson (ed.), *Managing the Modern Law Firm: New Challenges, New Perspectives* (Oxford: Oxford University Press, 2007).
87 John C. Coffee Jr., *Entrepreneurial Litigation: Its Rise, Fall, and Future* (Cambridge, MA: Harvard University Press, 2016), p. 1 and John C. Coffee Jr., "The Regulation of Entrepreneurial Litigation: Balancing Fairness and Efficiency in the Large Class Action" (1987) 54 *University of Chicago Law Review* 877, 882–883.
88 See Coffee Jr., "Securities Litigation Goes Global"; see also Hensler, "Future of Mass Litigation," p. 320 (describing the same types of actions as "mash ups").
89 Michael D. Goldhaber, "The Global Lawyer: Global Class Actions after Morrison," *American Lawyer* (Feb. 10, 2012).
90 Wet Collectieve Afwikkeling Massaschade (TK 31.762 nr. 1) (Dutch Statute). (The latter is described at length in Hensler, "Future of Mass Litigation," p. 311.
91 Goldhaber, "Global Lawyer" (citing leading members of the bar and of academia who are calling for an international treaty to deal with the coordination problems that the new patchwork of Canadian and European regimes now creates).
92 Government of the Netherlands, "Legislative Proposal Presented to the Dutch Second Chamber About Collective Compensation Actions" (Nov. 16, 2016), available at www.government.nl/latest/news/2016/11/16/legislative-proposal-presented-to-the-dutch-second-chamber-about-collective-compensation-actions.
93 John C. Coffee Jr., "The Globalization of Entrepreneurial Litigation: Law, Culture, and Incentives" (2017) 165 *University of Pennsylvania Law Review* 1895, 1904. See Coffee Jr., "Securities Litigation Goes Global."
94 See Coffee Jr., "Securities Litigation Goes Global."
95 See Coffee Jr., "'Securities Litigation Goes Global" (also describing the *Olympus* cases, which were brought by a group of largely non-Japanese institutional investors and settled in Japan in 2015). Yuri Kageyama, "Olympus Settles with Japan Whistleblower after 8-year Battle," *San Diego Tribune* (Feb. 17, 2016), available at www.sandiegouniontribune.com/sdut-olympus-settles-with-japan-whistleblower-after-8-2016feb17-story.html.
96 William Boston, "German Court Allows Lawsuits against Volkswagen to Move Forward," *Wall Street Journal* (Aug. 8, 2016).
97 Hof's-Amsterdam 29 mei 2009, NJ 2009, 506 m.nt. J.M.J. Chorus, M.P. van Achterberg en W.H.F.M. (Shell Petroleum N.V./Dexia Bank Nederland N.V.) cited and described at length in Hensler, "Future of Mass Litigation," pp. 313–319. Goldhaber reports that the plaintiff's lawyer opined that the Dutch court's "primary concern was that, after Morrison, investors would have no relief in the entire world." See Goldhaber, "Global Class Actions after Morrison." The court expressly cited Morrison as a consideration in its decision on jurisdiction. Hof's-Amsterdam 29 mei 2009, NJ 2009, 506 m.nt.

J.M.J. Chorus, M.P. van Achterberg en W.H.F.M. (Shell Petroleum N.V./Dexia Bank Nederland N.V.)

98 Hensler, "Future of Mass Litigation," pp. 314–316, 320. In addition to the association, claimants were represented by a shareholders' advocacy group and two Dutch pension funds, and a number of American and Dutch firms represented the various parties.

99 *In re Royal Dutch/Shell Transp. Sec. Litig.*, 380 F. Supp. 2d 509, 572 (D.N.J. 2005) and *In re Royal Dutch/Shell Transp. Sec. Litig.*, 522 F. Supp. 2d 712, 715 (D.N.J. 2007).

100 Hensler, "Future of Mass Litigation," p. 316–317.

101 As foreseen in Maya Steinitz, "Whose Claim Is This Anyway? Third-Party Litigation Funding" (2011) 95 *Minnesota Law Review* 1268, 1300.

102 Goldhaber, "Forum Shopper's Remorse," p. 63.

103 Whytock & Robinson, "Forum Non Conveniens," pp. 1448–1449. See also Mark A. Behrens, Gregory L. Fowler & Silvia Kim, "Global Litigation Trends" (2008) 17 *Michigan State Journal of International Law* 165, 166 (n. 4).

104 Eugene Gulland, "All the World's a Forum," *National Law Journal* (Feb. 11, 2002), p. B13.

105 Whytock & Robinson, "Forum Non Conveniens" p. 1449. See also Cassandra Burke Robertson, "Transnational Litigation and Institutional Choice" (2010) 51 *Boston College Law Review* 1081, 1130.

106 Henry Saint Dahl translates and discusses such Latin American laws in Henry Saint Dahl, "Forum Non Conveniens, Latin America and Blocking Statutes," (2004) 35 *University of Miami Inter-American Law Review* 21, 22–24. Specifically, he discusses, Ecuador's Interpretative Law of Articles 27, 28, 29 and 30 of the Code of Civil Procedure for Cases of International Concurrent Jurisdiction; Guatemala's Law for the Defense of Procedural Rights of Nationals and Residents; Dominica's Transnational Causes of Action (Product Liability) Act 1997; Nicaragua's Law 362, Special Law for the Proceedings of Trials Promoted by People Affected by the Usage of DBCP Base Manufactured Pesticides; Costa Rica draft Law in Defense of the Procedural Rights of Nationals and Foreigners (which was ultimately not enacted); and the Latin American Parliament's Model Law on International Jurisdiction and Applicable Law to Tort Liability. See also Gary B. Born & Peter B. Rutledge, *International Civil Litigation in United States Courts* (New York: Wolters Kluwer Law & Business, 2011), pp. 969–977.

107 William E. Thomson & Perlette Michèle Jura, "Confronting the New Breed of Transnational Litigation: Abusive Foreign Judgments," *U.S. Chamber Institute for Legal Reform* (Oct. 2011).

108 *Donziger*, 768 F. Supp. 2d 581, 599 (S.D.N.Y. 2011) (the EMA allowed for aggregation of claims).

109 Jeff Todd, "Phantom Torts and Forum Non Conveniens Blocking Statutes: Irony and Metonym in Nicaraguan Special Law" (2012) 43 *University of Miami Inter-American Law Review* 291, 308. The law enacted various procedural mechanisms to aid mass tort victims such as mandatory deposits by MNC defendants, minimum damages amounts, and presumptions that DBCP exposure was the cause of various illnesses or maladies.

110 Thomson & Jura, "Confronting the New Breed of Transnational Litigation," p. 3.

111 Hal S. Scott, "What to Do about Foreign Discriminatory Forum Non Conveniens Legislation" (2009) 49 *Harvard International Law Journal Online* 95, 100–101.

112 Thomson & Jura, "Confronting the New Breed of Transnational Litigation," p. 3.

113 See, e.g., *Osorio v. Dole Food Co.*, 665 F. Supp. 2d 1307 (S.D. Fla. 2009).

114 See Commission of the European Communities, "Green Paper: Damages Actions for Breach of EC Antitrust Rules" (Dec. 19, 2005), available at www.eur-lex.europa.eu/legal-content/EN/TXT/PDF/?uri=CELEX:52005DC0672&from=en.
115 Mark A. Behrens, Gregory L. Fowler & Silvia Kim, "Global Litigation Trends" (2008) 17 *Michigan State Journal of International Law* 165, 192.
116 See Introduction.
117 With the exception of Quebec, Canada, which allowed the class action in 1973. Other Canadian provinces followed suit in the 1990s, as did Australia in 1992. "If one looked out over the global landscape around 2000, that was about it with regard to [aggregate litigation]." See Hensler, "Future of Mass Litigation," p. 306.
118 Hensler, "Future of Mass Litigation," pp. 306–307.
119 Coffee Jr., "Entrepreneurial Litigation," p. 187 (n. 4).
120 Melissa R. Ginsburg, "First Opt-Out Class Action Underway in the United Kingdom," *Patterson Belknap* (July 7, 2016), www.pbwt.com/antitrust/antitrust-update-blog-2/first-opt-class-action-underway-united-kingdom/.
121 Deborah R. Hensler, "The Global Landscape of Collective Litigation" in Deborah R. Hensler, Christopher Hodges & Ianika Tzankova (eds.), *Class Actions in Context* (Cheltenham: Edward Elgar, 2016) p. 5.
122 Hensler, "Global Landscape of Collective Litigation," p. 5.
123 Hensler, "Future of Mass Litigation," p. 307.
124 See, EU Commission, Recommendation of 11 June 2013 on Common Principles for Injunctive and Compensatory Collective Redress Mechanisms in the Member States Concerning Violations of Rights Granted under Union Law (2013/396/EU) Official Journal of the European Union L201/60, para. 10 (hereinafter: "European Commission Recommendation). See also Christopher Hodges, *The Reform of Class and Representative Actions in European Legal Systems: A New Framework for Collective Redress in Europe* (Oxford: Hart Publishing, 2008), p. 115); John C. Coffee Jr., "Litigation Governance: Taking Accountability Seriously" (2010) 110 *Columbia Law Review* 288, 292.
125 Hensler, "Future of Mass Litigation," p. 309.
126 EU Commission Recommendation, para. 15.
127 Lisa Bench Nieuwveld & Victoria Shannon, *Third Party Funding in International Arbitration* (New York: Aspen Publishers, 2012), p. 177 (para 8.02).
128 Bundesverfassungsgericht (Bverfg), Beschluss des Ersten Senats vom (Dec. 12, 2006), 1 BvR 2576/04, Rn. (1–115), available at www.bverfg.de/e/rs20061212_1bvr257604.html.
129 See Amichai Magen & Peretz Segal, "Israel," in Deborah R. Hensler, Christopher Hodges & Magdalena Tulibacka (eds.), *The Globalization of Class Actions: The Annals of American Academy of Political and Social Sciences*, vol. 622 (Sage Publishing, 2009), p. 244–53.
130 The Right Honourable Lord Justice Jackson, "Review of Civil Litigation Costs: Final Report" (United Kingdom; Stationary Office Information Publishing, 2009), p. 334–335, available at www.judiciary.gov.uk/wp-content/uploads/JCO/Documents/Reports/jackson-final-report-140110.pdf.
131 Jasminka Kalajdzic, W. A. Bogart & Ian Matthews, "The Globalization of Class Actions: Canada," in Deborah R. Hensler, Christopher Hodges & Magdalena Tulibacka (eds.), *The Globalization of Class Actions: The Annals of American Academy of Political and Social Sciences*, vol. 622 (Sage Publishing, 2009), p. 41, 44.
132 Lord Justice Jackson, "Review of Civil Litigation Costs," p. 131.

133 James Surowiecki, "Companies with Benefits," *New Yorker* (Aug. 4, 2014). Going on to contextualize that "the desire to balance profit and purpose is arguably a return to the model that many American companies once followed. Henry Ford declared that, instead of boosting dividends, he'd rather use the money to build better cars and pay better wages. And Johnson & Johnson's credo, written in 1943, stated that the company's 'first responsibility' was not to investors but to doctors, nurses, and patients.... The rise of B corps is a reminder that the idea that corporations should be only lean, mean, profit-maximizing machines isn't dictated by the inherent nature of capitalism, let alone by human nature."

134 M. Todd Henderson & Anup Malani, "Capitalism 2.0," *Forbes Magazine* (Feb. 22, 2008).

135 James Surowiecki, "Moaning Moguls," *New Yorker* (July 7, 2004) (quoting the sociologist Mark Mizruchi, the author of *The Fracturing of the American Corporate Elite* (Cambridge: Cambridge University Press, 2014).

136 Brett McDonnell, "Benefit Corporations and Strategic Action Fields or (The Existential Failing of Delaware)," (2016) 39 *Seattle University Law Review* 263, 264.

137 See generally Archie B. Carroll, "A History of Corporate Social Responsibility: Concepts and Practices," in Andrew Crane, et al. (eds.), *The Oxford Handbook of Corporate Social Responsibility* (Oxford: Oxford University Press, 2008), pp. 19–46.

138 Carroll, "History of Corporate Social Responsibility," pp. 19–26.

139 Carroll, "History of Corporate Social Responsibility," pp. 24 (citing *Fortune*, Mar. 1946, 197–198).

140 Patrick Murphy, "An Evolution: Corporate Social Responsiveness" (1978) 30 *University of Michigan Business Review* 19, 12–15.

141 Carroll, "History of Corporate Social Responsibility," p. 26.

142 "Social Responsibilities of Business Corporations," *Committee for Economic Development*, June 1971, p. 16, available at www.ced.org/pdf/Social_Responsibilities_of_Business_Corporations.pdf.

143 See, e.g., Lee E. Preston & James E. Post, *Private Management and Public Policy: The Principle of Public Responsibility* (Englewood Cliffs, NJ: Prentice-Hall, 1975), p. 9.

144 Organisation for Economic Co-Operation and Development, "Corporate Social Responsibility: Partners for Progress," *OECD* (Oct. 15, 2001), available at www.oecd.org/cfe/leed/corporatesocialresponsibilitypartnersforprogress.htm.

145 OECD, "Guidelines for Multinational Enterprises," pp. 31–34, available at www.oecd.org/daf/inv/mne/48004323.pdf.

146 "Our Participants," *United Nations Global Compact* (March 11, 2017) available at www.unglobalcompact.org/what-is-gc/participants.

147 Graham Knight & Jackie Smith, "The Global Compact and Its Critics: Activism, Power Relations, and Corporate Social Responsibility," in Janie Leatherman (ed.), *Discipline and Punishment in Global Politics: Illusions of Control* (London: Palgrave Macmillan, 2008), pp. 191–213.

148 Brief of Joseph E. Stiglitz as Amici Curiae in Support of Plaintiffs, *Mohamad v. Palestinian Authority*, 566 U.S. 449; *Kiobel v. Royal Dutch Petroleum Co.*, 569 U.S. 108 (2011), p. 13, available at www.americanbar.org/content/dam/aba/publications/supreme_court_preview/briefs/10-1491_petitioner_amcu_stiglitz.authcheckdam.pdf (hereinafter Stiglitz *Kiobel* Brief) (citing Jonathan Isham, et. al., "Civil Liberties, Democracy, and the Performance of Government Projects" (1997) 11 *World Bank Economic Review* 219).

149 Shannon Lindsey Blanton & Robert G. Blanton, "What Attracts Foreign Investors? An Examination of Human Rights and Foreign Direct Investment" (2007) 29 *Journal of Politics* 143, 153.

150 Stiglitz, *Kiobel* Brief, p. 14 (quoting Blanton & Blanton, "What Attracts Foreign Investors?" p. 153.)
151 Stiglitz, *Kiobel* Brief, pp. 11–12 (responding to the US Chamber's argument in the Brief for the Chamber of Commerce as *Amicus Curiae* in Support of Defendants-Appellants, p. 28).
152 Brief of Amicus Curiae Joseph F. Stiglitz in Support of Plaintiffs-Appellees Seeking Affirmance of District Court's Decision, *Balintulo v. Daimler AG*, 2009 WL 7768608, No. 09-2778-CV, at *9 (2d Cir. 2009).
153 Stiglitz, *Kiobel* Brief, p. 12.
154 Brief of Amicus Curiae Joseph F. Stiglitz in Support of Plaintiffs-Appellees Seeking Affirmance of District's Court Decision, *Balintulo*, 2009 WL 7768608, at *9 n.7 (2d Cir. 2009).
155 Stiglitz, *Kiobel* Brief, p. 6.
156 Stiglitz, *Kiobel* Brief, p. 5.
157 Stiglitz, *Kiobel* Brief, p. 18.
158 Stiglitz, *Kiobel* Brief, pp. 19–20 (citing Paul J. Beck, et al., "The Impact of the Foreign Corrupt Practices Act on U.S. Exports"(1992) 12 *Managerial & Decision Economics* 295, 303).
159 Stiglitz, *Kiobel* Brief, p. 20.

5 INSTITUTIONAL AND PROCEDURAL FEATURES OF AN ICCJ

1 For these reasons, and because of space constraints, the suggestions are also conceptual and general rather than detailed and operational.
2 There is a wealth of literature on how (and why) international courts and tribunals hybridize common law and civil law. See, e.g., Colin B. Picker, "International Law's Mixed Heritage: A Common/Civil Law Jurisdiction" (2008) 41 *Vanderbilt Journal of Transnational Law* 1083.
3 William Tetley, "Mixed Jurisdictions: Common Law v. Civil Law (Codified and Uncodified)" (2000) 60 *Louisiana Law Review* 677, 685–686 (suggesting that, in fact, the distinction between "pure" and "mixed" legal systems and jurisdiction may be irrelevant since legal norms migrate into "pure" legal traditions). See also Kenneth G. C. Reid, "The Idea of Mixed Legal Systems" (2003) 78 *Tulane Law Review* 5, 7 and Picker, "International Law's Mixed Heritage," p. 1102.
4 See Tetley, "Mixed Jurisdictions," p. 680.
5 See Picker, "International Law's Mixed Heritage," pp. 1095, 1100–1102.
6 See Statute of the International Court of Justice, Ch. 1, Art. 31, p. 5, and Andreas Zimmermann et al. (eds.), *The Statute of the International Court of Justice: A Commentary* (Oxford: Oxford University Press, 2012), pp. 306–307.
7 Daniel Terris, Leigh Swigart & Cesare P. R. Romano, *The International Judge: An Introduction to the Men and Women Who Decide the World's Cases*(Lebanon, NH: University Press of New England, 2007), p. 99.
8 For this warning and for nuanced analyses of the differences and convergences between the world's legal systems see Mirjan R. Damaska, *The Faces of Justice and State Authority: A Comparative Approach to the Legal Process*, rev. ed. (New Haven, CT: Yale University Press, 1991), p. 3; George P. Fletcher & Stephen M. Sheppard (eds.), *American Law in a Global Context* (Oxford: Oxford University Press, 2005), p. 4; H. Patrick Glenn, *Legal Traditions of the World* (Oxford: Oxford University Press, 2000), p. 273 (n.130).
9 See generally, Manual for Complex Litigation, Fourth § 22 (produced under the auspices of the Federal Judicial Center).

10 See John H. Langbein, "The German Advantage in Civil Procedure" (1985) 52 *University of Chicago Law Review*, 823, 825.
11 EU Commission, Recommendation of 11 June 2013 on Common Principles for Injunctive and Compensatory Collective Redress Mechanisms in the Member States Concerning Violations of Rights Granted under Union Law (2013/396/EU) Official Journal of the European Union L201/60, para. 9.
12 Gary B. Born, *International Commercial Arbitration: Commentary and Materials* (2d ed., Kluwer Arbitration eds., 2001), pp. 1–10.
13 Francis E. McGovern, "The What and Why of Claims Resolution Facilities" (2005) 57 *Stanford Law Review* 1361.
14 See the Introduction, Section II "Incentives and Feasibility."
15 The precise contours of and boundary between the concepts of jurisdiction and admissibility are not universally settled, and the terms are sometimes given different or overlapping meanings even by the same court in different decisions. In this chapter I adopt the framework suggested by Yuval Shany. See Yuval Shany, *Questions of Jurisdiction and Admissibility Before International Courts* (Cambridge: Cambridge University Press, 2015), p. 7.
16 Of course, as mentioned in Chapter 4, research does not seem to bear out the thesis that stronger norms and enforcement lead to loss of investment. But the perception of the possibility of such a loss may nonetheless influence states' decisions about whether to join an ICCJ.
17 See generally, Rome Statute of the International Criminal Court, Rome (17 July 1998).
18 United Nations Convention on the Recognition and Enforcement of Foreign Arbitral Awards (1958).
19 "Recognition" means the preclusion of relitigation of the same issues. Enforcement goes a step further and requires that domestic procedures to enforce a judgment or an award be followed.
20 UNCITRAL Secretariat Guide on the Convention on the Recognition and Enforcement of Foreign Arbitral Awards, United Nations commission on International Trade Law (1958). As of this writing, 157 states have joined the convention and the New York Arbitration Center reports a 90 percent enforcement rate. See, The Convention on the Recognition and Enforcement of Foreign Arbitral, New York Arbitration Convention (10 June 1958), available at www.newyorkconvention.org/in+brief.
21 UNCITRAL Secretariat Guide on the Convention on the Recognition and Enforcement of Foreign Arbitral Awards, United Nations Commission on International Trade Law (1958), p.126. See also UNCITRAL Secretariat Guide on the Convention on the Recognition and Enforcement of Foreign Arbitral Awards, United Nations commission on International Trade Law (1958), n. 571 and 572 surveying court cases around the world and leading commentary. Even "an arbitrator's manifest disregard of the law, which constitutes a ground for vacating domestic arbitral awards under the United States Federal Arbitration Act" has been rejected as grounds for refusing to recognize or enforce international arbitration awards by U.S. federal courts. UNCITRAL Secretariat Guide on the Convention on the Recognition and Enforcement of Foreign Arbitral Awards, United Nations Commission on International Trade Law (1958), p. 127.
22 UNCITRAL Secretariat Guide on the Convention on the Recognition and Enforcement of Foreign Arbitral Awards, United Nations Commission on International Trade Law (1958), p. 125.

23 That could be accomplished in a number of ways. The most straightforward would be to specify, by name, a group of capital exporting countries some percentage of which would need to join before the treaty/treaties entered into force. If naming countries proved to be difficult, drafters could adopt an objective metric such as the ranking of FDI outflows calculated by UNCTAD. See "World Investment Report, Annex 2: FDI outflows by region and economy," United Nations Conference on Trade and Development, 1990–2015, available at www.unctad.org/Sections/dite_dir/docs/WIR2016/WIR16_tab02.xlsx. I thank Nathan Miller for suggesting the two-tiered structure.

24 Eric A. Posner & John C. Yoo, "Judicial Independence in International Tribunals" (2005) 93 *California Law Review* 1, 3.

25 Laurence R. Helfer & Anne-Marie Slaughter, "Toward a Theory of Effective Supranational Adjudication" (1997) 107 *Yale Law Journal* 273, 276–277; Laurence R. Helfer & Anne-Marie Slaughter, "Why States Create International Tribunals: A Response to Professors Posner and Yoo" (2005) 93 *California Law Review* 899, 901.

26 For a useful guide, see the *Burgh House Principles on the Independence of the International Judiciary*, Study Group of the International Law Association (2014), available at www.ucl.ac.uk/laws/cict/docs/burgh_final_21204.pdf. The *Burgh House Principles* provide guidelines on ensuring international judicial independence along four axes: from the parties to the cases; from their own states of nationality and/or residence; from the member states of the court or the organization of which the court is a part; and from the host state of the court. *The Burgh House Principles on the Independence of the International Judiciary*, Preamble.

27 International Court of Justice Statute, Art. 2.

28 See e.g., European Convention of Human Rights, Art. 21.

29 Judges of the ICJ, for instance, are elected by members of the General Assembly – all of which are also members of the Statute of the ICJ, something that happens automatically upon joining the UN (uniquely, the ICJ adds another layer of politics by holding a simultaneous election in the Security Council). See Members of the Court, International Court of Justice, available at www.icj-cij.org/en/members. At the International Tribunal for the Law of the Sea, the ICC, the African Court of Human and Peoples Rights, the European Convention on Human Rights, the Inter-American Court of Human Rights, judges are elected by the constituents of the court. See "Members, International Tribunal for the Law of the Sea," available at www.itlos.org/the-tribunal/members/; "Election of ICC and ASP Officials," *Coalition for the International Criminal Court*, available at www.iccnow.org/?mod=elections; "African Court on Human and Peoples' Rights," *African Commission on Human and Peoples' Rights*, available at www.achpr.org/about/afchpr/; "Judge of the European Court of Human Rights – Information Pack," *European Court of Human Rights*, available at https://jac.judiciary.gov.uk/sites/default/files/sync/basic_page/information_pack_final.pdf; and "Statute of the Inter-American Court of Human Rights," *Inter-American Commission on Human Rights*, available at www.oas.org/en/iachr/mandate/basics/statutecourt.asp. The statutes of the Common Market for Eastern and Southern Africa Court of Justice and the Court of Justice of the Economic Community of West African States merely provide that the members shall "appoint" judges (presumably leaving the appointments process up to the rules of procedure of members' plenary body. Community Court of Justice, ECOWAS, available at www.ecowas.int/institutions/community-court-of-justice/; Profile of the Court, COMESA Court, available at www.comesacourt.org/profile-2/. Judges on the Court of Justice of the European Union and

members of the Appellate Body of the World Trade Organization are appointed by consensus of the members of the organization. See "Court of Justice of the European Union Overview," *European Union*, available at www.europa.eu/european-union/about-eu/institutions-bodies/court-justice_en; and "Appellate Body Members," *World Trade Organization*, available at www.wto.org/english/tratop_e/dispu_e/ab_members_descrp_e.htm.

30 The ICJ nomination proceeds via national blocs with reference to membership in the PCA. Blocs must nominate three judges, of which only two may be of the nationality of members of the bloc. Members of the Court, International Court of Justice, The Court, available at www.icj-cij.org/en/members.
31 International Court of Justice Statute, Art. 9.
32 Rome Statute, Art. 36(8)(a)(i)–(iii).
33 Inter-American Commission on Human Rights Statute, Art. 7; Rome Statute, Art. 36(7).
34 International Criminal Court Rome Statute Art., 36(4)(b).
35 *The Burgh House Principles*, Art. 8.1.
36 See Karin Oellers-Frahm, "International Courts and Tribunals, Judges and Arbitrators," in Max Planck, *Max Planck Encyclopedia of Public International Law* (Oxford: Oxford University Press, 2012), para. 22.
37 See William Schabas, *The International Criminal Court: A Commentary on the Rome Statute* (Oxford: Oxford University Press, 2010), pp. 70–76.
38 See Schabas, *The International Criminal Court*, pp. 70–76.
39 See Schabas, *The International Criminal Court*, pp. 70–76.
40 The Permanent Court of Arbitration, "established in 1899 to facilitate arbitration and other forms of dispute resolution between states, ... has developed into a modern, multifaceted arbitral institution perfectly situated to meet the evolving dispute resolution needs of the international community." "About," *Permanent Court of Arbitration*, available at www.pca-cpa.org/en/about/.
41 International Criminal Court Rome Statute, Art. 11.
42 Vienna Convention on the Law of Treaties, Art. 28. See also Mark Villiger, *Commentary on the 1969 Vienna Convention on the Law of Treaties* (Boston: Martinus Nijhoff, 2009), p. 386.
43 Sadie Blanchard, "State Consent, Temporal Jurisdiction, and the Importation of Continuing Circumstances Analysis into International Investment Arbitration" (2011) 10 *Washington University Global Studies Law Review* 419, 422.
44 Louis W. McKernan, "Special Mexican Claims" (1938) 32 *American Journal of International Law* 457, 457.
45 As is the statutory definition in the American Multiparty Multiforum Trial Jurisdiction Act § a and § c(4).
46 Federal Rules of Civil Procedure 23.
47 See 28 U.S.C. § 1332 (diversity jurisdiction) and 28 U.S.C. § 1367 (supplemental jurisdiction).
48 The ICCJ statute should also provide that the court could make equitable determinations of "enterprise." Equitable power is the power to act as justice requires. It is flexible and discretionary and has developed in England, and later in other common law jurisdictions, to enable just results where the rigidity of the law prevents those.
49 See American Standard, SEC No-Action Letter, 1972 SEC No Act. LEXIS 3787 (11 Oct. 1972), p. *1 (indicating a person's ownership status as a "10 percent shareholder" is an indicator of control).

50 "Tort," *Legal Information Institute*, available at www.law.cornell.edu/wex/tort; see also John C. P. Goldberg et al., *Tort Law: Responsibilities and Redress* (4th ed., New York: Wolters Kluwer, 2016), p. 2.
51 See George P. Fletcher & Steve Sheppard (eds.), *American Law in a Global Context: The Basics* (Oxford: Oxford University Press, 2005), p. 440. The same is true beyond the West. See generally Dominic N. Dagbanja, "Customary Tort Law in Sub-Saharan Africa," Abdul Basir bin Mohamad, "Islamic Tort Law," and Hoa Jiang, "Chinese Tort Law: Between Tradition and Transplants," in Mauro Bussani & Anthony J. Sebok (eds.), *Comparative Tort Law: Global Perspectives* (Cheltenham: Edward Elgar, 2015), pp. 412, 441, 385 (which describe the main non-Western approaches to tort law). See also generally, Cees van Dam, *European Tort Law* (Cambridge: Cambridge University Press, 2013).
52 Robert L. Rabin, "Environmental Liability and the Tort System" (1987) 24 *Houston Law Review* 27, 29.
53 The vast majority of international courts and tribunals are specialized, meaning that they apply a specific body of law set forth in their constitutive documents. Generally, the International Court of Justice is regarded as the only general international court, as it has jurisdiction *ratione materiae* over any matter of international law. See Cesare P. R. Romano, "A Taxonomy of International Rule of Law Institutions" (2011) 2 *Journal of International Dispute Settlement* 241, 265.
54 Joel D. Goldhar & Mariann Jelinek, "Plan for Economies of Scope," *Harvard Business Review* (Nov. 1983), available at www.hbr.org/1983/11/plan-for-economies-of-scope.
55 See International Court of Justice Statute, Art. 36; Andreas Zimmermann et al. (eds.), *The Statute of the International Court of Justice: A Commentary* (Oxford: Oxford University Press, 2012), p. 633–711.
56 See Treaties, *International Court of Justice*, available at www.icj-cij.org/en/treaties; Jonathan I. Charney, "Compromissory Clauses and the Jurisdiction of the International Court of Justice" (1987) 81 *American Journal of International Law* 855, 855–887.
57 Yuval Shany, *Questions of Jurisdiction and Admissibility before International Courts* (Cambridge: Cambridge University Press, 2015), p. 64.
58 This shift in the paradigm of personal jurisdiction gave rise to what Karen Alter calls the "new international courts." See Karen J. Alter, "Private Litigants and the New International Courts" (2006) 39 *Comparative Political Studies* 1, 22, 25 (n. 5) and accompanying text. ("What I am calling the 'new style [international courts]' are the now very large number of [international courts] that a) have compulsory jurisdiction ... and b) allow private actors access. ... At this point, we can fairly say that most [international courts] fit this new-style model, and nearly every [international court] created since 1990 fits this new style.")
59 See "Practical Guide to Admissibility Criteria," European Court of Human Rights, 2014, available at www.echr.coe.int/Documents/Admissibility_guide_ENG.pdf; "Admissibility of Complaints before the African Court" (2016), available at www.fidh.org/IMG/pdf/admissibility_of_complaints_before_the_african_court_june_2016_eng_web-2.pdf; "Practical Guide African Court on Humans' and People's Rights" (2010) available at https://www.fidh.org/spip.php?page=spipdf&spipdf=spipdf_article&id_article=2067&nom_fichier=article_2067.
60 For a full taxonomy of the types of jurisdictions and relationships between national and international courts see Yuval Shany, *Regulating Jurisdictional Relations between National and International Courts* (Oxford: Oxford University Press, 2007), pp. 79–106.

61 Recall Petition for Writ of Mandamus, *In re Hugo Gerardo Camacho Naranjo*, No. 11-cv-0691-LAK (S.D.N.Y. 2011), n. 8.

62 "Complementary jurisdiction" is generally considered one of the most fundamental innovations and compromises that have led to an agreement on the ICC. See Rome Statute, Art. 17. As a compromise, and a fundamental feature of the court, both the principle and the application of complementarity are topics of quite some controversy. See, e.g., Laurence Weschler, "Exceptional Cases in Rome: The United States and the Struggle for an ICC," in The United States and the International Criminal Court 85 (Sarah B. Sewall & Carl Kaysen eds., 2000) (describing the positions of different groups with regard to jurisdiction issues, including complementarity); William W. Burke-White, "Proactive Complementarity: The International Criminal Court and National Courts in the Rome System of International Justice" (2008) 49 *Harvard International Law Journal* 53 (discussing opposition to complementarity as well as its conceptual and practical limits).

63 In the United States, for example, the evidentiary threshold for such determination is extremely low. A single adverse report might be enough; one federal court based its summary judgment rejecting the jurisdiction of Liberian courts on the US Department of State's annual Country Report for Liberia. Such reports typically devote between one and three paragraphs each to a host of human rights and rule of law issues that might be important in a given country. Maya Steinitz & Paul Gowder, "Transnational Law as a Prisoner's Dilemma" (2014) 94 *North Carolina Law Review* 751, 766 n. 60 (citing *Bridgeway Corp. v. Citibank*, 201 F.3d 134 (2d Cir. 2000)).

64 In the United States, as judges have found it necessary to adopt more and more case management techniques originally reserved for class actions some judges and scholars have come to view multidistrict litigations (MDLs), the main form of nonclass aggregation, as "quasi-class actions." See Charles Silver & Geoffrey P. Miller, "The Quasi-Class Action Method of Managing Multi-District Litigations: Problems and a Proposal" (2010) 63 *Vanderbilt Law Review* 107, 114.

65 See e.g., Rule 23 of the Federal Rules of Civil Procedure, which sets out the following conditions to certifying an action to proceed as a class action: "(a) Prerequisites. One or more members of a class may sue or be sued as representative parties on behalf of all members only if: (1) the class is so numerous that joinder of all members is impracticable; (2) there are questions of law or fact common to the class; (3) the claims or defenses of the representative parties are typical of the claims or defenses of the class; and (4) the representative parties will fairly and adequately protect the interests of the class. (b) [] A class action may be maintained if Rule 23(a) is satisfied and if: (1) prosecuting separate actions by or against individual class members would create a risk of: (A) inconsistent or varying adjudications with respect to individual class members that would establish incompatible standards of conduct for the party opposing the class; or (B) adjudications with respect to individual class members that, as a practical matter, would be dispositive of the interests of the other members not parties to the individual adjudications or would substantially impair or impede their ability to protect their interests."

66 28 U.S.C. § 1407. The writing on MDL is legion. Overviews are available, e.g., in Linda Mullenix, *Mass Tort Litigation: Cases and Materials* (St. Paul, MN: West Academic, 2008).

67 See generally, Mirjan R. Damaska, *The Faces of Justice and State Authority: A Comparative Approach to the Legal Process*, rev. ed. (New Haven, CT: Yale University Press, 1991). Additional nuanced analyses of the differences and convergences between the world's

legal systems include Patrick Glenn, *Legal Traditions of the World* (Oxford: Oxford University Press, 2000) and René David & John E. C. Brierley, *Major Legal Systems in the World Today: An Introduction to the Comparative Study of Law* (New York: Free Press, 1978).
68 Damaska, *Faces of Justice and State Authority*, p. 3.
69 James G. Apple & Robert P. Deyling, "A Primer on the Civil-Law System," Federal Judicial Center at the request of the International Judicial Relations Committee of the Judicial Conference of the United States (1995), pp. 26–27.
70 Michèle Schmiegelow & Henrik Schmiegelow, *Institutional Competition between Common Law and Civil Law: Theory and Policy* (Berlin: Springer-Verlag Berlin Heidelberg, 2014), p. 121.
71 Christopher Hodges, Stefan Vogenauer & Magdalena Tulibacka (eds.), *The Costs and Funding of Civil Litigation: A Comparative Perspective* (Oxford: Hart, 2010), p. 107 (and entire chapter).
72 Mathias W. Reimann, *Cost and Fee Allocation in Civil Procedure: A Comparative Study* (New York: Springer Science & Business Media, 2012), p. 30. See also Hodges, *Costs and Funding of Civil Litigation*, pp. 92, 102 (lawyers' fees are biggest expense in all systems).
73 See generally, Richard A. Nagareda, *Mass Torts in a World of Settlement* (Chicago: University of Chicago Press, 2007).
74 See Michael J. Saks, "Do We Really Know Anything about the Behavior of the Tort Litigation System – and Why Not?" (1992) 140 *University of Pennsylvania Law Review* 1147, 1212 (1992). See also Nagareda, *Mass Torts in a World of Settlement*, p. ix; Samuel Issacharoff & John Fabian Witt, "The Inevitability of Aggregate Settlement: An Institutional Account of American Tort Law" (2004) 57 *Vanderbilt Law Review* 1571, 1577–1599.
75 Gregory Shaffer, Manfred Elsig, & Sergio Puig., "The Extensive (but Fragile) Authority of the WTO Appellate Body" (2016) 79 *Law and Contemporary Problems* 237.
76 E.g., EU Commission Recommendation, para. 16.
77 The WTO Dispute Settlement Understanding, for instance, provides that parties may seek good offices, conciliation, or mediation and that the director general of the WTO may perform those functions. See "Dispute Settlement without Recourse to Panels and the Appellate Body," *WTO – Dispute Settlement Training Module: Chapter 8*, available at www.wto.org/english/tratop_e/dispu_e/disp_settlement_cbt_e/c8s1p2_e.htm. In the Inter-American human rights system, the commission may facilitate friendly settlements on its own initiative or on the initiative of the parties. See American Convention on Human Rights, Art. 48(1)(f); IACHR Rules of Procedure, Art. 40.1.
78 This language is taken from 28 U.S.C.A. § 1407, which created the federal Judicial Panel on Multidistrict Litigation (JPMDL). The stated purpose for the creation of the JPMDL was "to provide centralized management under court supervision of pretrial proceedings of multidistrict litigation to assure the 'just and efficient conduct' of such actions. The committee believes that the possibility for conflict and duplication in discovery and other pretrial procedures in related cases can be avoided or minimized by such centralized management.... for the limited purpose of conducting coordinated pretrial proceedings." See H.R. Rep. No. 1130, p. 2–3 (1968). In the United States, where the MDL is a mechanism devised to deal with the disbursement of federal courts across the fifty states, MDLs are limited to the pretrial phase. This limitation is irrelevant for an ICCJ, which will be a single institution.

79 See Howard M. Holtzmann & Edda Kristjánsdóttir (eds.), *International Mass Claims Processes: Legal and Practical Perspectives* (Oxford: Oxford University Press, 2007), pp. 210–211 (5.02 editors' commentary).

80 See Holtzmann & Kristjánsdóttir, *International Mass Claims Processes*, pp. 244–246 (5.06 editors' commentary) (also discussing additional methods that have been used in transnational claims facilities, such as matching claims data against verification data; computerized grouping of cases with similar issues; standardized verification and valuation by professionals such as accountants and loss adjusters who use "customized computer software to standardize the verification of claims and the calculation of the amount of awards").

81 Francis E. McGovern, "The What and Why of Claims Resolution Facilities" (2005) 57 *Stanford Law Review* 1361, 1371.

82 McGovern, "Claims Resolution Facilities," p. 1372.

83 Deborah R. Hensler, "The Future of Mass Litigation: Global Class Actions and Third-Party Litigation Funding" (2011) 79 *George Washington Law Review*, 306, pp. 307–308 (emphasis in the original).

84 The term 'private attorneys general' was first coined by judge and legal philosopher Jerome Frank in *Associated Industries of New York State, Inc. v. Ickes*, 134 F.2d 694, 704 (2d Cir. 1943) and it encapsulates the idea of private enforcement of the law through class actions brought by private attorneys who themselves finance the enforcement action.

85 Jules Stuyck, "Class Actions in Europe? To Opt-In or to Opt-Out, That Is the Question" (2009) 4 *European Business Law Review* 482, 491.

86 Samuel Issacharoff & Geoffrey P. Miller, "Will Aggregate Litigation Come to Europe?" (2009) 62 *Vanderbilt Law Review* 179, 184.

87 The Competition Appeal Tribunal Rules (2015), Rule 79(3), available at www.catribunal.org/files/The_Competition_Appeal_Tribunal_Rules_2015.pdf.

88 Hakim Bourlabah & Maria-Claire Van Den Bosche, "Belgium: Introduction to Class Actions Framework" (2017) 1 *Class Actions Law Review*, 21, 25, available at http://thelawreviews.co.uk/digital_assets/796e14a0-ce56-49e0-8156-6efa712eeb25/TLR---Class-Actions-1---Book.pdf.

89 Erik Werlauff, "Class Actions in Denmark" (2009) 622 *Annals of the American Academy of Political and Social Science* 202, pp. 202–208.

90 Government of the Netherlands, "Legislative Proposal Presented to the Dutch Second Chamber about Collective Compensation Actions (Nov. 16, 2016), available at www.government.nl/latest/news/2016/11/16/legislative-proposal-presented-to-the-dutch-second-chamber-about-collective-compensation-actions; "Overview of Legislative Proposal on Collective Action," (20 Feb. 2017), *Stibbe*, available at www.stibbe.com/en/news/2017/february/overview-of-legislative-proposal-on-collective-action-nl.

91 See Céline Lustin-Le Core, "Class Actions: France," *Getting the Deal Through* (Dec. 2017), available at www.gettingthedealthrough.com/area/82/jurisdiction/28/class-actions-france/; Duncan Fairgrieve & Alexandre Biard, "Focus on Collective Redress: France," *British Institute of International and Comparative Law*, available at www.collectiveredress.org/collective-redress/reports/france/sectoralcollectiveredressmechanisms.

92 See, e.g., Tina Leia Russell, "Exporting Class Actions to the European Union" (2010) 28 *Boston University International Law Journal*, 141, 150.

93 Samuel Issacharoff, "Class Actions and State Authority" (2012) 44 *Loyola University Chicago Law Journal*, 369, 371.

94 See Hensler, "Future of Mass Litigation," p. 309.
95 Elizabeth Oger-Gross et al., "Litigation and Enforcement in France: Overview," *Thomson Reuters Practical Law* (2017), available at https://uk.practicallaw.thomsonreuters.com/9-502-0121?transitionType=Default&contextData=(sc.Default)&firstPage=true&bhcp=1.
96 Christopher Hodges, Stefan Vogenauer & Magdalena Tulibacka, *The Costs and Funding of Civil Litigation: A Comparative Perspective* (London: Bloomsbury Press, 2010), p. 93.
97 See "Financial Assistance to Parties," International Court of Justice, available at www.icj-cij.org/en/financial-assistance-to-parties.
98 "The Services of the ACWL," *Advisory Centre on WTO Law*, available at www.acwl.ch/download/ql/Services_of_the_ACWL.pdf. See also James Ransdell, "Financial and Technical Support for Litigants in Inter-State Disputes: The Example of the WTO and the Advisory Centre for WTO Law," *Leiden University Law School* (Feb. 2017).
99 "Legal Assistance Fund," *Inter-American Commission of Human Rights* (2011), available at www.oas.org/en/iachr/mandate/basics/fund.asp.
100 See, e.g., "Electronic Document Distribution System of the United Nations," United Nations, available at https://documents-dds-ny.un.org/doc/UNDOC/GEN/N04/518/22/PDF/N0451822.pdf.
101 The "conditional fee," also known as "no win no fee," also shifts the financial risk of a loss to the attorneys. But should they prevail they receive their normal hourly based fee plus a success fee, which may be capped by law. (In England, a success fee can be no more than 100 percent of the normal fee, making the potential upside lower than in the United States.) See The Conditional Fee order 2000 § 4 (SI 2000 no. 823). Lawyers remain subject to the ethical rules of their jurisdiction, which means that whether or not they can enter into contingent or conditional arrangement may still be limited even if the ICCJ itself allows such arrangements.
102 Hensler, "Future of Mass Litigation," p. 309.
103 See James S. Kakalik & Nicholas M. Pace, *Costs and Compensation Paid in Tort Litigation* (Santa Monica, CA: RAND, 1986), p. 96 (reporting that 98 percent of individual plaintiffs in tort litigation paid on a contingent basis) and Nora Freeman Engstrom, "Lawyer Lending: Costs and Consequences," (2014) 63 *DePaul Law Review* 377, 379–380.
104 Reimann, *Cost and Fee Allocation in Civil Procedure*, p. 31. See also Catherine Elliott, Eric Jeanpierre & Catherine Vernon, *French Legal System* (Upper Saddle River, NJ: Prentice Hall, 2006), p. 178; Peter L. Murray & Rolf H. Stürner, *German Civil Justice* (Durham, NC: Carolina Academic Press, 2003), p. 261.
105 Howard M. Erichson, "A Typology of Aggregate Settlements" (2005) 80 *Notre Dame Law Review*, 1769, 1783 (quoting Oregon State Bar Legal Ethics Committee, Formal Opinion 2000–158, n.1 [2000]) (internal quotation marks omitted).
106 In the domestic American context see, e.g., McGovern, "Claims Resolution Facilities," p. 1361 and Kenneth R. Feinberg, *Who Gets What: Fair Compensation after Tragedy and Financial Upheaval* (New York: Public Affairs, 2012). Transnationally, see, e.g., Holtzmann & Kristjánsdóttir (eds.), *International Mass Claims Processes*; Permanent Court of Arbitration (ed.), *Redressing Injustices through Mass Claims Processes: Innovative Responses to Unique Challenges* (Oxford: Oxford University Press, 2006).
107 See, e.g., Herbert M. Kritzer, *Risks, Reputations, and Rewards: Contingency Fee Legal Practice in the United States* (Palo Alto, CA; Stanford University Press, 2014), pp. 139–180.
108 Under the Dutch WCAM, for example, "settlements are administered by private foundations established specifically for this purpose." See, Hensler, "The Future of Mass

Litigation," p. 311. In the United States, trustees or similar appointees are installed. See McGovern, "Claims Resolution Facilities," pp. 1368–1369.
109 McGovern, "Claims Resolution Facilities," p.1373.
110 McGovern, "Claims Resolution Facilities," pp. 1373–1374.
111 For examples of the extensive range of interim relief issued to constrain states see Don Wallace Jr., "Criminal Investigations: A Hypothetical Case," in Diora Ziyaeva et al. (eds.), *Interim and Emergency Relief in International Arbitration* (New York: Juris, 2015), pp. 199–208 (discussing investment arbitration tribunals enjoining states' regulatory action and staying domestic criminal investigations and prosecution); and Ian A. Laird et al., "Interim Relief in Investment Treaty Arbitration," in Diora Ziyaeva et al. (eds.), *Interim and Emergency Relief in International Arbitration*, p. 244 (discussing enjoining sovereigns from issuing regulation, which would be harassing, punitive, or made to sway the arbitration).
112 Gilbert Guillaume, "The Use of Precedent by International Judges and Arbitrators" (2011) 2 *Journal of International Dispute Settlement* 5; and Nathan Miller, "An International Jurisprudence? The Operation of 'Precedent' across International Tribunals" (2012) 15 *Leiden Journal of International Law* 483. To clarify, where an appellate level exists, its precedents are binding on the trial chamber within the court.
113 See Guillaume, "Use of Precedent by International Judges and Arbitrators," p. 12.
114 See *Burgh House Principles*.
115 Elizabeth Evenson & Jonathan O'Donohue, "States Shouldn't Use ICC Budget to Interfere with Its Work" (Nov. 23, 2016), *Amnesty International*, www.amnesty.org/en/latest/news/2016/11/states-shouldnt-use-icc-budget-to-interfere-with-its-work/.
116 At the time of the push to limit funding increases, South Africa, Burundi, and Gambia had announced their withdrawal from the Rome Statute. Since then, both South Africa and Burundi have revoked their withdrawal. "ICC Withdrawal Revoked after Court Ruling: UN," Al Jazeera (8 March 2017).
117 International Centre for Settlement of Investment Disputes Convention, Art. 17.
118 International Centre For Settlement of Investment Disputes, "Cost of Proceedings" (2017) https://icsid.worldbank.org/en/Pages/services/Cost-of-Proceedings.aspx.

CONCLUSION

1 United Nations Human Rights Council, Elaboration of an international legally binding instrument on transnational corporations and other business enterprises with respect to human rights, A/HRC/26/L.22/Rev.1 (25/06/2014).
2 Sara McLaughlin Mitchell & Emilia Justyna Powell, *Domestic Law Goes Global: Legal Traditions and International Courts* (Cambridge: Cambridge University Press, 2011), p. 10.
3 Mitchell & Powell, *Domestic Law Goes Global*, p. 11.

Index

Access to justice, 1–2, 3, 97, 143, 157–58, 167–68
Accounting, indirect costs and, 115
Ackerman, Bruce, 184n.2
Admissibility
  overview, 144, 150–51, 158
  complementarity, 160–61
  electa una via, 159–60
  exclusivity, 159
  exhaustion of domestic remedies, 159
  jurisdiction versus, 150–51, 222n.15
  "willingness to adjudicate," 160–61
Adversarial system, 163–64
Africa Watch, 25
African Court of Human and
    Peoples Rights, 223n.29
Aggregate litigation. *See* Class actions
Aggregate settlement, 174–75
Aguinda Salazar, Maria, 2, 65, 70
Algiers Accords, 31, 33, 188n.58
Alien Tort Statute
  Bhopal litigation and, 61
  cases filed under, 45
  Chevron–Ecuador litigation and, 65
  constitutional torts and, 90–91
  corporations, actions against, 73, 74–76
  evolution of case law, 72–73
  jurisdiction under, 74
  Kiobel case and, 4, 5, 72
  limitations of, 73–74
  presumption against extraterritoriality, 75–76
  reputation, harm to, 118
Alter, Karen J., 20, 225n.58
Alternative dispute resolution (ADR), 103, 166
AmazonWatch, 62
Americans Talk Issues Foundation (ATIF), 38–39
Americas Watch, 25

Amnesty International, 25, 48, 177
Appellate review, 165–66, 176–77
Arbitration
  in Chevron–Ecuador litigation, 68–69
  inadequacy of, 4–5
  international commercial arbitration, 12, 36, 100–02
  in US, 91–92
Argentina
  Consumer Law, 132
  punitive damages in, 132
Asia Watch, 25
Attorneys' fees
  conditional fees, 229n.101
  contingency fees, 97, 105, 134, 171, 173–74
  as direct costs, 111
  "English rule," 98, 173
  retainer agreements, 57
  shifting of, 98, 173
Australia
  class actions in, 133, 219n.117
  litigation finance in, 128
Austria, enforcement of foreign judgments in, 96–97

Backlash effects
  overview, 6, 127, 179
  blocking statutes as, 109–10, 131–32
  contingency fees and, 97, 105, 134
  entrepreneurial lawyering and, 128–30, 170–73
  litigation-enabling statutes as, 109–10, 131–32
  litigation finance and, 6, 110, 123, 127–28, 134
  punitive damages as, 132
Bangladesh, Rana Plaza disaster, 46, 104
Bassiouni, M. Cherif, 26
Belgium, class actions in, 133, 169, 170, 209n.72

Benefit corporations, 135
Bhopal litigation
    overview, 1, 2, 13, 47, 62
    adequacy analysis, 53–57
    Alien Tort Statute and, 61
    "boomerang litigation" in, 77
    claims processing scheme, 50–51
    collateral attacks on settlement, 60–61
    convenience analysis, 53, 58
    criminal prosecution and, 118
    deaths from accident, 48, 194n.21
    dismissal of US action, 51–52
    effects of accident, 48–49, 194n.21
    enterprise liability in, 59–60
    entrepreneurial lawyering in, 129
    forum non conveniens in, 50–53
    historical background, 47–50
    indirect costs of, 116
    injunctions in, 116
    injuries from accident, 48–49, 194n.21
    jurisdiction and, 155
    missing forum problem and, 3–4
    moral hazard in, 80
    negligence in, 49, 50, 61
    parallel and sequential litigation in, 47, 113
    private interest analysis, 58
    public policy analysis, 57–58
    standing in, 61
    strict liability in, 49
Bias, 99
Blocking statutes, 109–10, 131–32
Blueprint for ICCJ
    overview, 13, 139–40
    FDI and, 137–39
Bolivia, ICSID and, 119
"Boomerang litigation"
    overview, 77
    global preclusion and, 123–26
    ICCJ as solution to, 155
    missing forum problem and, 85–87
British Petroleum, 2, 81, 103, 124
Bulgaria, class actions in, 133
Burundi, ICC and, 230n.116
Bush, George W., 39
Business case for ICCJ
    overview, 13, 108–11
    backlash effects and (*See* Backlash effects)
    business ethics and, 134–37
    corruption and (*See* Corruption)
    direct costs and (*See* Direct costs of transnational litigation)
    global preclusion and (*See* Global preclusion)
    indirect costs and (*See* Indirect costs of transnational litigation)
Business ethics, 134–37

Cambodia, international courts in, 24–25
Canada
    class actions in, 133, 219n.117
    litigation finance in, 134
    Quebec as mixed jurisdiction, 142
Carter, Jimmy, 27, 30, 31
Case studies
    overview, 45–46
    Bhopal litigation (*See* Bhopal litigation)
    Chevron–Ecuador litigation (*See* Chevron–Ecuador litigation)
    Kiobel case (*See Kiobel* case)
    selection of, 45–46
Cassesse, Antonio, 26
Center for Constitutional Rights, 76
Challenges to ICCJ, 180
Champerty, 127–28
Chavez, Hugo, 119
Chevron–Ecuador litigation
    overview, 2, 13, 62–64, 70
    acquisition of Texaco by Chevron, 2, 64–65
    Alien Tort Statute and, 65
    arbitration in, 68–69
    "boomerang litigation" in, 77, 86
    criminal prosecution and, 118
    damages in, 130–31
    diversity jurisdiction in, 153–54
    effects of environmental contamination, 62–63
    entrepreneurial lawyering in, 129
    global preclusion in, 68–69
    goodwill, harm to, 119
    historical background, 64–65
    indirect costs of, 116–17
    jurisdiction and, 155, 156
    Lago Agrio litigation, 67
    leveraging political and diplomatic capital in, 69–70
    litigation finance in, 109
    missing forum problem and, 3–4
    moral hazard in, 80–81
    parallel and sequential litigation in, 77–78, 113
    "popular suit" in Ecuador, 67
    problems in enforcing judgment, 67–68
    ramifications for Chevron, 108–09
    RICO action in, 69
    US, dismissal of action in, 65–66

Index

Chicago Council on Global Affairs, 89
Chile, mixed claims commissions and, 33
China
  benefits of ICCJ, 7–8
  class actions in, 133
  FDI in, 40–41, 42
  ICSID and, 7–8, 41–42
  New York Convention and, 7–8, 41–42
  as potential holdout against ICCJ, 16, 39–42
  WTO and, 7–9, 41–42
Choice of forum. *See* Forum shopping
Choice of law, 95–96, 108
Civil Rights Act of 1871, 90
Claims Resolution Tribunals for Dormant Accounts in Switzerland, 9
Class Action Fairness Act of 2005 (CAFA), 91
Class actions. *See also* Collective redress; *specific country*
  contingency fees in, 171
  discovery in, 174
  entrepreneurial lawyering in, 170–73
  Federal Rules of Civil Procedure and, 226n.65
  globalization of, 133–34
  global preclusion and, 125
  growth in, 167–68
  in ICCJ, 43, 106
  jurisdiction over, 170
  litigation finance in, 174
  monetary relief in, 171
  opt-in/opt-out procedures, 168–70
  procedural features of, 162, 168
  punitive damages in, 171
  "quasi-class actions," 226n.64
  standing in, 168, 170–71
  structure of, 167
  "synthetic class actions," 129–30
  trust fund for, 173–74
Cold War, 23–24, 26–27
Collective redress
  overview, 143, 179
  in European Union, 97–98, 133
  in ICCJ, 43
Comity, 87
Committee for Economic Development, 136
Common Market for Eastern and Southern Africa (COMESA) Court of Justice, 223n.29
Complementarity, 113, 160–61, 226n.62
Composition of ICCJ, 147–49
Conditional fees, 229n.101
"Constitutional moments," 16, 19–20, 26–27, 184n.2
Contingency fees, 97, 105, 134, 171, 173–74

Convention Against Torture, 42
Convention on the Recognition and Enforcement of Foreign Arbitral Awards. *See* New York Convention (Convention on the Recognition and Enforcement of Foreign Arbitral Awards)
Corporate Social Responsibility, 4–5, 135–37, 180
Corporate structure, abuse of, 78–79
Correa, Rafael, 65, 68, 118
Corruption
  in developing countries, 123
  direct costs and, 121
  indirect costs and, 121
  missing forum problem and, 87, 99
  "prisoner's dilemma" and, 121–23
  rule of law versus, 120–21
Costa Rica, blocking statutes in, 131, 218n.106
Costs of transnational litigation
  direct costs (*See* Direct costs of transnational litigation)
  in ICCJ, 106, 110
  indirect costs (*See* Indirect costs of transnational litigation)
Court of International Trade, 142, 226n.67
Court of Justice of the European Union (CJEU), 20, 96, 223n.29
Crawford, James, 24
Cremer, Randal, 14, 17
Criminal prosecution as indirect cost of transnational litigation, 118
Cross-border mass torts defined, 46–47. *See also specific topic*

Daimler AG, 138
Damages
  monetary relief, 171, 175
  punitive damages (*See* Punitive damages)
Deepwater Horizon oil spill, 2, 81, 103, 124
Democracy, international courts and, 18
Denmark
  class actions in, 133, 169, 170
  enforcement of foreign judgments in, 96–97
  OECD Guidelines and, 104
Direct costs of transnational litigation
  overview, 5
  attorneys' fees as, 111
  corruption and, 121
  defined, 111
  forum shopping as, 111, 112–13
  increases in, 111–12
  parallel and sequential litigation as, 111, 112–13

Discovery
  in class actions, 174
  in ICCJ, 12
  in US, 92–93
Diversity jurisdiction, 153–54
Dole Food Co., 80–81, 108, 109, 118, 132, 212n.10, 214n.44
Dominica, blocking statutes in, 131, 218n.106
Dow Chemical, 61
Due process, 55–56, 87, 96, 196n.61

East Timor, international courts in, 24–25
Economic Community of West African States (ECOWAS) Court of Justice, 223n.29
Ecuador
  blocking statutes in, 131, 218n.106
  Chevron litigation (*See* Chevron-Ecuador litigation)
  Environmental Management Act of 1999, 65, 109, 131–32
  ICSID and, 119
  rainforest, devastation of (*See* Chevron-Ecuador litigation)
Electa una via, 159–60
Enforcement of foreign judgments
  "boomerang litigation" and, 85–87
  in European Union, 96–97
  global preclusion and, 125
  in US, 84, 86, 87
"English rule," 98, 173
Enron, 214n.46
Enterprise liability, 59–60, 153–54
Entrepreneurial lawyering, 98, 105, 123, 128–30, 170–73
Ethics
  of attorneys, 98, 101
  business ethics, 134–37
  of litigation finance, 127–28
  retainer agreements, 57
European Convention on Human Rights, 20, 96
European Court of Human Rights (ECtHR), 20, 102, 223n.29
European Court of Justice (ECJ), 18
European Union
  Brussels I Regulation (BIR), 94–95
  Charter of Fundamental Rights, 96
  choice of law in, 95–96
  collective redress in, 97–98, 133
  contingency fees in, 97
  enforcement of foreign judgments in, 96–97
  FDI and, 93
  "foreign cubed" cases in, 95
  "foreign squared" cases in, 94–95
  missing forum problem in, 84–85
  punitive damages in, 97–98, 105–06, 132
  Rome II Regulation (Law Applicable to Non-contractual Obligations), 95–96
Evidence
  admissibility (*See* Admissibility)
  discovery (*See* Discovery)
Exclusivity, 10, 113, 159–60, 170
Exhaustion of domestic remedies, 158, 159
Expropriation, 119, 120
Extraordinary Chambers in the Courts of Cambodia, 24–25
Exxon Valdez oil spill, 56

Feasibility of ICCJ, 8–9. *See also* Business case for ICCJ
Federal Arbitration Act, 91–92, 222n.21
Federal Rules of Civil Procedure, 52, 92–93, 153, 226n.65
Filártiga case, 73
Financing of ICCJ, 177–78
Finland
  class actions in, 133
  enforcement of foreign judgments in, 96–97
Foreign Corrupt Practices Act, 138–39
Foreign direct investment (FDI)
  backlash against, 119, 180
  in China, 40–41, 42
  European Union and, 93
  global preclusion and, 125–26
  ICCJ and, 1–2, 10, 42–43, 105, 137–39, 145, 156
  in India, 57
  Investor-State Dispute Settlement (ISDS) and, 100
  IUSCT and, 35
  South Africa and, 138
  US and, 5, 83
Forum non conveniens
  overview, 4
  adequacy analysis, 52–57
  backlash effects and, 6
  in Bhopal litigation, 50–53 (*See also* Bhopal litigation)
  "boomerang litigation" and, 85–86
  convenience analysis, 53, 58
  delay, effect of, 51
  private interest analysis, 53, 58
  public policy analysis, 53, 57–58

Index

in UK, 95
in US, 84
Forum shopping
  as direct cost, 111, 112–13
  entrepreneurial lawyering and, 130
  GATT and, 28
  ICCJ as solution to, 108, 158, 159–60, 161, 180–81
  as indirect cost, 119
France
  Civil Code, 95, 132
  class actions in, 133, 170, 171
  ICC and, 149
  litigation finance in, 128
  mixed claims commissions and, 33
  punitive damages in, 132
Functionalism, international courts and, 18

Gambia, ICC and, 230n.116
General Agreement on Tariffs and Trade (GATT), 18, 27–29, 38
Geneva Convention (1864), 22–23
Germany
  Capital Markets Model Case Law (KapMuG), 129, 130, 133
  class actions in, 133
  contingency fees in, 134
  enforcement of foreign judgments in, 96–97
  entrepreneurial lawyering in, 129, 130
  Kiobel case and, 88
  litigation finance in, 128
  mixed claims commissions and, 33
  punitive damages in, 132
Gibson Dunn (law firm), 108
Global Compact, 136–37, 180
Global preclusion
  overview, 126
  "boomerang litigation" and, 123–26
  in Chevron–Ecuador litigation, 68–69
  class actions and, 125
  courts, role of, 125
  enforcement of foreign judgments and, 125
  FDI and, 125–26
  in ICCJ, 6, 10–11, 110, 125–26
  parallel and sequential litigation and, 123–26
  "peace premium," 123–24
  thresholds and, 124, 216n.71
Goodwill, harm to, 119
Greece, enforcement of foreign judgments in, 96–97
Guatemala, blocking statutes in, 131, 218n.106

Guidelines for Multinational Enterprises (OECD), 45–46, 88, 104, 136
Gulf Coast Claims Facility (GCCF), 103, 124

Hague Peace Conference (1899), 21
Hague Peace Conference (1907), 21
Hariri, Rafik, 26
Helsinki Watch, 25
Hong Kong
  Law Reform Commission, 128
  litigation finance in, 128
Hudec, Robert E., 29
Human rights
  ICCJ and, 43
  NGOs and, 25
Human Rights Watch, 25, 43, 71
Hybridization of civil and common law, 141–42, 143, 144, 163–64

ICC. *See* International Criminal Court (ICC)
ICJ. *See* International Court of Justice (ICJ)
"Idea contagion," 24–25
Ideational theories of international courts, 18
Incentives for ICCJ, 5–8
Independence of ICCJ, 147
India
  Bhopal Gas Leak Disaster (Processing of Claims) Act 1985, 50, 51–52, 56–57, 60, 131
  Bhopal Gas Tragedy Relief and Rehabilitation Department, 48, 57
  due process in, 55–56, 196n.61
  FDI in, 57
Indirect costs of transnational litigation
  overview, 5–6, 113–14
  accounting and, 115
  in Bhopal litigation, 116
  bonds and, 114
  in Chevron–Ecuador litigation, 116–17
  corruption and, 121
  criminal prosecution as, 118
  distraction as, 117–18
  expropriation, 119
  forum shopping as, 119
  goodwill, harm to, 119
  injunctions and, 116
  investment climate, changes in, 119–20
  mergers and acquisitions and, 116
  reputation, harm to, 118–19
  restraint on business activities, 114–17
  stock prices and, 114–15
  uncertainty and, 114–17

Indonesia
  bilateral investment treaties and, 119
  class actions in, 133
Injunctions
  indirect costs and, 116
  as interim relief, 176
Inquisitorial system, 163–64
Institutional features of ICCJ
  overview, 141–44
  composition, 147–49
  enforcement treaty, 146
  independence, 147
  international organizations, relations with, 149–50
  statute, 145
  two-tiered structure, 145–47
Integration of civil and common law, 141–42, 143, 144, 163–64
Interactional theories of international courts, 18–19
Inter-American Commission of Human Rights (IACHR), 173
Inter-American Court of Human Rights (IACtHR), 148, 223n.29
Interim relief, 176
International Centre for Settlement of Investment Disputes (ICSID), 7–8, 35, 41–42, 99, 100, 177–78
International commercial arbitration, 12, 36, 100–02
International Commission for Penal Reconstruction and Development, 23
International Committee of the Red Cross, 22–23
International Court of Justice (ICJ), 19, 37, 142, 150, 173, 223n.29, 224n.30, 225n.53, 226n.67
International courts. See also specific court
  overview, 13, 14–16
  "constitutional moments" and, 19–20
  democracy and, 18
  development of, 8–9, 15–16
  features of, 184n.12
  functionalism and, 18
  ICC (See International Criminal Court (ICC))
  ideational theories of, 18
  interactional theories of, 18–19
  IUSCT (See Iran-United States Claims Tribunal (IUSCT))
  Jerusalem Arbitration Center (JAC), 15, 35–36
  political factors, 20–21
  rationalism and, 17–18
  self-interest and, 17–18
  theoretical models, 17–21
  WTO DSU (See World Trade Organization Dispute Settlement Understanding (WTO DSU))
International Criminal Court (ICC)
  overview, 15, 20, 186n.18
  admissibility in, 160
  appellate review in, 165–66
  applicable law, 155
  change agents, 25–26
  complementarity and, 160, 226n.62
  composition of, 148, 223n.29
  "constitutional moments," 26–27
  creation of, 22, 26
  criminal liability in, 8
  criticisms of, 211n.97
  financing of, 177
  geopolitical change and, 26–27
  historical background, 21–22
  international organizations, relations with, 149–50
  jurisdiction of, 150
  legal and institutional precedents, 22–25
  as model for ICCJ, 143–44, 145
  Rome Statute (See Rome Statute of the International Criminal Court)
  US and, 37, 39
International Criminal Tribunal for Rwanda (ICTR), 24–25, 38, 165–66, 176
International Criminal Tribunal for the Former Yugoslavia (ICTY), 24–25, 26, 38, 165–66, 176
International Emergency Economic Powers Act (IEEPA), 33
International Labour Organization (ILO), Declaration on Fundamental Principles and Rights at Work, 42
International Law Association, Burgh House Principles on the Independence of the International Judiciary, 148, 223n.26
International Law Commission (ILC), 23–24
International Military Tribunal (Nuremberg Tribunal), 23, 24–25
International Military Tribunal for the Far East (Tokyo Tribunal), 23, 24–25
International Monetary Fund, 20
International Tribunal for the Law of the Sea (ITLOS), 223n.29
Investor-State Dispute Settlement (ISDS), 43, 99, 100, 102–03, 180

Iran
  hostage crisis, 30–31
  Islamic Revolution, 30
Iran-United States Claims Tribunal (IUSCT)
  overview, 15
  Algiers Accords, 31, 33, 188n.58
  Claims Settlement Declaration, 31
  Constitutional challenges, 33
  criticisms of, 34
  historical background, 9, 29–31
  jurisdiction of, 150, 152
  precedents, 32–33
  success of, 34–35
Israel
  class actions in, 133
  contingency fees in, 134
  as mixed jurisdiction, 142
Italy
  class actions in, 133
  enforcement of foreign judgments in, 96–97
  punitive damages in, 132

Jackson, John H., 29
Japan
  class actions in, 133
  contingency fees in, 134
  entrepreneurial lawyering in, 129, 130
Jay Treaty (1794), 9, 32, 143
Jerusalem Arbitration Center (JAC), 15, 35–36
Judicial Panel on Multidistrict Litigation (JPMDL), 227n.78
Judiciary Act of 1789, 72
Jurisdiction
  overview, 144, 150–51
  admissibility versus, 150–51, 222n.15
  under Alien Tort Statute, 74
  applicable law, 154–56
  Bhopal litigation and, 155
  Chevron–Ecuador litigation and, 155, 156
  class actions, 170
  complementarity, 113, 160–61, 226n.62
  cross-border claims and, 153–54
  diversity jurisdiction, 153–54
  enterprise liability and, 153–54
  exclusivity, 10, 113, 159–60, 170
  of ICC, 150
  intentional torts, 155
  of IUSCT, 150, 152
  Kiobel case and, 155
  mass claims versus mass torts, 152–53
  negligence, 155
  personal jurisdiction, 73, 93, 108, 157–58
  under Rome Statute, 150, 151, 160
  subject matter jurisdiction (See Subject matter jurisdiction)
  temporal jurisdiction, 151
Jury trials
  in ICCJ, 12
  in US, 92, 93

Kiobel case
  overview, 13, 70, 138
  Alien Tort Statute and, 4, 5, 72
  diversity jurisdiction in, 154
  entrepreneurial lawyering in, 129
  historical background, 70–72
  jurisdiction and, 155
  missing forum problem and, 3–4
  parallel and sequential litigation in, 113
  reputation, harm to, 118
  in US Supreme Court, 75–76

League of Nations, 23
Lebanon, international courts in, 26
Legitimacy considerations, 87–89, 105
Lithuania, class actions in, 133
Litigation-enabling statutes, 109–10, 131–32
Litigation finance
  advantages of, 110, 123, 179–80
  backlash effects and, 6, 127–28
  in Canada, 134
  in Chevron–Ecuador litigation, 109
  contingency fees and, 97
  ethics of, 127–28
  ICCJ and, 174
Louisiana as mixed jurisdiction, 142

"Managerial judging," 142–43, 144
Mass claims versus mass torts, 152–53
McLane-Ocampo Treaty, 32
Mergers and acquisitions, indirect costs of transnational litigation and, 116
Methyl isocyanate (MIC), 47
Mexican-American War (1846–1848), 32
Mexico
  class actions in, 133
  mixed claims commissions and, 32–33, 152–53
Millennium Development Goals, 20
Missing forum problem
  overview, 3–5, 13, 83–84, 106–07
  alternative dispute resolution (ADR) as solution, 103

Missing forum problem (*cont.*)
 arbitration and, 91–92
 Bhopal litigation and, 3–4
 bias and, 99
 "boomerang litigation" and, 85–87
 Chevron–Ecuador litigation and, 3–4
 choice of law and, 95–96
 comity and, 87
 constitutional torts and, 90–91
 contingency fees and, 97
 corruption and, 87, 99
 discovery and, 92–93
 due process and, 87
 in European Union, 84–85
 foreign policy considerations, 87
 global courts, declining to act as, 87–89
 home courts, MNCs bringing actions in, 84–85
 ICCJ as solution, 104–06
 international commercial arbitration and, 100–02
 jury trials and, 92, 93
 Kiobel case and, 3–4
 legitimacy considerations, 87–89, 105
 litigation in courts of jurisdiction where injuries occurred, 99–100
 OECD Guidelines as solution, 104
 permanent court of investment disputes and, 102–03
 punitive damages and, 97–98
 self-regulation as solution, 103–04
 single-issue courts as solution, 103
 in US, 84, 89–93
Mixed claims commissions, 32–33
Mixed jurisdictions, 141–42, 180–81
Monetary relief, 171, 175
Moral hazard, 79–82
Moscow Declarations (1943), 23
Moynier, Gustave, 22–23
Multidistrict Litigation (MDL), 226n.64, 227n.78
Multinational corporations (MNCs)
 benefits of ICCJ, 5–6
 "boomerang litigation" and, 77
 corporate structure, abuse of, 78–79
 home courts, bringing actions in, 84–85
 lack of accountability, 2–3
 moral hazard and, 79–82
 multiple entities, abuse of, 78–79
 parallel litigation and, 77–78
 sequential litigation and, 77–78
 subsidiaries, abuse of, 78–79
Multiparty Multiforum Trial Jurisdiction Act of 2002, 91, 207n.35

Negligence
 in Bhopal litigation, 49, 50, 61
 in ICCJ, 155
Netherlands
 class actions in, 133, 169
 contingency fees in, 134
 Dutch Act on Collective Settlement of Lass Claims (WCAM), 129–30
 enforcement of foreign judgments in, 96–97
 entrepreneurial lawyering in, 129–30
 Kiobel case and, 76, 87–88
 litigation finance in, 128
New York Convention (Convention on the Recognition and Enforcement of Foreign Arbitral Awards), 7–8, 10–11, 41–42, 146, 222n.20
New York Uniform Foreign Country Money-Judgments Recognition Act, 52, 68, 199n.144
Nicaragua
 blocking statutes in, 131, 132, 218n.106
 Law No. 364, 132
Nigeria
 Kiobel case (*See Kiobel* case)
 Movement for the Survival of the Ogoni People (MSOP), 70–71, 72, 76
 "Ogoni Nine," 71
 "resource curse" in, 71
Non-governmental organizations (NGOs), 25, 43, 172–73
Non-monetary relief, 175–76
Non-representative collective litigation, 166–67
Norway, class actions in, 133
Nuremberg Tribunal (International Military Tribunal), 23, 24–25

Obama, Barack, 81
Oil Pollution Act of 1990 (OPA), 124
Ordre public, 96
Organisation for Economic Co-operation and Development (OECD)
 overview, 138–39
 Guidelines for Multinational Enterprises, 45–46, 88, 104, 136
Ortega, Daniel, 119

Parallel litigation
 overview, 77–78
 backlash effects and, 130
 in Bhopal litigation, 47, 113
 as direct cost, 111, 112–13
 global preclusion and, 123–26
 ICCJ as solution to, 10, 155, 158, 159, 161

Index

"Peace premium," 123–24
Peña-Irala, Americo, 73
Pennzoil, 114–15
Permanent Court of Arbitration (PCA), 68–69, 150, 224n.30, 40
Permanent Court of International Justice (PCIJ), 19
Permanent court of investment disputes, 102–03
Personal jurisdiction, 73, 93, 108, 157–58
PetroEcuador, 64–65, 67. *See also* Chevron–Ecuador litigation
Poland, class actions in, 133
Portugal, class actions in, 133
Preclusion. *See* Global preclusion
"Prisoner's dilemma," 121–23
"Private attorney generals," 228n.84
Private interest analysis, 53, 58
Private Securities Litigation Reform Act of 1995 (PSRLA), 207n.35
Procedural features of ICCJ
  overview, 11–12, 105, 144, 161–63
  admissibility (*See* Admissibility)
  aggregate settlement supervision and administration, 174–75
  alternative dispute resolution (ADR), 166
  appellate review, 165–66, 176–77
  class actions, 162, 168 (*See also* Class actions)
  integration of civil and common law, 163–64
  interim relief, 176
  jurisdiction (*See* Jurisdiction)
  monetary relief, 171, 175
  non-monetary relief, 175–76
  non-representative collective litigation, 166–67
  punitive damages, 12, 176
  remedies, 175–76
  routing of claims, 164–66
  screening of claims, 164–66
Proposal for ICCJ, 10–13
  definitions, 11
  discovery, 12
  enforcement treaty, 10
  exclusivity, 10
  global preclusion, 10–11
  jurisdiction (*See* Jurisdiction)
  jury trials, lack of, 12
  procedural features (*See* Procedural features of ICCJ)
  punitive damages, 12
  statute, 10
  two-tiered structure, 10

Public policy
  enforcement of foreign judgments and, 96
  forum non conveniens and, 53, 57–58
Punitive damages
  as backlash effects, 132
  in class actions, 171
  in European Union, 97–98, 105–06, 132
  growth in, 132
  in ICCJ, 12, 176

"Quasi-class actions," 226n.64
Quebec as mixed jurisdiction, 142

Racketeer Influenced and Corrupt Organizations Act (RICO), 69, 77, 204n.233
Rana Plaza disaster, 46, 104
Rationalism, international courts and, 17–18
Reagan, Ronald, 31, 90
Rehnquist, William, 33
Remedies in ICCJ, 175–76
Remembrance, Responsibility and the Future Foundation, 103
Representative actions. *See* Class actions
Reputation, harm to, 118–19
"Resource curse," 71
Retainer agreements, 57
Rome Statute of the International Criminal Court
  effective date, 22
  ICCJ, influence on, 143–44, 145, 149–50, 155
  international courts and, 20
  jurisdiction under, 150, 151, 160
  ratification of, 26
  US and, 39
Roosevelt, Franklin D., 23
Royal Dutch Shell, 4, 70, 71–72, 76, 111, 113, 130. *See also Kiobel* case
Rule of law
  corruption versus, 120–21
  in ICCJ, 105
Rwanda, international courts in, 24–25, 38, 165–66, 176

Saro-Wiwa, Ken, 71, 72, 111
Scotland as mixed jurisdiction, 142
Screening of claims, 164–66
Section 1983 actions, 90–91
Self-interest, international courts and, 17–18
Self-regulation, 4–5, 103–04
Sequential litigation
  overview, 77–78
  backlash effects and, 130

Sequential litigation (*cont.*)
  in Bhopal litigation, 47, 113
  as direct cost, 111, 112–13
  global preclusion and, 123–26
  ICCJ as solution to, 10, 155, 158, 159, 161
Settlement supervision and administration, 174–75
Shell Petroleum Development Co. of Nigeria Ltd., 72, 154. *See also Kiobel* case
Shell Transport & Trading Co., 72. *See also Kiobel* case
Shifting of fees, 98, 173
Sierra Leone, international courts in, 24–25
Singapore, litigation finance in, 128
Single-issue courts, 4–5, 103
South Africa
  apartheid in, 138
  FDI and, 138
  ICC and, 230n.116
  litigation finance in, 128
  as mixed jurisdiction, 142
South Korea
  class actions in, 133
  litigation finance in, 128
Spain, class actions in, 133
Special Court for Sierra Leone, 24–25
Special Panels of the Dili District Court in East Timor, 24–25
Special Tribunal for Lebanon, 26
Standing
  in Bhopal litigation, 61
  in class actions, 168, 170–71
  in US, 90–91
States, benefits of ICCJ to, 7–8
Statute of ICCJ, 10, 145
Stiglitz, Joseph, 137–39
Stock prices, indirect costs and, 114–15
Strict liability, 49
Subject matter jurisdiction
  applicable law, 154–56
  cross-border claims and, 153–54
  diversity jurisdiction, 153–54
  enterprise liability and, 153–54
  of ICCJ, 152–53
  intentional torts, 155
  mass claims versus mass torts, 152–53
  negligence, 155
Subsidiaries, abuse of, 78–79
Substantive law in ICCJ, 105
Sweden
  class actions in, 133
  enforcement of foreign judgments in, 96–97
Switzerland, ICC and, 149
"Synthetic class actions," 129–30

Taiwan, class actions in, 133
Temporal jurisdiction, 151
Texaco, 2, 62, 64–66, 67, 70, 114–15. *See also* Chevron-Ecuador litigation; Chevron–Ecuador litigation
Texaco Petroleum Company (TexPet), 62–63, 64–65, 66, 67, 153–54. *See also* Chevron–Ecuador litigation
Thailand
  class actions in, 133
  punitive damages in, 132
Theoretical models of international courts, 17–21
Third party funding, 110, 127–28, 134, 174, 179–80
Tokyo Round of GAAT Negotiations, 28–29
Tokyo Tribunal (International Military Tribunal for the Far East), 23, 24–25
Transparency International, 99
Treaty of Guadalupe-Hidalgo (1848), 32
Trump, Donald, 7, 42, 135
Trust fund for class actions, 173–74
Two-tiered structure of ICCJ, 10, 145–47

Uniform Foreign Country Money-Judgments Recognition Act, 52, 68, 199n.144
Union Carbide Corp., 47, 49–50, 52, 54, 55–56, 59–61, 80. *See also* Bhopal litigation
Union Carbide India Ltd., 47, 49–51, 54, 57, 59–60, 116. *See also* Bhopal litigation
United Kingdom
  class actions in, 133, 169, 170
  Competition Appeals Tribunal (CAT), 169
  Consumer Rights Act, 133
  contingency fees in, 134
  forum non conveniens in, 95
  Jackson Report, 134
  Kiobel case and, 87–88
  litigation finance in, 128
  Scotland as mixed jurisdiction, 142
United Nations
  Charter, 149
  Commission of Experts on the Situation in Yugoslavia, 26
  Compensation Commission, 9
  Diplomatic Conference of Plenipotentiaries on the Establishment of an International Criminal Court, 26
  Global Compact, 136–37, 180
  Guiding Principles on Business and Human Rights, 88

Human Rights Council, 43
Special Representative of the Secretary-
  General for Business and Human Rights,
  88, 103–04
United Nations War Crimes Commission
  (UNWCC), 23
United States
  Alien Tort Statute (*See* Alien Tort Statute)
  arbitration in, 91–92
  benefits of ICCJ for, 7
  Civil Rights Act of 1871, 90
  Class Action Fairness Act of 2005 (CAFA), 91
  class actions in, 91, 226n.64
  constitutional torts, 90–91
  contingency fees in, 173–74
  Court of International Trade, 142, 226n.67
  discovery in, 92–93
  enforcement of foreign judgments in,
    84, 86, 87
  entrepreneurial lawyering in, 129
  FDI and, 5, 83
  Federal Arbitration Act, 91–92, 222n.21
  Federal Rules of Civil Procedure, 52, 92–93,
    153, 226n.65
  Foreign Corrupt Practices Act, 138–39
  forum non conveniens in, 84
  GATT and, 38
  ICC and, 37, 39
  ICJ and, 37
  ICTR and, 38
  ICTY and, 38
  International Emergency Economic Powers
    Act (IEEPA), 33
  Judicial Panel on Multidistrict Litigation
    (JPMDL), 227n.78
  Judiciary Act of 1789, 72
  jury trials in, 92, 93
  Justice Department, 30–31
  litigation finance in, 128
  missing forum problem in, 84, 89–93
  mixed claims commissions and, 32–33
  Multidistrict Litigation (MDL), 226n.64, 227n.78
  Multiparty Multiforum Trial Jurisdiction Act of
    2002, 91, 207n.35
  New York Uniform Foreign Country Money-
    Judgments Recognition Act, 52, 68, 199n.144
  Oil Pollution Act of 1990 (OPA), 124
  as potential holdout against ICCJ, 16, 37–39
  Private Securities Litigation Reform Act of 1995
    (PSRLA), 207n.35
  pro-corporate trend of judiciary in, 93
  "quasi-class actions" in, 226n.64
  Racketeer Influenced and Corrupt
    Organizations Act (RICO), 69, 77, 204n.233
  Section 1983 actions, 90–91
  standing in, 90–91
  State Department, 69–70, 226n.63
  Treasury Department, 20
  WTO and, 38
United States Chamber of Commerce, 93, 118,
  121, 132
United States-Mexico Special Claims
  Commission, 152–53
Universal Declaration of Human Rights, 3
Unocal, 73
Uruguay Round, 28–29

Venezuela
  ICSID and, 119
  mixed claims commissions and, 33
Volkswagen, 128

"Washington Consensus," 20
World Bank, 20, 99, 137, 149
WorldPublicOpinion.org, 89
World Trade Center Disaster Site
  litigation, 124
World Trade Organization (WTO)
  Advisory Centre on WTO Law, 173
  Appellate Body, 102, 165–66, 176, 223n.29
  China and, 7–9, 41–42
  GATT and, 18, 27–29
  US and, 38
World Trade Organization Dispute Settlement
  Understanding (WTO DSU)
  overview, 15, 18, 19
  alternative dispute resolution (ADR), 227n.77
  historical background, 27–29

Yugoslavia
  Commission of Experts on the Situation in
    Yugoslavia, 26
  international courts in, 24–25, 26, 38,
    165–66, 176

Zhu Rongi, 41